I SAW DEMOCRACY MURDERED

I Saw Democracy Murdered is the memoir of Sam Russell (1915–2010), a communist journalist and a British volunteer with the anti-fascist Republican forces in the Spanish Civil War.

The book covers his experiences during the Spanish Civil War, his time as a journalist at *The Daily Worker* and *The Morning Star* newspapers, and his later disillusionment with Stalinism. In his capacity as a journalist, Russell travelled extensively and was frequently a front-row spectator at significant historical events, from the formerly occupied Channel Islands at the end of World War II to the show trials of communists in Eastern Europe in the 1950s. His report as Moscow correspondent on Nikita Khruschev's 'secret speech' condemning the crimes of Stalinism was lacerated by his newspaper's editor, as was his interview with the legendary revolutionary leader, Che Guevara. Sam, whose friends included Donald Maclean, the British diplomat who spied for the Soviet Union during the Cold War, also reported from Budapest in 1956 and Prague in 1968 during the Warsaw Pact invasions of Hungary and Czechoslovakia, and from North Vietnam during the Vietnam War, and in 1973 he witnessed the assault on Chilean President Salvador Allende's palace that signalled the start of the CIA-backed military coup. Sam's story was told to Colin Chambers and Chris Myant and has been edited by Colin Chambers.

This autobiographical account of a fascinating life will be essential reading for scholars and activists with an interest in the Spanish Civil War, the history of communism, and British radical history.

Colin Chambers is a former journalist and Literary Manager of the Royal Shakespeare Company (1981–1997) and is Emeritus Professor of Drama at Kingston University, London, UK. His stage writing includes co-authoring

Kenneth's First Play and *Tynan*, and adapting David Pinski's *Treasure*. Among his books are: *Other Spaces: New Writing and the RSC*; *The Story of Unity Theatre*; *Peggy: The Life of Margaret Ramsay, Play Agent* (first winner of the Theatre Book Prize); *Inside the Royal Shakespeare Company*; *Here We Stand: Politics, Performers and Performance – Paul Robeson, Isadora Duncan, and Charlie Chaplin*; and *Black and Asian Theatre in Britain: A History*. He edited *The Continuum Companion to Twentieth Century Theatre* and *Peggy to Her Playwrights: The Letters of Margaret Ramsay*, and co-edited *Granville Barker on Theatre*.

Sam Russell (1915–2010) was a Communist journalist who began his career reporting from Spain during the Civil War in which he had been wounded, fighting as an anti-fascist volunteer for the International Brigades to defend the Republic. He remained with *The Daily Worker* and its successor, *The Morning Star*, for more than 40 years, becoming Foreign Editor and covering many of the key historical events of the century.

Routledge Studies in Radical History and Politics
Series editors: Thomas Linehan, *University of Ulster, and* **John Roberts**, *Brunel University*

The series *Routledge Studies in Radical History and Politics* has two areas of interest. Firstly, this series aims to publish books which focus on the history of movements of the radical left. 'Movement of the radical left' is here interpreted in its broadest sense as encompassing those past movements for radical change which operated in the mainstream political arena as with political parties, and past movements for change which operated more outside the mainstream as with millenarian movements, anarchist groups, utopian socialist communities, and trade unions. Secondly, this series aims to publish books which focus on more contemporary expressions of radical left-wing politics. Recent years have been witness to the emergence of a multitude of new radical movements adept at getting their voices in the public sphere. From those participating in the Arab Spring, the Occupy movement, community unionism, social media forums, independent media outlets, local voluntary organisations campaigning for progressive change, and so on, it seems to be the case that innovative networks of radicalism are being constructed in civil society that operate in different public forms.

The series very much welcomes titles with a British focus, but is not limited to any particular national context or region. The series will encourage scholars who contribute to this series to draw on perspectives and insights from other disciplines.

I Saw Democracy Murdered
The Memoir of Sam Russell, Journalist
Colin Chambers and Sam Russell

For more information about this series, please visit: www.routledge.com/ Routledge-Studies-in-Radical-History-and-Politics/book-series/RSRHP

I SAW DEMOCRACY MURDERED

The Memoir of Sam Russell, Journalist

Colin Chambers and Sam Russell

LONDON AND NEW YORK

Cover image: © Top two photos, Ruth Muller's family archive; bottom photo, Marshall Mateer

First published 2022
by Routledge
4 Park Square, Milton Park, Abingdon, Oxon OX14 4RN

and by Routledge
605 Third Avenue, New York, NY 10158

Routledge is an imprint of the Taylor & Francis Group, an informa business

© 2022 material excluding the introduction, Colin Chambers and Ruth Muller; introduction, Francis Beckett

The right of Colin Chambers and Sam Russell to be identified as the authors of the material, excluding the introduction, and of the author for the introduction, has been asserted in accordance with sections 77 and 78 of the Copyright, Designs and Patents Act 1988.

All rights reserved. No part of this book may be reprinted or reproduced or utilised in any form or by any electronic, mechanical, or other means, now known or hereafter invented, including photocopying and recording, or in any information storage or retrieval system, without permission in writing from the publishers.

Trademark notice: Product or corporate names may be trademarks or registered trademarks, and are used only for identification and explanation without intent to infringe.

British Library Cataloguing-in-Publication Data
A catalogue record for this book is available from the British Library

Library of Congress Cataloging-in-Publication Data
A catalog record has been requested for this book

ISBN: 978-1-032-15272-1 (hbk)
ISBN: 978-1-032-12856-6 (pbk)
ISBN: 978-1-003-24338-0 (ebk)

DOI: 10.4324/9781003243380

Typeset in Bembo
by codeMantra

For Sam's grandchildren, Seán and Marika

CONTENTS

List of figures	*xi*
Acknowledgements	*xiii*
Preface	*xv*

	Introduction *Francis Beckett*	1
1	The Road to Spain	5
2	Fighting Franco	19
3	From Rifle to Typewriter	37
4	Defeat in Spain	62
5	The World Goes to War	82
6	Wartime Britain	99
7	Back at the *Worker*	110
8	Believing the Unbelievable	126
9	The 'Secret' Speech	140
10	Trouble in Moscow	158

x Contents

11 Farewell to Moscow	170
12 Meeting Che	188
13 Democracy Murdered	210
14 Back in Spain	223
15 Epilogue	242
Appendix: Letters from Abroad	*249*
Postscript: MI5 and My Family	*253*
Ruth Muller	
Index	*257*

FIGURES

1.1	Polly with her sons (left to right) Sid, Frank, and Sam	6
1.2	Sam's father Nathan in front of the family shop	9
1.3	Sam in Hackney, east London 1936	12
1.4	Sam (third on the left, third row from front) attending a residential school at Digswell Park, Welwyn Garden City, Hertfordshire, February 1936	13
2.1	Sam in his Officers' Training Corps uniform, Albacete, Spain	20
2.2	Sam in Spain with another Brigader, after being wounded	34
3.1	Sam's membership card of the Association of Volunteers for Liberty, formed in France by wounded Brigaders	38
3.2	Sam's radio work permit issued by the Catalan Communists	42
3.3	Sam's Spanish Communist Party card	42
4.1	Sam making a speech at the 2005 annual commemoration ceremony of the International Brigade Memorial Trust, Jubilee Gardens, South Bank, London	75
4.2	Sam (right) with his younger brother Frank in Spain, May Day 1938	76
4.3	Sam (right) with his younger brother Frank in later life	77
4.4	Sam (centre) and Margaret (behind *Daily Worker*) with comrades in Spain, 1938, after a special lunch of rabbit	78
4.5	Pass issued to Sam for the opera house in Barcelona where he took Margaret	78
4.6	Sam and Margaret at Brockweir, Forest of Dean, August 1951, the year of their daughter Ruth's birth	80
5.1	Sam at work in Paris, 1940	86
6.1	Identity card issued to Sam when he was working as a fitting shop inspector at the Napier factory, west London in 1943	100

xii Contents

6.2 Sam, Margaret, and their daughter Ruth in Finchley, north London, 1963, arriving for Sam's mother's 70th birthday   106

7.1 Pamphlet published in 1945 by the *Daily Worker* based on stories Sam uncovered about wartime collaboration in the occupied Channel Island   116

7.2 Programme for the *Daily Worker* twentieth anniversary dinner and dance   124

10.1 Sam with the Italian Communist and journalist Giuseppe Boffa in Lithuania   162

12.1 In Cuba, 1962, Sam talks to sailors ready to defend their country   194

12.2 Sam at a meeting in Cuba, 1962   194

12.3 Sam interviewing Che Guevara in Cuba, 1962   198

12.4 Sam on the Great Wall of China, 1979   206

12.5 Sam visiting a Chinese factory, 1979   207

15.1 Celebrating Sam's 40 years' service to the *Daily Worker/ Morning Star* with other staff members at the paper's offices, 75 Farringdon Road, London   246

15.2 Sam at 94, a year before he died   247

All figures except 15.2 are taken from the family archive. Every effort has been made to seek permission to reproduce copyright material where appropriate before the book went to press. If any proper acknowledgement has not been made, we would invite copyright holders to inform us.

ACKNOWLEDGEMENTS

Thanks, mainly, to Chris Myant; also to Richard Baxell, Josette Bouvard, John Green, Maggie Hanbury, Nicholas Jacobs, Francis King, Ruth Muller (particularly for providing the illustrations and the information about them), and Jane Noble; to Raimon for permission to reproduce his song 'Diguem no'/'Let's Say No', to Kevin Morgan for permission to quote from his essay in *Twentieth Century Communism*, to the *Morning Star* for permission to reproduce material published by the *Daily Worker*, and to Marshall Mateer for permission to use his photograph.

PREFACE

New to the world of journalism, I joined the staff of the *Morning Star* in 1973, aged 22, and found myself working in the newsroom a few yards from the paper's esteemed Foreign Editor Sam Russell. Despite the 35 years' difference in age, status, and experience, we ended up talking a lot during odd moments when the pace of work slackened, and as I came to discover the breadth and depth of his life through such occasional exchanges, I also came to believe that his remarkable story should be told in print. One problem: Sam did not want to tell it.

After I became the paper's Books Editor in 1980 and gave Sam space to air his views through reviews, often much to the annoyance of the editor, I felt able to ask Sam if he would agree to be interviewed at length, and I would then write his biography instead of him. Another shake of the head. We kept in touch after I left the paper, and over lunch one day in 1986 when he had retired from the *Morning Star*, I put the question to him again, and this time he agreed, somewhat sheepishly, but on condition that I did not tape record our conversations about his life. (This was the year he gave an interview to the Imperial War Museum, mostly about Spain, for the museum's Oral History programme, which was taped.)

The demands of gainful employment and fatherhood meant I had little time to devote to Sam, but I wanted to follow up his agreement before he changed his mind. I drafted some preliminary questions and a rough timeline of Sam's career to act as a steer, and, beginning in early 1987, we met for lunch on a regular but infrequent basis, though I ate little as I had to make notes of the Russell saga. Sam now had acquired a taste for recollection, piqued by the appearance of similar publications by comrades of his and, I suspect, feeling released by his retirement from the paper. He dealt forthrightly with the pain of confronting his political past but, aside from his childhood, not the personal past, and in particular felt guilt for ruining his wife Margaret's career when he became the paper's Moscow correspondent and took her abroad. The private Sam that can be glimpsed in

xvi Preface

the two letters printed in the Appendix was not on offer. Margaret's health was failing at this time and she died in 1990 while Sam and I were completing our series of interviews. When, not long after, we reached the present day in the story, and hence the conclusion, my own life left me no time to turn my written record into the promised book.

Following Margaret's death, Sam was offered increased support by Chris Myant, his former deputy on the Foreign Desk and later the paper's Assistant Editor, and Chris was able to go over Sam's story with him but this time with a tape recorder. When Chris typed up his interviews, we compared our accounts, which were remarkably alike, and we put together a version that Sam read and approved.

By the time of Sam's death in 2010, we had not found a publisher, nor had we added any material on Sam's personal interests (for example, his appreciation of contemporary artists such as John Hoyland and Terry Frost) or on his life since his retiring from the *Morning Star*, for example, his joining the Labour Party (and supporting the Iraq invasion to topple Saddam Hussein), his work with the International Brigade Memorial Trust, and his having to move into a residential care home serving the Jewish community (Nightingale House in South-West London where his father had died of cancer).

Chris and I continued to work on the book, with Chris checking what Sam had said against Sam's notebooks, cuttings from the paper, and other documents and sources, and, from 2012, the MI5 files on Sam, which were released. I edited the final text to a manageable length.

As was to be suspected of memories stretching back over 50 years and more, there were some details Sam got wrong, and a few times when Sam either gave slightly different accounts of the same event or even contradicted his own stories. I have tried to find the truth in these instances without losing his voice or intrusively imposing my interpretation, and there may well still be historical errors in the text. And the gaps remain. The memoir is not a complete autobiography. The story Sam wanted to tell, that he felt able to tell, was that of his time as a Communist journalist, and the overwhelming bulk of *I Saw Democracy Murdered* is just that, as told in his own words to Chris and me.

Colin Chambers

INTRODUCTION

Francis Beckett[*]

'I suppose', says the original angry young man, Jimmy Porter, in John Osborne's iconic 1956 play *Look Back in Anger*, 'people of our generation aren't able to die for good causes any longer. We had all that done for us, in the thirties and the forties, when we were still kids....There aren't any good, brave causes left'.

All the 'good, brave causes' had been eaten up by people like Jimmy Porter's father, who had fought and been wounded in Spain. In the 1950s, there was no Spain to fight in. Later came Vietnam, but it never provided the chance to fight and die for a better world, as Spain had done. Marching to the American embassy shouting 'Ho, Ho, Ho Chi Minh' was not quite the same thing.

Sam Russell was a man of Jimmy's father's generation, and he fought in Spain, and a lot more besides, and now his life has been faithfully recorded by younger colleagues. Some of his generation lived sheltered lives and saw very little of the blood-soaked times they lived through. A few saw a great deal of it, but very few saw as much as Sam Russell.

Born Manassah Lesser in 1915, to Orthodox Jewish parents who had fled persecution in Poland and had met in the East End where they ran a grocery shop, he came to Communism fighting the virulent anti-Semitism he found in London. He went to the front in the Spanish Civil War, first to fight for democracy in Spain, then to report on the war.

The outbreak of the Second World War finds him in Paris and then Brussels, reporting for the Communist newspaper the *Daily Worker* as well as Communist publications elsewhere in the world; he was effectively employed by the Communist International – the Comintern.

---

[*] **Francis Beckett** is an author, journalist, and contemporary historian. He has written several political biographies, including those of four of Stalin's British victims, and an account of the rise and fall of British Communism.

DOI: 10.4324/9781003243380-1

2 Francis Beckett

Post war, there's hardly a big story for which Sam did not have a ringside seat. He was in the Channel Islands just after the German occupying forces had left. At home he watched the battle for the National Health Service. He was the National Union of Journalists' Father of the Chapel (shop steward) at the *Daily Worker*, defending the uncomfortable compromise whereby *Daily Worker* journalists were notionally paid the union rate like other national newspaper journalists, but 'voluntarily' gave most of it back as a donation to the Communist Party, leaving them on subsistence wages.

As the *Daily Worker*'s Foreign Editor after 1953, he followed the show trials in Poland, Hungary, and Czechoslovakia before becoming Moscow correspondent in 1955, bang on time to be in the thick of it for the cataclysmic events of 1956, the year the Soviet Union invaded Hungary and Nikita Khrushchev's 'secret speech' exposed the crimes of Stalin.

His extraordinary capacity to be where it was happening brought him to Hungary later that year, and then back to Moscow again, in time to become a close friend of the British spy Donald Maclean, who had defected in 1951.

Back in London as Foreign Editor again in 1959, he was in Cuba in 1962 for the missile crisis and interviewed Che Guevara. He visited Vietnam twice in the 1970s, and travelled to China, Czechoslovakia, Chile (where he saw the coup that overthrew the left-wing president Salvador Allende), Poland, Italy (where he was in at the birth of Eurocommunism), as well as making a return visit to Spain and receiving Spanish citizenship.

And here in this book, for the first time, is what he made of it all, unmediated by the grey bureaucrats and political placemen who edited and mangled his journalism.

Along the way, though with no training, he turned himself into a fine writer, with the journalist's eye for both the story and the bit of colour that brings the story alive. But then he discovered that these were not the skills valued by the top brass at the *Daily Worker* (or the *Morning Star*, as it became after 1966.) He was disarmingly frank about this when I interviewed him in the early 1990s for my book *Enemy Within: The Rise and Fall of the British Communist Party*:

> People say, old Sam Russell's trouble is, he wanted to be editor. Damn right I did. I knew the trade. Communist Party leaders never completely trusted their own journalists. It was unforgiveable. If it was a question of loyalty they couldn't teach me anything about loyalty. The paper looked just like the CP organ. If there was a central committee meeting that would be the front page lead story, no matter what else was going on in the world.

So when he retired in 1984, he was the best editor the paper never had, with the possible exception of the great newspaper designer Allen Hutt, who had been its chief sub editor for many years. Both Hutt and Russell were passed over for people who knew a fraction of what they knew about journalism, but were considered politically reliable. Being editor is 'primarily a political job', Tony Chater, the last editor Sam worked for, told me. Chater knew little about journalism, and saw this as no great problem in his job.

In that, sadly, much of what we used to call the labour movement agreed with the Communist Party. In some of the big general trade unions, the general secretaries tended to regard their own journalists rather as Communist leader Harry Pollitt regarded Sam Russell. In my days working for the unions, I imagined some of the less imaginative general secretaries going into the corridor and shouting 'Hack!', expecting some humble functionary to come running, notebook in hand, tugging his forelock and licking his pencil. I suspect this attitude partly accounts for the fact that the trade unions have been in something like freefall since the mid-1980s.

In retrospect, I suspect that in his retirement, Sam wished he had rebelled, and not allowed his reports to be mangled. But in this book, we get the full benefit of what he saw and heard.

He brings alive the meanness and squalor of war, and I doubt whether the human story of the defeat of democracy in Spain has ever been told better. And he tells us what he did not tell his readers at the time, and did not know:

> Written in Stalin's own hand on a once-secret Soviet document are the simple words: 'this question is no longer of importance'.... It was his comment in February 1939 on the last, despairing request from the Spanish Republican Government for arms.

Along the way, Sam offers us a rather more sympathetic portrait than we are used to of the grim French commissar in Spain, André Marty.

Sam captures well the defeatist spirit in Paris in 1939, and the spine-tingling quote from General Weygand is new at least to me: 'Sooner Hitler than Thorez at the Elysée'. (Maurice Thorez was the French Communist leader.) He paints the immediate post war government in the Channel Islands as collaborators on the Vichy model.

About that time he seems to have decided that the *Daily Worker* News Editor, Douglas Hyde, was an MI5 mole, and felt vindicated when Hyde walked out in a blaze of publicity and into the arms of the Roman Catholic Church. He could be right, though personally, having interviewed Hyde, I think Sam was mistaken.

Sam became foreign editor in 1953, succeeding Derek Kartun. Alison Macleod, in a marvellous book about the *Daily Worker* office in 1956 called *The Death of Uncle Joe*, claims Kartun left the paper quietly, and editor Johnny Campbell appealed to the staff to rebut any suggestion that it was because he was Jewish, and replaced him with another Jew in Sam. She adds that Kartun was told to leave because of his particular friendship with *Daily Worker* journalist Claud Cockburn, who had been accused of being a spy.

He's rightly rather ashamed of the way he covered the show trials in Eastern Europe, and of having collaborated in keeping news of Khrushchev's 1956

4 Francis Beckett

speech exposing the crimes of Stalin from his readers. Interestingly, he seems to challenge Harry Pollitt's own account of what he knew and when. Pollitt claimed to know nothing of the speech at the time, having been packed off to visit a rubber factory – 'at my age I suppose that was a compliment'. But Sam says when they lunched together that day, he told Harry about the speech, though not its contents.

Of course the journalist in him lamented that, though he had the story, he was not able to get his paper to print it, and it was the Reuters correspondent John Rettie who got the scoop. The seeds of rebellion against Communist orthodoxy were starting to grow in Sam, but they were late flowering. He found his attempts to report truthfully from Moscow, and to describe the hardship and poverty he saw, irritated both the Soviet authorities and his editor.

Later that year finds him in Hungary, and I don't suppose I am the only reader who finds his account in this book of that part of his career defensive and unconvincing. Alison Macleod suggests that Russell was sent there to provide the politically reliable copy which the former correspondent Peter Fryer declined to do. Fryer, unable to get the real story into the *Daily Worker*, published it elsewhere and was expelled from the Party.

In Czechoslovakia in 1968, Sam's material was picked up and used by Radio Free Europe, and a furious Moscow apparatchik cut the order of the *Morning Star* from 12,000 to 9,000. 'It was a shot across the bows', Sam told me. 'At receptions people from the Soviet embassy would say, "I hear the circulation has dropped"'. It was restored two years later after George Matthews built bridges.

Sam writes beautifully about Vietnam in this book, and the reader cannot fail to be disgusted at the sheer cruelty of the US in wartime, but he went to Cambodia too, and he rightly observes: 'The US were bastards in Asia but they were not alone'.

In the end this is a ferociously angry book. Angry at the selfishness and cruelty of capitalism, yes. Angry at the secret and unaccountable power of the security services, which watched him all his life, yes. But angriest at the corrupt and rigid instrument the Communist countries, and the Communist parties, fashioned to fight capitalism, to which he had given his life.

1

THE ROAD TO SPAIN

Both my parents came from a little Polish village, Ropczyce, just down the road from Auschwitz, and left for Britain before the First World War. They came over separately and met again by accident in Whitechapel in the East End of London at a cousin's house. My father Naftali Leser stayed with relatives and found work as a button-hole maker.[1] He graduated to working on, and then repairing, Singer sewing machines. He spoke in Yiddish and read Hebrew. He hardly knew any Polish because he had been locked up in a ghetto-type existence in Poland in which Orthodox Jews considered the study of the scriptures and the Talmud as the be-all and end-all of their existence. And that was one of his phrases, a constant refrain: *ober goor, ober goornicht; either all, either nothing.*

In contrast, my mother Perla Weitzen spoke good Polish, as well as having Yiddish as her home language, and she was more worldly wise.[2] Her mother had died in childbirth, so she had been brought up by her grandparents, who had a big store for ironmongery, hardware and agricultural seeds, and had to do business with Catholic Poles. Her father had left Poland, come to England, got married again and raised a new family. He had visited her once in Cracow and didn't see him again until years later in England, when he was working as a ritual slaughterer producing kosher meat and came by to see her. Before coming to Britain, where she was a seamstress, she had worked in a baker's shop in Cracow, a city with a large Jewish population and a lively Jewish culture. She had particularly vivid memories of the Yiddish theatre there, and she passed on to her children her love of theatre. For her, it was heaven; for father, it was the work of the devil.

When the First World War broke out, they were both classified as enemy aliens because where they had been brought up – in what was then called Galicia – belonged to the Austro-Hungarian empire. The classification was lifted when the Allies agreed on the reconstitution of Poland. They moved from Whitechapel and

DOI: 10.4324/9781003243380-2

FIGURE 1.1 Polly with her sons (left to right) Sid, Frank, and Sam.
Source: Family archive.

The Road to Spain **7**

set up a grocery shop not that far away in Lauriston Road, south Hackney, which proved reasonably successful. It was seen as going up in the world, but it was a difficult existence for them. With not much time left for shows of affection, theirs was not a demonstrative relationship but it was a strong one. She was a hard working woman, in the shop up to the day before, or on the very day, that she gave birth. We were eight children, four boys and four girls, and I was the eldest, born in 1915.[3]

Though my father wanted to maintain a proper Jewish approach to life, he was obliged by economic circumstance to breach the strict rules of the faith. At first, the clientele at the shop was mainly Jewish and the shop closed for religious observance from dusk on Friday until dusk on Saturday. Unlike most shops in London at the time, it was open on Sundays, and gradually, more and more customers were non-Jewish. As the women were given the housekeeping money at the end of work on a Friday, they needed to buy their goods that evening, and it was a great inner struggle for him to have to open the shop to accommodate them. It caused trouble at the more orthodox Federation Synagogue he attended and, eventually, he switched to the more liberal United Synagogue. He attended English classes and, after many years of reading the Yiddish daily *Die Zeit* ('The Times'), he switched to the English-language *News Chronicle*, then the major liberal daily in London.

In the early days, when we were little kids, my father was still able to be more strictly religious. Jewish boys would wear a sort of small shawl with cotton tassels on the end as a reminder of prayers – when each prayer was said, you took out the tassels and kissed them. When I went swimming, there it was, most embarrassing until I got bold enough not to wear it. But one day my father found it under my pillow in bed and I got a beating.

I grew up speaking only Yiddish, but my father, then a Zionist, was strongly supportive of making Hebrew a living language again. I attended classes as a child at the synagogue's *cheder* or school every weekday night, other than Friday and Saturday, as well as on Sunday mornings. Later, I attended modern Hebrew classes at the Redman's Road Talmud Tora in Stepney, which I reached by tram. It was run by a Zionist and oriented to the return to the promised land. Here they taught the language by a kind of Berlitz method with everything spoken in Hebrew as soon as you went into the classroom. It made one learned, but with a knowledge that was entirely internal to Jewish life and of little or no help with the outside world. When I was a bit older I also went along to classes run by Habonim or Builders, a Socialist-Zionist youth movement.

I was pretty good at the religion, though each Saturday my father would check what I had learnt that week and greeted any mistakes with a clip round the ear. My development was also being watched from afar in Poland by my father's parents. He would write them dutifully long but proud letters in Hebrew or Yiddish. When I started to write in Hebrew, he made sure that I proved my progress with letters of my own.

A young man going through his bar mitzvah celebration of Jewish religious adulthood on his thirteenth birthday would usually read at the synagogue the last couple of paragraphs of the relevant portion of the Pentateuch for that week. My

8 The Road to Spain

father, who could recite all the five books of Moses from one end to the other, along with long sections of the Talmud, decided I was going to give a complete chapter for my bar mitzvah, not just a couple of verses, chanting the whole thing from heart. So there I was doing my school work, attending my Hebrew classes and getting special coaching for this performance, the money for which my parents could ill afford. There came a point when I told the coach I would not be coming again, but the next week when I did turn up, he asked me why: I had not dared tell my father I had decided to give it up. At my bar mitzvah, I also did a chapter from the Prophets. It was seen as something of a tour de force.

My father thought I should study to be a rabbi and so I was sent to classes at the Tree of Life Yeshiva – a Jewish seminary – in Whitechapel. Perhaps, it was his attempt to work out his own ambitions though me. On occasions, he had a most violent temper and I got some very harsh beatings from him. Thinking back, I can see that he was a frustrated individual, a person with great intellect, looked up to in the local Jewish community as a Talmudic scholar, but one whose hopes and aspirations were in conflict with the reality of his life. When things were difficult between us, my mother always acted as a sort of go-between. I felt that she understood, even though we never actually discussed such things.

The elementary school I went to was just across the street in Royston Road, so I was always late. Being Jewish made me stand out. My name Manassah gave me away immediately, even when the family name Lesser did not. A particular problem arose with the school assembly. Usually, I and the other Jewish children could stay out, but on Empire Day we were told that we all had to join in. I said I wasn't going to. There was an argument over why I did not want to take part. I remember the reason I gave – perhaps because it shows what a curmudgeonly sort of chap I already was. My particular objection was to the hymn 'Oh God, our help in ages past'. One line says, 'Be Thou our help while troubles last'. I took this to mean that when the troubles were over you would not need to worry about God any more. I strongly objected to that. One should stay faithful, even in good times. 'It's a matter of principle', I declared.

At the elementary school I took the scholarship exam, the equivalent of what became the 11 plus. If I passed, it meant that the London County Council would pay my fees for the local private grammar school. Neither I nor any of my brothers passed the scholarship exam, though our four sisters did. We boys all went to the local London County Council school, South Hackney Central, which offered a generally high level of education, including a foreign language. It was in easy walking distance across Well Street Common. By the end of the twentieth century, it had been converted into luxury flats.

In those days, compulsory education only lasted up to the age of 14, but if you went to the Central School, you had to agree to stay on until 16 when you took the School Certificate leaving exams. If you wanted to try for university, you needed to go to a school with a sixth form and sit the Higher Certificate exam. The Central did not have a sixth form and most schools that did were reluctant to let you in just for the two years it took to study for that exam. In the event,

FIGURE 1.2 Sam's father Nathan in front of the family shop.
Source: Family archive.

the only school I could get into was further away from home than the Central School. It was called George Green's in East India Dock Road, Poplar, and the number of Jewish kids there was relatively small.

The head came across as something of a religious fanatic who wore an enormous cross on his watch chain and had a copy of the Bible with him at all times and gave the impression that an important part of his duty was to save the Jewish boys for Christianity. Despite my disputes with the school, I became a prefect, edited the school magazine and took up cross-country running. This meant my day started by opening up the shop, then some running on the track in Victoria Park, which was at the top of our street, followed by school and after that, Hebrew classes. I also developed a love of music at George Green's, which had a grand piano, something I had never seen before and which, I discovered though never knew why, had been selected on the advice of the then well-known Communist composer Alan Bush.

I had to go into the fifth form in order to re-sit my school certificate because I had failed my Maths credit. I could only progress to the sixth form when I had passed all the credits, which I did at the re-sit but it meant I was a year behind. Arts was my chosen area of study as my French was very good, but, if I wanted to try for university, I had to have Latin, which meant cramming seven years of learning into just two years. There were some who did it, but I mucked it up, though I did very well in other subjects. The result was a scholarship to University College London to do history, but only on condition that I passed Latin at a re-sit. I did not manage this, and without the Latin, a full degree course was not possible.

10 The Road to Spain

UCL, however, had a special diploma course in Egyptology, which I took up in 1934, though I was never really that serious as a student. I lived at home and received 15 shillings a week from the London County Council and some additional money from a special Jewish grant – on condition I become a rabbi when I finished university. I was called before the responsible committee when reports were received that things were not exactly going in the rabbinical direction. The chairman was Sir Robert Waley Cohen, later a Lord Mayor of London. They were quite sympathetic but decided it was no go. I suggested they should be supportive as doing Egyptology meant continuing Hebrew studies and they let me continue on a reduced grant, though in fact I had abandoned the faith well before I went to university.

After the age of 13, a Jewish boy has to wear phylacteries, or *tefillin* in Hebrew, for prayers. These are two small leather boxes containing a sacred text on a piece of parchment. One is on a circular piece of leather which goes round your head. The other has a strip of leather which you wrap round your forearm, hand and finger when you pray on weekday mornings. Mine were specially made for me by my grandparents in Poland. My grandmother had embroidered a little black velvet bag, with my name in Hebrew surrounded with flowers, for me to keep them in. The house was cramped and we four boys were sleeping in a small room with two together in each of two single beds. I would get up, perhaps have a fight with my brother Frank, and then get these things on and start praying. But, as time went by, there were an increasing number of occasions when I was in such a hurry to get the tram to George Green's that I missed the prayers.

The first time I did not carry out the ritual I really thought I would be struck dead, but clearly I was not. I had a similar experience in the synagogue. Jews are supposed to be divided into three grades: the Cohens, the Levites, and the rest. The Cohens are called upon at a certain stage in the prayers for the Day of Atonement, Yom Kippur. They mount the *bimah*, a raised platform in front of the Ark of the Covenant, and pull their praying shawl, or *tallit*, right over their heads. They spread their fingers out in a certain order, supposedly in secret but everybody knows about it. While they are doing that, the rest of the congregation must not look. I was with my father. He had his praying shawl right over his head but I had accidentally looked up. When I realised I was still alive, the spell was broken.

My final fall from grace had happened at George Green's when I discovered the twin attractions of non-Jewish girls and non-kosher food. Because I could not get home for lunch once I had got to school – it being too far away – I would usually just eat a tin of baked beans to avoid eating non-kosher food. But one time when we were away at the school's annual camp, George, the guy who kept the school playing field in order on the Isle of Dogs and who became the camp cook, had me on kitchen duty, peeling potatoes. George was frying up some bacon.

'Why don't you eat it', he asked, 'It's good stuff. Try some'.

It was not bad and on camp George would give me two dinners, one kosher and one not. My father was already straying from the strict letter of observance, so I can't say that this rasher was what made me give up my faith. It might even have been a sort of laziness. I just got fed up with the *tefillin* and gradually came to realise that we were, as a family, not observant in the way we claimed to be.

My first political memories come from the time of the General Strike in 1926 when I was 11 years old. Before the strike, Victoria Park had been a sort of local Hyde Park with a Speakers' Corner where people would set up their soapboxes and tribunes every Sunday round the bandstand. I used to watch in particular the speaker from the Socialist Party of Great Britain because he had such a wonderful, curly pipe. At the time of the strike, the park was closed and made into a military camp. Tents were set up, troops stationed and units sent out to the docks. My father had won a contract to deliver bread every day to the soldiers and it was my job to take it. To see so many troops lined up in the same place where there had been all that talk only days before made a very powerful impression on me.

When I later went to George Green's, I had an 'enlightened' history teacher, Miss Downing, though not of the left, who offered social history alongside the Kings and Queens you needed to pass exams. The school debating society more directly introduced me to politics when I was in the sixth form and I bought a pamphlet from the local bookseller, *Democracy and Fascism* by the Communist Party theoretician Rajani Palme Dutt, to mug up for a speech in a debate.

The basic motivation for me politically at this time was the anti-Semitism I found around me. It took an increasingly ugly form in the shape of the pro-fascist Blackshirt presence in London. For any thinking young Jewish person, it had to be the central issue. The number of times I had been called 'Jew bastard' at school or told to 'Go back to Palestine', I cannot even start to remember. With my parents having fled anti-Semitism in Poland, we felt the issue particularly keenly. As small children, we were terrified of the moment in *Pesach* or Passover when the door is opened for Elijah because we had all heard stories of how, in Poland, Christians commemorating the Crucifixion would enter looking for Jews 'who killed Christ'.

Many people have forgotten how pervasive anti-Semitism was in British public life in those days.[4] Until the university authorities put a stop to it, there was a period in UCL when you had a group of supporters of the British fascist leader Sir Oswald Mosley wearing his black shirt uniform and parading in the college. They were particularly strong in the medical school and among the engineers. There were quite a number in the law faculty as well. Though it seems hard to believe now, UCL still had its Galton Society, named after the English statistician and eugenicist Sir Francis Galton, and the college Eugenics Department was still in operation – one of only two in British higher education focused on the idea that the population needed to be cleansed of people of 'poor genetic stock'.

In 1934, the year I went to UCL, the society's members were still conducting cranial measurements on new students at the Freshers' Fair in the college's Cloisters Hall where the fully dressed skeleton of the philosopher Jeremy Bentham sits on display. And they were still telling some of the students on the basis of these measurements: 'You are a Jew'. Taking measurements of the length and breadth of a person's head with specially designed callipers, calculating the ratio and then,

FIGURE 1.3 Sam in Hackney, east London 1936.
Source: Family archive.

depending on the figure, declaring them to be a Jew was not a student jape but a respected academic practice. The memory of the moment when I first saw that humiliating process has stuck with me over the years.

Coming from the East End of London, I had had the fascists on my doorstep. Hackney and Bethnal Green were hotbeds of Mosley's activities. The other side of Victoria Park to us, Victoria Park Square, was a favourite spot for Mosley, and there were many clashes there with the local Jewish population. As with a lot of young Jewish lads in the area, our idea was to give them a kick in the eye for what they were doing to us. There was no romance in fighting the fascists. It was something few of us saw as anything other than a straightforward duty. One fascist demonstration where I was protesting was at the Albert Hall. A group of us jumped up to ask a question, shouted it out and were immediately pounced on, dragged along, beaten and thrown out. The Communist Party, which had organised the protest, was widely seen in our area as the only political party that was fighting the fascists. I was the first in the family to join but it was the same for my brothers and sisters and, in the end, for both of my parents, too.

My father, who had been brought up in the Hasidic sect that believed Zionists were second-guessing the Messiah and were, therefore, wrong, was already well on the way to being a fully-fledged Zionist by the time he came to Britain. During my childhood, virtually every Jewish home had a little blue collecting box belonging to the Jewish National Fund. The collections were designed to buy land in Palestine from the then Arab owners and establish Jewish co-operatives, the kibbutz, on them. Every now and then someone would come round to our house and take the money, but my father had grown suspicious of those involved in the movement and he became more interested in British politics, supporting the Liberals. Then in 1933, when he had finally saved up enough money to see his parents in Poland, with whom he was in regular correspondence, he travelled there and back by train through Germany and returned home with frightening stories of the Nazis. As a naturalised British citizen using a British passport, he was not molested, but the experience was traumatic. He turned towards the Labour Party yet its line was to ignore the fascists, a policy that, for me, was total defeatism. Herbert Morrison, one of the great leaders of the Labour Party and our MP, said, 'Stay Away – ignore the Blackshirts'. It was not a surprise my father joined the Communist Party.

The letters from his parents stopped when the war broke out. If they survived the Nazis, they may have fallen victim to persecution when the Soviet Union occupied Poland. Presumably, only their killers know how they ended their days. For me, in 1934, this was still in the future. Like so many others faced with the dangers of fascism and the perils of anti-Semitism, the Soviet Union appeared as a beacon of progress and the obvious ally of oppressed Jews everywhere.

I joined the Communist Party at the end of my first term at university, in December 1934. I had spoken at union debates and was asked to join the student

FIGURE 1.4 Sam (third on the left, third row from front) attending a residential school at Digswell Park, Welwyn Garden City, Hertfordshire, February 1936.
Source: Family archive.

14 The Road to Spain

branch. The first comrade I struck up a friendship with was called Brian Pearce, who later became a leading Trotskyist. Together we cooked up the idea of going into the Officers' Training Corps (OTC) on the basis of a phrase we came across in our Marxist education where Lenin says that a working class that does not learn the use of arms deserves to be enslaved. The Party was campaigning against the militarisation of schools and universities, and was not alone in this. The British Labour Party and left movement had a long tradition of opposition to national service, but the two of us went our own way. Surprisingly, the OTC did not object to us joining. We were both well known as 'reds', but the OTC was so hard up for volunteers that it would even take us 'Bolshies'.

Arms drill became a regular thing on the college tennis court. The lefties would gather round and jeer at me and Brian flinging our rifles about. It was thoroughly enjoyable. We did all the things you have to do if you are in the OTC. There was a colour sergeant from the Grenadier Guards, a real tough guy who put us through our paces. There were weekends at a place at Princes Risborough in the Chilterns for target practice and an OTC summer camp was organised faculty by faculty, college by college across London University. The engineers were in artillery, the medical students in the medical corps, the rest in the poor bloody infantry. At a camp on the south coast with the whole university OTC – the largest in the country – the parades were very impressive. The honorary commander in chief of the University OTC, Earl of Athlone, the Chancellor of the University of London and brother in law to King George V, took the formal march past. I enjoyed it fantastically. I was even in the OTC detachment at the King's Jubilee in 1935 and eight months later at his funeral.

I was also invited to a course attached to the Durham Light Infantry, which the War Ministry had chosen to try out a mechanised machine gun unit. This was a new thing in those days in which a small armoured troop carrier made by the tractor company Carden Lloyd was fitted out to carry two Vickers machine guns. Having done well there, I went on to an attachment with junior officers of the Royal Scots at Dover Castle, where I was treated like one of their own and allowed to use the officers' mess. The Royal Scots was a Lowland regiment and wore tartan trews, but a battalion of the Argyll and Sutherland Highlanders, a Highland regiment with the kilt, was also at the castle. One day on parade, the Adjutant in charge of them gave the order 'Ground Arms', which he followed by 'Up Kilts'. At that time, it was a punishable offence to wear anything under the kilt. Our cry was that we were 'Nae bludy arse-rags', as I recall.

As I had done quite well, the Grenadier Guards sergeant back at UCL suggested I put my name down for the Supplementary Reserve of Officers. The only obligation was that those on the list would be the first to be called up in the event of another war, but, assuming that nobody would be stupid enough to have another war, I agreed, though it was counter to everything the Communist Party was preaching. Having been put on the list, I was allowed to wear a gold badge bearing the initials OCR, standing for Officer Cadet Reserve.

To make things easier for the weekend target practice, I would take a rifle home from the college armoury, but, because of my father, I had to smuggle the thing into the house and hide it in the bedroom I shared with my three brothers. The army was anathema to someone of his Hasidic background, and Jews, for him, were opposed to killing. My mother knew about the rifle, but never told my father. His opposition was so strong that, when I went off to fight in Spain, I did not tell him where I was going. My mother was in tears, but I asked her to say I was in Egypt on an archaeological dig.

I was at an army camp when I heard the news of the attempted coup against the Spanish government, though there was no talk of it in the mess. It didn't seem to impinge on the OTC, who were overwhelmingly right wing, but I was outraged.

The Popular Front government had won the Spanish election in February 1936. The coup by the generals of Spain's armed forces against the elected government in July 1936 failed to give them immediate control over the whole of Spain. One of the key players, Francisco Franco, quickly turned to Mussolini and Hitler for help. He had command over the powerful, well trained and battle tested military forces in Spain's Moroccan colony. The Government had the support of the navy where the ratings had removed those officers who had sided with the coup. Franco could not get his forces across the Mediterranean and into action against those forces who remained loyal to the Republic. Those opposed to the coup had control of the overwhelming mass of Spain and, with Franco locked in North Africa, failure was staring the generals in the face.

The Italian dictator dithered for a few days. After establishing that the British and French governments were not going actively to back the Madrid government, Mussolini provided transport and bomber planes to Franco. More came a few days later from Hitler. By the first week in August the Italian and German planes were ferrying thousands of Franco's elite soldiers across the sea and the following week were providing air cover for his troop ships to break the naval attempts to blockade them in the Moroccan ports.

The flow of arms to Franco, along with the active involvement of German and, in much greater numbers, Italian personnel and aircraft, gave the generals the opportunity to attack toward the centre of Spain and the capital Madrid from the south, and toward the Basque areas in the north from the bases in Northern Spain which the generals had secured in July. By early September, Franco's 'Army of Africa' had taken Maqueda, the last significant town on its route to Madrid, while, in the north, the Basque towns of Irun and San Sebastian were occupied after Italian planes engaged in heavy bombing of Irun.

The government's control over a coherent army had been destroyed and opposition to Franco came in the spontaneous formation of popular militias. Scattered individuals from various countries, mostly people who just happened to have been in Spain at the time, were active in these different militias. Among the international volunteers who died in this early fighting was the British artist Felicia Browne, killed in action in August.

16 The Road to Spain

The Republican government itself had sought help from France immediately after the coup. Both countries were ruled by Popular Front governments. Leon Blum, Prime Minister in the Popular Front cabinet in Paris, was reportedly persuaded by the British government during a visit to London to hold back despite Whitehall knowing – as reports released later show – of the immediate involvement by Germany and Italy.

The approach adopted by the British and French governments was one of 'non-intervention' combined with turning a carefully blind eye to the obvious and widely reported direct intervention by Hitler and Mussolini, who committed massive forces to Franco and were prepared to help defeat the Republic whatever the cost. A Non-Intervention Committee was established in London in September bringing together 27 governments to take action against those trading arms or sending forces to Spain. It failed to take any action against Germany or Italy whose direct military involvement was vital for Franco's forces.

Some have questioned how soon the British government recognised the scope of support Franco was receiving, but reading documents many years later in the National Archives in London shows what I believed at the time of the Civil War to be true: Whitehall knew from July 1936 on.[5] The ineffective Non-Intervention Committee was only kept going to enable the French government to avoid allowing the export of arms to the Spanish government and thereby they could argue this prevented the Civil War spreading to the rest of Europe.

In contrast to this bogus 'non-intervention', various left organisations immediately began to explore ways of sending help to Spain, but the serious numbers only came when the issue was taken up by the Communist movement. Key figures from the French Communist Party and the Communist International (Comintern to all of us) based in Moscow were in Spain before the end of August 1936, and on 18 September, the Comintern leadership voted to 'proceed to the recruitment, among the workers of all countries, of volunteers with military experience, with the intention of sending them to Spain'.

It was Jack Cohen, the Student Organiser of the Communist Party, who in September 1936 suggested Republican Spain needed me, though I thought Spain needed more arms, not more people. I had met Jack through setting up Party study classes in Marxism for students, and for me he was a mostly shadowy figure, someone I would see at the side of the street marshalling us in demonstrations and protests. Jack knew I was in the OTC, and, despite the Party criticisms in the past, he now appeared to see this as something in favour of me going to Spain instead of leaving for an archaeological dig in Egypt, as had been my original intention. He said an international unit was being formed with volunteers from all over the world. To overcome my objections, he persuaded me to go to the Party's head offices in London's King Street just beside the Covent Garden fruit and vegetable market, and see Harry Pollitt, the General Secretary. It did not take Harry long to convince me that an international force was necessary and that, with my military training, I could do a useful job. What clinched it for me at King Street was also talking to John Cornford.

By then, Cornford, one of the Party's student activists from Cambridge University, had already come back from Spain and was telling of his experiences in battle against the fascists alongside members of the leftist movement, POUM. I had met him at national student conferences where his knowledge of Marxism and the powerful way he put over his case was impressive. With all due respect to him, however, Cornford, like a number of those who went to Spain, appeared to see himself as telling the 'natives' how to run a revolutionary war, something of which he had no experience. Whatever his faults in this respect, he was the inspiration for the first round of volunteers. Though I found him too tense and nervous, I got to know him better in Spain as a splendid comrade.

The British Party official in charge of handling recruitment for Spain was RW 'Robbie' Robson, a member of the Party's Control Commission, the body elected at each congress to make sure the Party leadership followed the decisions of the congress and the Comintern. To cover expenses on the way to Spain, we were each given £10, which I never spent.[6]

I decided I would go to Spain in my OTC kit, though it was not the uniform of a revolutionary militia and I had not then fully paid for it. Bill Geyl, son of Pieter Geyl, the Professor of Dutch History at UCL, and a friend of the Communist Party with whom I used to have endless arguments, gave me a substantial rucksack, and a red pullover and brown corduroy trousers, which I put on over the uniform, puttees, and all. The Party branch held a collection to buy me a British Army officer's gas mask, which they got from the Army and Navy stores. Though it turned out to be a complete false alarm, there were already rumours that the fascists were using gas, and when I got to Spain the authorities were issuing gas masks.

Travelling alone via the Newhaven-Dieppe night ferry to Paris, I wanted to avoid French customs inspecting me too closely as there were already moves to stop volunteers, so I put the gas mask on top of my rucksack and buried anything political at the bottom. It did the trick, and when a suspicious customs officer at the French coast asked what the mask was for, I replied: 'You know what those dirty Germans are like'. He called over his superior, who looked at me and tapped the side of his head, uttering 'Ah, les Anglais!' as if to say 'they're all mad', and I went through without a hitch. Though the gas mask was never needed in Spain, the carrier for the mask proved very useful later as a sandwich box.

The address I had been given for the first stop on the journey turned out to be that of the French Communist Party headquarters in Rue Lafayette, Paris. The comrades there were organising rooms in small hotels and the like for the growing stream of volunteers passing through the French capital. Our orders for the journey were strict: we had to stay in small groups and pass via the Gare de Lyon to Perpignan in southern France, taking care not to talk to others so we did not give things away. Once I was on board, it became clear that the train was stuffed full of small groups all on their way to Perpignan, all trying hard not to give their real purpose away. Even worse than our own failures to travel incognito were

18 The Road to Spain

the actions of the track workers. As the train moved off, they raised clenched fists and shouted: *'Des avions pour l'Espagne!'* – *'Planes for Spain!'* But we got through.

We spent the night in Perpignan in a disused hospital. Each of us was given a Spanish name on the pretence that we were Spanish workers going home from France by bus. Mine was Raimundo Casado, which, ironically, turned out to be the name of the colonel who finally betrayed the Spanish Republic when he organised a coup against the government during the dying days of the war.

At that time, there was no need to hike across the high Pyrenees, as became necessary later, because the Non-Intervention Committee had not yet got into its stride. When it did, the French sought to close the frontier with Spain to any movement of volunteers or arms and thousands had to make a perilous night-time trek across the mountain passes. No one tried to stop us, and over the border we went.

Notes

1 In the Polish registration documents, the name was written Leser (pronounced like laser), which comes from Elizer, the Biblical figure who was Abraham's lieutenant, but in England the name became Lesser. In Britain, Naftali was known as Nathan.
2 Her original name was Pesel (or Pesla) Weitzen. The latter means wheat in Yiddish and came to be written in English as Whiteson or Witson. In Britain, she was known as Polly.
3 The eight children were: Manassah (born 1915), Efraim (1916), Salom (1917), and Isaac (1921) – and four girls – Queenie (1920), Ruth (1930), Shirley (1931), and Miriam (1932).
4 The MI5 record card of Sam's time in Spain says he was of 'Jewish appearance'.
5 Papers Sam consulted include reports to the Foreign Office from a British Consul in the Moroccan town of Tétouan (FO 371 20525, pp. 243 to 245), minutes of full Cabinet meetings e.g. 18.11.1936 (CAB 23.86) and 08.01.1937 (CAB 23.87), and dispatches to the FO from the Britannic Ambassador in Spain (e.g. 21.12.1936, FO371/20549, and 28.12.1936, FO 371/21281).
6 Sam said when the war was over he tried to pay back the £10.

> Robbie, as he was universally known, would have none of it. My brother Frank was teaching English at the Soviet Embassy at the time and could get things cheaply through a co-operative they had set up. The £10 went on a decent Swiss watch, which was so good it was still serving me long after I retired.

2

FIGHTING FRANCO

We were driven in a bus to Figueras, the first big town in Spain. We were billeted in the fine castle there, which, however, had appalling sanitary conditions. Amid the stench, the reality of my decision to go to Spain began to dawn.

A train took us right across Spain to Albacete, capital of La Mancha in the south-east, chosen as the base for what was initially called the 'International Column'. My group arrived on 17 October 1936. As our number doubled in a fortnight, the accommodation was quickly crowded out and the conditions in the barracks we were first allocated to became pretty horrible. Once again, the sanitation was appalling.

Also arriving at Albacete were Cornford, Bernard Knox, another student from Cambridge University, later Professor of Hellenic Studies at Harvard, and David Mackenzie, a student from Edinburgh University, whose father was an admiral and who later had the rare of honour of having his obituary published in the *Times* while he was still alive, following a mistaken report that he had been killed at the front in Spain. Knox, like me, had spent time in the OTC, but some in our group had done real military service. Jock Cunningham and Jock Clark, for example, had been in the Argyll and Sutherland Highlanders and the Black Watch respectively. Jock Cunningham regaled us with the tale of how in the Aldershot glasshouse prisoners had to polish the fire escape one day so it gleamed from top to bottom, then cover it with bootblack the next, ready for polishing once again.[1] He had other, more pertinent tales, so far as I was concerned, like how in the glasshouse they had been issued with only three pieces of toilet paper at a time – as he put it bluntly: 'One up, one down and a polisher'. My own training in the OTC had drummed into me that when you set up camp you made sure that the latrines were constructed properly right at the start, and that they were downwind from the cookhouse. Many of those going to Spain did not feel they

DOI: 10.4324/9781003243380-3

FIGURE 2.1 Sam in his Officers' Training Corps uniform, Albacete, Spain.
Source: Family archive.

had been called to dig latrines. They were there to fight fascism, they declared. Once the fighting began, the practical realism of the handful of former soldiers proved as important to those of us who bothered to listen as did the enthusiasm everyone shared.

Also in that first group was Freddy Jones, whose parents were in the fruit and veg line, though he himself had been in the Grenadier Guards before buying himself out, and Steve Yates, who was originally from New Zealand but served time in the British Army in India before ending up in London where he worked as an electrician. Many could give long histories of activities against fascism in Britain, some having been sent to prison for their efforts, and one or two had even wider experience. Joe Hinks, we discovered, had not only served in a Guards regiments but also with Communist Party forces in China. Our company commander was a good soldier called Fredo Brugère, a *gars du batiment* or building worker from Paris. Fredo, like virtually all the French volunteers, had done his military service in the French army.

The fact that some volunteers were students from Oxford and Cambridge universities has given the impression that those who went to Spain from Britain were all bright young intellectual things with glittering prospects before them, romantically putting their lives on the line in a moment of youthful enthusiasm. The truth is rather different. Among the small groups who fought in the first couple of months of the war in the summer of 1936 were a high proportion of students, intellectuals and people from professional walks of life – they were the kind of people who were likely to have been able to visit Spain in those days and be on the spot. But by the time the more formal recruitment process was in place, the vast majority of volunteers were industrial workers.

Another French Communist was in charge at Albacete. André Marty[2] had a hero status in the Communist movement because during the military intervention by the Western Powers against the young Soviet Republic immediately after the 1917 Revolution, he had led a mutiny among the sailors of the French Black Sea fleet. Marty welcomed us volunteers with a fiery speech, the first of more than a few I was to hear from him. His message struck a strong chord: 'A blow now may free civilization for all time from the curse of fascism but, remember, we are here to kill fascists, not to commit suicide in front of them'.

The first issue to arise was that of uniform. Most had come in their ordinary 'civvi' clothes, while, once I had removed my brown corduroys and red jersey, I was kitted out and accoutred in my OTC uniform with the letters OCR for all to see: Officer Cadet Reserve. The French teased me as 'Officier Cadet du Roi'. The other volunteers had a sort of navy blue uniform made of a thick woollen material with pair of baggy trousers and a top like the battledress that became familiar to all British soldiers during the war.

Who should be the commander of our little unit was the next question. Cornford was the name on everyone's lips, especially as he had already been in the fighting. But Freddy Jones, the former Guardsman, was the one appointed from on high, because of his military experience. Freddy could not speak French, so Bernard Knox took his first step towards that Harvard Professorship, acting as go-between with Fredo and the other French officers. He did a pretty good job until he got a bullet through the neck in the middle of fighting that December around the village of Boadilla. By amazing good luck, it did not kill him.[3]

The part of La Mancha around Albacete was the main centre for growing saffron, the stamen of a bulb of the crocus family, and saffron is one of the most expensive ways of flavouring food, but to prepare a proper Spanish paella, you need saffron. In the morning, women carrying great sacks picked the flowers, and during the intense heat of the afternoon they would sit in the shade picking the stamens out of the flowers – a labour-intensive activity, hence the high cost of saffron. We set out to help these Spanish women do the work – a most agreeable way, it seemed, of passing a war.

Almost immediately, however, the small group of British volunteers I was part of was moved to La Roda, a small picturesque town nearby, to start our so-called training. We were put in the machine gun company of the First French Battalion under Jules Dumont, who had arrived in Spain in August. At this stage, there were only two International Brigade battalions, one French, the other

22 Fighting Franco

German. There was another group of British volunteers, led by Giles Romilly, a nephew of Winston Churchill, who was with the German battalion, but they were unknown to us then.

Like our commander Fredo, Jules Dumont had military experience, and had been sent by the Comintern as a military advisor to the Abyssinian King Haile Selassie after the Italian invasion of Ethiopia in 1935. Later, during the German occupation of France, Dumont was shot by the Nazis for his resistance activities.

As an ex-Guardsman, Freddy Jones took us through a lot of formal drill. This caused problems. Former soldiers like Jock Clark had had enough of that in the British army: he was in Spain to fight the fascists not bash squares. Others just wanted to get to the front and fight. They did not understand the importance of training and discipline when it comes to battle. Reality interfered pretty quickly in the shape of the first rifles sent to us, which turned out to be a large quantity of old Austro-Hungarian empire rifles, Steyrs, from before the First World War. All were covered with thick 'verdigrease' from age and corrosion, and trying to get them ready to use, we were all doused in vast quantities of the stuff. We had to spend what seemed like days getting it off the rifles with endless buckets of boiling hot water, the only thing we had to hand. There were no magazines – those had been lost somewhere down the line – so we had to feed the bullets in by hand, one by one, but we found that the cartridges in the ammunition clips were also spoiled with the 'verdigrease'. Even after we had tried to clean them up, some of the charges would misfire in the barrel, causing very nasty injuries. As well as rifles that were as much a danger to our untrained selves as they might be to any enemy, we acquired a supply of a kind of home-made hand grenade. You lit a wick and waited until it was properly going before throwing it. As you might expect, several comrades had them blow up in their hands.

When we were leaving for the front some days later, a shipment of First World War US Remington rifles arrived, but with no magazine clips or bayonets. From the boxes they came in, it seemed they were leftovers from the British Army nearly two decades earlier. Remington was also the name of a famous typewriter, and the quip that passed through the ranks was: 'why are they giving us type-writers to fight the fascists?'

In spite of my resplendent uniform, my comrades did not see me as someone possessed of significant military qualities. Even on the butts in Buckinghamshire at Princes Risborough with the OTC, I was never exactly a crack shot, and what I would have managed in battle with one of the Remingtons, let alone the Steyrs, I hate to think. Luckily from that point of view, I was assigned to a machine gun unit.

It was a rather strange collection of machine guns that we had to train with. A real Heath Robinson object arrived with the declaration that it was a Hotchkiss. Familiar with the French Hotchkiss, I could not see much of a likeness, and it turned out that these were a Spanish manufactured version, which seemed to have cogs and springs everywhere, ready to fly out at the slightest touch. It was mounted high up on a most horrible, enormous and heavy tripod, quite unlike the convenient British Vickers machine gun I had been used to in the OTC.

After the fighting started for us, somebody said they had spotted some Lewis machine guns, which were standard British army equipment and carried the ammunition in a round drum fixed on top of the gun barrel – 'un camembert', the French called it – rather than being fed by a long belt of ammunition passed in through the side like most other machine guns. Edward Cooper – known to everyone as Burke, who had been an actor with the left-wing Unity Theatre and was killed in spring 1937 at the Jarama battle – suggested we see General Kléber, who was in charge of the International Brigade, and try to get our hands on the Lewis guns. Lo and behold, a few days later some arrived. 'As you British seem to know about them, you can have them', was the line. Pleased as punch, we set to work to get used to them. In addition, we got hold of some French Hotchkisses, which were easier to handle than the Spanish version.

Having heard about these French guns before leaving England, I had managed to secure a handbook in a book shop near the British Museum but when I started to read it, I discovered that four vital pages were missing. The bookshop owner told me it would take two weeks for a new replacement copy to arrive. I was due to leave for Paris within a week and the only place likely to have a copy was the British Museum itself, which housed the British Library, so I got myself signed in to the famous Reading Room where Marx had written much of *Das Kapital*. I intended to copy the relevant pages out but, in the event, I simply swapped the two books over as there was not enough time to do the copying. When I reached the front in Spain, I gave the book to our French comrades, although, as it was in English, it cannot have been of much help to them.[4]

Soviet food, such as tinned eggplant, arrived before Soviet arms but once the Soviet weapons came – they reached Barcelona late in October and were sent on directly to the front – we got a consignment of Soviet Maxim machine guns to add to our armoury. Confusingly, they operated in a reverse way to the British Vickers. On the Vickers, you pulled the cocking arm back twice to prepare the gun for firing, whereas on the Maxim you pushed it forward twice. Nonetheless, the emotional impact of receiving them was intense. Up till then, we had been facing elite troops supplied with the best weapons from the Nazis' factories while we had been armed with cast-offs picked up from international arms traders. But they were not just the real thing because they were often good weapons. They were the real thing because they were Soviet, because they came from the home of revolution, the inspiration that helped us believe victory was possible.

We had barely been formed as a unit, let alone properly trained, when 25,000 of Franco's advance forces reached the western and southern outskirts of the Spanish capital and Italian air force planes were bombing the city. Regular forces on the government side were still only just being organised in a new Popular Army and most of the fighting was undertaken by the independent militias, little better trained or armed than we were. Luckily Franco's forces had more experience in fighting in open country, and none in street fighting or house-to-house combat. The fascists were able to advance, but only slowly. On the night of 30 October, less than a fortnight after the International Brigades had formally come into existence, the Spanish government issued orders for us to be deployed to Madrid, whether we were properly ready or not. Three days later, by lorry and then by train, we were on the move.

As we disembarked in the early morning at Madrid's North Station on the other side of the city centre to the fighting, street vendors were preparing traditional *churros*, a sort of Catherine wheel shaped doughnut formed out of long strips of dough in a pan of boiling oil, a common breakfast in Spain to this day. The smell held in the air. It was still very misty. It did not really seem like war, though the sound of fighting could be heard in the distance and everyone knew the terror that awaited if Franco's troops won their way into the city. Assembled in our ranks outside the station, we paraded through the city along the Gran Via where the crowds shouted: '*Son Russos!*' – '*They're Russians!*' They thought real help was now on the way. Quickly they realised we weren't Russians and the word went round for a new cry to cheer us on: '*Son Internacionales!*'

A mere foot soldier has little idea of what is going on elsewhere in a battle, and each of the recorded histories of those first few weeks of fighting gives a different account. It was hard to remain heroic amidst the killing, and many of the details of the fighting got blotted out of my memories. Volunteers around me died before they knew how to act as soldiers or, in some cases, how to fire their weapons properly. Many of the volunteers had never handled a gun or worn a uniform, yet suddenly they found themselves in action against a trained, experienced and confident enemy. But that was no different to the circumstances of the overwhelming majority of the ordinary Spanish soldiers and militia volunteers alongside whom we were fighting. We were all, at that stage, a makeshift military force.

Early on, when our unit was lined up to move to an area under attack by the fascists, the remnants of a defeated Republican army unit came by in front of us. Most had only rags for clothes. They had not slept, most were in a dreadful state, but they were not running away, they could only shuffle along. There were hundreds of tired soldiers at the very end of their ability to cope. To watch a demoralised retreat by those who are on your side when you are about to go into battle is a frightening thing. Then, while this defeated gaggle trudged by us, two lorries driven by Spanish army officers arrived with a small car in tow. A woman and a couple of men in civilian clothes got out of the car. The woman climbed up on to one of the lorries and started talking to the soldiers. Some of us went over to hear what was going on. On the lorries were supplies of Soviet weapons and precious boxes of ammunition, and the woman was calling on those in retreat not to flee from the battle. She was telling those battered soldiers about the attacks on Madrid, about the dangers, about the sacrifices and about what would happen if Franco won. As she spoke, some in the shuffling horde began to respond; in ones and twos at first, they stopped, listened and shaped up. The officers got units formed, handed out new weapons, and it was not long before many of those from the rabble drifting into despair and defeat were once again a fighting unit ready to take the enemy on. Soon they were marching back the way they had come, the way we were about to go. We asked who the woman was and were told, La Pasionaria, or passion flower, Dolores Ibárurri,[5] the remarkable Communist leader I had already heard of, the symbol of the fight against Franco whose voice had been turning popular fear and rage into a determination that the fascists could be beaten.

Uncertain that the capital would hold, the government moved to Valencia on 6 November. The following day, Franco began what was intended to be his final assault, which would give him the ultimate prize of complete victory. He had been blocked at the working-class suburbs in the capital's south-west and now he chose what he hoped was the more open route of the Casa de Campo, the ancient hunting park of the Spanish kings, which, like London's Hyde Park, bagged by Henry VIII for much the same purpose, stretches into the heart of the capital and is mostly grass and scrub with bits of woodland dotted around. This suited Franco's troops, armour and artillery much better than the dense streets and flats of the working-class housing he had first attacked.

Franco's forces reached the River Manzanares beyond the park, hardly more than a glorified ditch or at best a small stream going north to south, which separates the park from the old city found on a slight rise above the river.

We were ordered to march through Madrid to key pressure points on the front line along the river on 8 November to help block this new offensive. We were less than 20 minutes from our triumphal welcome along the Gran Via, and the cheering there had given way to the sounds of gunshots. As we scuttled into position under enemy fire, we realised there was little by way of defence to shelter behind should we need to retreat.

For three days, we fought to and fro with the *Regulares*, Franco's elite colonial troops from Spanish Morocco, by the end of which they had been pushed back further into the Casa de Campo.

Our first night was spent in the open, in trenches under attack from the fascists. After that, we were billeted at the University City where we took over the Filosofia y Letras faculty. The building had only just been completed and was part of a modern campus financed by private donations, mostly paid for by the Majorcan millionaire Juan March, one of Franco's most fanatical supporters. As we were deploying, he was in Rome helping to fund the Italian arms that Mussolini was sending to Franco. The buildings he had paid for were now being torn apart by the artillery shells and machine gun fire he had also paid for. The architecture was quite beautiful to my eye at the time, but that did not stop me joining in knocking holes in its walls to get some firing positions, at the same time as we tried to make ourselves comfortable amid the lecture halls and the freezing cold stone floors. The faculty's modern quarters included bidets, which most of us had never seen before and thought were lavatories. As the sewage system had been destroyed in the fighting, their proper use became academic very quickly.

There were problems, too, of getting food and reinforcements into the building or our trenches. Communicating with our commanders, or even each other, was difficult. The Brigade had little in the way of telephone equipment and sending a runner was a hazardous exercise for even the fastest.

26 Fighting Franco

The one benefit was plenty of books. John Cornford, a real live wire in the unit with a very good sense of humour, uncovered a cache of English books and suddenly produced a number of *Everyman* volumes for our delectation. He also found some big tomes, which made a reasonably protective screen at the base of the large windows. Some wit had calculated that it took about 300 pages to stop a sniper's bullet, and in 2008, the History Channel took me back to the University where the camera crew filmed my surprise as they wheeled out from the library basement old volumes we must have used, with the bullet holes not always right through them.[6]

Back in 1936, in the lecture hall assigned to us, I also found some colourful tourist posters. One had a picture of the fountains at the Alhambra Palace in Granada with the slogan 'The sun is waiting for you in Spain' and another I recall carried a picture of a traditional style bullock cart with the slogan announcing 'Spain, the charm of the East with the comfort of the West'. I had only just stuck them up on the walls of the lecture hall and had gone back to my blanket roll in my allotted corner when there was an enormous wallop of an explosion and the room was instantly full of smoke and screaming. As the smoke cleared, John Cornford appeared, still standing but with blood streaming down his face. The cry of 'Stretcher bearer!' went up – a cry heard many times over the following weeks. Cornford looked most Byronesque when he returned a couple of hours later, his head in bandages. It seemed that the cause was 'friendly fire', an anti-aircraft shell fired by our own side, which had fallen short, come through the wall and burst.

It did not take long for us to discover the weaknesses of each of the weapons we had managed to collect. Our French comrades in the Commune de Paris Battalion had some St. Etienne machine guns that seemed designed more with the idea of emulating the Eiffel Tower than helping a soldier win a war. They had been replaced by the Hotchkiss pretty quickly during the First World War. Our British Lewis gun's 'camembert' drum trapped grit and dirt if you ever left it on the ground and the whole thing then had to be carefully cleaned out before it would work again – no good if the enemy is just about to rush your trenches. I ended up with a collection of instruction sheets for different weapons, all of which seemed to follow a simple rule: if we had the manual, we did not have the actual gun. The first of the Soviet machine guns we got were a boon, but they had their problems too. In *Chapayev*, a Soviet film about a Red Army partisan hero, they looked fine; I had seen it in London and, by chance, it had opened in Madrid a day or two before we arrived. But when you tried to trundle these guns around on the battlefield, it was a very different matter. Unless you were really careful, when you tilted up its low, wheeled carriage, the sights and front muzzle knocked into the ground. The only way to move the gun quickly and easily was to take it off its carriage and carry the barrel and the carriage separately. Both were very heavy and exhausting to cart around, whether on the rough ground of the park or on the stairways of the Faculty, and when you tried to put the two back together again, the grooves and the ridges on the two pieces had to be very precisely lined up, which, particularly under fire, was never easy. It had a proper belt feed, just like the British Vickers I used in the OTC, but it was water-cooled and could overheat quickly when the water had boiled away. The suggestion that one could piss into the cooling jacket turned out to be just a *Boy's Own* sort of story. When you got going with these Soviet guns they were tremendous, but the training was inevitably very limited and I made all sorts of mistakes. And instead of doing it as you were bid in the films – 'wait till you see the whites of their eyes' – everyone tended to pop off some rounds at the very first opportunity, giving away our positions and offering the excellent and highly trained snipers from Franco's Moorish regiments a chance to pick us off.

As is the case in any war, a day at the front could be very boring, too, and that might be fatal. When the attacks took place, with fighting house-to-house and floor-to-floor, the action was really fierce. When things were quiet, fear was always there, perhaps more so as moments of intense action stopped you thinking too much. A long moment of quiet might be broken by the sharp crack of a rifle fire as one of our comrades was hit. One had to get used to spending a lot of time just waiting and watching.

Three members of our unit were quickly killed when they sought to cover a retreat in the Casa de Campo: Robert Symes from London, 'Mac' McLaurin, a New Zealand scholar at Cambridge who had been managing the Communist Party bookshop there, and Steve Yates, also a New Zealander, who had been discharged from the British Army for insubordination and then worked as an electrician in London. It was also during these first moments that I came across a self-inflicted wound, or SIW. A Brigader next to me in the trench was wounded and sobbing with pain, so I called a medical orderly. When a French-Polish medical student came to bandage him up, he proved to be a wiser man than me. He explained that the powder marks around the wound showed he had put his hand over the muzzle and pulled the trigger. Ordered back into the line, my wounded colleague soon skedaddled off to Britain.

One night we were redeployed from the front line to Aravaca, just to the north of the park land, to try to attack from Franco's northern flank. The command was: 'No lights, no talking'. As we moved off across a small bridge over a railway line with a guide who was supposed to know the way, we became aware that behind us was what seemed like a truck, which every now and then flashed its headlamps. Freddy Jones ordered us to either side of the road, as we were not certain whether the truck was one of ours. They must have thought we were fascists as suddenly the lorry accelerated and those still in the road got thrown all over the place. When we picked ourselves up, we could not find Freddy. We had still not found him when we got to our new location. I was among those sent back to look for him when it was light. As far as we could tell, when the lorry had accelerated, its front mudguard must have caught some low-hanging telephone wires at the side of the road. They tightened and snapped, and the whiplash had torn Freddy's head off, a freak accident and gruesome death.

Our flank attack did not work. Its failure may have opened the way for a new thrust by Franco back through the Casa de Campo, across the Manzanares

28 Fighting Franco

and into the University City. This was the closest the fascists had yet got to the middle of Madrid. By 15 November, his Moroccan infantrymen were well established in the University buildings. We were deployed back to the area to help get them out, which meant close fighting, moving in and out of the different buildings and trenches in the area for nearly three weeks. My OTC training, mainly marching in step or on manoeuvres across open country, was not much use in this environment, but, in the end, we were able to push the fascists back out of the university area and then over a dozen miles to the west. A slight head wound from shrapnel in the University City did not keep me out of the fighting.

A lull came in the fighting and we were withdrawn for a moment of rest and reorganisation. The Brigade Commissar, who was charged with the political education and commitment of the troops rather than simply their military activities, told us we would be getting back pay at 10 pesetas a day, which we would be able to spend on leave in Madrid, as long as we took account of the dangers posed by toying with the ladies, a comment which sent the French volunteers rolling on the floor in laughter.

Jock Cunningham and I got a lift on a lorry to the end of the tramline and boarded the first tram. We didn't know our way round the city and got off at the last stop, the Puerta del Sol – the Piccadilly Circus of Madrid – in the hot sun. The fascist General Mola had boasted that a cup of coffee was waiting for him at a cafe in that Puerta, but, instead of the fascist general, we were there.

Much of life still appeared to be carrying on as usual, even though public buildings were sandbagged and guarded, and every spare piece of ground seemed to have people practising drill. There were already plenty of signs of the damage from shelling and bombs, but people were strolling from street to street, enjoying the clear weather. Despite the war, with the street organ players filling the air with, among other things, the strains of the 'Internationale', it seemed utterly sensible for Jock and I to join in enjoying the sun and the coffee and the sense that we could walk upright without worrying about a sniper's bullet. On that particular day in the sun at Puerta del Sol everyone seemed to be having their shoes shined so we thought we would join in too.

Someone came up to us and asked whether we were English. It turned out to be Sefton Delmer of the right-wing *Daily Express*, one of the bigger names of Fleet Street in those days, at least big enough for the two of us to have heard of him. Delmer had got wind of the fact that there were British volunteers in the fighting and took us for a most welcome meal at the Marichu, a Basque restaurant that was a regular haunt for journalists. He made me as sick as a dog on my first cigar. After we had eaten, he invited us to the Telefonica in the Gran Via, the central telephone exchange where the censorship office operated and the journalists could send their reports. A 14-storey tower, it was higher than any office block I had seen in London, and from its upper windows, you could get a splendid overview of the fighting in the Casa de Campo.

Jock and I had agreed on the quiet that we would not tell this class enemy anything. At the Telefonica, Delmer introduced us to the New Zealander

Geoffrey Cox, who had arrived in Madrid for the anti-Franco *News Chronicle* not many days before we had. He seemed hardly any older than me, and years later went on to become the first editor of ITN and boss of Yorkshire TV. Jock and I decided in a whispered conversation that he was someone we could talk to. We got into cahoots with him, telling him what had happened to us so far. It was Cox's first interview with any British Brigaders and gave him the chance for the first full report from Spain of a British unit in the International Brigade, beating even Claud Cockburn, the legendary sniffer out of news, whose stories from Spain appeared in the *Daily Worker.* We might have thought that we had succeeded in denying Delmer his grand scoop, but he managed to file a decent story, which reported that I, though unnamed, was still equipped with my OTC uniform.

All too soon, trucks came and we were taken back from Puerta del Sol to the Casa de Campo and the front. Hearing there was some Lewis gun ammunition available at the Brigades HQ in the former royal golf club in the Casa, I was sent to pick it up. Waiting around until I could get my hands on it, I was able to procure some spare horse blankets, which were wonderfully warm but light, and get a warm shower. There I came across a unit of miners from Oviedo in the Asturias, Spain's coal region, who used their explosives to take apart the tracks of the fascist tanks, and in the showers we compared marks and wounds. The big body next to me, however, turned out to be General Kléber, the military commander of the 11th Brigade.[7] He spoke very good English and was at that moment pretending to be a Canadian. Naked under the water with the much taller Kléber towering over me, we were deep into conversation on the effectiveness of Lewis guns and the availability of suitable ammunition when in rushed his aide de camp, a Czech called Joe, who also spoke good English.

'The German comrades have gone mad', he shouted. Kléber and I dashed out, pulling our clothes on. Kléber told me to join him in the motorcycle and sidecar that was to take him to the trouble spot. The aide began to explain what had happened as we drove along. Following a lecture from their Political Commissar, the German Battalion had decided that falling victim to one of the particular diseases he had said you might get from 'toying with the ladies of Madrid' would be the equivalent of desertion in the face of the enemy. Even though they knew what the punishment was for that in time of war, the battalion had supported this policy with a unanimous vote. After they had been shoved back in the front line as we had been, and when the appropriate incubation period of a few short days had run its course, a sergeant and a second lieutenant were found to have the symptoms of the pox. A meeting of the battalion had carried a motion – again unanimously – that the agreed policy should be implemented.

When we arrived, the two were standing ready for execution before the firing squad and a Commissar was reading out the decision. Kléber rushed over and tore away the paper. The Commissar protested that the doctor had given evidence on medical issues and that sentence of death had been passed with the two culprits agreeing that this was the correct punishment. Kléber would have none

30 Fighting Franco

of it and the two were sent to hospital before being put back to fighting the real enemy. 'Don't you realise', Kléber barked at the Commissar, 'that if this was to become policy, I would have to shoot half the Spanish army'. Proper discipline, of the kind that was a help in fighting, was not an easy thing to learn. Kléber, calm and collected under fire, was a model for us.

In the trenches at Madrid, as well as weapons and good food, there were two other things we really wanted. One was letters from home, the other was the *Daily Worker*, and I used my French to pester the Brigade's Political Commissariat to get them both. And so, amidst the chaos of war in imperilled Madrid, 'Camarade Lesser 2° Bataillon, C° Mitrailleuse, 4° Section' exchanged carefully typed letters with Giuseppe Di Vittorio, a former Communist MP in Italy who took the name Nicoletti in the Commissariat. Despite all that went on, I kept his letter, formal, neatly laid out, with a detailed explanation of everything he had done to get our letters to us. It was an oddly reassuring correspondence as the carnage carried on around:

> Your desire to have, from time to time, the Communist newspaper, the *Daily Worker*, is completely justified. I was already busy with this question before receiving your letter and I am pleased to be able to tell you that the first copies of this paper have already come to us. We have immediately sent them to the political commissar of your battalion and we think that you must already have them in your possession.

We had been in action to halt another attack through the village of Boadilla, to the west of Madrid. The fascists hoped they would return to the Casa de Campo but, at the cost of more of our lives, they did not. Franco decided he was not going to win in a direct assault on the capital and the front to the west stabilised quite a bit. But, of the first group of 28 British volunteers I had been with, only five were still fit to fight; hundreds of the 2,100 Brigaders who had left Albacete five weeks beforehand were dead or wounded. Stopping Franco, and our small part in that, was an immense boost to Republican morale, but the toll in lives was terrible. It was only a portent of what was to come.

While some of us were keeping a slim hold on life, His Britannic Majesty's Ambassador to the Spanish Republic, His Excellency Sir Henry Chilton, was sending carefully typed reports to the Foreign Office in London on our collective efforts to defend Madrid against Franco's raids. No wonder the British government was so ill informed if they relied on his evidence, which in December 1938 including the following gem:

> In one of these attacks, the Government troops are reported to have loosed a pack of ferocious hounds on the enemy. Most of the dogs, which are alleged to have come from Russia and had been trained not to bark (or had their vocal chords been cut?) were eventually killed, but the experiment - which was not ineffective - has aroused interest.

Not only did Chilton think it worthwhile to include such risible drivel in his reports but seemingly no one back in London raised any objections once he had.

Journalists writing for the Fleet Street dailies were in Madrid while Chilton had retreated to Hendaye just inside the French border with Spain. London could get better information, as is so often the case, from journalists than from official sources. Even the *Daily Express*, then Britain's biggest selling daily, carried back page picture features giving dramatic evidence of the bombing of Madrid and stories of the cruelty of the war as well of our efforts in the International Column, as the paper termed us.

On 7 December, we were withdrawn from Madrid and returned to Albacete, some 150 miles to the south-east of the capital, and then to our own new training base at Madrigueras, 20 miles further away and smaller even than La Roda. Once there, we were reinforced by a new influx of volunteers from Britain and Ireland. These were about the last group to be able to cross from France without the hike over the mountains. The expectation was that, as a new unit, we would form a full British Battalion. A few weeks later, in January 1937, the government in London threatened British volunteers with prosecution under the Foreign Enlistment Act despite the invasion of Spain by German and Italian forces. This made the journey from Britain to Spain a bit more difficult, but did not reduce the numbers coming.

It might seem a small point all these years later, but the naming of this unit was a problem. The Irish, who formed a great part of the unit – and, when one looks at the names of those who died in the fighting over the following few weeks, a great part of the casualties – strongly objected to being called British or English anything. When the US Abraham Lincoln Battalion was eventually formed a lot of the Irish in the British units went off and joined it, though quite a few stayed in the eventual British Battalion. Indeed, it seemed to me that many of those who stayed in it were IRA men, like Frank Ryan, who had been a prominent Republican leader back at home.

Even for those of us who were British or English, the specific name of the unit posed a question too. Most of the International Brigade units were named after some hero or leader on the left – the Dimitrov, the Dombrowsky, the Thälmann, the Garibaldi Battalions. For a while, the British Battalion was known as the Saklatvala Battalion, but nobody had really heard of the first Communist Labour MP from the 1920s, Shapurji Saklatvala, so the name was dropped. All the way through it was in fact just known as the British Battalion. Even worse, so far as the Irish were concerned, this first reformed unit was known that December as the Number 1 English Company. After terrible losses sustained at the later battle of Jarama it was visited by Clement Attlee, the Labour Party leader, and was then named the Number 1 Major Attlee Company. To the Spanish and the French the whole battalion was always just known as 'los Ingleses' or 'les Anglais'.

I was also just starting to find out about some of the political problems in Spain, which, to a soldier at the front who doesn't speak Spanish, filter down

32 Fighting Franco

rather slowly. I had learned French and a little Latin at school, so I was able to pick up Spanish quite quickly – enough after a few weeks to read a newspaper. I found reflected there the political difficulties of the Popular Front government, issues of authority and the need for a unified command. The Republican forces were made up of forces that zealously guarded their own independence, and I could see that, to put it mildly, it did not help to form an integrated defence of a place like Madrid or to fight any kind of war. For example, the anarchists didn't want to be commanded by General Miaja, commander of the Madrid Front, let alone by the Communists. They thought Miaja was a suspicious character having been a general in the old army, most of whose officers had gone over to Franco. As the Republic became increasingly stretched, such problems had more serious consequences for its future survival.

For our unit, instead of a long period of training and building up of numbers, as many of the volunteers as could be mobilised were brought together in Albacete, and towards the end of December we were rushed south by train some 200 miles towards the Córdoba front. Major George Nathan, an ex-army officer complete with pipe, the British Army's traditional Sam Brown belt, and swagger stick, commanded the new company. Few of the new recruits had fired a shot in anger. Many had still not even fired a gun during training. In fact, we were presented with our weapons at midnight the day we set off.

We dismounted at Andújar about 15 miles from the front line, and then marched and trucked to a point near the village of Lopera where the fascists were said to have broken through. The area was one of extensive olive groves. The trees were planted in neat, straight lines, which immediately revealed any group of soldiers to the enemy planes over head. We were machine-gunned and strafed from the air straight away, even as we were getting out of the trucks.

When those who had not already been hit got to the front, we were told to advance across some rolling open country. We reached a slight crest and, suddenly, it dawned on us that we were the only ones that far forward. Machine gun fire was coming at us both from our French comrades who, being some way behind our position, mistook us for fascists, and also from the enemy somewhere out in front.

I was on the ground firing my rifle as best I could when I felt this knock. It was as if something had fallen on me. I got up to run forward and keeled over. I realised I couldn't walk. I saw blood coming out of my boot and felt it seeping along my back. I had been wounded in the foot and the backside. I shouted to Jock Cunningham that I'd been hit and he dragged me by my good leg from the no-man's land, as it had become. It was quite a long way he had to pull me, and all the time I remember hearing people calling repeatedly in French '*brancardier, brancardier*' – or, '*stretcher-bearer, stretcher-bearer*', even though stretcher-bearers were a rare commodity at the front.

My bowels gave out, as happens at moments like that, which did not make things any more comfortable or dignified. Finally, Jock did find a stretcher-bearer. A few moments later a man came up in full uniform. It was my first meeting with

Fighting Franco **33**

the Polish General Walter,[8] the commander of the 14th International Brigade to which we were then attached, who asked how I was and how it happened. John Cornford and Ralph Fox, both important Communist Party intellectuals, were killed at the same time as I was wounded, though in the confusion I knew nothing of that. For a while, I was listed as dead as well.

Of the 145 British and Irish volunteers who set off for Lopera, only 67 were able to return to Albacete. In all the fighting at the Córdoba front, some 300 volunteers were killed and another 600 wounded, coming from 19 different nations. The Republic never managed to retake Lopera, but we did stop the offensive, and that stabilised the southern front for quite a while.

It was a rocky 40-mile ride for me to the hospital at Linares de Jaen in a lorry that had obviously been used to transport farmyard manure. When we arrived, there was a huge welcoming party, wanting to shake our hands. We were the first volunteers they had seen, yet all we wounded wanted to do was lie down and rest. The hospital, like most in Spain at the time, was a religious foundation, but all the nurses were nuns, which was an exception. In other hospitals, the nursing nuns had either been chased out or had left of their own accord. Indeed, according to Franco's propaganda machine, the nuns who put me back together again had all either been murdered or been the victims of Republican rapists.

The following day, the place was chock-a-block with people bringing gifts of grapes, soap, combs, toothpaste and toothbrushes, pastries, and wine. It was a fantastic feeling of support. Though our losses had been heavy, the fascist drive had been blocked and these people were more than grateful. Kept in the hospital longer than the others because my wounds meant I could not be moved, I had time to learn Spanish more thoroughly, helped by a nun who read out vast chunks of *Don Quixote de la Mancha* in the original language.

A local businessman, who spoke good English, was honorary British consul, and, at first, refused to see me. He was telling the British volunteers that, if they wanted to get back to dear old Blighty, he could arrange it for them. He turned out to have pictures of Hitler and Mussolini on the walls of his office. As soon as I could hobble that far on my crutches, I gave him a piece of my mind. I told him he was organising desertion, which he denied. The fighting we had been involved in would have been bad enough for fully trained soldiers, so it was not surprising that several of the volunteers did not want to stay.

In contrast, I got to know a local woman working in the hospital and she introduced me to her mother, who soon let it be known that my attentions were not welcome. Later she barred me from entering the house.

After a couple of weeks, I was shifted to another hospital 80 miles to the north in Ciudad Real. During the war, the name was changed to Ciudad Leal, Loyal City rather than Royal City. There were quite a few French Brigaders in the hospital and the hospital Political Commissar was French. A meeting one day of the walking wounded brought together complaints about the food and the French were particularly indignant that there was not enough wine. They wanted *un quart* (a quarter of a litre) with each meal. One bloke got up and said he knew the hospital down the road not only gave the *quart* regularly, but also had chicken almost every day. Demanding the right to speak, I said I had not come to Spain to drink wine or eat chicken. I could barely stand from my wound and had to be rescued by the nurses from my fellow patients who rushed me at this declaration. The French Political Commissar ordered my arrest and I was taken under guard to Albacete.

When I had been put in the barracks there, Peter Kerrigan, the Commissar of the British Battalion at Albacete, turned up.[9] He brought unwelcome news. He told me of the deaths of Cornford, Fox and the others in the Lopera fighting. But he got me out of the barracks, and I slept the night in his office. My treatment by the French was taken up with André Marty as the overall boss of the Albacete base, and the next thing I heard was the French Political Commissar at the hospital had been arrested.

'Big Peter' as he was known, became a friend and helper to me over many years. I started working, as well as sleeping, in his office. The wound remained pretty bothersome and I had to have it dressed every day. For many months, there was no chance of walking without a stick.

FIGURE 2.2 Sam in Spain with another Brigader, after being wounded.
Source: Family archive.

I was telling Kerrigan the story of General Kléber and the German comrades, when a rather far-away look came into his eyes.

'I've got a little job for you', he said. 'There's this Number One Hospital here. It's the pox hospital and quite a few of our people are in there'. Till then, I had not even heard of the place.

The food for the British patients there was a real problem and so were the cigarettes. (The Spaniards themselves called their cheap cigarettes *matacintos*. It was a term deriving from the custom under the military conscription rules in Spain that meant everyone was liable for conscription but only every fifth man was called. So these cigarettes were 'fifth' or 'recruit' killers.) We weren't used to food cooked in olive oil, you could hardly ever get tea and we just did not drink coffee in those days. There was no beer and the wine was too alcoholic for us. We did not even have things like packs of cards. Whatever came went to the front and the poor bastards in the hospitals with wounds or those recovering afterwards were getting little. Letters, sending them and getting them, were also a problem, especially with the existence of the postal censorship in and out, which often caused complaints over silly changes or cuts. At the pox hospital, they were getting nothing. Kerrigan wanted me to go there and give them a bit of a morale boost as well as some supplies.

It was in the days before penicillin or even before sulphonamides and I got a quick lesson in how gonorrhoea was treated in those days. The French called the method *lavage* and it involved a solution of permanganate of potash, which was squirted into the penis twice a day. The first thing I noticed at the hospital was the awful stink. Most of the hospitals stank, given the suppurating wounds of those days, but this was a particular stench, given the nature of gonorrhoea. The second thing was the surprisingly large number of leading comrades who were in the hospital, including a couple of German political commissars, part of the very group which had voted unanimously for the death sentence for such transgressions.

By the time I was properly assigned to Kerrigan in February 1937, the battle of Jarama was well underway. When the first list of casualties arrived, it was a horrendous moment. The French had already taken very heavy casualties in earlier fighting, but this was the first time the number of British deaths was similar – the battle at Lopera being in comparison a side show – and it was the first fighting in which British volunteers had taken part in such large numbers. Kerrigan decided I had to go back to London with the casualty list so that it could be personally delivered to the Communist Party leadership and the news properly passed on to relatives of the dead. With my leg still in plaster, I remember standing and watching Kerrigan just repeating, 'How can we tell them? How can we tell them?'

Notes

1 Glasshouse is a British term for a military prison.
2 André Marty (1886–1956) was Political Commissar of the International Brigades. In Spain, he earned a reputation as paranoid and ruthless, the latter trait sometimes exaggerated by others; Sam said 'he could indeed be brutal, but war is cruel in the extreme'. After Spain, Marty went to the Soviet Union, then in 1943 to Algiers as the

36 Fighting Franco

French Communist Party's representative to the Free French Forces before returning to France when the war was over. He was expelled from the Party in 1952 on a charge of being a French police spy (a charge described by Sam as 'ludicrous').

3 After Spain, Knox went to the US and became a captain in the Office of Strategic Services, the American special forces unit, which used quite a number of ex-Brigaders. He was dropped into Brittany to work with the French Resistance and then sent to northern Italy to fight alongside the Partisans where the commander of one unit he was attached to turned out to have been in the Garibaldi Battalion in the Brigades. When the war ended, he decided to return to classical studies and applied to Yale University only to be told when he said that he had been in Spain that he had been identified as a 'premature anti-fascist', later discovering the phrase was an FBI term for Communist.

4 This enterprising sleight-of-hand constitutes one of the first entries in Sam's MI5 files.

5 Dolores Ibárurri (1895–1989), Spain's best known Communist leader, became the international symbol of the Republican struggle. She coined the rallying call '¡No Pasarán!' – 'They Shall Not Pass'. She joined the Spanish Communist Party on its founding in 1920, and in 1939 went into exile in the Soviet Union where she became the Spanish Party General Secretary (1940–1960), then its President, a post she held until her death. She returned to Spain in 1977 and was elected to the Cortes (Parliament) for the same Asturias region she had represented during the Civil War.

6 The television documentary, made by Max Arthur, is called *The Brits Who Fought for Spain* and his interview with Sam is printed in his book *The Real Band of Brothers* (London: Collins, 2009).

7 Born Manfred Stern in Bukovina, later part of Romania and then the Ukraine, Kléber left with his family for Toronto and became a naturalised British citizen, fighting in the Canadian forces during the First World War. Sent in a Canadian unit to Siberia as part of the intervention against the Bolsheviks following the 1917 Revolution, he had deserted and joined the Red Army, rising to become a prominent commander. Having served the Comintern in Germany (during the 1923 Communist uprising in Hamburg), the US, China (where he commanded a Red Army unit fighting the Japanese in 1935), and now in Spain, he was recalled to Moscow in 1937 and disappeared in Stalin's purges, dying in the Gulag after 15 years in the camps.

8 Karol Świerczewski (b. 1897), who took the name 'Walter' in Spain, had served in the Red Army during the Russian Revolution and then became a teacher in a military school at Moscow. He later became the commander of the 35th Division in the Republic's army. He left Spain in 1938 before the end of the war. During the World War he also played a prominent part, becoming the Deputy Defence Minister in Poland after 1945. He was killed by anti-Communist guerrillas in fighting in eastern Poland in 1947.

9 Kerrigan, a trade unionist in Glasgow from as early an age as he could be – he joined the engineering union as a 16-year-old apprentice – had been called up into the Royal Scots in 1918 and had served in Palestine. As soon as he got out of the army, he joined the Communist Party, was sent to Moscow for training, and served on the executive of the Comintern. He had been a grass-roots organiser in Britain, and organised a Scots Hunger March to London, before heading for Spain.

3

FROM RIFLE TO TYPEWRITER

Back in London, I handed over my material, and arrangements were made for me to see a top orthopaedic specialist in Harley Street – this was before we had won the National Health Service. He turned out to be Lord 'Tommy' Horder, none other than the Physician Extraordinary to the King who was later a resolute opponent of the National Health Service. He was credited with saying, 'I would treat Beelzebub himself if he came into my consulting room'. I don't know whether he saw me as Beelzebub or whether he had a genuine feeling for the Spanish Republic and democracy, but he got me an appointment with specialists at Hammersmith Hospital in West London. My foot gave me some trouble in later life, but the doctors there enabled me to get back to reasonable fitness. It was not quick, though. Hanging around while I recuperated seemed to take forever. I was desperate to get back to Spain. During the few months I was in London, the bombing of Guernica took place as well as what the Republican government described as an attempted putsch against it by the POUM, the United Workers' Marxist Party with which George Orwell was associated and the rival Marxist organisation to the Communist Party.

When I was cleared to return, at the end of July 1937, the hike across the Pyrenees had become necessary but this was impossible for me, as my wounds still held me back. Instead of getting back to Spain immediately, I was directed to work with the organisation in Paris sending the volunteers on their way. The call from on top was always for more volunteers, but I did not think the quality of those being sent always met the demands of the war they were about to fight. Each man was given ten francs on arrival in France, and most of those I was responsible for seemed to spend it on wine, drinking the stuff as if it was English beer. On more than one occasion, my work involved collecting drunken British volunteers from the local police station before sending them on to Spain. Despite

DOI: 10.4324/9781003243380-4

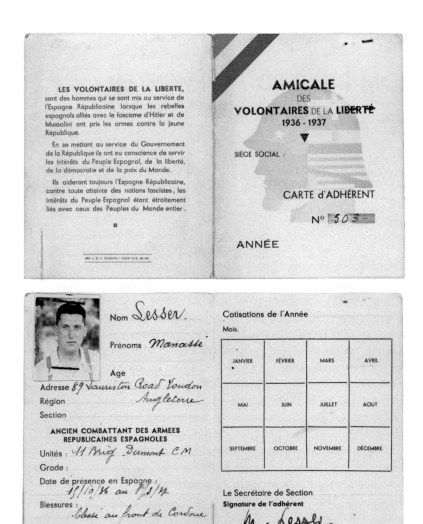

FIGURE 3.1 Sam's membership card of the Association of Volunteers for Liberty, formed in France by wounded Brigaders.
Source: Family archive.

posting off frantic messages in a feeble code back to Robbie Robson, the key Party person in the recruitment network in London, and saying something along the lines of 'The last batch of literature was totally unsatisfactory', things did not change while I was working in Paris.

At long last, I had a message via a French comrade that I could go to Spain, though there was something in his voice that told me it was not going to be that simple. 'There is a little job you can do on your way', was the giveaway. It turned out that a number of young women from different countries had volunteered to work as nurses or medical orderlies in Spain and it was felt they could not be expected to go across the Pyrenees on foot. Giving me my train ticket to Perpignan, still the main jumping off point for volunteers crossing into Spain, my French contact said that, when I got there, the comrades would tell me what my role would be. Further, a young, blue-eyed, blonde Polish woman was stuck in Paris and I was to escort her to Perpignan. She could speak nothing but Polish, a language which, despite my parents' birthplace, I did not know a word of. All she would say was 'Apteka', which in the end I realised was chemist. She found one and went in. The problem then was she could not make the man behind the counter understand what she wanted. Rather to my surprise, we eventually found a chemist with the sign *Apteka* above the door and in she went to ask for 'henna perska'. In those days, I had never heard of henna, let alone Persian henna, and I had certainly never thought hair dye might be a useful item to take to a war.

In Perpignan, my instructions were to gather the women together and get them to a tiny fishing village, Agde – which later became a major holiday complex – where a local fisherman in the Communist Party would help us. There were a dozen or so of them, Polish, German, Italian, and a woman from Palestine, all going to the front. It was a beautiful summer Sunday afternoon. The chap with the boat explained we would be travelling all the rest of the day and through the night and he hoped we would arrive on the Spanish side some time the following morning. Unfortunately, the motor would not start and his mate went off to find some spare part. While we were stuck in the harbour, a woman lent out of a top storey window and shouted over, inquiring whether the boat had space for a party who just wanted to have a cruise around.

'I'm busy', the fisherman replied, only to be told that she had spoken to his wife who had said he was free. A booking had come up, he said, and there was nothing he could do.

'I hope you are not going to Spain', she bellowed back, 'You know it's illegal'. Unfortunately, some of the women could understand French well enough to make sense of this and they began to panic. But before they got really worried, the part was found and off we went.

Out in the Mediterranean, the boat sometimes travelled so slowly some of the women were able to take a swim around it. I got chatting to one of them in particular, Dora Birnbach, a Polish Jew who had gone to Palestine as a Zionist but had joined the Communist Party there, only to be arrested and thrown out by the British authorities. Arriving in Paris stateless, she had volunteered for Spain. We talked into the night as the moon rose over the summer sea with politics at the heart of our conversation and the war we were going to seemingly a million miles away. We stayed friends over the years.[1]

When dawn came, the German women on our boat panicked again. They could see smoke rising on the horizon. Perhaps it was a non-intervention patrol coming to arrest us? Or a ship from the Italian navy or one of Franco's own growing force of warships, which were sinking vessels they thought were supplying the Republic? But, as we turned to move in toward the coast, we saw an

40 From Rifle to Typewriter

enormous fire – the smoke was coming from a bombing raid that had set a pine wood along the coast ablaze. It did not stop us landing or prevent me from delivering my strange cargo.

Back in Barcelona, I was told to report to the medical authorities. Bitter disappointment came the following day when I was informed that I could not return to the front. Instead, I was to replace a comrade who had been doing English-language short wave radio broadcasts to Britain and who had left the day before. Arriving at the offices of Radio Barcelona at 10 am, immediately after my final medical inspection, the only thing I was told by the German comrade in charge of its foreign language broadcasts was: 'You're just in time. There's your typewriter. You're on air at 7 pm for half an hour'.

He gave me a desk and told me to start by translating the military communiqué for the day, which was in Spanish, and then add in whatever else I could find. I had barely used a typewriter before and the text had to be copied in full a number of times, as it needed to go through censorship before being broadcast. That was my start as a journalist. Now I really was fighting the fascists with a typewriter, but whether or not this one was a Remington, I cannot remember.

The main slogan for anyone who I thought might have been listening – and I must have repeated it hundreds of times – was 'Save Spain, Save Peace, Save Britain'. Looking back, that always seemed to me to have been correct. Hitler used Spain as a testing ground for his preparations for the world war he expected would leave Nazism victorious. Had his protégé, Franco, lost in Spain and the Republic won, history could have been very different, and Nazism might have been defeated more easily. Indeed, that was a core conviction all of us in the Brigades shared.

Everything was subject to censorship, naturally – this was a war, and a very divisive civil war at that, which meant there were plenty of spies, agents and supporters of the other side prepared to give away secrets, name possible targets and undermine operations. When I read out a script for broadcast, the censors followed what I said with a text in front of them. They could switch off the broadcast if they chose at any time. Much of my material came from the central editorial service of the Spanish government radio. Some items had to be included in all broadcasts, whether in German, French, Italian or English. They were compulsory and I had to fit them in, no matter what. Others, I could select for my English-language broadcast. The first item remained the military communiqué and then there was often an item about developments away from the front within Republican Spain – stories about help for children, refugees, crèches, kindergartens, agrarian reform, and progress in social services. There was, for instance, a great literacy campaign that the Republican government conducted throughout the war. It was easy to forget in later years, but Spain was 90% illiterate at the start of the 1930s. One of the Republic's great achievements was its enormous education programme, of which this literacy campaign was just a part.

Half an hour of solo speech might not sound much, but it takes time to prepare, especially when it all has to be typed up, and I quickly discovered that the German comrade's words had been quite correct. If I did not get working pretty early in the morning, I would not have everything ready in time. Given that I had to do this for a broadcast every day, it was not possible to get out and about and do much by way of direct reporting. On one occasion, I did manage to visit the Battalion at the front, travelling the whole way on top of a load of cabbages in the back of an open lorry, but usually my reports came from office-based work. Once in a while, I got to interpret for some of the Comintern big shots or get to big rallies and meetings, which might give me an item or two. Occasionally, I tried to broadcast a bit of music, but the technical facilities were very rudimentary and this was not easy.

Studio guests could also be testing. Passing through Barcelona in August 1937 were Jock Cunningham and George Aitken. Two very different comrades they might have been, but it seemed a good idea to have them in my programme. Aitken had been at the Lenin School in Moscow and was someone of considerable character and had real standing in the Party. Cunningham was an absolutely fearless, almost foolhardy, man. I owed my life to that, but when he became the Battalion commander in February 1937 he was quite out of his depth in the role. The two turned up at the appointed hour. George was a much quieter chap and had a neatly written text, which was more than serviceable. Jock had nothing. He proposed to ad lib. Somehow, I got the censors to agree to the arrangement. However, the result was chaos almost as soon as Jock tried to speak. I interrupted him and he lost his temper. I managed to usher him out of the studio before too much damage was done. Knowing the way Jock was liable to criticise anything and everything that he thought stood in the way of victory, I felt we could have ended up broadcasting something that, in those days, might have got you shot. I suppose I had returned the favour he had done me at Lopera.

It was radio broadcasting that gave me my professional name. At home, I had always been called Manny Lesser and that was the name under which I joined the Brigades. After I had been refused a return to the Brigades because of my wounds, as well as working for the radio, I was assigned to Bill Rust, one of the leading figures in the British Communist Party, who was officially the *Daily Worker* correspondent, though he was also the British CP representative in Spain. For some reason, he always called me Sam.

My radio work was for the Republic's central government, which had been moved from Valencia to Barcelona, and it so happened there was a short wave radio transmitter there controlled by the government of autonomous Catalonia, which was thought to be capable of broadcasting to the US. The Central Committee of the Catalan Communists wanted someone to broadcast in English on that service and chose me.[2] When I was given the news by Pedro, the Comintern advisor to the Catalan Party, a Hungarian whose real name was Ernő Gerő, he said I needed another name, as the Catalans would not be happy if they thought the same person was doing broadcasts for their service as well as for the central Spanish government. I had to choose a new name immediately so that I could get to work straight away. Turning Lesser round the other way and using Rust's nickname was how I became Sam Russell, though for other work, I still used my own name.[3]

42 From Rifle to Typewriter

FIGURE 3.2 Sam's radio work permit issued by the Catalan Communists.
Source: Family archive.

FIGURE 3.3 Sam's Spanish Communist Party card.
Source: Family archive.

My Catalan radio work turned out to be a job unlike any before or since. One night, when I had finished my broadcast at 1.30 am and was really shattered, the engineer in charge of the broadcasts invited me for a cognac. He was the same engineer in charge of the Spanish government broadcasts and he complained to me about his life: he could not get his leather boots repaired; he could not get soap; he could not get all sorts of things. I had just received a parcel from my mum and it had not been pilfered by the customs, as was usually the case. She had sent me four bars of Sunlight soap, and I gave him two. It then became a habit for us to have a snip of cognac after the broadcasts were over. Relaxing one night, he suddenly said to me:

> You know it may be more than my life is worth, but you have been working away so hard at this for weeks and I just want you to know that not a single word you are saying has actually been broadcast on the short wave system. As soon as you start speaking, I just switch the transmitters off.

He was acting, he explained, on the instructions of the organisation that secretly controlled the transmitter, by which, I took it, he meant the POUM, which the government had banned following what they considered to be an attempted putsch.

The following morning, I had to go to a meeting with Pedro. I stormed in to complain. 'I know', he told me. As I spluttered and raged, he said it was very important that I continued to do the broadcasts. The CP knew the illegal POUM were in control of the station, and that it had me switched off every night, but the Party was certain that if I just gave up, the POUM would immediately put in their own person, someone for whom they would switch the transmitter on. It was my duty, he explained, to do my nightly broadcasts in order to ensure that the transmitter stayed off. I protested vehemently and was given in return a lecture on the sacrifices we all had to make. What could I say? I carried on doing the Catalan broadcasts for a bit, but, fortunately for me, an American turned up and took over the work. I never found out whether the transmitter was turned on for him.

Once I got used to the rhythm of the broadcasts, I plunged into other news projects, particularly for the bulletin service of the Catalan Communists. This, which, became incorporated into the Spanish arm of the news and propaganda agency created by the legendary Comintern public relations and campaigning partnership of Willi Münzenberg and Otto Katz (of whom I saw little, if anything) and which became the body paying my wages. Along with receiving 10 pesetas a day, the same as my rate as an ordinary soldier, I also got a meal ticket at the restaurant for full-time political workers, where I ate mostly on salt codfish and chick-peas – it was a great day for me when spuds arrived.

I lived rent-free in a small flat that had been passed on to me by some Spanish nurses, who had moved out because the fascists regularly bombed near that part of the city. I felt it was safe enough as the bombing was heaviest further away in the downtown area nearer the port, which was where I first witnessed the deliberate bombing of civilians. A large group sheltering in a police station thought the raid – possibly by Italian pilots – was over; they came into the open under a line of lime trees in full blossom when a second round of bombs fell. The gutters really did flow with blood, and its smell mixed with the stench of the explosions

44 From Rifle to Typewriter

and the beautiful, heady scent of the limes. No matter where I was, every spring for years after, when the limes came into flower I could not escape the thought of that smell and the oozing blood.

I was on my own in the flat at first, but as there was plenty of room, I invited Bill Rust to share it with me. Bill had been a professional journalist before joining the CP in its very early days, and was the first editor of the *Daily Worker* when it was set up in 1930. The Party had sent him to Barcelona to double as correspondent and Party representative in the spring of 1937. Somehow all of this, I discovered, meant he had the bed while I slept on the floor. He did, however, once let me have a piece of his excellent Côte d'Or plain chocolate. I later took a bit more and later some more still, and he never forgot this, even years afterwards. Nevertheless, he did leave me his typewriter, a sturdy Imperial portable, when he went back to Britain. Over the years, I took that inheritance with me on virtually all my assignments abroad as a journalist.

Some German comrades who had nowhere to go also joined us in the flat. Not long after, one of them, Artur Becker, leader of the German Komsomol or Young Communists, told me they had been in touch with the municipality of Barcelona, which had said they were welcome to the flat but they needed to pay rent, and pay it back to the time when I first took the place over. Becker said that the days of just taking over housing were long gone. There needed to be proper Republican order and the British Party should pay up for the time when it had occupied the flat, that is, before the Germans moved in. Rust exploded when I told him of the proposal, but the argument continued and I decided to move out to lodge with an Italian comrade.

As well as writing the radio and propaganda articles, I began helping Bill Rust with the reports he was sending to the *Daily Worker*. When Rust was called back to London, Peter Kerrigan, though not a journalist, was made the *Worker* correspondent as well as British Party representative. Neither Bill nor Peter spoke proper French or Spanish and that gave me entry into their work. When Peter himself went back to London in the early summer of 1938, I became the correspondent, just 23 years old and fully ready to tell the world how it should be run. My actual role, however, was unclear: was I the British Party representative, as had been the case for Bill and Peter, both of whom seemed nearly twice my age and had mixed with the greats in Moscow, whereas I only had to my name five weeks in the front line at Madrid and a bullet wound from an Andalusian olive grove. Arthur Horner, the Communist leader of the South Wales miners who happened to be visiting Spain at the time, put me right. He got me to type out on headed notepaper of the South Wales Miners' Federation, and then himself signed, a brief note declaring: 'Sam Russell is the representative of the Communist Party of Great Britain'. That sorted matters out in my own mind, if in no one else's.

I had watched Bill and Peter prepare stories, and, nothing daunted, had filed stories of my own when acting as Peter's leg man, which the *Worker*, much to his annoyance, printed under his name, but the only 'training' I got came from

Ernie Wooley, a metal worker, who had worked for the Comintern in the Soviet Union and was in Barcelona re-assembling Soviet fighters. They could not be safely flown to Spain so they had to be sent in pieces by sea. Ernie had done bits of writing for the *Worker* and told me the first sentence had to be the most important point of the story. I have always tried to follow his advice.

When Kerrigan returned to London, I got accreditation with the Foreign Press Department, and may well have been one of the longest lasting of the foreign correspondents in Spain. Most of the newspaper reporters tended to stay only for short periods, retreating from the bombing back over the French border every so often. Sefton Delmer of the *Daily Express*, Henry Buckley, who was there for the *Daily Telegraph* and whose face was distorted by a Bell's Palsy, Willy Forrest of the *News Chronicle*, and Keith Scott Watson of the *Daily Herald* all seemed to get home leave. That never came my way.

Forrest had been sending vivid reports from Madrid for the *Express* up to the beginning of November 1936 but was then suddenly withdrawn and replaced by Delmer, who had been reporting from areas Franco had already conquered and was more suited to the paper's right-wing politics. Delmer became the doyen of the foreign correspondents in Spain. He was one of the many curious characters that Lord Beaverbrook, the owner of the *Express*, used to build up the paper's reputation and readership. He was a personality, and promoted as such by the paper, as well as being a good reporter who had written powerful pieces about the burning of the Reichstag in the first moments after Hitler grabbed power. For many years, his rather sinister looking profile, with a trilby hat tilted, gangster-like, over one eye, appeared beside his stories. Once, when he had a story he knew he would not be able to get past the censor, he went on board the destroyer HMS *Devonshire* and got permission to file from the ship's radio. Such behaviour earned him our nickname of 'Seldom Defter'.

When Forrest returned to Spain in 1937, it was for the *News Chronicle*, taking over from Geoffrey Cox. Forrest was an 'underground' member of the CP – his father was a Glasgow labourer and his mother was already involved with the Party when he was a very young journalist. Forrest had been in contention as editor of the *Worker* at one time. He helped me a great deal in my early days as a journalist, with advice, with contacts, with background knowledge, and above all by convincing me I could do it, and do it with commitment while always trying to get at the facts. Scott Watson had been a local newspaper journalist in Britain but had joined the Tom Mann Centuria, a unit of British volunteers in Barcelona, and went with them to Albacete when the Brigades were first being formed. He was with the German Battalion in the first fighting in the Casa de Campo but left the Brigades when his spirit was finally broken after his unit experienced an intense artillery barrage. He was quite straightforward about it, saying he just could not take it. I thought his reports were generally a disgrace and we called him Scott Shitson. Buckley, though working for the *Telegraph*, and another of the gang, Herbert Matthews of the *New York Times*, who came with the reputation of having been awarded by Mussolini for his coverage of

46 From Rifle to Typewriter

the Italian conquest of Abyssinia, were both definitely not pro-Franco. They were honest journalists who taught me much about the trade, or, as they would probably have said, the craft.

It being war conditions, newspaper journalists had to submit all their stories to censors and have them stamped as approved before they could be sent. They all had to be phoned from the Foreign Ministry. The Sub-secretariat of propaganda of the Ministry had within it the Foreign Press Department headed by Constancia de la Mora, reputedly the first woman in Spain to get a legal divorce. Her former husband became head of Franco's Press Department. She came from an aristocratic family and had learnt her English from an Irish nanny. Indeed, she always seemed to me to speak her excellent English with a definite Irish accent. When provoked, as she often was by British journalists, particularly Delmer, she would come out with a string of violent invective in English that shocked even me.

Even a journalist as green and young as I was had the opportunity to mix and meet with those at the heart of affairs. As the *Worker* correspondent suitably armed with my accreditation from Horner, I had access to key figures such as Jawaharlal Nehru, the leader of the Congress movement for Indian independence, and Paul Robeson, the Black American activist and singer who performed for the Brigades, as well as those from abroad who were centrally involved in the fight, like Palmiro Togliatti, the future architect of post-war Italian Communism. He was then acting as Comintern adviser to the Spanish Communist Party under the name Alfredo, rather than his Comintern name of Ercoli. My most frequent meetings were with Pedro, the Hungarian, and the Italian Luigi Longo, known in Spain as Gallo, the Inspector General of the Brigades, who, with André Marty, was directly responsible to the Comintern for the Brigades.[4] These were impressive people to be among.

All my stories were dictated by phone to the stenographers at the paper's offices in London. That was quicker than the cablegrams I had to use when sending copy to papers in the US. The amount of time one had to spend typing up stories, dealing with the censors, preparing cablegrams, shouting over bad phone lines to get 500 words dictated, was something that surprised me. In those days, and in the difficult conditions of the war, it could turn out to be longer than the time it took you to get the story in the first place. Later, when I eventually got back to Britain, comrades at the *Worker* told me there was always a sense of emotion when I came on the phone. Radio reports were very limited, there was no television from the war, just some news films in the cinemas, and even a country as close as Spain seemed like another world. People would sometimes listen to me dictating my story, crowded close around the little cubicle where the stenographer worked. In contrast, phoning London sometimes made me very homesick.

I was also filing stories for our American comrades in New York, both for their paper, also called the *Daily Worker*, and the magazine *The New Masses*. These I had to type before getting them telegraphed, another lengthy process.

My reporting work meant getting out and about, so I soon gave up the broadcasts, handing on the job in July 1938 to a former Brigader from Newcastle called

Frank Graham, though he contracted typhoid a few weeks later and had to resign from the post. In my role as the Party rep, I managed to wangle him into the private English hospital run by a British businessman who had made his money introducing greyhound racing into Spain. For reasons that, at the time, I did not fully understand, representations I made to the British Consulate to have Frank repatriated were suddenly successful and an instruction came that he should be ready as the Navy was about to send in a ship to take him out. The last thing I heard was that a chauffeur-driven Rolls Royce had gone to pick him up. Clearly something fishy, as they were not going to do that just for a sick former Brigader.

When we met again in Britain, he told me the whole thing had been a set up. The Rolls took him to a deserted beach well north of Barcelona. The destroyer sent a boat ashore. While an embassy official walked him down to the shoreline, Frank realised they were being followed by two well-dressed middle-aged Spaniards. Whether by chance or by foresight of the Republican authorities, there was a Spanish soldier standing guard at the point where the British boat had beached. He let Frank go aboard, but not the two others who Frank had worked out were rich Barcelona factory owners and were probably the real reason why the whole show had been put on, Frank being just the excuse needed to gain the permission from the Republican government. Frank got to travel to France on the destroyer by himself.

After giving up my broadcasts, my first major assignment was covering what turned out to be the Republic's last big attempt to turn the tide of the war in its drive across the River Ebro in the summer of 1938.

Having secured the west of Spain, the far south and the Basque region at the western end of the Pyrenees in 1937, Franco and his German and Italian allies had moved round the north of Madrid and pushed east to the Mediterranean coast, cutting the part of Spain held by the Republic in two. They finished this operation by the end of March 1938. The region held by the Republic stretching from Madrid, in the centre, to the Mediterranean, was a wedge about the size of one third of Spain. The second region held by the Republic was Catalonia in the north-east, centred on Barcelona, Spain's largest city at the time. It was the only part of Republican Spain that had an international border. There were several attempts by the fascists to push deep into the central wedge, but the crucial fighting developed around Catalonia. On the night of 24 July 1938, the People's Army, as we had come to call it, started to attack south across the Ebro, Spain's largest river and which marked the southern boundary of this Catalonian territory.

The offensive appeared to begin well, but soon bogged down in bitter fighting in searing daytime heat in the steep, rocky, mountainous territory. In the days immediately after the start of the offensive, I was just behind the Republican advance, watching the fascist prisoners being brought back in their hundreds. German and Italian aircraft attacked the advancing Republicans repeatedly. We were showered with bombs from dawn till dusk. From my position in one of the myriad of trenches, I watched the white puffs of the bursting anti-aircraft shells against a beautiful blue sky. Several times that day, one of Mussolini's bombers

48 From Rifle to Typewriter

turned into a sickening spin, crashing to the ground with a thud that shook everything except our spirits. The troops around me seemed to take less notice of the fascist planes than their commander's horse was taking of the flies that were trying to bother it.

It was a titanic Republican effort. Great pontoon bridges and cable ferries were flung across the river. Heavy guns, armour and masses of disciplined regular troops moved across. The initial attack across the Ebro had achieved complete surprise. A few days later the Republic attacked westward out of Catalonia across the River Segre, this time without any advantage of surprise. The troops involved told me they had been able to hear the fascist officers warning their own soldiers of the dangers of an attack. In some places, the rival trenches and strong points were only a few yards apart.

The Ebro offensive had been undertaken by regular soldiers from the People's Army with the International Brigades playing their part. The second offensive was by the shock battalions of the Carabineros, the specialist frontier guards, who I watched creeping forward in their olive green uniforms. They had been silently moving up to the riverbank throughout the day. At 4 am the first units slipped across, some wading through the water with their rifles held aloft. They were lightly equipped, orderly, eager, and noiseless. There was no silence, however, when the artillery opened up. Not only were there the guns, but nature delivered its own onslaught. The sky had been getting blacker and blacker as the night progressed and a storm broke that unleashed such thunder that, at times, the roar of the heavy artillery was drowned out. Flashes of lightning made the exploding shells look like candle flares. As the battle raged throughout the day, the river rose dangerously, swollen by a torrential downpour. Despite this, and the enemy shells and bombs, troops and tanks continued to cross over the river while I watched prisoners being brought back in the other direction.

In both offensives, the fighting soon ground to a halt. This meant, inevitably, that the pendulum would swing against the Republic on the battlefield. Though Franco and his allies lost huge numbers of soldiers in their counter attacks, the casualties on our side were devastating. The International Brigades lost hundreds upon hundreds, killed, wounded, and captured. Eventually in mid-November, the People's Army pulled back north across the Ebro and east across the Segre. True, it had taken the fascists three and a half months to regain this bitterly fought territory, but the return to the north side of the river meant that the veteran forces of the Republic were now in strategic retreat.

The war in fact lasted until the first moments of spring in 1939 following battles in which tens of thousands died on both sides. Hitler and Mussolini tested new weapons and military skills. They used Spain to battle harden their elite units, though, in Mussolini's case, the results were on occasion inauspicious, as when his professional soldiers were bested by the anti-fascist Italian exiles of the International Brigade's Garibaldi Battalion at Guadalajara.

The Spanish government had tried in vain to get an international agreement on mutual withdrawal of volunteers on our side and of German and Italian forces on the fascist side. At the end of September 1938, as Chamberlain was capitulating in Munich before Hitler's demands over Czechoslovakia, the Republic switched strategy and Juan Negrín, the Prime Minister and Defence Minister of the Republic, announced a unilateral withdrawal of the volunteers. The withdrawal was not an easy decision, and the Spanish government was just trying to save something from the war they were losing. The military contribution from the Brigades had become insignificant, the People's Army was now well-trained and well-organised, and the Republic gambled on gaining political leverage by leaving Franco as the only one with foreign supporters on the battlefield.

On 28 October, Barcelona put on a mass parade to say goodbye to the Brigades. I watched from the balcony of the Foreign Ministry as vast crowds stood along the Diagonal, the wide boulevard that cuts through the heart of the city from east to west, as people mobbed the Brigaders whose heroism was celebrated in the most incredibly powerful speech by 'La Pasionaria'. An air force fly past showered the streets with postcards carrying a poem written 'To an international volunteer fallen in Spain'. A march past by Spanish forces was followed by the International Brigades, many with bouquets of flowers in their arms, not weapons. The final ranks of the Brigaders were the doctors and nurses, in their clinical whites. The crowds surged after the marching volunteers, blocking the way for the armoured vehicles that were supposed to end the march past. It was an incredible outpouring of emotion.

All of us who had served in the Brigades received a presentation version of a farewell address to us by Dolores Ibárurri. She spoke directly to my heart. And she spoke of my own experiences that November in Madrid when I had first seen the power of her oratory:

> In the hardest days of the war, when the capital of the Spanish Republic was threatened, it was you, gallant comrades of the International Brigades, who helped save the city with your fighting enthusiasm, your heroism and your spirit of sacrifice. You can go proudly. You are history. You are legend. You are the heroic example of democracy's solidarity and universality. And when the olive tree of peace puts forth its leaves again, entwined with the laurels of the Spanish Republic's victory – come back! Come back to us. With us, those of you who have no country will find one, those of you who have to live deprived of friendship, will find friends.

It was one thing to bid farewell to the Brigades, another to get the home governments to allow them back, and for those who were refugees from fascism at home, the situation was especially difficult. For weeks after that farewell parade, Brigaders remained holed up in the small town of Ripoll high in the foothill of the Pyrenees and just ten miles south of the French frontier. I was to and fro from Ripoll throughout those weeks, just as most of the volunteers spent their days visiting factories, schools, refugee children's colonies and the Republican towns all around, trying to keep everyone's morale up.

50 From Rifle to Typewriter

One of the miracles of that encampment for the British Battalion was the work of the cook, Hooky Walker – he conjured up the most amazing meals, as he had when the Battalion had been on the other side of the Ebro and his kitchen seemed to have had a fascinating attraction for the Italian bombers! Hooky gave me a break from salt fish and beans.

One night, when I had to return late to Barcelona, Sam Wild, the Battalion Commander, walked with me a good way out of town along a road with a mountain street rushing alongside. A young merchant seaman, he had first gone into action at Jarama after I had been wounded out of the Battalion. We had got to know each other well. The only light was the stars in the clear and cold sky above, but Ripoll was a working town and competing with the gurgling stream was the hum of the local textile factory which worked night and day. Sam, in his straightforward way, told me of his plans to 'make Britain hum' with the message of Spanish resistance once he got back home. I had particularly liked Sam, probably both the most effective and most popular of the Battalion commanders, ever since I had watched him dancing in one of the giant tubs used to squash the grapes as the first stage in wine making. He was with the mayor of a small village near where the battalion had been based at the time, dancing and singing a mixture of sea shanties, Spanish love songs, and revolutionary chants as the grapes began to ooze up between their toes.

As well as the British and Americans, there were 300 Canadians, some Australians, New Zealanders, and Jews from Palestine. I acted as the messenger boy for them all, sending telegrams they had composed here, there and everywhere, to the authorities in Ottawa, Canberra, and, above all, in London.

A month after the Barcelona parade, and still stuck facing a possible winter in the Pyrenees, a frustrated British battalion elected a delegation to lobby the British consul in Barcelona. The junior foreign minister, R A Butler, had just told the Commons that the Foreign Office was still not in a position to give a 'definite date' for when the preparations for the return could be completed. I went along with the delegation to hear what the diplomat had to say. He offered all sorts of specious arguments, claiming that the Health Ministry in London needed to have everyone checked for infectious diseases and that French authorities were stopping any train with returning volunteers from crossing the frontier – ridiculous, as the American Abraham Lincoln Battalion had been told by all concerned that it could leave the following day. He even claimed a general strike north of the border was the real problem, telling me that 'With all the influence you have, it is a pity you did not use it to stop the strike in France'. Leaving Barcelona to get back to Ripoll, our train was held up, not by French strikers but by more Italian air raids, two of them.

As light was just beginning to break over the bleak Pyrenees the following morning, I marched with the Americans through the town's streets to the station against a bitterly cold wind but amidst a rousing send-off from the local population. At the station entrance, British volunteers lined up to salute the departing Americans. The train pulled out slowly to the strains of a band playing 'Himno de Riego', the national anthem of democratic Spain. It was a moment of great emotion on both sides.

Though not many of the original volunteers had survived, the first Americans had arrived at the Spanish battlefront on 17 February 1937 during the fighting at Jarama. The British Battalion had been blocking a fascist drive to take a vital bridge and gain control over the road between Madrid in the heart of Spain and Valencia on the Mediterranean coast, and the American volunteers were crucial reinforcements for the British and the Republic.

The British turn to leave finally came a week later. A trainload of 304 men crossed the border into France on the morning of 6 December. I typed my story on the return journey to Barcelona in one of the goods wagons commandeered by Sam Wild after the passenger train that had been arranged for the journey broke down. The Battalion had paraded for a final roll call in the square at Ripoll, replying one after the other as their names were read out while the first streaks of a cold dawn crept across the sky. As I listened, I could only think that more men from the Battalion were lying in graves across Spain than were standing before me.

The men marched to the station with banners aloft, the town's folk cheering from their windows. At the station, the column was welcomed by the local leaders of the parties in the Popular Front, their own banner taut against the bitter December wind. There were stirring speeches, thanks and hugs – and a commitment by the British volunteers to act, as the Spanish Government had asked, as ambassadors for the Spanish cause as soon as they were back home. Everyone burned with anger and regret at the failure of the leaders in London and Paris to understand that what was happening in Spain would happen to them if Hitler, Mussolini and Franco were allowed to win.

At every hamlet and village along the way, people came to the side of the line to say goodbye. Farm labourers, tiny children, and old women with tears in their eyes clenched fists in the air in a final salute. On the road alongside the track were ten mobile anti-aircraft units from the People's Army moving with us, machine guns at the ready, their commanders scanning the skies for any enemy planes that might think of attacking. It was a gesture of support that moved the volunteers greatly.

At Puigcerdà on the frontier, André Marty came to make a final speech. Of those present, perhaps I alone had heard him give his address when the first volunteers for the Brigade arrived in Albacete in October 1936. Tears were running down the cheeks of some of the toughest men I ever met. Then, as they gave three cheers for the troops of the People's Army who were now going to face the fight alone, the Battalion crossed into France.

The unlucky Canadians were still in Spain at Christmas in deep frustration. For my part, I remember being peeved in the extreme when someone in the relative calm and comfort of our London office told me they were going to run a story Claud Cockburn had filed from the French side of the border, rather than mine phoned later from Barcelona, but that is just part of the rough and tumble of daily journalism.

52 From Rifle to Typewriter

Back in Barcelona during those weeks at the end of 1938, I saw heavy bombing by Italian airplanes intensify. Since an Anglo-Italian Pact in April 1938, Chamberlain, who became infamous for his appeasement of Hitler, had assiduously courted Mussolini by giving way to his demands, with each of Chamberlain's *démarches* being followed by, or sometimes even accompanying, an escalation in Italy's military involvement in Spain.

The city was attacked three days after the Barcelona parade for the Brigades, on 1 November. The air raid warning system could give no more than four minutes notice of the approach by ten Italian Savoia bombers coming in two waves. In addition to the anti-aircraft fire, a chaser – as we called fighter aircraft at the time – went up to take them on, diving at speed on the second wave. The pilot misjudged and collided with one of the bombers. Both planes spiralled down into the sea followed by another bomber he must have been able to hit with his machine guns during his dive. In all, the planes managed to drop about 30 bombs on the harbour district, hitting several homes.

One house I rushed into to help the rescue workers had its top two floors wrecked with the roof beams collapsed down bizarrely onto freshly made beds. The family had got up, done the housework and were ready to flee when the air raid warning sounded. Even so, we heard that one person had died in this raid.

Perhaps surprisingly, the city's farewell to the volunteers had not been attacked by the Italian planes. Indeed, as the Brigades were being pulled out there had been a deceptive moment of calm at the fronts, on the Ebro some 60 miles or so south-west of Barcelona, and on the Central and Southern fronts from Madrid to the coast. It was just the quiet before the final, shattering storm. Berlin and Rome both wanted now to wrap matters up quickly in Spain. Neither they, nor Franco, had expected the war to threaten to go into a fourth year.

One indication of what was to come was an announcement we heard on 3 November over Radio Salamanca, Franco's broadcasting service, that 137 towns and villages in the Republican rear-guard were going to be bombed. The names of all the target villages were read out, one by one. It was not an empty threat, but a careful change of tactics. Guernica had shown what aerial bombardment could do. At the same time, the Republic estimated it had brought down some 200 German and Italian planes during the Ebro battles in the summer through a combination of air force and anti-aircraft artillery. That may have been an exaggeration, but whatever the real figures were, the enemy had been losing planes over the big cities as I had seen in Barcelona.

Now the German and Italian commanders must have decided to turn on less easily defendable targets as well. Barcelona, Madrid, and Valencia continued to be hit, but they had anti-aircraft batteries and a degree of air raid shelters. The villages and small towns were quite unprepared. The Republic's tiny force of chasers could not take on these dispersed bombing raids. By the time I was able to file my first report about the Radio Salamanca announcement a few hours after it had been made, news had already come in of attacks on 15 of the target villages. Fear spread, naturally, to all of them.

One morning later in the middle of November, I was out in the open in the Plaza de Cataluña, Barcelona's equivalent to London's Trafalgar Square, when the sirens started.[5] People around me ran quickly but orderly to take shelter in the underground station nearby. An old lady in difficulty with a big bundle of cabbages was helped by a bronzed soldier off a tram that had stopped at the first sound of the siren – we had only that four minutes between the first warning and the arrival of the bombs in which to get everyone to relative safety. As she got her feet to the pavement, the guns began to boom and, almost immediately, there was the whistle and rattle of the bombs. Cowering with me in a doorway, she could not control a shriek of horror as the shock waves hit us.

The following day, the sirens sounded early, around 9 am. The Italian bombers started with their usual target of the housing in the port area and the old town, the more densely populated parts of the city sloping down from the Plaza to the sea. They managed to drop about 40 bombs there but, faced by an intense barrage of anti-aircraft fire, they moved off to leave the rest of their load on a small village just beyond the Barcelona boundary, killing 20 people. I walked down the Ramblas, the ancient street that splits the old town in two, where its working class in peaceful times went for their evening stroll, and which now took me to the harbour. One of the bombs had hit a British ship, the *Lake Holwell*. That was about the only bomb that had fallen on the actual port. The rest had hit homes.

In the old town, the streets were often less than 15 feet wide and the housing rose to six or seven stories. In one narrow street, a lorry had been crushed under falling masonry. While I was navigating round it, the whole roof of another house crashed down. A bit further on, I found a street where I had been with Peter Kerrigan the week before. He was back on Party business and wanted a present for his little daughter, Rose. We had found a small shop selling beautifully engraved Toledo-work brooches, and 'Big Peter', in a sentimental mood, bought two of them. Now it looked as if the shop and the house above had escaped any damage – all the windows were intact. Yet, when I opened the door to find the shopkeeper, the Mediterranean sun was shining on a tremendous pile of rubble. The entire back of the house had been blown out. It was then that I saw the smears of blood on the doorstep. Scattered all around were the remains of the stock of Toledo trinkets. Congealed stains were the only sign left of the shopkeeper and his family.

A bit nearer the port, a tenement building had its top stories shattered by a bomb that had walloped through the front wall. A young woman, her hair dishevelled, pushed her way through the crowd, panting and clutching a shopping bag. She had left her only child with her younger sister when she went to queue for food. She just kept muttering 'Mi niña, mi niña' – 'My child, my child'. Firemen appeared carrying a form covered in a sheet. Following them was a Red Cross man carrying another, smaller, form wrapped in a blue-striped blanket. The young woman shrieked out 'No puede ser' – 'It cannot be'. Wrenching herself free from neighbours who were trying to hold her back, she rushed forward.

54 From Rifle to Typewriter

Her shaking fingers ripped back the coverings. Her sister, not more than 13 years old, had been horribly maimed by the blast that killed her, while her child in the blanket lay still, waxen white, with only the tiniest trickle of blood oozing from its mouth. The Red Cross man shook his head and the young woman collapsed, crying, on the two bodies. As she did so, her shopping rolled out along the gutter, a few tomatoes and two tins of milk.

As I did every day then, I went back furiously to type out my story. There was a queue forming up for the afternoon show at the theatre and a clothing factory where the young women were already back at work and singing as they did so. Despite the bombs, a 'normal' life continued. For me, it was a good discipline imposed by the need to have the censorship approve what I was going to phone over to London: typing the story was something that focused my rage. I could not dictate to the stenographers at the *Worker* without the censor's stamp on my copy.

I was not only sending stories to the *Worker* in London but also both to our American comrades in New York, whose paper was also called the *Daily Worker*, and to their *New Masses* magazine, for whom Joe North, the editor, would often send a telegram demanding, perhaps, something as simple as a fifteen hundred word interview with the Prime Minister Negrín and expecting that I could send the worked up text by return a couple of days later. That meant typing up the story in telegraphese for the keyboard operators at the Direct Spanish Telegraph Company who then could copy it accurately, key stroke for key stroke. And it all had to pass through the censor's office in time for me to rush the copy to be cabled or to get to a free phone booth to dictate to London. It could easily take half an hour to put the copy over and longer for me to type it up on Bill Rust's trusty portable. That, amidst the sounds, the tensions and the realities of war. Just once in a while, I passed a scribbled note through the censors when a last minute piece of news from the front was worth it, but those easy occasions were rare. This work at least kept me together and gave me the feeling that I was still fighting the fascists.

But I found I was writing the same story I had had to write on previous days and would have to write for some weeks yet. One time, I went to the hospital where the greater part of the wounded from the last 24 hours had been taken. The chief surgeon had been in the theatre all night doing what he could for the victims. He took me on his round of the wards. If only, I wrote, it had been Chamberlain with that surgeon and not me; perhaps the British Cabinet should be made to live in these homes crowded down by the harbour and hit day after day by the cargoes of death.

In the first ward, the doctor pointed to a child whose face was swathed in bandages. He had not yet recovered from the anaesthetic. Two years old, he had been playing at sandcastles in the Plaza de Cataluña and was caught out in the open when the bombs fell. There was no hope that the surgeon could save his eyes. He would be blind for life, if he managed to survive. Nearby, a tiny child in a cot began to cry. Her mother had been struck by falling masonry as she ran with the child in her arms to take shelter. The mother died, the child was only

From Rifle to Typewriter **55**

lightly wounded. A young woman moaned in her sleep in the next bed. There was nothing I could say. Nothing I could do. In the street outside, I found myself in the middle of a crowd of relatives, heavy-eyed and silent as they waited for the nurses to look through their lists of the wounded survivors. Everyone in that crowd hoped desperately that the names they hesitated to give those nurses were not among the hundred plus names of the dead.

Fury over the traitors to democracy on the international scene was paralleled by fear of the fifth column on the local scene. It was not always easy to distinguish panic from betrayal and sometimes in a war the only way of halting panic is to be as harsh with spreading panic as one is with traitors. In mid-November, while I was visiting the front with Joseph Swire of the Reuters news agency and Herbert Klein from the Basel *National Zeitung*, we got the chance to interview the local commander, Lt.-Col. Sebastián Pozas Perea, over breakfast. He set about denouncing the way the war was run. His anger was particularly directed against the Fifth Army Corps and its leadership of Generals Modesto, Lister and Campesino, who all happened to be Communists. Perea waxed lyrical over the theme that nothing could move, no one could attack, aside, he claimed, from the Communist generals of the Fifth Corps. Swire and Klein did not see that they had a story, but I felt it my duty to type up a detailed report for the comrades in the Party. Swire thought that if he gave any kind of report, then Perea would get into serious trouble. Actually, despite my attempted denunciation, the Lt-Col was still the commander of the Republic's forces in Figueras in the last week of the fighting in Catalonia.

The Servicio de Información Militar, the Service of Military Information, the key security agency trying to root out real fifth columnists, had bigger and properly nasty fish to fry. They announced in the middle of December that they had broken a major fascist spy ring in Catalonia and that some 200 would be executed. The Service said the ring had pinpointed targets for the Italian planes and had supplied military details to the Franco side. In the rush of those final weeks, I don't recall whether the sentences were carried out.

That winter was already the coldest in many years. In most Republican areas, there were severe food shortages. The authorities estimated by then there were half a million refugee children in Catalonia alone. I visited refugee hostels that were being supplied with food by volunteer women, sometimes helped by parcels and donations from abroad. It was a pitiful sight, children, many of them orphaned and all without enough clothing or food.

But these humanitarian concerns were cut short just before Christmas Day. There had been some weeks of relative calm on the ground, before the fascist offensive duly opened up with a vengeance on 23 December. Italian planes did the bombing. German and Italian artillery did the shelling and on the ground it was fresh ranks of Italian soldiers that did the fighting. Two of the initial Italian thrusts were held. The main one advanced some nine miles, but, even there, the fighting was hard for them and the People's Army took quite a few prisoners, some of whom I had the chance to interview. One, a Lieutenant of Engineers,

56 From Rifle to Typewriter

Ladislau Edilli, came up with a new explanation for me as to why the Italians were in Spain: it was to end British and French influence over the Republic!

There was little time for festivities on Christmas Day. My own was spent first at the front seeing how the troops were holding up against a new onslaught and then, in the evening, at Ripoll with the 300 Canadians still holed up in the Pyrenees. They had decided to cut their rations and had saved up enough food to make a feast of sorts for some 500 refugee children also billeted in the village.

Pressure by the fascist military was inexorable, both on the infantry at the front and the civilians in the city. From the beginning of the New Year, Barcelona experienced more gruesome air raids. On New Year's Eve itself, for half an hour in the evening darkness, the planes circled above the city. From the fourth floor of a building in the middle of Barcelona, I watched searchlights stabbing the sky to try to pick out the bombers and give the anti-aircraft batteries a clear sight on their targets. Above the mournful wail of the sirens came the whistle of the first bombs and the whole centre of the city was lit up by the lurid flash of the blasts as they fell right along a line that went through the heart of the main residential district. Mussolini's pilots then returned to attacking the Plaza de Cataluña. They had left it alone since the previous March. Then, a series of murderous raids had left hundreds killed and wounded. This time, I counted a quick succession of some 25 bombs.

Rushing through darkened streets to where I had seen them fall, with the ambulance bells clanging in my ears as the crews raced to help the wounded, I thought of all those people in Britain hurrying home to welcome in the New Year in their homes safe and sound. Here was I groping my way through the acrid smoke that hung in the street like a pall, a street where the Red Cross were already at work, where on one bench they were tending a young woman, bleeding from an internal wound while in the road, prone, her husband lay in a pool of blood, far from any aid. The bombs had fallen in the open streets, rather than being targeted on houses. They appeared to be fragmentation bombs designed to kill people rather than destroy buildings. While the wounded were being gathered in, the anti-aircraft guns boomed again, and this second raid was beaten off.

On my way back up town, at the last bomb crater I passed, I stopped to pick up some fragments and read 'Rheinische Stahlwerke 1937'. Franco's war, Mussolini's planes, but Hitler's bombs. The intention of the raiders had clearly been to kill civilians, and that night 83 were killed instantly. Small beer, perhaps, compared to the war that was to come, but it was as stark a warning as one could possibly want of what bombing could do to civilians.

That there remained some small degree of hope did not seem an entirely foolish dream. The People's Army launched a major offensive in the far south, aiming to force the fascists to ease the pressure on Catalonia. The drive was from east to west, threatening to cut the fascist communications passing through Estremadura from the south towards the north. For several days, the Republican troops pressed ahead, capturing a great deal of weaponry.

It was a boost to be able to report victories for our side in the south, but it was clear that the main battle was taking place in Catalonia. The *Worker* office in London told me that some of the London papers were giving lavish reports of the successes in Estremadura and I hastened to damp down the enthusiasm, a most unusual role for me. Mussolini had wanted Republican Spain on a plate as a fait accompli before Chamberlain came on his visit to Rome on 10 January.

In Barcelona, the Under Secretary of Land Forces, Colonel Cordon, set out for us journalists the government's view that, whatever happened in the south, the fascist military planners were not going to let up in the north. 'It is Catalonia that the enemy has selected for the main attack against Spanish democracy', he argued. The enemy strategy, he said, was to accumulate overwhelming aviation, artillery and tank forces and deploy motorised columns whenever that superiority gained an opening in the Republican defences – a trial run perhaps for the Nazi blitzkrieg strategies of the following year across Belgium and northern France. The day after Chamberlain returned to London from Rome, the Italian push towards Barcelona resumed in an avalanche of bombs, shells and tank fire.

Making my way that day towards the front line at Lérida, 60 miles inland in the west of Catalonia, I was held up for three hours, sheltering from intense bombing by Italian planes. Even when I was still ten miles from the front, the ground trembled with the shock of the bombs and exploding shells. Flight after flight of planes passed overhead. The troops I met shortly after were still in good shape and their determination was still strong, despite everything.

Passing through the small town of Borjas Blancas, on the road from Lérida to Tarragona on the coast, it was difficult to pick out a house that had not been severely damaged by 11 days of continuous bombing. The final bout had come the day before and had amounted to little more than an attack on a cemetery. Those who had not been able to flee already, lay buried under the ruins of what had been a charming Catalan town. A short way further on, Esplugas had been bombed that afternoon and we watched as rescue workers scrabbled to pull apart the rubble and free those still trapped in their ruined homes. One group of soldiers waiting there told me how they had just pulled out of Santa Coloma to the heights above it; they had had to watch Italian troops enter the village and herd perhaps as many as 250 women, children and old men onto a threshing floor at the village outskirts where they were machine gunned. No wonder that when I saw Vincente Uribe, the Minister of Agriculture, later that day he spoke fiercely of the determination to resist. 'Many times in the course of this war we have astounded the world when we have been given up for dead. But Spain will not die so easily'.

Huge Italian reinforcements were the reason why Republican advances in the southern sector did not force Franco and his Nazi strategists to let up in their pressure on the Barcelona pocket in the north. When the final fascist offensive began, there were about 50 tanks available to the Republican commanders. Against them were at least 500 armoured vehicles. The Republican artillery, around 300 guns, could only fire at an average rate of one shell per gun every five

58 From Rifle to Typewriter

minutes. That was not because the Republicans did not know how to operate their guns effectively. It was because they lacked the ammunition. Franco and his German and Italian strategists had deployed some 3,000 cannons and a quarter of a million infantry along the front. His generals could therefore pick and choose where to thrust, and their losses, even when heavy, could be replaced, as they regularly were, with fresh troops and new weapons. Ours could not, especially as Soviet arms were stockpiled at the French frontier in the name of 'non-intervention'.

The problem, even at that late moment, did not appear to be a lack of enthusiasm or people, but a lack of arms. I translated and sent off appeal after appeal from trade unions, mass organisations, political parties and others trying to mobilise international support to have arms freed for use by the Republic. The French government relented only when it was too late, just before the fall of Barcelona.

Going back up to the front after the Italians had taken the town of Valls, a dozen miles inland from Tarragona, I saw the extent of the damage all those fascist guns could do. One hill in the defence system round Valls was said to have been hit by 7,000 shells. The town had literally been pounded to bits. As we came up to a crossroads about five miles east of Valls, two batteries of enemy artillery opened up, their shells bracketing the crossroads. I lay flat in front of a stone wall with General Modesto's Brigade Commissar Luis Delage at my side. Four shells fell in a row about 20 yards in front of us and four more about the same distance behind. We had just lifted up our heads when the whine of another batch told us that a third battery was opening up. This time round the shells were much closer, one of them hitting the wall we were using as cover, and we were both smothered with dirt.

At the same moment, a People's Army artillery unit came rushing down the road, having left a position that it seemed to me no human being could ever have dreamed of holding. The whole process was disciplined. Having been in the trenches in bitter battle, I could sense when troops knew what they had to do and could set about doing it under the command of good officers. These artillerymen were brave and calm. While Delage sang their praises to me, I watched as staff officers controlled the replacing of the guns and the 'transmission men', the runners with messages from the command, set off to make sure that Modesto's officers knew what was going on. At Modesto's HQ a short while later, the atmosphere was business-like and determined.

But going back through Tarragona, I found a wrecked town with only a few people left, taking shelter in refuges where some of them had been stuck for three days. What valuable machinery and equipment there was in the town had already been dismantled and moved the 60 miles to Barcelona, even as the Italian bombers came over. While I was looking around, those planes came back for their ninth raid that day.

By 15 January, the pressure was too much and the second line of defence had been lost. Tarragona had to be abandoned to the Italian generals. They sent an immediate boastful message to Mussolini from, as they put it, the shores of *Mare*

Nostrum, Our Sea. Though the troops I watched pulling back from Tarragona were in good order and spirit, this really was the beginning of the end.

Barcelona itself was plastered with posters declaring *¡Todos a fortificar Barcelona! – All for the fortification of Barcelona!* But it was not to be. There was no one in the city who could have had any doubt as to what defeat would mean, but the will to resist was being ground down. By January 22, Italian units had advanced to within 30 miles of the city and some of Franco's troops were trying to encircle it by passing round in a vast arc to the north. If they had been successful, any hope of escape to France would have had to be abandoned. There were 16 bombing raids on Barcelona that day alone. We could see the dog fights in the skies above as Republican planes tried to bring the German and Italian planes down before they could hit the city. People came out to cheer the Republic's planes as they successfully shot down three Junkers bombers and two Messerschmitts. Unfortunately, I had to watch as two of our own were also brought down, something the Republic could not afford, while Hitler and Mussolini could always send more.

The Republican authorities in the city declared a state of war and tried to mobilise the population while evacuating civilians from the least protected areas. But as the civilians streamed out of the city to the French frontier 100 miles to the north, the Italian armour and artillery proved irresistible, not least because this was accompanied by 44 major bombing raids in the final four days of the assault.

With Willy Forrest and Henry Buckley, I went to the top of a hill just outside the city. Buckley had a pair of good binoculars. We were able to see the fascists advancing – and see that there was nothing to stop them. There were no defences in place and as far we could see no effort being made to put any in place. Unlike in Madrid, where the Republic had mobilised the population to build fortifications and trenches, nothing was being done. Leaflets were being distributed calling on people to defend Barcelona, but, finally, no one was taking any notice. There were long queues at the bread shops and heaps of rubbish piling up in the streets. The city itself was, at last, demoralised.

I got to the Spanish Communist Party headquarters a short while later. Togliatti was in his office with his then wife, Rita Montagnana, standing as if on guard at the door.[6] I asked if I could see him. I told him what we had seen and asked him what the situation was.

'You've seen the situation', he told me. But I protested: 'Nothing's happening'.

'That's right', he said 'Nothing is happening'.

'Aren't we going to defend Barcelona?' I asked passionately. He just replied: 'What with?' I declared that we had defended Madrid.

'Barcelona', he observed, 'is not Madrid'.

It is curious how little things stick in your mind, but while we were talking Montagnana came in several times with hot milk and biscuits.

There had been a wave of panic in the rear-guard forces of the Republic, who gave up their positions in Barcelona and moved north, forcing the troops at the front to pull back. There was then a further wave of panic among these

60 From Rifle to Typewriter

second-line forces, who retreated across the French frontier in their thousands. Even doctors left their patients. Civilians trying to flee commandeered the lorries that had been sent for food, water and munitions. I wrote that those escaping had had their morale undermined 'by enemy agents, Fifth Columnists and Trotskyists'. There probably were plenty of Franco's agents at work, but the truth was that people were just more realistic about the military realities than I was. They had no choice, whereas I did.

Recognizing the time had come to leave Barcelona, I managed to get a phone call through to London and asked for advice. I spoke to Dave Springhall, the former political commissar of the British Battalion. His reply was blunt but useless: 'Stay to the last possible minute'. Green though I was and over-optimistic I may have been, but something told me that such things were easier to say in London than to practice in Barcelona. What on earth would be 'the last possible minute'? How was I to tell when it had arrived?

I finally left Barcelona on 25 January with Scott Watson. Whatever I might have thought about some of his stories, he had a car *and* had been prepared to wait until 'the last possible minute'. By the following evening, all of Barcelona was in Franco's hands. The final copies of the Communist Party papers hurriedly printed off in Barcelona, then on presses that were moved to the north in Gerona and finally in Figueras, just 15 miles from the French frontier, were continuing to call for resistance, but the great city of Spanish revolt had finally, in complete exhaustion, given up the struggle.

At some point along the road north, I have no idea exactly where, we had to leave the car and go by foot because of the sheer numbers of refugees making for the border. The night was very nasty, wet and cold, and with no means of transport and no money, we made slow progress. We feared the fascists would be upon us at any moment. We walked for hours along that coast – known today as the Costa Brava – with Franco's navy and Italian ships shelling the road from time to time from the sea. When, eventually, we arrived at the final control on the Spanish side, it was still raining and all around us were babies crying and women dying at the roadside, as the remains of a defeated and beaten people, many of whom had not slept or eaten for a week, moved slowly along.

Notes

1 Dora Birnbach, later Lewin, was interned by the French, but managed to reach Yugoslavia and worked for the medical services as part of Tito's partisans and then returned to Poland after the war. Like many Jews who returned to the new Poland, she fell victim to a vicious anti-Semitic campaign there in the 1960s and, finally, she went back to Israel.

2 In Spain, Sam held a membership card for the Catalan Communist party (known as the Unified Socialist Party of Catalonia) in the name of Manuel Lesser, Funcionario in Propaganda, and one for the Communist Party of Spain in the name of Manassé Lesser, both issued in Barcelona in 1938.

3 Sam's brother Salom was in the navy during the 1939–1945 war, and, according to Sam, everyone called him Salome, much to his disgust and annoyance, and he

changed his name to Sam. The brothers argued over many years as to who first took the name Sam but when the war was over Salom became Sid to distinguish himself from his older brother. It took MI5 some time to work out that Lesser had become Russell and one they had, they decided it showed how devious and dangerous a Communist he was.

4 Longo, a founder member of the Italian Communist Party, fought the Germans as a partisan in Italy and became an Italian MP and secretary-general of the Italian Party after the death of Togliatti in 1964.

5 Sam sometimes used Spanish names rather than Catalan (e.g. Plaza de Cataluña instead of Plaça de Catalunya, Ramblas instead of Rambla) and sometimes the reverse (e.g. Sant Ferran instead of Castillo de San Fernando). They are reproduced according to his usage.

6 A founder member of the Italian Communist Party, Rita Montagnana established *La Compagna*, the organ of the Party's women's section, and later became the section's leader.

4
DEFEAT IN SPAIN

The frontier turned out to be the best part of two miles further on. It was guarded by a unit of soldiers from the West African French colony of Senegal who did not appear to speak any French. As we approached, a hand was thrust into our faces and we were not allowed to proceed. Then a white French officer, very elegantly turned out, came out of a little hut nearby where he had been sheltering from the weather, and, on realising we were not Spanish refugees, said in impeccable English, 'I'm very sorry, gentlemen' and invited us into the hut. He explained that, as we would obviously understand, he had had to close the frontier for the night, but that we, of course, would be allowed through. Watson had married in Spain and his wife was with us. He said he wasn't going to leave Spain without her. So, thanks to the impeccably polite officer, we stayed until the morning on the Spanish side amid the noise of a foul January night and the strained sounds of thousands of desperate, hungry, and despairing refugees.

Throughout the days that followed, there was a direct assault on these refugees. As they made their way on foot to the north, they were shelled by fascist artillery or machine-gunned by German and Italian planes. To add to their suffering, the weather remained ghastly – rain sleeting down as women gave birth at the roadside in the cold winter weather; bitter winds blowing a gale as struggling columns of children, barely old enough to walk, carried bundles of the few things they still possessed. By their thousands they were all moving to the frontier where the French troops had been blocking their entry. To prevent this desperate mass from passing, the French army was lined up, two deep, with rifles at the ready. A Republican soldier, with both legs blown off by an earlier bombing raid, bled slowly as the French commanders stuck by an order that the frontier could not be opened until 7 o'clock the following day. Beside him another soldier, blinded, his head swathed in blood-soaked bandages, lay in a dead faint,

DOI: 10.4324/9781003243380-5

Defeat in Spain **63**

having fallen to the ground in front of my eyes. There was no food, no warmth, no shelter, and no welcome. The moans of thousands of women, children and wounded, replaced the constant sound of gunfire, shells, bombs, and tanks that had marked for me the final days of Barcelona. The ear-splitting echoes of war gave way to these pathetic wails.

No one could forget the sight that greeted me after that dawn: our elegant officer and his perfectly dressed colleagues supervising the disarming of the desperate and bedraggled refugee soldiers and civilians trying to escape the danger of death at the hands of Franco's forces, their desperation reinforced by the echoes of the bombs and guns of the steadily advancing fascist front sometimes audible from the far distance.

Just before the fall of Barcelona, the French government had belatedly lifted the ban on Soviet arms going to Spain through France. The final insult to those who had pleaded for the Republic since July 1936 was that now much of that weaponry simply fell straight into the hands of the victorious Franco forces. Most remained piled up just inside France, the majority of the guns still in their wrappings and grease. I was not sure what made me more angry, the treatment of the refugees or this astonishing decision by the French authorities, something they only did when it no longer mattered.

The Military Commission of the League of Nations' Non-Intervention Committee that had supervised the withdrawal of the Brigades was overseeing the retreat of the Republican soldiers. It required all those who crossed into France to lay down their arms. This humiliating process was adding to the vast quantities of weaponry accumulating in heaps on the French side of the boundary. The two piles told the tale. One, dropped by the retreating soldiers, was mostly of second-rate, second-hand arms. The other, of brand new weapons that had been blocked from entering Spain, was made up of just the sort of things the defeated soldiers arriving from Spain had needed were they to have ever had any chance of winning. While I stood transfixed by the sight, a particularly obnoxious Persian captain in a sky blue, tightly fitting uniform, pocketed a pistol with a mother of pearl handle, which one of the soldiers had been made to discard. Having fired a few shots in the air from it, he had asked the officer in charge if he could keep it 'as a memento'. Of course he could.

I spent the next night on the French side of the frontier. Other journalists had hotels to stay in, but I didn't. Fortunately, I happened to bump into Tom Driberg, who I knew as the journalist behind the 'William Hickey' column in the *Daily Express* in which he covered the wilder goings-on of the rich and infamous. He was ostensibly there in his role as a reporter. At that moment there were two things I did not know about him. The first I quickly learned. He was really there helping to get food to the Republican army and had a letter from Harry Pollitt, General Secretary of the British Communist Party, as his warrant for this work. His press credentials from Lord Beaverbrook were just a cover. When he offered me a share of his hotel bed, I accepted, desperate for some rest and comfort. And, surprising as it might be, despite sleeping together all night

64 Defeat in Spain

long, I never came across the other thing about him that I did not know, his homosexuality. At that time, I was not consciously knowledgeable about homosexuals, and I became possibly one of the few young men to share his sheets and escape with that ignorance completely unscathed.

Basing myself in France, I went back into Spain but had to phone my stories from the French side of the border, usually in the small port town of Cerbère, though a couple of times I had to go further back to Perpignan, 20 miles north of the frontier. Luckily, there were Spanish comrades with motorcycles prepared to take me around. Throughout that week, I was to and fro across the frontier. As the phone lines were not always open, I had already done this a couple of times during the final weeks of the fighting around Barcelona, even though it meant a round trip of more than 200 miles just to phone a story across. When I did manage to get through to the paper, I tried, with what skills as a journalist I had, to rouse in the readers the same pitch of anger I felt.

For the moment, there were two routes I could take back to Spain. We had come from Barcelona by the roads that kept as close to the coast as possible, passing through Figueras but then crossing the frontier between Port Bou and Cerbère, both small Mediterranean fishing ports. From Perpignan, there was a more direct route south and inland but it crossed higher up in the mountains, going through the village of La Jonquera and then directly down to Figueras. Either way, refugees lay at every roadside between the frontier and Figueras. Shattered human beings, the wounded from the front line now without hospitals to go to in the rear, made their way slowly forward. The certainty of a fascist bullet awaited them, if they could not complete that terrible last journey. Once in a while there were international volunteers with them, mainly doctors and nurses, driven like me to stay to that very last minute.

A week after the fall of Barcelona on 2 February 1939, the Cortes, the Spanish Parliament, held a session in one of the dungeons under the Sant Ferran Castle at Figueras, the very building where I had spent my first night in Spain. With a small group of other foreign correspondents, I watched as a strained and tired Premier, Juan Negrín, told the 62 MPs present that he had seen the heroism of the troops who had re-formed and turned to face the enemy.

> I have seen them this morning. I have seen how many of them have had to fight without arms, have had to wait until one of their comrades fell before taking up a rifle. It is impossible to put up an effective resistance with unarmed heroism and this has been the cause of our misfortunes.

I headed my story with another quote from Negrín: 'The fate of the world is being decided here in the foothills of the Pyrenees'.

The days that followed were a truly ghastly experience. Every street and house in Figueras was still crowded with refugees. The air raid shelters were so full that women and children were reduced to getting what protection they could in passageways and staircases. There had already been three bombing

Defeat in Spain **65**

raids on the town by the time I got back there after crossing the French border to phone my story. The planes had targeted people waiting around the railway station for trains to France. Wounded victims were lying everywhere. The hospital had taken two direct hits and most of its medical supplies were destroyed. After surveying the scene around the station, I was back in the town's main street when the alarm was sounded again. Screaming with fear, women and children tried to find shelter. Huddling in doorways, women had tried to put their bodies between their children and the bombs. Even before the street was clear, the bombs began to fall. Managing to get into the offices of what was still functioning as a press centre, I was then thrown to the floor by the force of an explosion. This is the story I phoned to the paper, when I managed to get back to Le Perthus on the French side of the frontier. It appeared in the *Daily Worker* on 6 February 1939:

> Covered with debris and broken glass, choking with the acrid fumes of the explosion and almost blinded by the dust and smoke, I saw that a bomb had come right through the ceiling, not more than three yards from where I had fallen. It had dropped in a curve and exploded in the house next door, otherwise this story would never have been written. The place was a shambles. Exploding in the middle of a room where a refugee family had been preparing a meal, the bomb had killed nine people, only the old grandmother escaped, and she was moaning softly to herself as we dragged out the killed and wounded. All around, these scenes were repeated. Although the bombs were comparatively small, they had completely destroyed some ten of the small and fragile houses and debris completely blocked the narrow streets, while blood trickled from the ruins.
>
> It was impossible to see anyone in the avenues and the air was filled with the cries of the wounded and of demented mothers looking for their children. Through the smoke a woman rushed past me, trying to stem the blood that came oozing from the stump of her right arm.
>
> As I walked on in a daze, I stumbled over a first aid man. He was kneeling over the body of one of the women I had seen a few moments before trying to protect her baby. She had succeeded, but at the cost of her life. A piece of shrapnel had blown her leg off and wounded her horribly in the stomach. She died as we bent over her and all we could do was to pull out the baby, not more than three months old, covered in its mother's blood.

The town was bombed six times that day, and three times on the next day. Who could disagree when I wrote that the only reason for the raids 'was just plain murder, to massacre those who had left everything, rather than live under fascism?' I calculated that in Figueras at the time there were some 5,000 refugees, most of them women and children. The frontier village of La Jonquera to the north of Figueras was also attacked with bombs and machine-gunned from the air that Saturday. La Jonquera was hosting 35,000 refugees, 15,000 of them

66 Defeat in Spain

reportedly already wounded. I have no idea as to how many were victims of those raids, but it must have been hundreds.

Those last moments of the fighting in Catalonia saw great suffering, but from a purely journalistic point of view, there were strong stories to be had. My anger continued to help me focus and sharpen my writing, and, indeed, the only occasion in my entire career that I received a straightforward letter of congratulations from the paper for the work I had done came after I telephoned that Figueras story. It was precisely the moment when Harry Pollitt visited the *Worker* editorial office. As I realized over the years, however, there are regrettably few things more useless than a vote of thanks from the management.

There were still units in the People's Army thinking of putting up a fight. I watched as some of them moved back south to face the enemy, chatting to troops whose constant refrain was: give us the weapons and we will do the fighting. Despite the obstacles, the government managed to get many of the refugees to France both for their safety and to clear the roads for military use – but those roads remained largely empty of the lorries bringing the hoped for munitions and food from the north.

On 6 February, I crossed back into Spain, walking some five miles along the road to La Jonquera to try to meet up with the military leaders of this last ditch stand, the Communist generals Modesto and Lister. I was with a correspondent from a French agency, Havas, when I saw a face I knew well. It was Lon Elliott, a Cambridge man who had served in the Brigades and who had been working at the Spanish Party headquarters after being invalided out of the front line. I had helped Lon and several other comrades a couple of weeks earlier pack up the archives of the International Brigades in Barcelona and stack them into large crates, marked in black painted letters ODESSA, the Soviet Black Sea port. Included were files on each individual, the personal histories we volunteers had written out as part of the records. It took us three days and nights to put all the stuff in, trying to add to every box an inventory of the contents.[1]

Now, here he was in the middle of the road. He had been assigned as an aide to André Marty, and, I thought, if Lon's here, Marty cannot be far away.

At first, Lon would not tell me what he was doing there, which only confirmed my suspicion. When I slipped in the apparently knowledgeable question: 'Where's Marty?' his guard dropped and he blurted out: 'How did you know?' After a bit, from a little hut at the side of the road, out came the man himself, wounded. As it turned out, he was not the only one there. Gallo, or Luigi Longo, the future leader of the Italian Party, was with him as well as a number of other leading figures from the Brigades who had not yet been able to get out of Spain. There were Germans, Austrians, Czechs, Poles, and Bulgarians. If France kept them out, their future was going to be bleak, for these were all countries already in Hitler's grip or run by right-wing dictatorships. Explaining to Marty who the Havas guy was, I asked if he would like to talk to him. Marty agreed, but bristled immediately when the journalist's first comment was to say that the Republican forces were in retreat.

'Retreat? Retreat? What retreat? We can defend this position,' Marty declared, his usual blustering self, announcing it would be a fight to the death, while all along the roads around was streaming a defeated majority of the Republic's army. Events had taken their toll on poor Marty's mind, even more than they had on mine. When I filed my story, I put it that 'I found him true to his post'.

I went on, riding pillion on a motorbike. The road became deserted. The further south we drove, the louder came the sound of the artillery at the battle-front. We got to Figueras, for me now the city of death, just as night fell. The bombing had inflicted further heavy damage on the housing. The only people we passed on the streets were two old women hurrying along, keeping close in the shadow of the walls. Going up to the castle, we could see houses still burning from raids that morning. Other than that, it was the silence of the graveyard over this battered town. In the distance, some five miles further south of Figueras, Republican troops were still giving battle, their bravery protecting the flight of their demoralised comrades and those tens of thousands of refugees.

Back just across the frontier, those who had escaped the bombing and fighting were still out in the winter open under the guard of French troops with fixed bayonets. I tried to get to see the concentration camps the French authorities were hastily throwing up at Le Boulou and Argelès, just a few miles north of Cerbère, but the local Prefect in charge was refusing to allow even Colonel Molesworth, the President of the International Commission, to have a look, and my chances of getting a peep were therefore nil.

The final report I sent – on 12 February – was my last from any sort of front line. The day before, I had walked as far as possible along the coast with Henry Buckley, Willy Forrest, and other journalists. We could see the house where Premier Negrín had held a meeting of the cabinet of the Spanish Republican Government. Now, the building was draped in the Franco flag. It was a terrible blow to us. Buckley, although a *Telegraph* man to the core and an ardent Roman Catholic, could not cope with the sight because it made clear that defeat was being finally and totally imposed on the Republic.

The main rear-guard elements of the People's Army in Catalonia had crossed into France in a disciplined manoeuvre when the fascists were still some ten miles away. They were beaten on the battlefield, but most of the soldiers still seemed undefeated in spirit. Standing on the heights at Cerbère on the French side of the border, I could see the men of the 11th and 35th Divisions covering this final retreat, wrecking the heavy equipment they could not bring out, de-molishing phone lines and the like and blowing up the bridges one by one as the final units retreated to the north. Dawn was just breaking as a huge fire broke out in the direction of the Colera Bridge, five miles south of the frontier, followed a few moments later by a violent explosion that shook the ground I was standing on. This last big bridge had been taken out along with a number of ammunition dumps.

They marched past in a continuous stream, orderly and disciplined, many of them still singing Republican battle songs. I chatted to the ordinary soldiers.

68 Defeat in Spain

Their aim, they told me, was not to sit in a French camp but to get back to fight in Spain. 'Do you think it will be long before we get to Valencia,' I was asked time and again. Former sawmill worker General Modesto and his Commissar Luis Delage had left the last town in Spain, Port Bou, 800 yards as the crow flies from the border, and they came through with the last units up the winding road on the steep hillside. They were full of praise for their troops, as was Lister, the stonemason turned general, and his Commissar, Santiago Alvarez. Lister was exhausted. He could hardly keep his eyes open as we talked. Modesto had only had two weeks away from the battlefield since the war began, and that was in hospital to recover from a wound. Delage hugged me, saying he needed to see a comrade at a time like that. The last time we had been together had been some three weeks before when Republican units were pulling back to Tarragona and the shells were falling dangerously close around us.

It was to be 33 years before the next time I set foot in Spain again.

Reflections on Spain

Though I witnessed other wars, other defeats and other attempts to change the world, the experience of Spain remained the constant theme of my life thereafter, both personal and political. It set me on my course as a Communist journalist and became the key to my attitudes on many other matters, for example on the importance of unity and political alliances. The volunteers from Britain like me were fighting to save Britain from fascism as well as defend Spain, and I still believe that if we had stopped fascism in Spain the Second World War could have been prevented.

I had been generally optimistic about Spain and the chances of success even at the time of the Munich agreement between Chamberlain and Hitler. For me, justice was on our side. Looking back on it, I realise that I more or less discounted the fact that the fascists had the overwhelming military force with non-stop supplies from Germany and Italy along with trained troops. Just after Munich, I was talking with Fermina, a comrade who had been appointed my secretary for my radio work. She said: 'Chamberlain's signature means the end for the Republic'.

'Nonsense,' I declared. 'How can you possibly say that?'

But by the end of February, the governments in London and Paris announced they were recognising the Franco rebellion as the legitimate government of Spain. Franco finally saw his troops enter Madrid on 28 March, just a week after Hitler had occupied Czechoslovakia; emboldened by events in Spain, Hitler was putting in place his final preparations for the world war to come, and in the first week of April, Mussolini invaded Albania with the battle-hardened troops he had just brought back from Spain.

In contrast to the supine surrender of the British and other governments that should have known better, the Soviet Union stood by the Republic, at least until the cause was clearly lost. Stalin was right when he said that the cause of Spain was the cause of all progressive people. The Soviets did not send arms in order to take over Spain, which was in south-west Europe and the Spanish Party only a small if influential organisation.

Yet, written in Stalin's own hand on a once-secret Soviet document are the simple words: 'this question is no longer of importance'. Hidden for decades in the Kremlin archives, it was his comment in February 1939 on the last, despairing request from the Spanish Republican Government for arms. By this time, Stalin believed Spain was a lost cause, but the Republicans were determined to fight on. Spain became a possible stumbling block in the way of an option clearly already present in Stalin's mind: a deal with Hitler that would get round the Munich appeasement approach of the British and French, and would manoeuvre the Nazis into an attack on the Western front first, rather than on the eastern. Stalin signed his pact with Hitler in August 1939 and the fate of the Spanish Republic, which had collapsed in March, was sealed.

But for Communists fighting in Spain, defending the Soviets was not only a practical priority in terms of their support for the Republic but it was also a political priority, as the Soviet Union was the only state that had broken from the capitalist world and was trying to build a Socialist alternative. It was first Soviet food and then Soviet weaponry that kept the Republic going at all.

As far as British participation in the International Brigades was concerned, the Communist Party was running the show and it was my impression that non-Party members of the Brigades were more than happy with this. Deserters who condemned Party dominance of the Brigades were regarded by non-Party members who stayed in as traitors in the same way that we did. For me, and for many Spaniards, the Communist Party offered a disciplined approach without which the war was never going to be won.

Having lived in my Barcelona flat with German comrades, I knew their discipline was fantastic. Many of their compatriots were Communists who had already been living in exile in France following Hitler's rise to power in 1933. Others had come directly from Germany to the Brigades. The Poles were another group with a very strong sense of discipline. For the French it was rather different.

It seemed to me at the time that the German comrades had still not got used to the fact that they were no longer top dog in the Comintern outside of the Soviet Party. The Nazis had been in control for over three years already and the German Party had been broken inside Germany and outlawed. A number of leading German comrades were in Spain and had set up a German Party organisation. At the start of the war, what had been the Italian fascist club in Barcelona was taken over and made into an anti-fascist club. One of the German comrades invited me down for the evening and I was rather surprised when I was given the card for the club to see that it was in German. It turned out that everything else in the club was as well. They had their own journal and had their clear, separate Party structure.

Yet it was a rule in the Comintern: one country, one party. André Marty declared that in Spain the Germans had no right to a separate organisation. In

70 Defeat in Spain

fact, the Germans collected their own Party dues on the basis of a percentage of the pay of their members. Given that a fair number of the officers were Germans, they had some substantial funds. In negotiations over the matter it was impossible to argue with Marty and he put a stop to it.

There had also been a conference of Commissars at the base in Albacete on the issue of discipline in the town. Drunkenness was a particular problem. Volunteers were billeted in villages around the town and would come into the central camp barracks during the day for training of one sort or another and go to the only available bar in the evening. The results were inevitable. The conference did not manage to resolve the issue, so Marty chaired a meeting of commissars from the various units in Barcelona when they all happened to be there. They decided to take measures to deal with the problem, including the establishment of some kind of detention centre.

Rust attended in his role as British Party representative in Spain and I was called in to act as his interpreter. John Gates, the political commissar from the US unit, was also there, though he had not been at the original Albacete meeting. Each commissar reported in turn on the situation in his unit. Gates started off his report saying the American comrades were behaving all right but the problem was with the French, who were always drunk. Rust kicked my ankle hard under the table and indicated with his eyes that I should look at Marty who was going slowly purple. Gates was going blithely on, totally unaware of the explosion about to come.

'Ah!' Marty suddenly shouted. 'The French, always the French ….Has not Dimitrov said that the number of French comrades who have fallen in the cause of liberty was greater than those of any other nation…?'[2] Gates was reduced to a stuttering silence.

The drinking was to be expected as an escape from the bitter realities we were facing. Young people had come to Spain full of illusions about a war against fascism and the dangers involved, and, especially in the early days, the shock could be destructive. The Spanish war was a particularly bloody and testing one, facing gunfire and death in a foreign land in the terrible heat in the summer and the incredible cold in the winter. It was so cold during the battle of Teruel, between December 1937 and the end of February 1938, the medical staff told me that if they did not get to a wounded soldier within five minutes of him falling, he would be frozen to death. Many did not get used to even the simple fact that, while it might be hellish hot in the day, it could be terribly cold at night. Many comrades just put aside their warm clothes, only to lose them as we advanced or retreated. Quite unusually, I managed to come back in the greatcoat and OTC uniform I went out in.

There were other simple lessons which some volunteers just did not understand, lessons that professional soldiers have drummed into them during their training, things commanders make sure they will do even in moments of panic. In the very first moments of our fighting in the University City, for example, a sudden order came to withdraw immediately. Bugger the guns, was the reply, when I said it would take us only a few moments to dismount them. I could not get my number two on the machine gun to carry the wheels, but I managed to

Defeat in Spain **71**

take out the firing bolt to disable the weapon. The other gunners failed to do that and, as a result, all the fascists had to do as they took over our positions was to turn those machine guns round and open fire on us as we fled.

Some also had the attitude that, as they had come out of their free will, so they could leave of their own free will when they felt they had done their stint. There was no oath, no agreement signed. That meant that some who had just had enough, simply walked away or did what the fellow next to me in the trench at Madrid did and inflict a disabling, but relatively minor, wound on themselves. Though ordered back into the line, my wounded colleague soon skedaddled back to Britain.

This raised a challenging question for us: if someone who might be seen as a deserter was caught, would one treat them in the way that deserters were then treated in a time of war? Would one start shooting people, as the British and French armies had done in the World War only 20 years earlier? The Republic's authorities recognised this could not be done, and started penal battalions and set up prisons for those who had offended against military discipline. There was one individual from the British Battalion I heard of who was supposed to have been caught not just attempting to desert, but also on his way to cross to enemy lines in possession of maps showing our positions and plans. He was shot by firing squad.

Some volunteers did leave against orders. In the later stages of the war, I had to handle several such cases. This all meant negotiating with the Republican authorities, the Catalonian government and the British consulate staff, which presented all sorts of challenges. Most of the time, though, volunteers just let the tensions and uncertainties of the war express itself in grumbling of the kind I heard one time I was with Kerrigan at Albacete and a large group of British volunteers was singing 'Take me over the sea, Where Franco can't get me ...' as they relaxed at the end of a hot day. That did not mean they were about to desert.

It was also the case that some senior volunteers were withdrawn, as with Battalion Commander Fred Copeman – there were 11 different battalion commanders at different times – and his Battalion Commissar Bert Williams. Bert was a nice enough bloke who had been the CP organiser in Birmingham but he was not the right kind of person for a post at the front in a war. Fred had been one of the leaders of the Invergordon naval mutiny in 1931 and was a tough character. He was a rather brutal man, which, unfortunately, is a quality sometimes required in war. An argument of some kind had broken out in the brigade and the result was they were to return to Britain, officially to do propaganda for the cause. An official order of the day hailed them both for their great work at the front and so on.

I was told things were not in fact quite like that. There had been a row involving Fred and Bert and one of the Soviet military advisers. Sending the two of them home was seen as the best solution to it all.

The two arrived in Barcelona and it fell to me to get the appropriate papers for crossing the frontier into France. There was always a degree of tension between the government of the Spanish Republic and the government of Catalonia. As I knew from my radio broadcasts, there were two authorities to deal with in the city. The Catalans insisted that it was they and not the Republican government

72 Defeat in Spain

who controlled the Catalan frontier with France. My job was to get all the papers in order so that people could get across the frontier without problems from the French, the Catalans or the Republican government.

Having arranged to see an official I knew from the Military Commission of the Catalan Party, I took Bert and Fred over to get the relevant papers. The Party's headquarters had been an aristocrats' club with a vast entrance hall, now decorated with enormous painted portraits of Marx, Engels, Lenin and Stalin. Fred demanded in a loud voice to know what the hell we were doing. Bert tried to keep him quiet, which only seemed to make him more obstreperous. 'Bug whiskers Marx' and other insults began to fly from Fred, which, very luckily, no one else could understand or there would have been trouble. They got their papers.

On those occasions when I was aware of military discipline being exercised, it did not seem that those on the receiving end had much of a proper trial or court martial. The badly coordinated advance on the Córdoba front, during which I was wounded, resulted in the arrest of our Battalion commander, Gaston Delasalle. It was claimed he had fascist documentation on him and, later, that he was working for the French state intelligence service. With the assistance of Marty, a fierce disciplinarian, Delasalle was convicted at a drumhead court martial and summarily shot. All hell broke loose in France; his family protested and the matter was raised in the French Assembly by some right-wing Deputies. Marty, who was a French Communist Party MP as well as a commander in the Brigades, was at the centre of the storm. I was in hospital while all of this raged, but I know I would have supported Marty in his actions, if I had been asked. By one of those ironies of fate that dogged many leading Communists from the 1930s, Marty was expelled from the French Communist Party on a ludicrous charge of himself being a French police spy. That was in 1952 when it was claimed that Marty, whom the Party had held up as one of its truest heroes until that moment, had been a spy since 1919.

The Communists believed it was absolutely necessary to maintain the unity of the Popular Front during the Civil War and accepted compromises to do so, which, if they had been running the show as some pretend, they would not have done. But the opponents of Franco were made up of groups and organisations that zealously guarded their own independence and spent much, in some cases most, of their time denouncing everyone else. To put it mildly, this did not help to form either an integrated defence needed for a place like Madrid or to fight the kind of protracted conflict that the war turned into. Although there was conflict within Republican forces and growing dissent as the war was being lost, I think too much subsequent emphasis has been put on the political disputes in Spain, a false presentation as if the whole country was taken up in a fight between leftists and Communists.

The Spanish Communists were only a small part of the Popular Front and many of the Party's leading members had been anarchists before they changed their approach as they saw the need for discipline and alliances if Franco were ever to be beaten. The greater part of the government and many in the country were Socialist, as seen in the influence of the general trade union body, the UGT. The anarchists were very strong in Spain, particularly in Barcelona but the Communist Party grew in both the number of its members and in its influence as the war continued. Before the war, the majority of the country's workers, agricultural and industrial, were influenced by the anarchist ideas of the small and semi-secret Spanish Anarchist Federation and were organised by the CNT trade union confederation. There was tension between the Popular Front and the leftists and anarchists as well as between the Communists and Socialists. Whichever group was in control of a particular place, be it a factory, a restaurant or a hotel, it would keep that place for its own supporters. A porter would check for a UGT or CNT membership card and only let in the appropriately affiliated person.

The sole aim as far as I was concerned, and as far as I am aware of the majority of Brigaders, was to defend the Popular Unity government against fascism, to defend the Republic. Others on the left took a different view and believed revolution was the most important thing. For me that was so much hot air while fascism was crushing democracy and had to be defeated. This became the key to my attitude on many other situations and in particular the problems caused by those whose only answer to any situation seemed to be to demand an immediate and complete revolution, however little support that might have had and however unclear an idea there might have been in their own heads about what 'revolution' might actually mean.

The anarchists produced some fantastically heroic fighting units and individuals but – and I don't say this to score points – in my experience, they did not like military discipline. They were quite capable of fighting only when the mood took them. On two occasions we were sent out on patrol to find out what had happened to an anarchist unit guarding one flank only to discover the majority had gone off to the cinema because nothing was happening.

After I was wounded and returned to London through Barcelona, I saw other examples. With the fascists having been beaten off in Barcelona, which was Spain's great industrial city, members of the POUM were parading, some with immaculate uniforms, machine guns, heavy weaponry and vehicles that would have helped us no end – and they had smart new ambulances, while we had been brought back wounded from fighting the fascists in shit carts. It made me more than angry. I was also asked to speak at a factory that had been taken over by the CNT. It was a small works making pots and pans, and the central government wanted it to switch to producing shell cases. With raw material hard to come by but provided by the central government, the CNT cut down on the number of hours everyone worked to ensure jobs and refused to accept they should make the much-needed shell cases. The anarchists and far left seemed to have lost sight of the fact that the fascists were steadily crushing the left across most of the rest of Spain and that they needed to join in if we were to defeat Franco.

The roughly 35,000 Brigaders in Spain were mostly not involved in battles with other left groups or in the Comintern's then unknown to me orders to eliminate them, although I knew the Soviets did recruit individual Brigaders as agents.

74 Defeat in Spain

Similarly, the Brigades were infiltrated by fascist spies. I was not aware of any activity in Spain by the Soviet secret police, nor that the Spanish military security was run by the Soviets, as was later claimed. I was hobbling about in London when some in the POUM and among the anarchists carried out what the Popular Front parties called an attempted putsch and those responsible said was a defence of the workers' control approach that had swept through Barcelona workplaces in response to Franco's rebellion. The upshot of the clashes was a number of deaths, much bitterness, the banning of the POUM and the murder of its leader, Andreas Nin, probably under torture.[3] I did not attend the subsequent trial of the arrested leaders, though I did broadcast reports on it taken from the Spanish government news agency. Evidence was put forward in the trial to implicate them in direct collaboration with the fascists. In the tense atmosphere of a vicious civil war where there was a lot of chaos and much by way of a real 'fifth column', this was something I and those around me accepted as true. I was against them not because I thought they were agents of fascism, as was the Comintern line, but because of what they were doing in Spain, keeping, for instance, their new ambulances and artillery when they were needed at the front. I believed the case against them had been answered but I now believe the evidence to be suspect and that it was a show trial like the ones held in the Soviet Union, which I accepted at face value.

The show trials of Stalin's purges were going on while the war was being fought in Spain, but I knew nothing of what was happening inside the Soviet Union. Yet it was all too easy to believe that those who criticised in such a bitter way the 'first workers' state' – the state that was effectively our only ally – were on the side of our enemies. No one who tries to understand the politics and the atmosphere of those days can do so unless they remember that this attitude was not confined to us Communists, but was shared by many of those involved, and that it was reinforced as the months progressed by the ever-present sense of the fascist danger around us and the sacrifices being made in the fight against it. The unpardonable behaviour of Soviet agents in Spain has overshadowed the vital and unique contribution the Soviets made, isolated as they were in the international community and with whatever mixed motives they may have had.

The situation in Spain had generally seemed to me to be desperately shambolic and makeshift. But since then I have seen what happens in other armies and other wars. After all, if I had not been struck off the British Army supplementary reserved list of officers, I would have been drafted into my old OTC training regiment, the Royal Scots, and probably would have become dead meat on the road back across northern France in the chaos of the retreat to Dunkerque or part of the massacre by the Japanese of the other battalion of the Royal Scots in the conquest of Hong Kong two years later.

When I was a correspondent in Moscow in the 1950s, my first secretary Lyosha Lipovetsky told me about his days after the end of the World War in 1945 when he was called up to a cavalry unit. The ruthless discipline in the Red Army meant that they were called out in the middle of the night without warning and sent off on manoeuvres for several days, having to clean everything including the

FIGURE 4.1 Sam making a speech at the 2005 annual commemoration ceremony of the International Brigade Memorial Trust, Jubilee Gardens, South Bank, London.

Source: Family archive.

horses to a point at which an officer wearing white gloves could come round and stroke the horses flanks without getting his gloves in anyway dirty. Lyosha always claimed that Red Army discipline was based on a saying of Marshal Suvorov, one of the Russian marshals in the war against Napoleon: however badly you treat a soldier in time of peace, it is nothing compared with war.

However distasteful such a thought may appear, it is absolutely true. No matter what training you do, war itself is so horrible that nothing can compare. Bringing yourself to the point of being able to kill another human being is hard enough in itself. Experiencing the fear, slaughter, and chaos of war is unique.

Years later, in 1996, I visited the mountainous battlefields beyond the Ebro where my brother Frank had fought and which I had never been able to get to as a correspondent during the Civil War. This was a rocky, dry, and dangerous area at the best of times. From a soldier's point of view, the topography was merciless. The Brigade units had fought in the heat of a Spanish summer, attacking up steep hillsides in the Sierra de Pàndols. I could only marvel at how those who had served there somehow managed to hold off the professional soldiers of the Nazi Condor Legion and the Italian army, backed by their planes and heavy artillery, not to mention Franco's own troops. I was more than humbled. I had only been a few weeks in the front line, and it is one of the ironies of warfare that people

76 Defeat in Spain

like me were very lucky to have been wounded. I got what they called in the First World War a 'Blighty One' wound: it did not kill me, but took me out of the front line and left me in what, everything considered, was a very cushy job compared with the devastating experience of those who remained in the line of battle.

I was in Spain on that trip with Jack Jones and other Brigaders to receive honorary citizenship promised to surviving Brigaders by the Spanish government after the death of Franco.[4] I was asked to say a few words, which I did – in Spanish. Much to my great pleasure, the local papers reported that my Spanish was 'more than acceptable'. And when in 2009 only seven of us surviving International Brigaders could attend a ceremony at the Spanish Embassy in London to receive honorary Spanish passports in recognition of our actions in the conflict, we again did so in the name of all the 2,500 who had volunteered from Britain more than 70 years earlier.

On the personal front, I met up with my brother Frank during the Civil War. Coming to Spain long after I had first made the journey, he had taken the midnight climb across the Pyrenees. We had always fought as kids and, for a while, he had kept his life private from me. I saw his name on a list of the wounded one day. I went to see him in hospital. I am not even sure that I actually knew he was in Spain until then, such is the way brothers sometimes treat each other.

FIGURE 4.2 Sam (right) with his younger brother Frank in Spain, May Day 1938.
Source: Family archive.

FIGURE 4.3 Sam (right) with his younger brother Frank in later life.
Source: Family archive.

He recovered sufficiently to go back to the front for the bloody battles at the River Ebro. He did not return to Britain until December 1938 after the final decision to wind down the International Brigades. Before Frank went back into the line, I sent home a May Day photograph of the both of us in 1938 via Geoffrey Bing, a lawyer who had business with the Republican government and who became a Labour MP in 1945 and afterwards Attorney General of Ghana.

It was also in Spain that I first met Margaret Powell, who more than a decade later I would marry. I was visiting the headquarters of the British Medical Aid committee where a pianola was playing Mozart's 'Turkish March' over and over, and there she was. A young woman born on a Welsh mountain farm in the village of Llangenny, Margaret had gone to London to train as a nurse, which she did, and she had just completed her midwifery qualification when she volunteered in March 1937 for medical work at the front line attached to a Spanish unit. She spent more time at the front, more time in deep danger, than ever I did.[5]

Surgery at the front was carried out in makeshift circumstances, to say the least. Often she had the job of the triage nurse, the one who inspected the wounded and would have to decide who could be saved, who would have to be left, who might benefit from treatment, and who was beyond hope.

One wounded soldier she instructed be operated on was condemned by the surgeon as an SIW (Self-Inflicted Wound).

'Can't you see the powder burn on his wound?' shouted the surgeon. 'Just clean him up and send him back to the front!' The following day he was back with a bad stomach wound. 'This time it's for real,' the soldier told her. He went in for surgery but did not survive. The nightmares over that came back time and again.

78 Defeat in Spain

FIGURE 4.4 Sam (centre) and Margaret (behind *Daily Worker*) with comrades in Spain, 1938, after a special lunch of rabbit.
Source: Family archive.

FIGURE 4.5 Pass issued to Sam for the opera house in Barcelona where he took Margaret.
Source: Family archive.

Defeat in Spain **79**

One of the perks of my job was getting a pass for the opera. I took Margaret but I was too bashful to press my suit at that time and we lost touch.

When her unit was in retreat in February 1939 she lost everything, including her passport. They had been moving by night to avoid the aeroplanes, and when she eventually reached the border, she was treated as Spanish, and that meant treated very badly. The French colonial troops herded them all into a makeshift camp on the beach. There was no food or water and no proper sanitation. After a fortnight their state was desperate. A group of Quakers, which had heard of a British nurse with the refugees, eventually came to her rescue. She was able to get back to Britain and we did not meet up again until a few years later. It was always on my conscience that I hadn't gone back to look for her at the border.

Back in London after Spain, Margaret served in the Air Raid Precautions as a nurse and then did secret work for the postal services because of her Catalan language skills. She volunteered for the United Nations Relief and Rehabilitation Administration and was sent in October 1943 to Sinai in Egypt working at the El Shatt camp for the families of partisan refugees from Yugoslavia. They were housed in tents and children were dying of simple diseases. Margaret bought medicines, even bed linen, with her own pay, and discovered a Communist network among the refugees. She helped to train many young Yugoslav women as nurse aides.

After accompanying the refugees home to Split in early 1946, she was transferred to the American zone in Germany, taking charge of maternity and child welfare services in a number of camps for displaced persons, who were kept in terrible conditions. In one camp, particular problems were being created by a group of teenagers without parents. No one could understand their language. Margaret thought they were talking Spanish, but the boys at first could not understand her Spanish. In fact, their language was Ladino.

When the Jews were expelled from Spain in 1492, they took their Spanish with them. Like Jews in northern areas of Europe such as my parents who spoke a developed archaic German, or Yiddish, these youngsters spoke a language derived from an archaic form of Spanish. The boys had probably been deported by the Nazis from Hungary. Using her Spanish, Margaret was able to work with them, trying to help them be more responsible. One day she was called to their hut, as one boy had got a female German cleaner on the ground by the throat. He was dragged off. The others explained that the cleaner had come in while they were playing around and had shouted what for any camp victims were the terrible words: '*Raus! Raus!*' – '*Out! Out!*' The boy had completely lost his self-control. He sobbed his heart out. The following morning, he was found hanged. Margaret carried a sense of guilt ever after – all she had been able to do for the young man was give him a tablet.

These were not the only memories that haunted her. Coping with them was not helped by the work she did in London later as a health visitor trying to assist women trapped in what were often appalling conditions, or by her time spent in Moscow when I was working there.

FIGURE 4.6 Sam and Margaret at Brockweir, Forest of Dean, August 1951, the year of their daughter Ruth's birth.
Source: Family archive.

Margaret had married a Catalan, a member of the Spanish Communist Party, but, after the World War when we met up again – her sister worked at the same factory as me – I discovered the relationship was over.[6] We saw more and more of each other. After the divorce from my first wife, Nell, came through, Margaret and I were married in 1951 and our daughter, Ruth, was born later that year.

The spouse of a busy correspondent who has to be available for work at all hours – and some of that for carousing at receptions – has a pretty awful time, and for Margaret in Moscow, it was worse. She had not wanted to go to Moscow and gave up an interesting, important, and rewarding career in nursing to accompany me. She refused to come until a proper flat was available in place of the hotel room I had been allocated. When she got there, we effectively had no money. We did not even have enough to buy her a proper warm coat for the first winter she spent in the Soviet Union. To make ends meet, she had to take up correcting and proof reading English translations while stuck in a small flat with few friends, a tiny child to care for, a news printer churning out copy round the clock that made a terrific noise, and, sometimes when I was away, having to take down by hand the stories I phoned into her, which she then had to phone to London.

In the long years that followed after she died in 1990, I missed with a sense of increasing loss her presence, her criticisms, and her ways. More than once, she saw things much more clearly than I did. At one stage, she tried to persuade me to train to be a carpenter – a useful trade, she argued, not like journalism. We should probably have swapped trades and she should have done the journalism, though I think I would have made a better job of it as a carpenter than as a nurse.

Notes

1 The idea, Sam said, was that one wrote out one's personal and political history on a form as part of 'self- criticism' intended to sharpen one's commitment to the Party line. As it was something one did every so often, it also meant that people spinning yarns might get caught out, forgetting what they had written the last time. For this to work, you were not meant to keep a copy. 'I kept a copy of mine,' Sam said, 'and made sure I said the same things each time I had to fill one out'. Sam also said, 'When the Italian Communist leader Luigi Longo planned to write a history of the International Brigades, he asked to see the archives we had bundled up, but Moscow said no one knew where they were'. They came to light after the end of the Soviet Union and are available on line at sovdoc.rusarchives.ru. The website is in Russian; the documents are in a variety of languages.
2 Georgi Dimitrov was head of the Comintern.
3 It was established in 2010 that Nin was murdered by an assassin of the Soviet secret police, NKVD.
4 Jack Jones, who had organised protests in Liverpool against fascism, joined the British Battalion of the International Brigades in 1936 and was wounded at the Battle of the Ebro in 1938. He subsequently became General Secretary of the Transport and General Workers' Union, President of the National Pensioners' Convention and President of the International Brigade Memorial Trust.
5 She had volunteered before finishing her training but was advised to complete it first, which she did. In recognition of her work as a nurse in Spain, she was made a Dame of the Order of Loyalty to the Spanish Republic by the Spanish government in exile. Her name appears on a plaque that was unveiled in 1986 in the London Borough of Southwark's Mayor's Parlour commemorating those who went to Spain. The plaque was moved to a Southwark library, the John Harvard Library, in 2016.
6 It seems the marriage was not legally recognised. Sam's MI5 files say that in 1941 the British police warned the Catalan to stop claiming he was married to Margaret. On Sam and Margaret's marriage certificate, Sam is listed as divorcee and Margaret as spinster.

5
THE WORLD GOES TO WAR

While I was rushing around like an idiot in the final mayhem of the battle for Catalonia, the comrades at the *Worker* sent my instructions for the following weeks. Waiting, Poste Restante at Perpignan and dated 30 January 1939, was a message of the kind I got to know so well over the years that followed: carry on working but do it on a shoestring so short it won't hold anything together:

> We are enclosing £5 and hope you will be able to manage things on this. We shall let you know as soon as we have decided about your future. Would you get in touch with your former employers as soon as possible to see whether they are re-opening a service?

The 'former employers' were the Comintern news agency, my paymasters in Barcelona, but, given the state of play, I could not immediately contact them. The paper's apparent generosity had a sting in the tail: I was now to phone them myself from France 'instead of our phoning you, as it is much cheaper to do it from your end, owing to the exchange'. A few days later, the inevitable happened in the shape of a telegram with the terse message: 'Impossible send more money – return immediately'.

My own wandering, however, was apparently over and I was at the paper in London's Cayton Street just two days after I had spent a good part of that £5 phoning my last story from Cerbère. I went straight to a desk and hammered out an article, a howl of frustration at the Chamberlain government but with a message of confidence for Spain. The paper pictured me at the typewriter, one that was as old and about as efficient as the first guns we had had at Madrid. The introduction to the piece declared boldly: 'He knows what he is talking about'. The following day, the paper's fighting fund column celebrated 'Sam's Tonic … full

DOI: 10.4324/9781003243380-6

of hope and based on first-hand knowledge and real facts'. Hope, yes, but facts? Unfortunately, the Republican Spain that I declared could still win the war was in truth on its last legs.

As the song says, 'Don't mourn, organise', except in my case it was 'report'.

Harry Pollitt had decided I should go to Paris for the *Daily Worker*. My leg wound was still giving me trouble despite all the treatment I had received in London and Barcelona, but it was not going to stop me. I was to double up as correspondent for the New York *Daily Worker* as well as working in the English-language section of the news agency Agence France-Monde. After some protests on my part that others had a greater right to what seemed to me to be a privileged posting, off I went in March 1939. Agence France-Monde was, in effect, my 'former employers', being the French end of the Comintern's international news agency operations that I had worked for in Spain, and, as in Spain, the agency paid my wages and upkeep. My official position was head of the British journalists attached to the agency, and my work was similar to the agency work in Spain: preparing stories for the paper and writing up reports to be circulated to Communist and left-wing publications around the world.

A veteran Hungarian Communist, Julius, or Gyula, Alpàri, ran the office. He had been the Commissar of Education for a short-lived revolutionary government in Budapest in 1919. He was now in his late 60s and was known to all of us as 'le vieux', the old man. My immediate boss was Fritz Runge, who spoke English with a perfect Yorkshire accent, having been a prisoner-of-war there in the First World War, and who had remained a devoted follower of Yorkshire County Cricket Club. He was in France with a *carte d'identité* on the basis of a false Australian passport. Though born in what became Czechoslovakia, he did not speak the Czech language, having been born and brought up in the German-speaking Sudetenland.

As someone coming from the Spanish war, I was treated with great respect and Fritz held a party to mark my arrival. When he suggested that we go to a night-club after the meal, I did not know what to expect. I had not even by then been in many proper restaurants as opposed to canteens. The first place was called La Boule Blanche and the next club was, I discovered afterwards, a top-class brothel. Champagne was ordered and after a few moments I could not help but notice there were lots of mostly naked women walking about. Fritz explained that if I fancied one I could go off with her. Genuinely shocked, I got up and strode off, putting on the heavy black leather overcoat I wore in those days. It had been presented to Bill Rust by the Lancashire district of the British Party before he went off to Spain and he had bequeathed it to me. It was the sort of thing that senior commissars wore and, perhaps, I felt that it gave my exit greater moral authority.

The following morning, I arrived at the office and walked through the first room where the staff were all French, producing the cyclostyled agency bulletin. I called out 'Bonjour camarades' and noticed a snigger. The snigger volume grew louder as I walked on through the offices. When the first pay day came

84 The World Goes to War

up – Fritz gave us our pay in Swiss francs every month – I tried to talk to him about that evening. 'Say no more', was all he was prepared to offer. For my part, I kept thinking of a Maupassant story, *Le Rosier de Madame Husson*. It tells of an old widow who arranged a reward every year for the local girl who was the prize virgin. One year they could not find a female virgin so they chose a young man instead, Rosier. I still felt very stupid. I knew such places existed, but it was another matter to be introduced to them by those I thought were the moral leaders of a new world.

There was often not a great deal I could do to fulfil my duties as a reporter for the *Worker* – it was only six pages, roughly tabloid in size, and space was always at a premium – and I got very little advice from London. I was desperate to know whether or not my stuff was liked, and desperate for some supportive guidance. I wrote to Pollitt: 'Paris is a much more difficult job to handle. It's not as straightforward as just going to the front and seeing what's on. I've made mistakes and missed the boat too often on stories'. My focus for readers in Britain was mostly on the continuing dreadful plight of the Spanish refugees with some about those under the boot of Franco in Spain itself. One such was the German Communist, Artur Becker, with whom I had shared the Barcelona flat for a good few months. Captured by the fascists in 1938, for a long while his fate was unknown. Finally the news came in June 1939: he had succumbed to his Gestapo torturers in Franco's Burgos jail. His death touched me particularly strongly.

For most of my time, I lived just half an hour's walk, or a few minutes in the Metro, from the agency's offices in Rue Buffault near the Faubourg Montmartre, which, in turn, was just round the corner from *l'Humanité*, the daily paper of the French Communist Party, in Rue Montmartre. Home was a flat beside the Buttes Chaumont, a landscaped park (the largest in central Paris), and a wonderful place for a stroll. I was living with the family of Maurice Choury, a journalist on *l'Humanité* who became leader of the resistance on Corsica. His wife was from the island and they went back there after the Germans occupied France. Her sister, Danielle Casanova, leader of the Communist Party organisation for young women who was to die in Auschwitz in 1943, was also in the house with her husband Laurent, a Party functionary and later a minister in the immediate post-war French governments. The ménage was completed by Pierre Pagès, a leading Communist militant in the giant Renault factory at Billancourt who also became a resistance figure in Corsica during the occupation. With them, I was plunged into the life of the French Communist Party, for which I developed a great admiration.

Just as the Spanish war ended and many people hoping to get out of the country had retreated down to the coast towards Alicante, the French Communist Party sent one of their MPs, Charles Tillon, to try to help.[1] In the end no ships came and a large number, including Tillon, were put into camps by the Franco authorities. There was an immediate campaign to get the MP freed. When it was successful, the French CP put on a hero's welcome for his return to Paris at the Gare d'Austerlitz and the following week organised a splendid show in the Latin Quarter at the Mutualité, the left's main conference hall, complete with a special 'vin d'honneur', a French Party tradition that, over the years, I very much warmed to.

A few days before the celebration, there had been a debate in the House of Commons during which the British Prime Minister Neville Chamberlain had announced general conscription in Britain. There was a big argument in the British CP as to what line of action Party members should follow. The Young Communist League was absolutely against accepting conscription. Willie Gallacher, the Communist MP elected in 1935 for West Fife, spoke in the Commons against it. Chamberlain got up and started reading out comments from the foreign press on the British government's action, the first time in peace there had ever been conscription in Britain. Among the quotes he gave was one from Gabriel Péri in *l'Humanité*, the daily paper of the French CP, approving the British government's decision. Péri was the paper's Foreign Editor and a person of some significance in the French CP. Gallacher jumped up and said: 'I repudiate him completely'.

Knowing nothing of this, I turned up at the celebration in Paris for the release of Tillon. While I was savouring a glass of the excellent 'vin d'honneur', Gabriel Péri and Maurice Thorez, the French Party's General Secretary, advanced on me. Péri angrily flourished a copy of *The Times* with a report of Gallacher's remark, as if I was personally responsible. They insisted on an explanation from me there and then. They demanded I get in contact with Gallacher immediately to get the repudiation put right. When Péri writes something in *l'Humanité*, it means it is the policy of the French Party, Thorez declared angrily, adding ominously: 'This is a very bad business'.

The tradition of the British labour movement was against conscription, whereas the French tradition was different. Not only was conscription a general practice on the Continent, but it was also justified politically by the various Communist parties with a phrase of Lenin's about the working class needing to learn the use of arms – the very justification Brian Pearce and myself had used when we joined the OTC in University College London. At this point in 1939, before the trauma of the Nazi-Soviet Pact, the French Communist Party was in favour of fighting an anti-fascist war and so conscription was a logical corollary for them. The row at least meant that I was now easily recognised by Thorez, which came in useful later on.

My first story from Paris that had been published in the *Daily Worker*, which turned out, unsurprisingly, to be on Spain and the refugees, on the continuing efforts to help the human casualties of the war, got me into trouble with the powers-that-be. The war had only been over a fortnight and I had sat among the sand dunes at Argelès on the Mediterranean coast where thousands of Spanish refugees had been herded and left by the French authorities. We listened together to the radio from Madrid reporting on Franco's victory parade along the Gran Via, the road I had marched along on my way to the front. The French treatment

FIGURE 5.1 Sam at work in Paris, 1940.
Source: Family archive.

of these refugees was sordid and cruel, and after I had visited a camp where many of the refugees were children crammed into horse stables, I described the horrors I saw, which led to a summons from the French Foreign Ministry. A very arrogant official condemned my story as an attack on the French government 'which cannot be permitted'.

'Was what I wrote untrue?' I asked.

'I give you warning, if there is any repetition of this, you will have 24 hours in which to pack your bags and leave the country', was all that the official would say. But how could I lay off?

I did earn another summons to the Foreign Ministry but through no fault of my own. Richard Kisch, who had also been wounded in Spain, was a colleague working in the agency with me in Paris. He was disgruntled that he had not been made the number one in the British group there, having been working at the agency for some time before I came over from London, but he did send reports to the paper on weekends that I was off. The French Party had an initiative at the time designed to draw small shopkeepers into a Popular Front organisation. Dick wrote a report that was rather over top about a demonstration this organisation had held one weekend. I saw a copy of the report when I arrived for work on the Monday and felt there would be trouble for me with the Ministry. Dick had used my name. The report gave the impression the revolution was about to break out at any moment under the leadership of this gaggle of shopkeepers. The gross exaggeration led to a summons from the Ministry but I pleaded the report had not been written by me, and said the subordinate responsible was being dealt with. It got me off the hook.

The attitude of the officials in the Ministry reflected the panic in official France at the time in the summer of 1939. Few believed that there was not going to be some kind of sell out by the French establishment to the Nazis. When, for example, a British submarine, the *Thetis*, sank on a trial run early that June, people immediately remembered that a US Navy submarine, the *Squalus*, had gone down the previous month. Then a French submarine, the *Phoenix*, sank off Vietnam, and tales of sabotage seemed perfectly plausible to me. I wrote from Paris in the *Worker* that sources in the US

> consider as highly possible the existence of an international group of saboteurs in the pay of certain countries who are carrying out these attacks against the navies of the democratic states. American naval circles also consider that the loss by fire of the French liner *Paris* is possibly the work of the same group.

A few days later I was able to report a story of faults on the French sub which had been noticed over a long period, and to point out that an Italian agent had been arrested and shot in the sub's home port of Toulon a month before it sailed for the Far East.

This sense of suspicion and fear was real and pervasive. The theme of the Fifth Column was constant and encouraged by the activities of those who either seemed to be prepared, or actually were prepared, to accept the dominance of the Nazis rather than pay the price of resistance. Documents surfaced purporting to be evidence of such plots on the part of the anti-Semitic right. True or false? One never knew, but they fitted the political realities of the moment. The trial of those thought to have been responsible for the fires that sank the *Paris* circled round the theme of German agents inspiring the sabotage. While it was going on there were a number of bomb attacks on power lines around Bordeaux. One story ran for several days highlighting the links between the German representative in Paris, Otto Abetz, who was expelled under suspicion of bribing newspaper editors, and leading French politicians, who included at least one Cabinet minister. The business manager of the right-wing daily, *Le Figaro*, was arrested. It was said that he had gone to Berlin with another journalist to bring back large sums of cash to finance this network. Official secrets legislation made it impossible for me to fully report all of what followed but there was more than enough to enable me to make the splash on the front page.

Very quickly the French right tried to turn the tables on the left and twist the affair into a witch-hunt of the Communists. *L'Humanité* had been first with the news of the arrest, and Lucien Sampaix, the journalist at the centre of the

88 The World Goes to War

paper's exposé, was himself arrested and formally charged under laws banning the publication of information on treason and espionage cases. The business manager of *Le Figaro* then died in detention, so removing a key potential witness as to what Berlin and the French right had been up to.

When it came to the Sampaix trial, Gabriel Péri appeared as a witness, citing foreign press disclosures of the links between the Nazi spies and members of the government – disclosures made by one of the spies in interviews given to British papers.[2] Speaking in a strikingly calm manner, Péri denounced the French Foreign Minister Georges Bonnet saying: 'With a certain minister at the heart of the Government, one does not need to go hunting for spies'. Bonnet had been a regular target for Péri's powerful prose throughout the time I was in Paris, and, by the standards of British journalism and public debate, his remarks might have seemed almost tame (particularly as there was plenty of public evidence to support them), but the French authorities claimed that what Sampaix and Péri were doing was nothing short of treason. Defending Sampaix was the top lawyer in France, Maître de Moro-Giaffera, who won an acquittal.

Audiences were flocking to the Hollywood film *Confessions of a Nazi Spy* and I interviewed the star, Edward G Robinson, who played an FBI chief. Born in Romania as Emanuel Goldenberg, he grew up like me speaking Yiddish as his first language. In America, he changed his name to Edward G – for Goldenberg – Robinson, and several of his films aimed at undermining anti-Semitism. 'It is necessary to unite all our forces against the menace of Nazism', he told me. He also talked to me about an idea for a film on a Jewish member of the Vienna city council who had been sent to Dachau after Hitler's Anschluss, but, as far as I know, he never got to make it.

The atmosphere of panic and mistrust was encouraged by an infamous remark of the French military hero General Weygand: 'Sooner Hitler than Thorez at the Elysée', the French equivalent of Buckingham Palace, and a few weeks after my grilling by Thorez at the Tillon event, I was invited into his den, a small, paper-filled room in the Party offices overlooking what seemed to be one of the busiest streets in Paris. Against the noise from the traffic and hubbub outside, he set out for me the reasons why he considered the anniversary of the storming of the Bastille so significant in the France of 150 years later. The Bastille Prison had been the symbol of royal power. King Louis XVI had been forced to accept the convening of a parliament but tried to keep it as three equal, separate chambers, the commons, the aristocracy, and the church as this could give him a chance to continue to control events. When the commons declared themselves to be a national assembly representing the whole people, and the king mobilised his troops against the commons, the poor of Paris took the Bastille, symbol of royal power, and opened the way for the development of popular power. International reaction mobilised to try to restore royal power, but, said Thorez, its defeat at by the new army of the French Revolution 'proved the vitality of the first country to adopt the principles of the Rights of Man as the fundamental principles of state'. He argued that France was now the France of the Munich Agreement, governed by those who had allowed Franco to win in Spain. Such rulers, he said, could not allow this anniversary to be a moment when France might recall what lay behind that victory because they wanted to 'calm the susceptibilities of the dictators in accordance with the spirit of Munich. Commemoration of the Revolution would mean praising the victorious struggle of the people against the foreign aggressor and against the enemy agents within'.

Then suddenly, in August, the situation changed for all of us. Hitler's Foreign Minister, von Ribbentrop, went to Moscow on the 22nd and signed a non-aggression pact on the 23rd between Nazi Germany and the Soviet Union. On Friday – the 25th – a colleague rushed into our office to announce breathlessly that the Communist evening paper, *Ce Soir*, had been seized. A few moments later we learnt that the daily *l'Humanité* was also being stopped. The decree under which both papers were banned was not published until after the police had entered the buildings. On the Saturday, all the papers run by the French Party were banned. Arrests of Party members followed – and this was before war was declared.

It was like a thunderbolt but there was no time for reflection as events moved so rapidly. Communists everywhere were deeply confused – the Soviet Union up until then was seen by all of us as committed to active resistance to fascism – but I, and most of the comrades around me, did not immediately interpret the pact as meaning we should stop trying to make our governments fight Hitler. Neither the pact, nor the arrests, nor the ban on the papers prevented the Communist deputies in the National Assembly voting for the war budget on 2 September, the day after war against Nazi Germany was finally declared. I believed it was a capitalists' war and that comrades had to prepare themselves to overthrow the capitalist regime and ensure the victory of Socialism, as had already been achieved in the Soviet Union.

It came as no surprise that there was a terrible resignation among ordinary people in Paris when war was declared on 3 September 1939. The tension was difficult to endure. It seemed to me that everyone was sitting on the edge of the seat in the bus or the taxi. The declaration was followed immediately by general mobilisation, sending a trauma right through the population. All French males were required to do military service and every family in the land, almost without exception, was directly and immediately affected.

At the Gare de l'Est, which I passed on my way to the office, there was pandemonium day after day. Those mobilised were trying to make their way, either to the Maginot Line along the frontier with Germany between Switzerland and Luxemburg or to bases between the line and Paris. I saw old soldiers in moth-eaten uniforms that had been dragged out of chests. Families were sobbing, girlfriends weeping, children screaming.

My first story from France at war – 'the fourth day of the war against Nazi Germany', as I put it – was about Spanish Republican refugee soldiers volunteering for the French army. Holed up in a concentration camp at Gurs in the far south-west of France, they said they were asking for one thing only, 'to be in the front ranks'. Their spirit was incredible. With them were Austrian, German,

90 The World Goes to War

and Italian anti-fascists along with Poles and some 500 Czechs, who, like the Austrians, Germans, and Italians, no longer had a country they could return to.

By complete chance, I met up with Fermina, the young woman who had been my secretary in Spain, who had resisted my blandishments there because she had had a husband in the Republican army. As happened with so many Spanish families, his brother was in the Franco army, not by choice but because he had been conscripted. When the defeat came, Fermina's husband went to the new authorities saying he had been conscripted and they accepted his story. He wrote asking her to return but she could never go back to Spain under Franco, and soon we got together. There was just one complication, which, at first, did not add up to much. In public, one had to carry a gas mask but they were only issued to those foreigners with proper documents and Fermina was in Paris illegally. I gave her my mask as I felt I was safe if any gendarme questioned me, while she might run the risk of being sent back to Spain or at least to a camp.

One night when the air raid sirens sounded, the others in the flat dragged me off to the local metro station, our designated shelter. A man came by on a bike whirling a rattle, the warning signal for gas, and everyone started putting on their masks. People were signalling to me with strangled cries: where was mine? The soldiers guarding the Botzaris metro demanded to know why I had not got a mask but, before I could say anything, one of them grabbed me with one hand, turned round while doing something with his other hand and then in what seemed like one movement turned back again and slapped on my face a warm, wet cloth. The stench told me that he had pissed in his handkerchief. It was a supposed precaution against poison gas he had presumably remembered from the trenches of the First World War. Worse followed. The press of people forced me down into the station where everyone else in their masks decided I would be safest in the tunnel where I was kept for the rest of the night amidst the most incredible shit and slime. Such was the cost of helping a damsel in distress.

The French authorities continued to chase Communists and the appointment of Georges Bonnet from the far right of French politics as Minister of Justice was a portent of worse to come, as was the discovery by the French Communist leadership that their initial attempt to combine resistance to the repression directed against them with support for the declaration of war against Nazi Germany was not at all what Stalin wanted.

On 27 September, the French Communist Party was banned and the 73 Communist MPs removed from Parliament. I saw several Party offices raided the following day, their files carried off, presumably to help the police identify suitable subjects for more arrests. Over the weeks that followed, the several hundred local government bodies that had Communist majorities were abolished and replaced by central government commissioners. The French equivalent of the shop steward system was abolished. As the months went by, any organisation that could be tainted with a relationship to the Communists – trade union bodies, cultural organisations, tenants' leagues, even holiday camps – were banned or broken up or had their leading personnel dismissed, if not arrested.

The World Goes to War **91**

My 'former employers' were an early victim of the government's attempt to stamp out the Communist Party. I helped Fritz Runge destroy all his papers, including his false Austrian passport. He registered at the Czech embassy in his real name and booked into a hotel. The police came for him at 4am and he was interned, the fate of a good number of the foreign Communists in exile in Paris. The French officials who put them behind barbed wire were often those who went on to serve the occupation regime a year later, taking their prisoners with them. Many of those prisoners eventually disappeared, being among those consumed by the Nazi death machine, some leaving behind them, like my grandparents, no record. Fritz, however, escaped and ended up in Czechoslovakia after the war.

Our agency stopped issuing its bulletins. The French male staff were called up and the rest of the British section quickly returned over the Channel. My instructions were to stay in the office, looking after the vast amount of mail that was still coming in from around the world and filing a lot of reports.

On my own in the large suite of offices one day, I heard a huge racket. Three thugs came in through the door. The one in front shouted 'Commissaire de Police' and produced his papers, announcing he was going to be making a search. I showed my papers and was told to stay put. In anticipation of just such a raid, we had cleared everything out from the desks. There was one cupboard where we had stored old copies of the agency bulletin and the works of Marx, Engels, Lenin – and Stalin, of course – in various languages none of us could read. They pulled out this stuff and angrily banged through the empty draws as one declared, 'Ah, les salots, ils ont fait une bonne nettoyage!' We had, indeed, cleaned up well. But then they discovered a little cupboard hidden in a corner which had been used by the stenographers, two English women comrades. I had forgotten to check it over and panicked. One policeman went at it with an air of great excitement and pulled out its contents and on to the floor tumbled a mass of unused sanitary towels. He let out a Gallic howl of anger.

The agency chief Alpàri's immediate response to the raid was somewhat Shakespearean: 'Sam we must to post. This is a testing time and we must prove worthy'. He spoke in a strangulated way because of a throat operation he had just had in Moscow, and that only made his way of speaking English all the stranger. 'To post' for me meant going to the Belgian capital, Brussels. I cleared Alpàri's instructions with London and was given the name and details of a contact there with whom I could deal. After leaving Paris, I never saw Alpàri again. My Hungarian boss had created a complete French identity for himself as a retired gentlemen but, I discovered after the war, he was arrested in the summer of 1940 shortly after the Nazi occupation. He was ordered to write out the history of the Comintern, and reputedly took ages, tearing up what he had written day by day until the Gestapo got fed up and he was sent to the Sachsenhausen death camp where he was shot in 1944.

I needed a permit to leave Paris and fully expected to be arrested but the French authorities granted me the visa. Fermina saw me off at the railway station

92 The World Goes to War

that October. She had agreed to return to Spain at the request of the Spanish Communist Party, which was looking to re-establish the movement against Franco. We corresponded for a while but then lost touch. I never found out what happened to her.

I destroyed all the papers I had in the name of Russell and registered in Brussels as Lesser, the name in my passport. Belgium was neutral and the Belgian CP was still functioning openly, though its paper was banned the following month. Belgium provided safe houses for various French Communist Party figures and for some Comintern agents. I booked myself into a hotel as my work was above board and I did not need to hide. My Belgian Party contact was René Blieck, a lawyer in the Brussels appeal court but who was also editing a number of anti-fascist papers and had published a couple of books of poetry. A Sephardi Jew, he spoke excellent Spanish and, when at home, Ladino. He was arrested by the Nazis on the day Hitler invaded the Soviet Union and was killed at the end of the war.

Through Blieck, I had regular meetings with Eugen Fried, the Comintern advisor to the French Communist Party, who I knew from Paris where we used to call him Pudding Face.[3] His cover name was Clement and he had reached Brussels before me. One of an extraordinary band of Communists who came out of the ferment in central Europe at the beginning of the twentieth century, he was a heavy-jowled Czech, and he died at the hands of the Gestapo in Brussels in 1943.

At the same time as reporting from Brussels on what was happening to the French Communists, including wholesale arrests, I prepared reports on the situation in Britain for a network of illegal papers that Clement was running in France. There was a WH Smith newsagent in Brussels which had the main Fleet Street titles and, strangely enough, sometimes the *Daily Worker*. Upstairs was an Olde English Tea Shoppe where I could sit and read. I had no idea then that Clement was a link in the chain along which key materials from the British Party made their way to the Comintern in Moscow. Years later, I was told that some short, coded messages went via the Soviet Embassy in London or via a radio hidden in south London but lengthy documents, like verbatim transcripts of British Party leadership meetings, had to be physically sent as typescripts.

One day, not long after I got to Brussels, he passed me a document of many dozens of pages. He told me to read it overnight and give it back straight away. It turned out to be a verbatim transcript of the debate on the war in the British Party's Central Committee meeting of some three weeks earlier.

Although it was known that the Comintern view differed from that of the British Party, the meeting had started off on the basis of its existing line, which had been encapsulated by the General Secretary Harry Pollitt in a quickly produced booklet *How to Win the War*. Pollitt began by arguing for an active anti-fascist front against Hitler as well as opposition to the Chamberlain government. Rajani Palme Dutt, the Party's main ideologist, argued against Pollitt but was in the minority among those speaking. After the meeting had been going for a couple of days (there were less than 30 people involved, but Communists can talk the hind legs off even the most political of donkeys), Dave Springhall returned from Moscow to say the line of the world Communist movement had changed and that the British Party would have to follow suit.

The Central Committee adjourned while the smaller political bureau discussed the matter. It received a short-written thesis from the Comintern, which said the war was now 'an imperialist and unjust war' like the First World War. The Central Committee reconvened with a majority of the political bureau convinced that the Soviets must be right. Dutt took up this new line with enthusiasm but Willie Gallacher, the Party's only MP and one of its most prominent public figures, said he had 'never at this Central Committee listened to a more unscrupulous and opportunist speech', and that, having seen how Dutt had behaved, would never trust him again. After more debate, Pollitt made his final remarks before a vote was taken and called on the committee not to try to think of the way Comrade Stalin would think but of how they were going to justify their vote to the British working class. On losing the vote 21 to 3, Pollitt stood down as General Secretary and Dutt temporarily took his place – a move in the view of some, including those who backed the Comintern line, that had been Dutt's true purpose. So we did the public somersault and denounced the war.

At first, I had found the argument set out by Pollitt very helpful but the first thing I had consciously read which took me towards Communism was a pamphlet by Dutt, who was the Party's ideological mastermind. Particularly after 1956, the magic of that dry, cynical interpreter of the holy texts of Marxism had vanished, but in 1939 it was still there, and the onslaught on the Communist Party in France gave strength to the Comintern line. Clement put it to me:

> You know quite well what is going on in France at the moment. How can anyone say that the war is an anti-fascist one? Obviously, we are against Hitler. But Chamberlain wants to turn this into a war against the Soviet Union. That is the biggest danger at the moment.

Clement evidently decided I had a role to play in the French Party's response and, out of the blue, he asked me teasingly one day: 'Would a great journalist like you want to have an interview with Maurice? If you are interested, I might be able to arrange it'. I had interviewed Maurice Thorez, the French Party General Secretary, earlier that year in Paris on the 150th anniversary of the French Revolution but since then the situation had changed dramatically. He had been called up after war had been declared and had joined his regiment but key leaders of the French Party, who were hiding in Belgium, had decided he might be 'accidentally' killed by the French authorities if he stayed in the army and told him to go on the run. A hue and cry ensued across France for the deserter and I was being asked if I wanted an interview with him.

I submitted some questions in writing and then a message came: I was to be in a certain café in Brussels at a given moment. Sitting in one of the Belgian capital's

94 The World Goes to War

classiest spots on the Place de Brouckère, I could see it had been carefully chosen as it was on a corner and with two entrances, both with revolving doors opposite each other. I chose a table where I could see both doors. Clement came in through one, pretended he had not seen me, and then went out of the other door. Then a chap appeared whom I had known in Paris as 'Le Gros Maurice', the Big Maurice, whose actual name was Maurice Tréand. He was Thorez's bodyguard and had been running a clandestine network for the French Party since 1932 in case the CP was banned, but this network had all but vanished and the Party was trying to re-establish it. 'Le Gros', now sporting a thin moustache, passed me by and went out through the other door. Clement came in and told me to follow 'Le Gros', who would be at the wheel of a car I was to get into. After a long night-time drive in the rain, to where I do not know, we came to a house. I went in and after a few moments Thorez appeared with a glass of wine and written answers to my questions in his pocket. I read through the answers, which were basically all I needed, but we chatted for an hour and a half in a very relaxed atmosphere.

Clement was insistent that the interview was to go into the British Party weekly, *World News and Views*, not the *Worker*. I could not see why, but I sent a covering letter explaining this when I dispatched the interview directly to the weekly via the hopefully secure route of the home address of Rose Schechter (later Grant), one of the two British secretaries who had worked at the agency with me in Paris. Most unusually, at my next meeting with Clement, he had a broad smile across his pudding face. He congratulated me for being a good journalist and produced the latest copy of the *Worker*. The Thorez interview was the splash. As is often the case as a reporter abroad, I never found out why my careful instructions on how the story was to be used were so completely ignored. Not only had they put the story in, but they had carried a picture of Thorez, too. Clement's calculation had paid off.

The interview was described in the introduction – not written by me – as 'the biggest story that has come to any newspaper from "Somewhere in France" since the war began'. Thorez rejected the accusation that he was a deserter – though technically, he *had* deserted from his unit – as the reality, he argued, was that those in power had deserted the cause of France. It was a declaration of the Communist Party's determination to continue its activities come what may. The core argument was simple: Hitler's regime of violence was hateful, but how could the 'Men of Munich' claim be the leaders of anti-Hitlerism at the same time as they were introducing fascist-type measures in France?

Over the weeks that followed, my interview appeared in copies of *l'Humanité* printed on hidden presses ('Reprint and hand around', declared the masthead). I discovered later that readers of the *Worker* in the British Expeditionary Force based in northern France also passed the paper on to French Party members who circulated copies widely through the Party network inside France, giving the first indication to many of its members that Thorez was still alive. Shortly afterward, a row blew up in the French Chamber of Deputies led by a fascist called Taittinger. Thorez was on the run as a deserter from the French army, he said, and *l'Humanité* is banned in France, and yet interviews with Maurice Thorez are being circulated all over France. These clandestine leaflets even got themselves into a novel – in the series by Louis Aragon entitled *Les Communistes.*

One morning, not long after the Thorez interview appeared, there was a knock on the door of my Brussels apartment. The concierge said a gentleman had arrived to see me. Still in my pyjamas, I could do nothing before in came an official declaring he was from the Commissariat de Police. He looked around and commented what a nice room it was. He gave no hint as to what he was after me for or why I needed to go with him.

'You have to go and see the Chief of Police', was all he would say. As I had another meeting with Clement coming up I managed to fob him off, agreeing I would come the following week.

At the Commissariat, I was asked whether I realised that any foreigner living in Belgium and not registering with the police was guilty of a serious offence. I pleaded innocent of any such misdemeanour, protesting that I had registered properly. Did I realise, I was then solemnly asked, that any person, foreign or otherwise, who knows of a foreigner living in Belgium who is not registered with the police and who does not report this to the police is equally guilty of a serious offence? I had, I assured him, always assumed that to be the case. Did I know Maurice Thorez?

'Do you mean the General Secretary of the French Communist Party?'

'Yes, the very same'.

'Are you inquiring about the interview with Thorez that has appeared under my name in the *Daily Worker?*'

'What do you mean, *under your name?*'

'Well, I have heard about the article and have sent a strong protest to my editor. Sam Russell is my *nom de guerre* and *nom de plume*, but it is also a name used by my colleagues in the office where I worked'. Knowing Dick Kisch was safely in England, I fingered him for a second time as the perpetrator.

The prefect repeated his statement about reporting non-registered foreigners and gave me his card. I gave him mine, and left.

It was obvious the Belgian police were following me, so I had to be careful not to lead them to Blieck, Clement, and their contacts. The French authorities had also started looking for me, assuming I was still in France as I was still reporting on the arrests of Communists there, and presumably hoping they might get to Thorez through me. They went round various offices of foreign correspondents in Paris to see if anyone knew where I was, as one mate of mine, an undercover Party member in the *Daily Telegraph* office, told me many years later. At the United Press office, one of the journalists pointed out that I was filing stories for the New York *Daily Worker*. All the police had to do was check with Western Union or Cable and Wireless to see where I was sending my telegrams from. In this way, the French police were able to track me to Brussels. Indeed, one day, I had been visited in Brussels by a chap from Western Union's local office who wanted to know whether I was satisfied with their service. I did not use it that

96 The World Goes to War

much – the funds that Clement was able to give me did not allow too many cables to New York, but I must have sent enough to let the police discover my whereabouts without too much difficulty.

When the Soviet Union had gone to war with Finland at the end of 1939 I had discussed with Clement the possibility of going to Moscow to cover the fighting. Moscow never answered his messages and, luckily for me, I never went or I might not have survived to tell this story. Now, there was no alternative but to go back to London. In March 1940, a year after I had disembarked from the ferry in France, I set off, landing at Shoreham airport near Brighton unaware that in a fortnight the Nazis would invade Norway and that, a month later, the countries I had just been working in – Belgium and France along with the Netherlands – would also be over-run.

Some 40 years later, my time in Brussels unexpectedly came back into my life. In 1979, on the anniversary of the British Communist Party's change of line on the war, the Party's History Group organised a meeting on the change. I was flabbergasted by the remarks of the only two surviving members of the Central Committee, Idris Cox and Ted Bramley, who had both voted with the pro-Comintern majority. Neither made any reference to the points put so fiercely by the other side that I remembered from the transcript, so I gave my account. As it turned out, the British Party did not have a copy of the transcript to check who was right. The Party supposed the text was only available in Moscow and was locked up – as far as anyone was prepared to predict in those pre-Gorbachev times – for ever. Moscow, however, was not the only place where an archive held the text, something I soon found out by 'accident'.

As a *Daily Worker* and then *Morning Star* journalist attending Foreign Office News Department briefings and going on various FO facility trips, I had got to know fairly well a FO career civil servant Denis, later Lord, Greenhill. We engaged in a kind of chummy, joking relationship. After he had graduated from university, he had first gone to work on the railways. One day he needed to get to the marshalling yards in Sheffield quickly, and the controller said he should take a trip in the guard's van of a goods train due any moment. 'But watch out for the guard', the controller warned. 'He's a bit Bolshie'. 'I was thunderstruck when I got in', Greenhill told me. Shardloe (he only remembered the man's surname), who 'had left school at 14 and had taught himself everything he knew', was a member of the Communist Party and had fitted out his van with bookshelves and a table, which was covered with notebooks. 'We talked for hours about literature and history and stories of Merrie England', said Greenhill.

Perhaps that was why Greenhill often asked after the paper and seemed permanently amused by a man who advertised insurance policies in the *Worker*. Rather surprised, I once said, 'You must read the paper closely', to which he replied: 'In a professional capacity, and mostly the back page' – which meant the sports section, noted especially for its racing tips by Cayton. This was during the UN peace-keeping operation in the Congo immediately after independence from Belgium, and Greenhill then took out his wallet and extracted an 'Our

Alfie' cartoon, carefully cut from the paper. It showed Alfie descending in parachute gear asking, 'Where is this 'ere peace keeping operation?' I asked if Greenhill would like the original and duly handed it over a few days later.

Soon after the 1979 history conference, when I was coming out from a midday Foreign Office news briefing, I 'bumped' into Greenhill in the entrance lobby. By that time, he was the Permanent Under Secretary at the FO and also Chair of the Joint Intelligence Committee, which brought together agencies like MI5 and MI6 with GCHQ, the British secret radio and telephone monitoring centre, and Defence Intelligence. People of that rank are not paid to loiter in Whitehall entrance lobbies.

'Care for a drink?' he casually asked.

We ended up in his vast room overlooking Horse Guards Parade. There on the desk was the framed Alfie cartoon. After the opening pleasantries, he pushed over to me a pink folder. 'Do you recognise this, Sam?' he asked. In it was a copy of the covering letter I had sent with my Thorez interview. I recognised it immediately before I had even read it as I had typed it on the Imperial portable I had inherited from Bill Rust in Spain, and the results on the page were always very distinctive.

'Oh', I said, 'I didn't know you were so interested in my activities that you wanted to inspect my private correspondence'.

'You were suspected of being a Soviet sleeper'.[4]

'I hope by now they've realised I wasn't a sleeper but was actually fast asleep the whole time'.

He withdrew the folder and then said he understood I was very interested in what had gone on in the Central Committee regarding the change of line. They could help with my interest, he explained, as they might have one or two 'pertinent' items.

'If you are interested, we can arrange for you to have a meeting with one of our chaps'.

In due course I got a letter inviting me to the old War Office in Whitehall. They had the complete verbatim transcript of the meeting typed by the Party's stenographers, the same document I had seen a carbon copy of four decades before. The explanation I was given was that the transcript had belonged to Palme Dutt. He had kept a copy of the document and when his secretary's house was raided the transcript was found in a trunk under her bed. The truth, as it subsequently turned out, was perhaps even more startling: the secretary was actually an agent for MI5, providing her supervisors with copies of anything important she typed up for the Party leadership.

Over several visits, I was allowed to read through the blue files containing this complete copy, which, as it happened, confirmed my memory of the Central Committee discussion. I could have the lot, they said, and, indeed, the suggestion was gently made, I might even be interested in writing a book for which they might even be able to arrange a publisher. My response was that I wanted to discuss the idea with Johnny Gollan, then the British Party's General Secretary.

98 The World Goes to War

Excellent thought, was the reply. Gollan's response, however, was abrupt and delivered in most untypically crude language, which gave me the impression that I might not have been the first person to seek his advice on such a project.

My final meeting with the 'contact' was in a room in the Charing Cross Hotel over *oeufs florentines* and a bottle of wine. At that stage of my life, I told him, I did not fancy being taken in hand by Greenhill's goons. The full publication of the material had to wait a decade when Mikhail Gorbachev's perestroika and glasnost opened the books in Moscow, and what was left of the Communist Party decided, some 50 years late, to finally publish the lot.[5]

Notes

1 The war officially ended on 1 April 1939.
2 Péri and Sampaix were both eventually shot by the Nazis in December 1941.
3 In one of Sam's MI5 files (KS 2/3741; 31a), there is a letter from him ('Manny' at the Hotel Anspach, Brussels) to a London contact, using what appear to be coded references, including 'Pudden Face'.
4 Sam's MI5 files (KV 2/3742; 64a) show that it wasn't until February 1940 that MI5 established 'pretty well' that Manassah Lesser and Sam Russell were one and the same. They had seen the likeness between the photos on Sam's journalist's card and his passport (in the name of Lesser). Additionally, they saw a resemblance in the handwriting and spotted that Russell is very near to Lesser reversed. 'We have had several examples of this method of choosing aliases among Communist Party members'.
5 *About Turn: The Communist Party and the Outbreak of the Second World War. The verbatim records of the Central Committee meetings, 1939*, edited by Francis King and George Matthews (London: Lawrence and Wishart, 1990).

6

WARTIME BRITAIN

Back in Britain after leaving Brussels, I found my mother had kept all the letters that had come for me while I had been away. One I *had* expected to find was a letter telling me to report for duty. The rule was that if you were abroad when your call-up papers came, then you had to report immediately on your return, which I did. My wounds were well enough healed and I passed the medical. But nothing happened and I was never called into the Forces. Instead, after a few weeks, I got a letter from the War Office telling me my name had been removed from the supplementary reserve for officers, and my dream of a military career culminating as a general in the Royal Scots was over. It was only after my 'accidental' meeting with Denis Greenhill all those decades later that I surmised I had been turned down because I was suspected of being a Soviet sleeper.[1]

I tried to interest the *Worker* in pieces on France, and in June 1940 I went to St Austell in Cornwall to meet a representative of the French Party travelling with other refugees by boat across the Channel who had a message to deliver. I stayed with a local doctor who was in the Party and who had to carry out health checks on the new arrivals. Streams of people were coming ashore. Most of them did not know a word of English. 'Pas malade?' 'Kein krankheit?' the doctor would call out as the queue shuffled forward. I borrowed one of his white coats and looked out for my contact. A man came over and slipped me a piece of paper. The contact was made. I never found out how he worked out who I was. The paper was a statement from the French Party Central Committee on the need for resistance. I took it back to London, translated it and gave it to the *Worker* to publish. I wrote that the Party statement had reached the *Worker* through a correspondent in Sweden. I also produced one or two issues of a bulletin in English and French with French Party members who had come to Britain after the fall of France. The French comrades opposed the collaborationist authorities

DOI: 10.4324/9781003243380-7

of Vichy France under General Pétain and were critical as well of the Free French forces that General de Gaulle was trying to organise from London.

The *Worker* had limited funds and did not seem too happy with me hanging around trying to be a reporter in Britain. Fed up with not having a proper job to do, I went to Harry Pollitt, who was working in the London docks not far from my home, who thought I should get some factory experience. 'You've had enough of war', he said, so, in October 1940, I was sent to see Walter Swanson, the Amalgamated Engineering Union (AEU) shop stewards' convenor and tool room man at the key Napier aero-engine factory in Acton, West London. I had no skills whatsoever as a production worker but the firm was looking for people who could manipulate a slide rule and I became a trainee inspector. 'Swannie' or 'Gloria', as he was known, after the then popular star Gloria Swanson – a wonderful character, someone to whom the term 'natural leader' really could be applied – squared everything with management. Under the pressure of wartime production, factories were looking for labour. The AEU had come to an agreement with the employers on the introduction of trainees, provided they joined the AEU, and after a week's course, I began – and finished up as an inspector in the fitting shop. This meant, at the age of 25, accepting or rejecting the work of people far more experienced than I was, who, to become time-served engineers, had passed through traditional apprenticeships lasting many, many years. My first pay packet I still remember contained £14, calculated as an average of the wage received by the production workers, whose money was calculated on a payment-by-results basis.

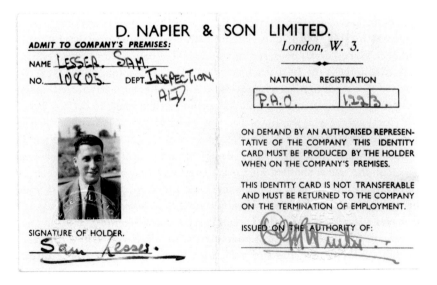

FIGURE 6.1   Identity card issued to Sam when he was working as a fitting shop inspector at the Napier factory, west London in 1943.

Source: Family archive.

The first time in a machine room is absolutely terrifying. The Napier workshops had overhead gantries operated by manually controlled chains to move heavy castings around the shop. There was constant noise, dust, and movement. Drive belts seemed to be on the go everywhere. The air was thick with the smell of burnt oil, grease, and solvents. It was another university for me.

There was already a strong Communist Party group there. Even during the period of the Nazi-Soviet pact, the Party branch grew. Contrary to the general allegations made against the Party during that period, there was no attempted sabotage of the factory, though it would obviously have been a prime target had that been what we wanted to do. The branch developed rapidly after Hitler's attack on the Soviet Union in June 1941 when the Party line reverted overnight to not only supporting the war, but also campaigning for it to be pursued with ever greater vigour. A ban on the *Daily Worker*, which had been imposed in January 1941 because of its anti-war position, was lifted in August 1942. For a while, the largest Communist organisation in any workplace across Britain was in the two Napier factories in London, and some in the branch even began to see Napier as the cradle of proletarian power in London, naming it the Putilov of the British revolution after the famous factory in St Petersburg where the Bolsheviks had enjoyed such strong support in October 1917. The strength of the Communist Party at Napier, and of the shop stewards committee, was based on ordinary men who had learned their trade unionism and politics in the factory, often the hard way, and who set out to improve the conditions of their colleagues on the shop floor as much as to transform the world.

The chair of the stewards committee was Fred Arter, a long-standing AEU man in the grinding shop. Like many of the long-standing Napier's workers, his lungs were full of the metal and carborundum dust. The grinders had suction fans by the carborundum wheel, sucking away the fragments that would come off the wheel. The suction never managed to catch all of them and the air in the shop was full of pernicious dust and fragments of metal. Arter's lungs, like those of many of the older men, were full of the stuff and they were forever coughing it up. He had a large lump of cotton waste placed by his machine each day so he could spit it up onto the waste, and the first job each day for one of the millwrights was to see to Arter's wad.

Another old Napier hand I became friendly with, Len Misseldine, was a highly skilled tool room operator able to work any machine. Elected a shop steward for many years, he eventually joined the Party. He was above all a grinder and his way of dealing with the effect of the dust was to chew tobacco as he found that gave him more saliva with which to spit the dust out.

There were other Spanish war veterans at Napier; for example, Bob Walker, who had been a well-known footballer before volunteering for Spain, was working in the grinding shop. More important for me personally, was Peter Kerrigan, the former commissar to the British Battalion, who was working in the experimental branch of the factory. He had sided with Pollitt in the 1939 debates on the war and was now, like Pollitt, back on the shop floor. He lived just

102 Wartime Britain

down the road from the factory gate, and I would often share an evening meal with him and his family. There was much to make me feel close to them. Rose, his wife, was Jewish and she used to sing to her small children the same Yiddish cradle songs my mother had sung to us as children.

Everyone seemed to smoke, something I did not do when I arrived. After each engine block was finished, the men would hand round cigarettes and, in the end, I gave in. For days on end, it made me sick as a dog.

I was elected shop steward for the inspection department of the fitting shop and was involved in the traditional, seemingly very limited but actually very important role of pushing management to improve the quality of the factory toilets and canteen. In one food poisoning crisis, half the factory was off for days and there was a long row over the running of the canteen, which had been contracted out. It appeared that one of the assistant managers was taking kickbacks in the form of a regular under-the-counter ham from the canteen manager, a bribe, which in the days of rationing, was worth something. Good food and clean toilets were priorities that had been drummed into me in my days in the Officers' Training Corps and then in Spain, both of which gave me plenty of points to use in the confrontations.

But there were bigger things as well, particularly after the change in the Party line on the war with Hitler's invasion of the Soviet Union. The two principal campaigns we became involved with then were the drive for higher production and the campaign for a Second Front, the demand that Britain and the US should not wait until the Red Army had 'torn the guts out of the Wehrmacht', as Churchill was to say, but invade Nazi-occupied France at the earliest possible moment.

When the *Worker* resumed publication at the start of September 1942, the war was at its most critical moment: Rommel was at El Alamein with his Afrika Korps dangerously close to Cairo and the Suez Canal; the Japanese were at the gates of India; and we were all aware that a titanic struggle was just beginning on the Russian front around Stalingrad. If Stalingrad fell to the Germans, it was hard to see what would stand in the way of a final, total victory for Nazism. For me, that was the force behind the argument for the Second Front, which I campaigned for vigorously.

Word went round one day that there was going to be a royal visit to the factory. Even if we had not heard the rumours, the signs became obvious. The plant was an old one and the wooden floors were soaked with ages of grime, grease, and oil. No royal foot could be allowed to slip, even if us lesser mortals could. Along with the clean-up, white lines were carefully painted to guide the Party. We decided on a counter stroke. A new blast wall had been built in the fitting shop to protect the degreasing tanks, should the factory be hit by any bombs. Across the wall we pasted a magnificent display of Party posters demanding a 'Second Front Now'. Managers talked of knocking the wall down to get rid of the display but, because it was there for safety reasons, they had to leave it in place. What the Duke of Kent thought when he came round with the company boss one could not tell, but the top brass was petrified.

Wartime Britain **103**

This Second Front campaign did not please everyone. There were voices that said we Communists were keen to shout about fighting, but were reluctant to do it ourselves. With my fellow Brigader and shop steward Bob Walker, I put the argument in the *Acton Gazette*, our local paper where other readers had been writing in to jeer at our demand. Both of us had been refused any opportunity to join the forces along with many other Spanish war veterans. Some had even been dismissed from the forces or blocked from joining the Home Guard. I was in the Home Guard and saw it as a real duty, not a *Dad's Army* knock-about joke, and all of those I was close to were eager to fight.

If Bob and I were not allowed to pull our weight in the trenches, we could certainly do so in the factories, and we pushed the issue of production from the summer of 1941 on. This campaign was a sharp contrast to the previous role of unions, which had not seen it as their job to organise production. A movement was launched for joint production committees across the country bringing together shop floor representatives and management, with Napier in the forefront, under the leadership of Walter Swanson. For us it meant big arguments with others on the left, particularly the Trotskyists, who were arguing for workers' control. Our campaign, which was covered in the monthly magazine, *New Propeller*, culminated in a national war production conference in the Stoll Theatre, Kingsway in central London. More than 300 factories were represented and Swanson presented the main report. It was a masterful performance.

'Our task is nothing less than the saving of the British people', he announced. The conference must be such a 'turning point in Britain's productive effort as shall amaze the world'. What more immediately amazed some of his fellow engineers, men each and every one of them, was his direct demand for the integration of women into the industry. They should be welcomed, he said, and paid the same rates as men. Every plant should have full trade union membership and joint production committees. Flexibility of work – no strict demarcation lines between one craft and another – should be welcomed wherever it meant the removal of restrictions that hampered better production.

We Communist shop stewards in Napier felt a particular responsibility, as the Acton plant was at the forefront of the technological effort for the war. Our relationship with RAF pilots and mechanics was a close one. They fed their criticisms back on a regular basis. On one occasion, the entire workforce – all the different shifts brought together – heard first-hand from a couple of pilots using Sabre-powered Typhoons, then the fastest single-engine fighter plane anywhere. Decades later when kids were taught how the RAF's brave pilots helped win the war, they did not learn how the ordinary men and women who made their planes set about creating production records in the process. You cannot understand the strength of the shop stewards' movement in Britain right up to the days of Margaret Thatcher if you do not grasp the importance of the wartime experience. Engineering factories were both at the heart of the production drive for the war effort and at the heart of the rank-and-file surge, where skilled workers already had confidence in themselves. It spread to the mines, the shipyards, the tank factories,

104 Wartime Britain

and the aircraft works. It challenged the sluggish attitude of civil servants and of managers who preferred to make profits rather than weapons to defeat Nazism.

There was a downside to this intense political commitment. One could not be a Party member in industry without being involved in union elections. Over the years, the Party and others on the left in the unions got themselves into a terrible mess cooking the books. My experience of this came one day when I rolled up at an AEU branch meeting being held upstairs in the Acton Arms pub. Jack Lawrence, secretary of the Acton 5 branch, was organising the ballot for a union election. Jack had worked very hard as secretary in the face of an enormous expansion in the numbers of members and he asked me to act as doorman. Members were coming in and marking their ballot forms and leaving quickly. They did not want to hang around because of the Blitz. After the meeting ended and others had drifted off to other things, I was the only one left with Jack. Once he had finished filling out his books, he came over to me and said the number of completed ballot forms did not look very good considering the size of the branch. Could I fill in some more to build the numbers up? There were two ballots, one for a Party candidate and one for someone else. I duly set to, filling them 50/50, matching a ballot for one with a ballot for the other. Although Lawrence had been a Labour Party member, man and boy, he was swept up by the 'Tanks for Joe' atmosphere and said I should have done them all for the Communist candidate. After putting only the pro-Communist ballots in an envelope, he signed his name across the seal and sent it off to head office. That occasion always stuck in my mind. The right-wing networks were guilty of much ballot rigging by one means or another, but that did not justify our doing the same.

During my time at Napier, I was living in a flat in north London with my brother Frank and his wife Mira, a Jewish refugee from Germany. Our road led directly onto Hampstead Heath and was just round the corner from the railway station. In peacetime, the journey from Hampstead Heath to Acton was simple, no more than a few minutes on the north London railway. With Luftwaffe attacks, the journey was a different matter. Aside from the line itself, the German pilots were targeting a number of industrial concentrations close to the route. If the line itself was ever cut, a bus service was laid on, and, though many Napier workers and their families suffered in one way or another from the Blitz and what followed, the factory itself was never put out of action.

On one occasion when I was visiting my parents' home, a phosphorous incendiary bomb landed on the roof of a neighbouring family – one of whose members had volunteered for Spain and died in the terrible winter fighting at Teruel in the opening weeks of 1938. The bomb failed to go off and I climbed onto the roof and threw it into their back garden with my bare hands – whereupon it promptly exploded and thankfully just fizzled out.

This was the second time I was living and working in a city under aerial bombardment. I often thought of the days in Barcelona and that slogan I repeatedly used in my radio broadcasts: 'Save Spain, Save Peace, Save Britain'. Even when I was saying that, I had never thought that London's turn would come so soon.

The Blitz was not the only thing that recalled my days in Spain. Living with Frank and Mira was also Nell Jones, 20 years my senior and widow of my first company commander in Spain, Freddie Jones. She was a switchboard operator at the *Worker*, so I had known her voice since I had begun reporting for the paper from Spain, and in 1946 we eventually got married.

Like any family in London, the war touched us in many ways. That was especially so for my relatives living still in the East End. Queenie was at university and my three youngest sisters were evacuated to Cornwall, but the shop was kept running throughout the war, largely without the help of us boys. Frank had been called up and joined the RAF as a ground crew member but then slipped off the wing of an ice-covered plane and was invalided out. His brother-in-law, however, went on to become an RAF pilot and was eventually killed in 1944 when his plane blew up with a full bomb load on the way to bomb Caen during the Normandy invasion. My youngest brother Ivor was in the army while, at the time of Munich in 1938, my younger brother Sid had joined the Royal Naval Volunteer Reserve. This meant that when the war began, he was called up into the Navy and had to break off a teacher training course. Put on mine sweepers, the small vessels used to clear mine fields laid by the Germans to trap merchant ships bringing in supplies across the Atlantic, he was blown up a couple of times. Once, after his ship had finished a sweep near Portsmouth and was nearly back in port, Sid and several other ratings dived in the sea for a swim. He was just back on deck and drying himself down when the sweeper itself hit a mine and he was catapulted back into the water, stark naked. Rescued and kitted out at the quartermaster's stores in Portsmouth, he was sent home on leave with congratulatory free drinks from everyone he seemed to meet. By the time he got to Liverpool Street station, he was legless.

I happened to be at home that evening. There was a knock at the door and I opened it to a messenger with a telegram. My father came up and asked what it was. I gave it to him. It was from the Admiralty telling my father they were sorry to inform him but his son Sid had been killed. Mother was upstairs and asked what was going on. We were standing there trying to think what we were going to tell her, when the bell rang again. There was Sid, rocking on his heels, absolutely blotto. My father smacked him right across the face, roaring half in anger, half in relief, 'Drunken sailor!' After his leave, Sid was sent up to Scapa Flow, the huge Royal Navy base in the Shetlands. By the time he arrived, his ship had gone – fortunately for him, as it was torpedoed in the Atlantic with all hands lost.

My father died from cancer in 1942 at the age of 51.[2] One of our neighbours, the local newsagent who had always referred to the paper my father had bought from his shop as 'the Jew boy's *Chronicle*', helped us carry him out, tears running down his face, repeating to us all: 'Your Dad was a good man'. For the funeral, the four sons carried the coffin: one in the RAF, one in the Navy, one in the Army, and myself, a civilian war worker. My mother took over the business and really was quite remarkable, perhaps doing better than he had. She taught herself to drive a van to do the grocery deliveries and kept the shop going through the war. Polly Lesser, as she was known, and her shop became the centre of a network of talk and friends.

FIGURE 6.2 Sam, Margaret and their daughter Ruth in Finchley, north London, 1963, arriving for Sam's mother's 70th birthday.
Source: Family archive.

I did not last the whole war with Napier. When I came into the fitting shop one day in October 1942, an engine was laid out on a bench with red paint all over it. It had obviously failed a test, been dismantled, and the problem parts of the cylinder block had been marked in red. Summonsed to the manager's office, I was shown records that appeared to prove I had signed off the cylinder block in question. Once a block was assembled, inspectors like myself had to sign for each of the nuts and each of the split pins fixing them in place to hold the cylinder sleeves. The record sheet showed I had signed for each of the 16 nuts and that I had recorded each of the 16 split pins as being in place and properly bent so they and the nut could not slip off. Yet the managers claimed the pins had not even been put in place and that, when the engine was run, the nuts flew off. I could not, and cannot, believe that I would have signed 16 times for pins that were not there.

The management could not sack me, as I was a shop steward, but I was eventually transferred to the Aldenham plant. However, I was also hauled before a Party tribunal chaired by Johnny Mahon, industrial organiser of the Party's London district committee. There was no electricity when it met, only candles in bottles for light. Mahon argued the Party had to investigate my behaviour because this could have been sabotage of the war effort. He said I would have been shot in the Soviet Union for this offence and I remember getting the impression that he appeared genuinely put out that he could not do the same in my case. However, he said, I could be expelled from the Party. Desperate, I went to see Bill Rust, the *Worker*'s editor. He was not a friend, but we had been together in Spain. I also happened to know that he had little time for Mahon and so might be a good ally in this argument. He told me not to worry. I remember long conversations over the phone with Kerrigan who told me he had discussed my case with the Party's Control Commission, the final arbiter on discipline, and I was relieved to learn that I would not be kicked out. For better or worse, I remained a member of the Party until it decided to wind itself up 50 years later.

My troubles, however, did not stop there as far as Napier was concerned. Aldenham had been provided to Napier as a maintenance shop for Sabre engines that had seen service and needed repair or modification. One day, having done my report on an engine showing it was working correctly, I went to lunch and didn't sign the report until I got back. I was then instructed to report to the superintendent's office where I was told the timing on the engine was out of phase and I should not have signed it off. I was sacked and this time it was final.

When years later I met up with Denis Greenhill at the Foreign Office, I became convinced that my sacking at Napier had been a set up. I asked him why I had been allowed to work at Napier. 'Accidents happen even in the best run organisations', he said. 'Then you decided to get rid of me', I countered. 'I don't know anything about that', he replied, in a tone of voice that I felt implied he clearly did.[3]

Having got the sack from Napier, I had no other job to go to. After the excitements of my time as a reporter in Spain, Paris and Brussels, journalism was still something I did not want to leave. The ban on the *Worker* in 1941 had meant I spent much of my time over the following year campaigning for the ban to be lifted. During the ban, I was involved in a minor way in discussions about producing the *Worker* illegally. Nothing came of this, and a cyclostyled publication called *Industrial and General Information* was produced instead. Its couple of pages of duplicated typescript became our key reading material on the shop floor until the ban was lifted. When the paper reappeared I was not on its staff but I had not abandoned journalism altogether.

While at Napier, I had gone back to radio, where I had begun my journalism. In the spring of 1942, the BBC asked the AEU to put out a call for someone among its members who might know French and be prepared to do talks about what was going on in Britain's armaments factories. These would be part of the daily 'Ici Londres' broadcasts produced at Bush House, the home of the BBC World Service in the heart of London. That interested me greatly and I jumped at the chance. As the job at Napier could hardly be described as tiring, and I got time away from the factory to chase and write up the material, I had plenty of energy to spend on pursuing the stories I wanted to suggest for my talks. I knew this time round my audience could hear me, while the pay at 4 guineas a go was better than anything I had ever seen in Barcelona. For some reason, the BBC

108 Wartime Britain

Accounts Department thought I was 'Dr Sam Lesser', awarding a qualification though I had left university without one.

To prepare a broadcast, we met at Bush House swapping some ideas in a rather clubby-like atmosphere. There was a wide variety of people, all of whom had come together to help win the war. Beforehand, and after the war was over, we might have found ourselves in deep conflict, but while the war was at its sharpest, we were a team. There was an exciting and very inventive group of French exiles who did most of the stuff put on air. The ultimate boss was Richard Crossman, the future Labour Cabinet minister, but the man who corrected my French scripts was William Pickles, a lecturer at the London School of Economics just across the road. Our broadcasts were a small part of the activities run by the Political Warfare Executive whose London offices were upstairs in that wonderful, ornate building. To the outside world it was the innocent sounding Political Intelligence Department, but for many of those on the inside it was an opportunity to engage in the dark arts of deception, the complicated double cross and counter-information work designed to disrupt or confuse the Nazis (and much of that was led by the *Daily Express* journalist who had interviewed me at the start of the fighting in Madrid, Sefton Delmer). The part of the work I was involved in was, on the face of it, much more straightforward, traditional broadcasting designed to inform an audience of what they would not know because of German or Vichy censorship. Others might have had the special code phrases in their scripts placed to inform Resistance activists of one thing or another, but I did not.

The nearest I got to that was when a report specifically mentioned Maurice Choury, my host in Paris before the war. He was on Corsica and a key leader of the *maquis*, as the resistance fighters there were known, taking the name from the scrubland that covered much of the island. When the news came through in August 1943 of the uprising that liberated Corsica – a move pushed by Communists like Maurice instead of waiting for Allied landings – the BBC put forward the idea of a personal broadcast by me to the *maquis*: 'Alo, Maurice c'est moi!' What it meant to Maurice to hear my voice, I hate to think.

The first of my talks went out on May Day 1942. The presenter's introduction announced: 'Un délégué d'une usine d'aviation de la région londonienne vous parle' – a delegate from an aero-industry factory in the London region will talk to you – and I was followed by Paul Robeson and the 'Internationale'. My aim was straightforward. I set about highlighting the way in which the war was being conducted on the engineering front in Britain, just as we were trying to do it at Napier, and, through that, to inspire those in Occupied France. Over the following months I took the message directly from the shop floor at Acton and put it on the air. Swannie's words at the Stoll Theatre, which had helped launch the Joint Production Committee movement, set the tone for many of my talks and I quoted him at length, telling those under the Nazi jackboot in occupied France what we were doing to help free them and how the Sabre-powered Typhoons they could see in action in the skies above them were all the better for the hard work my fellow workers were putting in.

Wartime Britain **109**

There was also the new decisive role of women workers to cover. I visited a shipyard in the north of England where women were filling the jobs of the men called away to the forces and 'have declared they will defend the principle of equal pay for equal work'. One young woman had lost her husband in the final fighting on the Dunkerque beaches, another 'knew that the ships she was helping to build would take supplies to her husband fighting in the Eight Army in North Africa'.

There was sometimes grim news to report. Wal Hannington, leader of the unemployed movement in the 1920s and '30s and, during the war, National Organiser of the AEU, helped me put together a piece in the summer of 1942 on the execution of the Paris engineering union leader Jean-Pierre Timbaud. He was one of the group of 48 hostages held by the Germans and shot at Châteaubriant in reprisal for the execution of a senior German officer. Hannington had met Timbaud in June 1939 when he had been shown round a special engineering training centre set up by the French Metal Workers' Union.

I had marked the 1,000 bomber raids Churchill sent against Germany in 1942 when there seemed no other way for British forces to strike at Hitler's war machine, by saying, 'We have only just begun. My comrades in the factory have sworn to build all the planes that may be needed to demolish all the war factories of Hitler: in Cologne, in Essen …'. And as the guns of war died away in 1945, I got to see the terrible destruction inflicted by those air armadas I had promised on the Essen after I finally had got back on the staff of the *Worker*.

The fee for the broadcasts was not enough to keep me going after being sacked from Napier, so I spent several months working in the London office of TASS, the Soviet news agency, before Bill Rust as editor of the *Worker* (reluctantly, I think) agreed to take me on as a general reporter on home news stories.[4] His one condition was that I agreed to use the name Sam Russell. I agreed and the name has stuck with me ever since.

Notes

1   A memo dated 9 May 1940 in Sam's MI5 files confirms this. An earlier memo, from 1939, describes him as 'a dangerous civilian Communist' whose 'presence in the army would be a serious menace to morale and discipline' (National Archives KV 2/3742).

2   The year before, a letter from Sam's father to Sam – erroneously believed to be in code – was intercepted by MI5 and given to a specialist code breaker, who prepared a note on it [KV 2/3742]. Nathan talks about his parents being in the town of Oswiecim (Auschwitz) with one of his sisters. Another sister is in Frankfurt and gets letters from their parents, who are 'crying for help but she can't help them'. Her husband and two sons are in concentration camps. Nathan asks Sam to write and gives the address in Oswiecim.

> I don't know if it is still called Galicia … You say you have very little to do and lots of time to do it in … You will have to give your grandparents your address so they should send the letters to you and you will send them on to me.

3   Russell's MI5 files suggest Greenhill would have known about the sacking, though bizarrely they suggest Russell sought the sack in order to return to journalism.

4   Sam believed Rust was interested in his wife-to-be Nell, who worked at the paper, and thought perhaps that this lay behind his reluctance to employ him.

7

BACK AT THE *WORKER*

When I got back to the *Daily Worker* in 1944, the editorial office was in Swinton Street, near London's King's Cross station. Its former print works and offices in Cayton Street behind the Moorfields Eye Hospital had been wrecked during the Blitz while the paper was banned. The new place was just round the corner behind the Ear, Nose and Throat Hospital in Gray's Inn Road where a 21-year-old rotary printing press that had previously been used to print the *Sunday Worker* was lying idle. As part of the London Caledonian print works, it had been sold to the Communist Party by the steel trade union in the days after the ban was lifted.

It was all very cramped. There were two floors. Upstairs were the reporters and sub-editors almost sitting on top of each other. Downstairs was what we called the 'Lions' Den' of the paper's big names, with Walter Holmes, who wrote a daily diary piece, his *Workers' Notebook*, Ben Francis the Industrial Correspondent and Johnny Campbell as Assistant Editor. There was also my brother Frank, the Forces Correspondent handling a stream of letters the paper was getting from those in the services. Old timers, including some of the great names in the profession like Allen Hutt, perhaps the best newspaper design specialist of his day, and Claud Cockburn, whom any national title would have been keen to employ, sat cheek by jowl with us much younger ones.[1] Sales were high. The print run reached over 100,000 a day – and it would have been much higher but for paper rationing – and there was scarcely a factory in Britain to which a copy of the *Worker* did not find its way.

My first story of note came by chance. One of the rota of volunteer lawyers who checked the *Worker* every day for libel had been trawling through the *All England Law Reports* and found a court case between a company called Magnesium Elektron and the Inland Revenue. Before the war, it seemed the company had been formed as a joint venture between ICI and the German chemical firm IG

DOI: 10.4324/9781003243380-8

Farben under which IG Farben agreed to ICI producing as much magnesium as it wanted through this joint subsidiary. There was just one condition: ICI could not sell the caustic soda that was being turned out as a by-product in markets where IG Farben was already trading. IG Farben would compensate them for the losses that resulted. The 'mutual market protection' agreement carried on right through the war. Inland Revenue argued that this compensation was taxable, hence the court case.

My take on the story was the work IG Farben had done for the Nazis, and so the paper published a small item on the case. In response, Judd Cohen, a Communist Party member in Manchester who was an industrial chemist, wrote to say he had made an interesting discovery. The ICI plant funded by government money to produce magnesium required for aircraft production was pumping out its caustic soda into the estuary of the River Lune on the Lancashire coast. The implication was clear: ICI should have used the caustic soda for the war effort but instead was wasting it because of its deal with Farben and was being helped by the government to do so.

Having put me on the scent, the lawyer would not let me write this up on Cohen's say-so and demanded direct proof before allowing the copy to be printed. The *Worker* had very high standards of factual accuracy – this was in the days before tape recorders – and was praised for this by many of its opponents. I went up to Lancashire at weekends over a two-month period and with Judd tracked the entire 27-mile route of the pipeline from the factory to the sea where we saw the outfall across an enormous expanse of mud. The following weekend we waded through the mud at low tide. I used some litmus paper to give me an idea of whether I was onto to something, and when that showed positive we filled two jerry cans full of the liquid coming out of the pipe. Independent chemical analysis proved Judd's claims and we published. The Ministry denied it was happening so we had a Labour MP ask questions in the Commons and as a result secured an eventual government confession that it was true.

My story, however, could not stop the practice. ICI and the government claimed there was a surplus of caustic soda, though experts I spoke to denied this, and in the courts, the ownership of Magnesium Elektron was not so clear.

The Nazi war effort, of which IG Farben was such a key part, had not relented despite Germany's losses, and one of my next jobs was to report on the continuing damage in the capital inflicted by Hitler's terror weapons. He hoped the V1 flying bombs and the V2 rocket bombs would turn the tide in his favour, even at that late hour. I had known wartime censorship in Barcelona, and covering the British response to Hitler's final desperate lunge at London was my introduction to how media control was done in Britain. The V1 bombing was at its height in the summer of 1944 but in early September Allied forces had captured the German launch sites in northern France and there was widespread confidence the threat was over. Then, out of the blue at the start of November, London was hit by a new danger, the V2s or 'ghost bombs', so called because there was no sound before the blast as the rockets moved faster than sound. I saw the explosion

112 Back at the *Worker*

of what I believed to be the initial bomb. We splashed on the news and even included a picture of the crater it had made.

Each reporter covering the attacks, including myself, was then given a typescript of detailed guidance from the Chief Press Censor at the Ministry of Information. We would get a daily bulletin (so be 'in the know') and, in return, would stick to precise rules: we could talk only of 'bombs', not mention V1s or V2s, could not say where they had fallen or when ('recently' was as near as we were allowed to go), and could never mention the existence of a crater. Part of the motivation for the official manipulation was the great game of military deception played against the Nazi high command by the British, and no journalist wanted to let Hitler's military boffins get any information that would help their war machine become more efficient, but it was also part of the less justifiable tradition of deception practiced against the public, the belief that the only ones responsible enough to be in the know were those in power.

Soon I got the chance to see what *our* bombs had done. Alone in the newsroom on a Sunday morning in April 1945, I took a call from the Air Ministry offering the chance to go on a mercy mission to Holland where German forces had reduced much of the population to starvation. Could I be at the aerodrome with my passport that afternoon? As they could not guarantee the plane would not be shot down, I would have to wear military uniform in case of capture.

Aircrews had competed to be on these missions delivering supplies, even though none could be certain they would survive. My two pilots were Australians, both from Melbourne, but the rest of the crew, five of them, came from city streets around England that had felt the heat of Hitler's Blitz, including Jimmy Rowland, the 19-year-old bomb aimer from Eltham in south London whose job it was to make sure the sacks of food were on target. We were in Lancaster F for Freddie, the fourth off the ground at 5pm in bad weather, ready to drop enough food for over a million people for a day. The first mission had gone across the day before and had dropped just half the amount we were carrying. The English coast went beneath us at 1,500 feet as the rest of the squadron streamed around. Flying with 400 Lancaster bombers, I had no more idea whether I would be alive in a few hours' time than I had in the fighting at Madrid. Although I did not know it at the time, it was the day Hitler committed suicide.

Some of the crews ahead had to drop their cargoes in heavy rain. For us, the sun burst through the clouds as we passed over the Dutch coast. People were welcoming us as we flew over. From one small factory, hundreds were streaming out of the gates and cheering. Sheets, bunting of all colours, and orange strips guided us towards our target. Children cycling on their way home from school got off their bikes to take their handkerchiefs from their pockets to join this frantic waving and cheering as we dropped to just 50 feet above the ground. Then came the strange order over the intercom: 'Spam doors open!' Jimmy aimed the sacks round a white cross in the middle of the field. As I watched, the lump in my throat was nearly as large as the sacks that fell to the welcome below.

Days later there was another facility trip, care of Bomber Command, this time in brilliant sunshine over the 14 towns of the Ruhr, or rather what was left of this industrial heartland of Germany after three years' attention by these same bomber crews. At a height of 800 feet we crossed over Krefeld and Duisburg, then, flying roughly in a gigantic letter M, we covered Hamborn, Sterkrade, and Bottrop; Gelsenkirchen, Herne, Dortmund, and Bochum; Essen, Mulheim, Hagen, and Elberfeld, with the last lap bringing us across Remscheid, Solingen, and Düsseldorf. The briefing before the flight, from the RAF station at Wratting Common in the flat farmlands just to the south-east of Cambridge, had given us the names of all these towns making up the greatest industrial concentration in Europe, known ironically to the bomber crews as 'Happy Valley'. It had been Bomber Command's priority target, visited, we were told, by no fewer than 41,600 aircraft sorties, which had left behind them a grand total of 143,000 tons of bombs and a great deal of destruction. It was exactly what I had promised my French radio listeners.

Those were the figures. The results had to be seen to be believed. In the main city areas, the devastation was complete. The pilot took us in lower and the abomination of desolation stretched as far as the eye could see. First came Duisburg, the largest inland port in the world, with its great docks on the rivers Rhine and Ruhr now a wilderness of gutted warehouses, broken locks and deserted waterways. Sunken barges lay where they had been bombed at their moorings and already a green scum was beginning to form over them, mingling with the huge patches of oil that still covered the water. At the sprawling marshalling yards, rails, locomotives and trucks were piled in rusting heaps as if they had been flung together by some giant's hand. At the central railway station, great craters pitted the permanent way amid a jumble of smashed buildings. At nearby Hamborn, the great Thyssen steel works reared its ruins to the sky. At Gelsenkirchen, the centre of the synthetic oil industry, I could see the damage done to two of the most important plants, where what roofs remained were a patchwork of red tiles and rusting corrugated iron sheeting. We did not see any sign of life in the Ruhr until we got to Dortmund. There, from the piles of rubble, broken glass glittered in the sun in a myriad of points of light. The only undamaged buildings appeared to be two multi-storey air raid shelters in the centre of the town, and around them a few people were pottering about. Then, along the roads, many of them obliterated by debris and overlapping bomb craters, I could make out a number of small groups of people dragging a few belongings in pushcarts of various sorts. Otherwise the town was deserted in spite of the fine weather.

All this devastation paled into insignificance when we came to Essen, the largest town in the Ruhr and home to the Krupp armament works covering much of the northern part of the town, a site of over 2,000 acres. I recalled my French broadcast on the promised demolition as we flew over machine shops, rolling mills, steel foundries, and the great locomotive shop, reputedly the largest in Europe, all of which lay gutted. Not a building was undamaged. Acre upon acre of rusting metal stretched below, great girders lay in a crazy criss-cross

114 Back at the *Worker*

of torn roofs and the whole area was pockmarked with craters, completing a fantastic and horrible pattern. After that even Elberfeld, 97% destroyed according to the statistics I was given, seemed small beer. Only over the Rheinmetall-Borsig armament works at Düsseldorf did we see anything like it – 20,000 tons of bombs had been dropped in an attempt to cut off its contribution to the German war effort. There was a grim but deep sense of satisfaction in seeing the damage our forces had inflicted on the Nazi war machine.

My first opportunity back at big reporting on my own came a few months later. The Channel Islands were just about the last place to be liberated at the end of the European war, as the German garrison only surrendered *after* Victory in Europe. Home Secretary Herbert Morrison quickly visited the islands with a media circus in train, followed by the King and Queen. This was the only bit of British soil that had been under the Nazi yoke and myths needed nurturing, in particular, the myth that suggested sturdy Britishers would never turn into abject collaborationists, like some of the French, even when ground down by the heel of Hitler's jackboots. The press was prompted to run stories of heroic actions under the occupation of Island leaders such as Mr Alexander Coutanche, the Bailiff of Jersey, and CW Duret Aubin, its Attorney General. But Norman Le Brocq, the leading Communist on the island, wrote to the *Worker* editor and convinced him there was a story on what had really happened.

As soon as I had voted in the general election at the beginning of July 1945, I was on the ferry. I found the islands seething with discontent. Wherever I went on Jersey, the walls were chalked with the slogan 'Out with the States', the island's ruling body. People told me of the intimidation used against them if they joined the Jersey Democratic Movement (JDM), formed illegally under the Nazis and, in the weeks after liberation, the driving force for democratic change. Le Brocq painted a very different picture to the one in the press: not one of heroic resistance on the part of these establishment figures, but one of collaboration by the very same individuals. There *had* been a heroic resistance by the JDM, many of them Communists along with Red Army and Polish POWs and Spanish Republicans taken to the islands as slave labour, but they were not the ones getting the medals.

Stories exposing life on the islands under the Nazis were there for the taking. All I had to do was go to the office of the local Jersey paper, the *Evening Post*, and look through the back numbers. There one could see the orders of the German *Kommandatur*, printed over the signature of the Nazi occupation commander and counter-signed by the Bailiff or the Attorney General, on topics such as banning listening to the BBC, death if you were caught in possession of a bicycle, or orders to name Jews. The *Evening Post*, which printed the decrees of the occupiers, condemned the JDM and would not publish its manifesto, even as a paid-for advertisement. On neighbouring Guernsey, I found in the *Evening Press* an order from the Bailiff Victor Carey offering a £25 reward for information as to who was chalking the letter 'V' anywhere.

Human interest stories were something special to me as the *Daily Worker* correspondent. The people involved would not have talked to the rest of the media.

I spoke to Spaniards, for instance, who recounted how, under cover of darkness, they had tipped a particularly nasty German guard into the concrete they were laying. Le Brocq told me of two old ladies, White Russians, who had ended up in Jersey running a millinery shop, who agreed to hide two escaped Soviet POWs. Then there was the rich farmer's daughter who had formed a liaison with a German officer and was given a short back and sides when the war was over; she was living in fear of her life when I met her. The farmer's son, though, had been with the resistance.

What added zest to the material was a photograph I was given by my farmer friend showing Coutanche greeting the German commander as he arrived by plane. There was a group shot of SS officers being presented by the Attorney General with a small terrier dog. This all showed what might have happened had a Nazi invasion of Britain succeeded. Worse, the Bailiff and the Attorney General claimed they were acting under instructions from the British government in their collaboration.

The War Office, which had charge of the Islands, got more and more hot under the collar about what I was writing (although the stories were appearing without my by-line, as was the custom then) and issued a statement denouncing the *Worker* reports. The War Office HQ on the island summoned me for a dressing down. I simply made the point that I was just reporting what had been appearing in the local paper over the previous years.

Before I had set out for this trip, Barbara Niven, the organiser of the *Daily Worker* Fighting Fund, had told me that a woman on the islands had been sending a shilling a week to the paper for some years before the war. After liberation, when the mail was re-instated, she had written to Barbara sending £13, representing a shilling a week collected carefully across each one of the 260 weeks of the occupation. 'We are free at last', she said. Could I look her up, Barbara asked, thank her for her efforts and find out how she was?

After some asking around, I discovered that Cissie Cave worked as a cleaner at the offices of the Guernsey State Electricity Department in St Peter Port. I found her with a tin of polish in one hand and a duster in the other, cleaning the brasses on some of the fires on show. She quickly hushed me when I said I had come from the *Worker*. Rather than talking in front of her employer, she asked to me to go to her house the following day after she had finished work. For a woman whose only income was from a poorly paid cleaning job, saving a shilling a week for the paper's fund must have been a hard enough task, but to meet someone who had done so under the Nazi occupation from the summer of 1940 to that of 1945, left me with a feeling of deep humility. There had been real starvation on the islands under the occupation – potato peelings had fetched a more than handsome price. Yet week in, week out, she had added a shilling to the growing sum in the tin on her mantelpiece.

On my return to London, I was incensed when the new Home Secretary, Labour's Chuter Ede, backed the policy of collaboration and defended the administrators. Several of the leading figures on the islands were given

FIGURE 7.1 Pamphlet published in 1945 by the *Daily Worker* based on stories Sam uncovered about wartime collaboration in the occupied Channel Island.
Source: Family archive (courtesy of the *Morning Star*).

knighthoods. I turned the stories into a pamphlet, 'Spotlight on the Channel Islands', yet for decades the history of defiance and resistance vanished. In the 1990s when a new war crimes unit at Scotland Yard began to investigate the collaboration, it was clear the true story had long been suppressed, especially by the British civil service, and ignored in books on the islands. Britain had let down the islanders during the war, and the deportation of Jews and other islanders who were imprisoned, perhaps for listening to the BBC, had conveniently been forgotten.

On the home desk, it was generally a lot harder to get good original stories, which not only had political bite to them but were also news and were different to those of other papers. I reported mainly on health, education, and housing, and the home story I was most passionate about was the formation of the new National Health Service. It was a bitter battle between the British Medical Association (BMA), the powerful professional body of Britain's doctors, and the new popular mood for change. From the spring of 1944, when the wartime coalition government tabled the first official proposal for an NHS, to the end of the decade, it was my duty to attend every BMA meeting I could physically get to, every Ministerial briefing I could bluff my way into, and meet every official and politician with a possible story to tell who I could lobby, telephone or discretely buy a drink for. After the Health Service White Paper was published, BMA leaders announced they would call on doctors to refuse to co-operate with Aneurin Bevan, the Health Minister, and my splash intro was direct: 'War has been declared by the BMA on the Government, Parliament and people'.

At the BMA AGM that year, a consultant called Lawrence, who was dressed in a way that to most people would have been a caricature of a consultant – a morning coat with a carnation in his button hole, wing collars, and cravat with diamond pin – denounced Bevan's plans as 'state medicine'. His peroration was an elaboration of his own idea for what should be done instead of a national health service – 'total workers insurance for total sickness' – a gift to a journalist as the initials spelled out T-W-I-T-S, which I duly wrote up as 'a service for the twits of the nation'. When a Communist Party doctor, Sam Smith from Tower Hamlets, who had secured election as a delegate, got up to speak, ranks of delegates began stamping their feet making such a noise that he could not continue.

The great character in the whole debate was Charles Hill. From humble origins, he had a very earthy and popular touch and had become famous as *The Radio Doctor* from his wartime talks on the BBC when broadcasting rules meant he could not use his own name. His official post was General Secretary of the BMA, and later he became a Tory MP as well as heading both the ITV and BBC boards. Although he was against the NHS, at a personal level I got on well with him, picking up stories like his private confirmation in March 1945, before the rest of Fleet Street knew, that the wartime coalition's plan for the NHS had been abandoned. The diehards were confident they could kill the whole project, but the sweeping Labour majority in the general election dashed their hopes.

My feeling was that Bevan in the end gave way far too much in order to placate what was a very powerful and vociferous lobby. The Socialist Medical Association within the Labour Party had been working for years preparing plans for an NHS, and particularly for an industrial health service based on prevention, but most of their work was discarded because of the root and branch opposition to their proposals by the BMA. In such a situation, many will say that Bevan had little choice but to compromise but the consequences of that compromise have been with us ever since.

One that angered me greatly was the failure to push through the original proposals for health centres as community-based hubs for the promotion of good health. Churchill's personal physician Lord Moran declared at one BMA session in April 1945 that it would be 'years and years' before these centres would see the light of day. I was first with the news a year later that Bevan was intending to stick to the idea of setting up an initial wave of hundreds of these centres and I could write with real enthusiasm that the troglodytes of the private medical profession were getting slapped down. But it was not to be. The principle remained,

118 Back at the *Worker*

but the means were gravely weakened, and Lord Moran had the last laugh. By the end of 1947, I was running a rueful story that, out of 225 that had been planned for London, only four centres were to be created.

In the opening months of 1948, as we moved toward NHS vesting day on 5 July, Dr Guy Dain, the BMA chair, and Lord Horder, the King's physician, pushed within the BMA leadership for total opposition to the new service. Having built up good contacts within the BMA Council, I was able to give exclusive coverage to the fact that they were at last in a minority. So, when the post from Land's End to John o' Groats included pamphlets to every household in the country setting out what the NHS would be delivering, the profession accepted the change, even if, in many cases, with ill grace and a determination to keep their private practice on the side. That was far from the end of the battle. Without the health centres, NHS hospitals were over-stretched and the system was left picking up the patient after disease or accident had struck rather than pushing good health practice into every community and workplace. Worse, the NHS was trying to run itself on sweated labour, not the doctors, of course, but the nurses. As the NHS started up, for the first time in their lives nurses took to the streets demonstrating for better pay and conditions. I was with a group of student nurses from St Mary's Hospital in Plaistow who kicked off the protests, but soon it was a mass movement and I had dozens of nurses telling me of the circumstances in hospital after hospital. I felt a real pride in my work when two weeks after vesting day I could report a Health Ministry official saying of a decision to grant a pay rise: 'In view of the state of affairs disclosed by the *Daily Worker*, we thought it better to make the announcement immediately'.

Pay was not the only one of those arguments from the founding days of the NHS that never went away. The BMA employed a PR man called Colin Hurry, who affected a cravat with a diamond pin. Always very jolly with me, he would buttonhole me and complain about my articles. His refrain was simple, but it has persisted: the trouble with you Socialists is you want this all under the control of the state when really the way to help people have access to a good medical service is to see that they have enough money in their pockets so they can buy whatever medical service they want.

If I needed a reminder of why a health service was a thing to fight for, I got it when visiting the slums around London where health needs were equalled by those for decent housing. People there did not have enough money to put the food they needed in their mouths, let alone fill the pockets of Mr Hurry's medics. Blitzed homes were repaired at a slow rate, the work held up by inefficient private enterprise, spivs, and speculators. Thousands of families continued to live in ghastly conditions. The wartime government had promised 'a military operation to get the job done' but the reality was certainly no competition for the Normandy landings. Popular anger led to a unique squatters' movement, invading army bases and former refugee camps as well as some empty fancy housing in the middle of London. Communist Party local councillors and tenant activists organised this latter group of what came to be called the 'Duchess Squatters', named after the Duchess of Bedford House that was one of the mansions taken over in the summer of 1946. Accompanying a giant march that September of newly demobilised soldiers and homeless families and their supporters that stretched all along Oxford Street, I could hear tale after tale of desperation. Empty luxury housing was also being occupied in Willesden, Islington, and other London borough. Government departments were said to have enough empty housing on their hands, inherited from wartime arrangements, to immediately provide homes for some 10,000 families. Instead of opening those doors, Ministers denounced what they termed 'organised lawlessness' and set about having the leaders of the movement put on trial for 'inciting persons to trespass on property'. Tough police action and promises to build more homes brought the movement to an end.

Housing was for a while in the same ministry as health, and Nye Bevan started a system under which all local authorities had to prepare a monthly statement on the number of houses started, the number under construction and the number completed but the ministry did not regularly bring together the statements. The government, however, began claiming the housing problem had been solved, when I could still walk the parts of London I grew up in and find shored-up, bomb-blasted hovels with families waiting for decent homes. In November 1948, the ministry asked each council to send in its waiting list figures but only after having written to everyone on the list to find out if they were still waiting. The trick was that, if the council did not get a reply, it was to delete the name. The councils were meant to have sent in their statistics by the end of March 1949. Months went by and the ministry kept refusing to divulge the results. There were some 1,400 housing authorities across Britain and I decided in the quiet moments of Christmas week that we should write to a comprehensive selection of each type of local authority to get the latest monthly statistics. It was hard work and, for those days, an unusual approach among newspapers but, in the end, we got a large number of responses, which showed that any such claim was totally false. Following cuts in funding for house building announced in October, I estimated that, at the rate of house building now proposed, it would take nearly 12 years before those on the existing lists would be housed. It gave me a series of articles and a front-page Saturday splash.

Despite the MI5 delusion that I was a Soviet sleeper, I was allowed to attend the first open day for the press at the Harwell atomic research centre in March 1949.[2] We were told that a low-powered atomic pile had turned out enough plutonium to produce an atom bomb. As we walked around, a Ministry of Supply official told me that when it came on stream it would be able to produce enough for a new bomb once every 25 days. Which horrifying thought gave me a front-page splash covering the resources being put into weaponry while the Chancellor of the Exchequer was looking to cut state expenditure and keep wages frozen. Did this mean that Marshall Aid was really Martial Aid, as one factory worker I spoke to at the time asked?

120 Back at the *Worker*

Marshall Aid was the US programme of loans designed to refloat the post-war economies of Europe but doing so on the basis that Washington wanted. Stalin had made the countries of Eastern Europe opt out. In February 1949, Washington had sent all the governments getting its aid a 'request' that they clamp down on trade with the East. When I got wind of the story, I chased from one Whitehall department to another, each one passing me on to the next. By the end of a hard day's work on the phone, I knew that the Board of Trade was about to issue a long list of items that could not be sold, mirroring the restrictions Washington had imposed on US industries. That was why Soviet orders for engineering goods that could be turned out by British factories were caught up in the delaying tactics that the British civil service could deploy at the drop of a bowler hat. The problem that I tried to underline was that British engineers could not find the markets they needed for their exports so Britain could earn the cash to import the food we needed when in fact there were governments prepared to provide the food exports and take the engineering goods, only they were in Warsaw, Moscow, and Prague.

East-West trade was a subject I banged away at in the paper, highlighting the seesaw nature of our government's approach. In February 1948, I had gone to Millwall Dock, which handled most of the grain brought to the Port of London, for the first cargo of grain from the Soviet Union in ten years. Rationing continued after the end of the war and the food situation was not at all good. A Board of Trade official had told me the year before that the Soviet Union was offering a million tons of wheat, if Britain was prepared to buy. There followed months of haggling over the price. The Board claimed Moscow wanted to charge too high a price only for me to be able to point out in the paper that wheat prices on the Chicago spot market were by then even higher. This shilly-shallying over trade with Russia particularly annoyed me as the Board's officials seemed at the same time to be doing a lot to promote trade with Franco Spain. However, the minister in charge, the future Prime Minister Harold Wilson, eventually flew off to Moscow and signed a deal. The Ministry of Food started chartering British freighters in January 1948, but there, in Millwall Dock at 8am on a February morning, it was a Soviet ship that was disgorging a golden rain of maize into the barges waiting alongside. A crowd of some 200 had gathered to cheer Captain Ivanov and the crew of the *Baku*, which included, I noted, a woman doctor. The dockers handling the cargo thought it was good, but the grain brokers' representatives were a lot more cautious. 'Never judge a sausage by its skin, nor a cargo by its top layers', was their motto intoned to me by one. Luckily for Soviet prestige and my stories, the lower layers proved good and the holds of the *Baku* were quickly sucked empty. Even so, I was able to show that in the first half of 1949 we took more imports from Franco Spain and its colonies than we did from the whole of Eastern Europe and the Soviet Union put together.

In the years after the end of the war and before the Cold War really set in, the *Daily Worker*, thanks to the Soviet Union's role in the war, had a much higher standing than ever before. As journalists, we were treated as a proper part of the newspaper trade, and the paper itself was expanding in its ambition. The idea that things were going to change fundamentally in post-war Britain gave rise to what was very soon shown to be a grossly mistaken, over-blown plan for the paper's future on the part of the editor, Bill Rust.

The major change was in the ownership of the paper. It had been created by the Communist Party in 1930, though it was technically owned by a small company, Keable Press Ltd. Now, war time feelings of popular unity led to the idea of the People's Press Printing Society (PPPS): a co-operative of individual members and labour movement organisations that could take over ownership of the paper from the Party so the *Worker* could be a voice of the wider movement. There was already an advisory Editorial Board with prominent names such as the playwright Sean O'Casey, the actress Beatrix Lehmann, the Dean of Canterbury Hewlett Johnson, and the scientist JBS Haldane, one of the best writers the *Worker* used, and the idea was to build on this broader appeal even though real control would remain with the editor, always a member of the Communist Party leadership.

Formation of the PPPS was announced in September 1945. 'The only paper owned by its readers' became our proud boast, emblazoned underneath our masthead and later in a huge banner on a new building in Farringdon Road on a site acquired in the summer of 1946. Many of these new owners we never heard from, but others were very active, and the PPPS gained its 25,000th member by October 1948. You could buy a share, attend an annual general meeting, take part in debates and pass resolutions on the content and conduct of the paper and, in the process, have a pretty direct go at those of us working for it. On the one hand, these reader activists were vital to us. They sold the paper where they worked or in the streets where they lived at the weekend. They paid into our Fighting Fund. Some were also our 'worker correspondents' phoning in stories from strikes, union conferences, tenants' mobilisations or football matches. They were constantly harried to get more readers, a task that was never ending. But, on the other hand, just as we did not let them relax for a moment, they might equally have a go at us, and those most likely to do so were those who were also the most committed to the idea of a *political* rather than a *news*paper.

As a result we were in a constant battle with ourselves over the kind of paper we wanted to produce. Our model was never *Pravda*, the Soviet Party daily paper, as some cynics might have thought; it was always the best of the Fleet Street competition, even though we were only too well aware that, in the words of Alan Hutt, our Chief Sub-Editor, 'much of the news we handle is somebody else's propaganda'. We determined the *Worker* should never be a propaganda sheet of interest only to the most committed, but should be livelier, more popular and interesting, as well as giving the news on the political and trade union issues of the day. There was Alf Cayton, our racing tipster, an asset we boasted of constantly – for decades he scored more winners than those

122 Back at the *Worker*

working for our Fleet Street rivals. We had cooking columns, nature notes, sports reports, radio and book reviews, travel features: everything a complete newspaper should have.

Being like other newspapers brought other troubles, though. When one of our chief sub-editors, Reg Weston, was sacked from the staff, he went to the National Union of Journalists (NUJ) to state formally that we were not being paid the union minimum rate, as claimed publicly by the paper, but a lower Party rate. The NUJ had a strict policy: members had to be paid at least the agreed minimum rate for their sector. The Communist Party firmly supported this approach when it came to anywhere other than the editorial and admin staff of the *Worker*. Reg's move came at the height of the Cold War and bitter battles followed in the union's Central London branch in which I, as Father of the Chapel (shop steward) of the *Worker*'s editorial staff, defended the paper's position as best I could.

Eventually, a formal union inquiry determined that every NUJ member had to receive at least the union minimum but that what individual members then did with it was their own affair. From then on *Worker* journalists would 'covenant' back to the paper the difference between the union minimum and the Party wage. This left us with a pay so poor that we all had to take jobs on the side or depend on much better-paid spouses. Some worked for trade union journals, others for the media in the Socialist countries, such as Warsaw Radio, which I did stories for. The disadvantage with the latter was that the currency in which I was paid was not convertible and could only be spent in Poland.

We had a new Goss rotary press, which had a capacity beyond what anyone else was then producing, but, as paper rationing was eased, a right-wing campaign against advertising in the *Worker* hit our income just as other papers began to increase the number of their pages significantly. The growing confrontation between the Western allies and the Soviet bloc meant we steadily lost sales, and when, many years later, the Goss press was sold, it earned a reasonable price because it had never been used to its full power.

To accommodate the new press we settled on a Victorian warehouse previously used by a brush manufacturer at 75 Farringdon Road. This was just outside the traditional area for national newspapers in Fleet Street but still convenient for the railway stations we needed to use to get copies out across the country. Ernő Goldfinger, one of the leading modernist architects of the day, a left-winger who had designed the British Party headquarters in King Street, was brought in when it was found the building was not as structurally sound as had been thought.

To welcome the first Farringdon Road issue of 1 November 1948 crowds arrived from midday the day before and spilled over into surrounding streets, filling the nearby Clerkenwell Green – famous for us because Marx House is there, the building where for a few months Lenin had edited the Bolshevik paper *Iskra* or Spark. Many of our readers wanted to see whether their sales efforts and Fighting Fund contributions had been put to good use in what was described as the 'most modern newspaper building in Britain', and requests came in for visits to the paper. As one of my reporting responsibilities had been to cover the conversion of the warehouse into the new building, I was asked to provide conducted tours for special visitors. These became something of a feature of life at the paper.

In those days, newspapers buzzed with physical and mechanical activity. Hot-metal typesetting and plate making for the giant print machines was exciting to watch, and an example of workers acting in close co-ordination with each other to turn a product round in double quick time. From the typists in the stenographers box, the 'copy' would move through the hands of a 'copy taster', whose job it was to sort out the good stories, and a news editor, whose job it was to co-ordinate these with the work of our own reporters, then to a chief sub editor, who had to decide how it all might fit into the page, and then to a sub editor, who had to correct, rewrite and 'mark up' the 'copy' so the linotype operators would know how to 'set' it in metal, one line at a time, and fit it into what space there was, all that in just a few minutes. The slugs of metal were then assembled in a rectangular 'form' that was the size of the final page, which was used to create a mould from which to make the plates for the print machine. When it ran on full speed, that press made the whole building shake as well as filling it with the smell of hot lubricating oil and ink. It could be as little as 15 minutes when edition times were pressing and the planes, trains or vans were waiting for the first copies, between the moment a stenographer could start taking a story from a reporter like me to the appearance of the first copies. To add to the atmosphere, news agency 'copy' arrived by ticker tape machines and teleprinters that clattered away the whole day and night. If you were in the newspaper trade, there was no end to the noise. It was compelling enough for those of us on the inside; it must have been exciting for our visitors.

The idea of official visits had arisen when the 'Red' Dean of Canterbury Hewlett Johnson ceremonially started the new presses. The relevant print union, NATSOPA, which was very right-wing, would not allow him to press the start button as that was a job for their members. Nor would they give him a special temporary membership card, saying his application for union membership had gone in too late. So the Dean just tapped a NATSOPA member on the shoulder who then pressed the button.

The machine room staff who were not hired for their political affiliation were not always on the best of terms with the Party editorial staff, and the solid wall of pornographic pictures in their locker room did not always make it easy with visiting delegations that happened to catch sight of it. On one trip, I had to escort Lady Moorea Hastings, a left-wing aristocrat in her early twenties who later married the right-wing politician and journalist Woodrow Wyatt. Wearing a full-length luxurious fur coat, she exuded waves of the latest Paris perfume, something unprecedented in a newspaper machine room. Her visit earned me the jeers and the leers of those men for many years after.

FIGURE 7.2 Programme for the *Daily Worker* twentieth anniversary dinner and dance. *Source*: Family archive (courtesy of the *Morning Star*).

Another memorable visitor was Nnamdi Azikiwe, the future president of Nigeria always known as 'Zik'. He and his colleagues helped us with stories from within the country on the horrors of colonial rule and the struggle for independence. Already an influence in his own land, he came in with his robes and his bodyguard, and that evening it was my responsibility to act as the host. The linotype operator set his name in metal and the slug was still surprisingly hot when it was dropped into his hand. He jumped and the bodyguard looked as if he would deal severely with all of us immediately. The visit, however, must have left some favourable impressions. When Independence Day came for Nigeria, an invitation arrived at the paper saying the new President particularly wanted the gentleman who conducted him around the *Daily Worker* to represent the paper at the celebrations, if possible. Everything was laid on and I got some tropical gear – the heat when I got out of the plane and stepped on to the tarmac hit me in the face like an oven.

The chief celebration on 1 October 1960 was held on the main racecourse with be-wigged and be-robed dignitaries sweating away. At the table with me was Kingsley Martin, then still editor of the *New Statesman*, and Bernard Levin of the *Times*, carrying on in his usual snotty, bombastic style. In his speech at the reception, Zik went out of his way to mention DN Pritt, the prominent lawyer close to the Party who had taken up many court cases for liberation leaders in Africa, and me. The President had, he explained, invited from all parts of the world 'agitators and troublemakers' whose life's object was the betterment of human existence, and among those was the representative of the *Daily Worker*. He told of his visit to the paper and how he wanted now to see a 'spirit of inquiry' among young people in Nigeria, adding: 'Anyone who is an intellectual or politician who has not read the works of Karl Marx is a political illiterate'. In reality, Zik was far from sharing my politics, and Nigeria, like other African states formed on the boundaries of the old colonies, did not fulfil its early promise. Land reform came to little, the models offered by the Soviet Union and its allies proved more often damaging than appropriate, entrepreneurs moved in, corruption was terrible, and a bitter civil war around Biafra all meant that, for much of the time, colonial authority over Nigeria was replaced by a mediocre military dictatorship rather than by democracy.

Notes

1 For Sam, Cockburn's most memorable achievement was his exposure of the Cliveden Set of pro-fascist appeasers in the 1930s at the heart of the English establishment but he also found him 'a phoney self-promoter' whose brand of journalism – 'that it was better to lie than tell the truth if necessary because the cause was more important than the truth' – seriously harmed the cause, particularly as regards Spain.
2 Sam in his turn believed MI5 had a stooge at the *Worker* and hit upon Douglas Hyde, the news editor, for whom Sam would occasionally deputise. When Sam told the editor, Bill Rust, of his suspicions, Rust gave him a dressing down, then not long after, in March 1948, when Sam was due a day off, the phone range and it was Rust telling Sam he was right. Hyde had 'done a bunk' and became a notorious Catholic anti-Communist. Sam said Hyde later appeared at meetings of the International Brigade Association and made some kind of atonement, giving money to the Communist Party Library and placing advertisements in the *Morning Star*, successor to the *Daily Worker*.

8

BELIEVING THE UNBELIEVABLE

For me at the *Worker* in the years after the war had finished, my desire to move on from the home desk resulted in other options being mooted. I was even to have gone back to Paris – my bags were packed and everything was ready but the posting was cancelled by the editor without explanation. There was a short stint of only a few months in the Parliamentary Lobby – where I remember meeting secret Communists who were Labour MPs, like Stephen Swingler, brother of the writer Randall who was at the *Worker* – before being replaced by a comrade who was regarded as more reliable. Then, in May 1950, just a few weeks before the start of the Korean War, which isolated the paper in a way not seen since the Nazi-Soviet pact, I was appointed Diplomatic Correspondent and my destiny was shaped.

Being Diplomatic Correspondent meant exactly the same approach was expected of me when it came to my relationship with government as had been the case when I had briefly been Parliamentary Correspondent. Short as my time was at Westminster, it had put me on the inside of the 'Lobby', that mysterious, restricted group of journalists who were accredited to Parliament and shaped the way papers reported government actions and opinions. The trick from my point of view both at Westminster and the Foreign Office was not to get taken in by the spoon-feeding, but not to push matters so far that I might be excluded from the feeding trough. I had to learn the rituals and the incantations, the ways things could be written to hint at who was saying what without naming names. In return for the little extra bits journalists got in these briefings, they were happy to abide by the rules of the game, which meant that 'off the record' remarks by ministers in special private briefings or by officials could be reported directly by journalists as fact or as their own opinion, rather than the tendentious statement of a government figure. The overall effect of the system was to enable

DOI: 10.4324/9781003243380-9

successive governments to put out their messages in ways that made it appear as if the message was coming from an independent media rather than a self-interested government. Nowadays it is called 'spin'.

The difference, I discovered, between the 'mere reporting' that most journalists went in for and the mysterious and magical arts of the lobby correspondent was protecting one's informants. The principle drummed into your head as a starting journalist that the story should set out 'Who, What, Where, When, How', was here to be brushed aside when it came to the 'Who'. Further, you had a duty to protect the lobby system itself. No matter how many times I might walk under the splendid arch into the courtyard of George Gilbert Scott's nineteenth-century palatial offices where the Foreign Office resided, each visit I made as a member of the FO lobby group had to remain a supposedly delicious little secret between me and its masters.

The situation remained the same when I became Foreign Editor in 1953 and subsequently attended several Cold War conferences on East-West relations, whether focusing on the status of Berlin or disarmament, but at one conference – in Geneva in 1959 – I decided to expose the charade.

At this conference of Foreign Ministers of the 'Big Four' – the US, Britain, France, and the Soviet Union – in addition to the set-piece, open daily press conferences and briefings given by the media head of each delegation, there were also closed sessions. These formed part of the 'off-the-record' briefings for different and jealously guarded 'lobbies' of journalists, a system based on a recognised pecking order. As a journalist writing for a paper like the *Worker*, I was half in and half out.

Few of the 'in-crowd' journalists, nicknamed the 'Trusties', bothered with the general briefings because they had their own individual and separate sessions. In Geneva, the general drill for the British was slightly different to the London set-up because there was not time to hold as many separate briefings and allow all the journalists concerned to meet their deadlines. Instead, the privileged few – me not included – came together as one group after the main briefing, which did include me.

At a moment of deadlock in the talks, journalists from different countries were sitting around the enormous horseshoe bar of the Maison de la Presse, swapping ideas on what they might lead their stories on, when suddenly WN Ewer of the *Daily Herald* appeared. Known as 'Trilby' Ewer, he was the self-appointed doyen of the British foreign correspondents.[1]

'Come on you chaps', he shouted, 'time to go to the briefing'.

It was the call for the British reporters to file over to the Beau Rivage Hotel and get the line from the British government officials. A magnificent hotel on the shores of Lake Geneva, the Beau Rivage had been used as an HQ by British delegations since the days of Lord Curzon in the 1920s. I had never been invited to these private briefings but Willy Forrest of the *News Chronicle*, a friend since our days together in Spain, said I should go along. So I did.

128 Believing the Unbelievable

'Colleagues' like Nicholas Carroll from the *Sunday Times* and the BBC diplomatic correspondent Tom Barman, a British intelligence man, had a distinct air of disquiet as the briefing got under way and several others present were glancing at me quite obviously. I assumed they were worried in case my unauthorised presence might deny them juicy nuggets of information. As it turned out, nothing of consequence was said, whether because of me or not I do not know. Eventually we dispersed.

Later at the same horseshoe bar, Trilby came up and asked me for a 'word'. He took me across the road to a different bar, which claimed to be another one of Lenin's pubs. (They seem to be scattered around the various cities of the world where he was a refugee, like The Crown in London's Clerkenwell Green just off Farringdon Road.) With Trilby I found myself embroiled in a Kafkaesque conversation. His admiration for me apparently knew few bounds, but there was a bit of a problem when I attended something like the briefings between the British government officials and the diplomatic correspondents. 'It creates great difficulty for us', he said. 'It's nothing against you. But it's the chaps of the Foreign Office. They might well think that anything they tell us off the record you might go and report it to...'

'... Kensington Palace Gardens?' I interjected helpfully, giving the location of the Soviet Embassy in London.

'Something like that', Trilby said. I was fed up with this and told Trilby I reserved the right to report publicly anything further he might say to me. I had come to Geneva to do a job and either I was treated on the same basis as other correspondents or I would reveal what was happening to deny me my right to do my job. He went on and on trying to press the point that he had nothing against me personally, which only irritated me even more, and I went off for a bite to eat.

When I got back to the Maison de la Presse bar, Peter Hope, head of the News Department at the Foreign Office, came on the phone for me. Obviously very concerned to pacify me, he kept mentioning Carroll and Barman, who certainly had not wanted me at the briefing.

'Say whatever you have to say to my face', I declared. So we met, and Hope also went on in the same vein as Trilby: 'Look Sam, we have nothing against you personally...' So I told him, as I had Trilby, that I reserved the right to use publicly anything he might then say to me.

I showed Willy Forrest the piece I had determined to write exposing the system, which included him. I had named the names and found myself saying, 'Look, I have nothing against you personally...' He said he had no objection and that he would have done the same in my position. The story carried the headline: 'Trilby's Troupe of Terrible Pterodactyls'. It created a sensation in the small pool of political journalism.

The following day the word spread among correspondents from around the world and they came looking for copies of the *Worker*. Like me, they were fed up with the special treatment given by the Foreign Office to the inner circle of British correspondents. The ludicrous position was arrived at where I ended up being given a separate briefing with Hope all to myself. What was said to me may well have been quite unlike the points made to the others.

I would not accept that Carroll and his colleagues, whatever their views of me, had been the ones responsible for my earlier exclusion. I believe Trilby had been acting as Hope's stooge, which was not surprising.

My one-to-one arrangement with the FO persisted in a haphazard way for some years. On one occasion when Sir John Russell was head of the Foreign Office News Department and we were at a conference in Paris, I was waiting dutifully, ready for his dulcet tones after he had given his briefing to the main group. Finally, when he saw me he apologised. He had forgotten all about me.

'Now that you have thrown your pearls of wisdom to the swine who have just departed, am I not to get the benefit also?' I asked. He protested that he had to get changed for a formal occasion but invited me to his bedroom to talk while he got dressed for the dinner and told me of the earlier exchanges around the ministerial tables as he pulled up his trousers.

Reporting the Show Trials

As soon as I had become became Diplomatic Correspondent in May 1950, I had faced another kind of 'spin', which I failed to expose and which played a much more important part in my life.

During an editorial executive discussion just after my appointment, the editor's secretary came in and whispered in his ear. The Czechoslovak Embassy had been on the telephone. There was a very important trial starting the following day. It was essential somebody report it for the *Worker*. The trial would prove a group of Social Democrats were enemies of the new Czechoslovakia. The editor said I should go; a plane was ready on the tarmac and it would wait while I picked up my things and went to the embassy. An official was waiting for me the moment I got out of my cab. Pavel Kavan, a Communist Party member, I knew from the war when he was in England as a refugee. We renewed our relationship after the war when he returned as a diplomat and I was chasing stories about trade. He was standing with the Embassy stamp ready to thump down on my passport. 'Now we've got the bastards, and we'll show them', he declared. 'We have all the evidence we need for this trial, proving they have been in touch with American and British intelligence'. An Embassy car took me at top speed to Heathrow.

A bit of background. After the defeat of Nazism, millions across Europe had shared in the great hope that a new beginning could be created. I had written about how people were trying to build a new Britain, but it all ended pretty quickly. Churchill had made his Fulton 'Iron Curtain' speech at the start of 1946 and had hinted the US should use its nuclear weapons against the Soviet Union. In 1947, Stalin established the Cominform with an elite group of Communist Parties, which did not include the British Party (whereas, before the war, the Comintern had included every Communist Party, however small or insignificant, but Stalin had dissolved it in 1943 when he looked to please his wartime allies). He

130 Believing the Unbelievable

decided to form the new bureau because more than a few leading Communists in Eastern Europe did not want to follow his policies of forced collectivisation of agriculture and the rushed development of heavy industry and armaments factories. Worse, some had expressed interest in getting a bit of the vast funds the US was putting on the table for European reconstruction. In a speech by the leader of the Soviet delegation to the Cominform's first meeting, Andrei Zhdanov spoke of a 'world divided into two camps'. By this time, the French and Italian Communist Parties were out of government while across most of Eastern Europe Communist Party leaderships had assumed complete control in place of alliances that came to power after the war.

For just a little while longer, Czechoslovakia had been different. Communists had gained 114 of the 300 seats in parliamentary elections there in 1946 and continued in a coalition government. Six months after Zhdanov's speech, through a 'constitutional coup' in February 1948, they 'persuaded' the President that, rather than call new elections, he should replace any ministers not prepared to dance to the Communist tune.

In June 1948, Yugoslavia was expelled from the Cominform and denounced as disloyal to the doctrine of Marxism–Leninism. Stalin moved to put the leaderships of all the East European Communist Parties under his control and to stamp out any 'nationalistic deviations', in other words, any attempt to create a society that did not look like a mirror image of the Soviet Union. The Hungarian leader Mátyás Rákosi was a particular ally in this.

The Hungarians who fought in Spain had named their unit after him. The political commissar for the unit was László Rajk who, after the fighting finished in Spain, had returned to Hungary and became the leader of a tiny Communist organisation that managed to survive under the local fascist regime of Admiral Horthy and then under full Nazi occupation. After spending 16 years in Hungarian prisons, Rákosi had been in Moscow during the war years, then returned to Hungary in the baggage train of the Red Army at the beginning of 1945. He got the top job, while Rajk became Minister of the Interior and then Foreign Minister. Rajk held that last post for less than a year before he was arrested, put on trial in September 1949 as an agent of the US, found guilty and executed. The paper's coverage of the trial accepted the official version, as did I. We took it for granted that such conspiracies existed. The challenge was to uncover who the actual traitors were.

What had been unearthed in Hungary must exist elsewhere, Rákosi declared in a private letter to the new Communist Czechoslovak President, Klement Gottwald, and named several leading Czech Communists as 'imperialist agents'. Gottwald either did not believe him or decided to move with caution. This I write with a lot of hurtful hindsight because, at the time, I accepted all the Rákosi arguments, along with the 'facts' put forward to defend them, and had no inkling of the terrifying machinations, tortures, and cruelty that lay behind the trials.

The first significant arrests in Czechoslovakia were in September 1949, but were not of Communist Party members. Instead, people from other parties were targeted. The following summer came the first trial of four Social Democrats on charges of treason, which was the reason for my trip. I had been to Prague before, for a few days in September 1948 for the International Trade Fair, one of central Europe's biggest trade events. Now I was to attend what came to be known as the Horáková trial after Milada Horáková, the chief accused, one of the leading figures in Czechoslovakia's main social democratic party and a former MP. She reminded me immediately of my history mistress at school, and, poor woman, seemed to be lost, never appearing to know where she was.

The trial was quickly over. It began on a Wednesday and ended on the Thursday of the following week. I reported it in detail. I even picked out for praise the 28-year-old prosecutor, Ludmila Brožová-Polednová, a worker who had been given a special course of legal training for the job, and I reported it relatively straightforwardly, as did the correspondents from Reuters and other international news agencies. Looking back, this may seem hard to accept, but many were deceived by what happened in the courtroom.

There were no physical signs of the torture that lay behind the defendants' courtroom performances, and I never suspected any. Two officers accompanied each of the accused. These I later realised were the 'rehearsers', that is the torturers-come-interrogators who took the defendants through the script for the trial until they were word perfect. The performance of the defence lawyers was poor, to say the very least, but on the face of it, the formalities of a trial were followed. The judges delivered four death sentences, including one on Horáková, who was hanged just three weeks later, and for the others decades in jail. Clearly, I was both foolish and wilfully blind to what was going on, but at the time I was convinced, as were other journalists in the courtroom who were not Communists like me.

My next experience came in the summer of 1951 when dozens of senior Polish military figures were brought before the courts in a series of cases, the key one of which I was invited to cover. Among those on trial were officers who had served with the British forces during the war, having escaped from Poland in the first weeks of the Nazi onslaught. Others had served with the Red Army. Some had fought on in Poland against the Nazis but under the flag of the Home Army, loyal to an exile government in London. There were a few who had fought under all three flags.

One of the aims behind the trials was to discredit the exiled anti-Communist leader General Anders but the trial I attended was mainly being used to build a case against Władysław Gomułka, leader of those Communists who did not think Poland needed to copy everything Stalin had inflicted on the Soviet Union. Everybody in Warsaw, and that included even me, knew he was being detained, under house arrest, if not in jail, though nothing had been officially announced. He had just disappeared from sight.

The main accused were three generals. The key question for the prosecution was: 'how come these officers of the Polish army, who had served with the

132 Believing the Unbelievable

British army, had not only been allowed to come back to Poland but very quickly had won leading positions in the new Polish armed forces?' The answer was obvious: because their appointments were officially authorised. 'But by whom?' was the pointedly posed follow-up question. Call the next witness: General Marian Spychalski, former Mayor of Warsaw and, up to the previous summer, Minister of Defence and a leading member of the ruling Communist Party. He also had simply vanished from public view and no one seemed to know what had happened to him. All eyes turned as he came in. 'Name? Number? Present address?' To which he replied, 'Prison'.

'Do you know the accused?'

'Yes'.

'Who authorised their appointments?'

'I did'.

'You must have discussed it with someone?'

'Yes'.

'Who?'

'Gomułka'.

There was a curt: 'No further questions', and out he went. The expected verdict was duly reached.

Spychalski and Gomułka were spared, probably in a bargain with Stalin and then by the dictator's death in 1953. They both emerged from prison after Khrushchev's denunciation of Stalin in 1956, Gomułka to resume the leadership of the Party and Spychalski back as Minister of Defence.

On visits to countries like Poland, I would be put up in a hotel with an ever-ready minder, an official who was meant to stay with me at all times and be my sole means of meeting and talking to any local people. If simultaneous translation were not provided at a trial, they would be at my elbow whispering. I, however, always wanted to go off on my own. It was not because I disagreed with them – I just never liked being told what to do. In Poland, I got an unofficial view of the country from a woman I knew in Warsaw through my work for Warsaw Radio. She went so far as to tell me that large numbers of people were in prison without cause. After inviting me to her house because her mother had been in Britain during the war and wanted to see me, she phoned on the day to say perhaps we should put it off. The local priest would be round and I might not like to be with him. A priest was no problem for me, and he spoke very good English. 'It is not for nothing', he said, 'that Poland is known in the Church, and has been known for centuries, as its most favoured daughter. Poland is always a faithful daughter of the Church'. Banging the table, he declared, 'I could tell you the names of Politburo members who, while they conduct the affairs of state, send their children to be confirmed at communion in villages far from where they live'.

I saw how powerful the Catholic Church was and realised that Stalin's re-organisation of Poland had made it even more homogenously Catholic, an important factor in the eventual downfall of the Communist Party there. During my visit I was taken around the Wawel Castle in Cracow when one of the Polish

Cardinals died. The authorities thought they would stop any large funeral and all trains to Cracow were cancelled. Huge barriers were put up. But people came from all over Poland and formed a crowd of tens of thousands that broke through the barriers. At the time, I could still put that down to the backwardness of much of the Polish population.

Another espionage trial the following year, in 1952, meant I was back in Czechoslovakia. This time it was of 14 leading Communists, including Party General Secretary Rudolf Slánský, who was accused of being the centre of a vast conspiracy against Socialism. The trial only lasted seven days and consisted of a series of confessions backed up by witnesses like Pavel Kavan of the London embassy, who, some six months later, was rewarded for his pains with a life sentence when he himself was prosecuted.

One of the accused, Otto Šling, secretary of the Party in Brno, was married to an English Communist, Marian. He had been wounded in Spain and had escaped to Britain after the Nazi occupation of his country. Otto and Marian, who had written articles for the *Worker*, were close friends of John Gollan, the future British Party General Secretary, and his wife Elsie; Marian and Elsie had been students together. She and Otto had come to the *Worker* offices at the end of the war and had written articles for the paper.

I knew personally another of the accused, Otto Katz. Using the name André Simone, he was part of the Comintern circle in Paris for some of the time I was there. One of the inspirational, but also completely unscrupulous, propagandists who worked for the Comintern, Simone/ Katz, had helped mobilise some of the Hollywood giants against Nazism and by all accounts inspired the characters Kurt Muller in *Watch on the Rhine* and Victor Lazlo in *Casablanca*, both anti-Nazi heroes. Now he was confessing to being a British spy and saying he had been recruited by none other than the playwright and composer Noël Coward when Coward was based in Paris working for British intelligence against the Nazis at the beginning of the war. Katz added that among those he had passed 'espionage information' to was the *Manchester Guardian's* man in Paris before the war, Alexander Werth, the author of powerful stories from the Russian front which he later collected into one of the most moving books about the sacrifices of the Soviet people in the struggle to defeat Nazism. I had read his stories during the war. They had been a source of great hope. Now he too was an anti-Soviet spy.

The trial was broadcast live on the radio almost in its entirety, and, I was told and I believed, was being listened to by workers at the factory bench. Certainly, all manner of resolutions and letters came from factories and workplaces across the country demanding the death sentence. It made me feel that the tone of outrage used by the prosecutors and the judges was something shared by the whole country.

The verdicts were delivered on the eighth day. There were 11 death sentences, including Slánský and Šling, and three of imprisonment for life. While I was on a plane back to London, the executions were quickly carried out in Prague's Pankrác Prison, where some of the executed had been held during the Nazi

134 Believing the Unbelievable

occupation and the Gestapo used to finish off its victims. Another seven major trials followed, and the last execution took place in 1954.

A major link between the accused in the Prague trial was that 11 of the 14 were Jewish. This was in no way hidden. All reporters at the trial were given copies of the indictment. Each of the accused had a characterisation printed against their names. These included things such as 'Jew', 'petit bourgeois' and so on. I should have understood what this meant, but it simply did not strike me at the time. Instead, I reacted to accusations run in the *Daily Telegraph* during the trial about its anti-Semitic nature, denouncing this as a 'stunt to hide spies' guilt', and adding a few days later: 'I can say categorically that all the allegations about "an outbreak of anti-Semitism accompanied by a wave of suicides of prominent Jews" (in Prague) are a pack of lies from start to finish'.

It so happened that Fritz Runge, my immediate boss when I was working in Paris for the Comintern, turned up, seemingly out of the blue. At my request, he arranged an interview for me with the Chief Rabbi of Prague, a Dr Gustav Sicher. On the Monday of the week that 11 of the accused were hanged, the *Worker* ran, as a front-page splash, the interview I had had with Dr Sicher. We had met in his offices next to a 1,000-year-old synagogue. The poor man denied all the *Telegraph's* claims: 'I would just point out', he said, 'that criminals can be of Jewish origin as well as non-Jews'. The extremity of some of the claims of those arguing that Czechoslovakia was home to rampant anti-Semitism, such as the alleged block on all Jewish religious practice, which was manifestly untrue, made it possible for me to believe the counter claims that there was no anti-Semitism. I quoted the porter at the synagogue:

> I, as a Jew, know that, if anyone did make an anti-Semitic remark, I would have the full support of the State Security Police in taking action against them – which is more than any Jew in Britain or America can say.

The *Worker* splashed on my interview, declaring it was 'the only paper to print the truth about the Czech trials'. My words, and the Rabbi's replies, went round the world, picked up by the Communist press and reprinted more times than I care to remember. When I returned to London, the British Party asked me to do a number of meetings on the trial. Margaret, my wife, came to one, much against her will. She was already not that convinced about the trial and, after listening to me, was even less so. After one meeting, a comrade, Chimen Abramsky, came to me privately because he recognised the anti-Semitism that was becoming apparent in the Communist movement (the so-called Doctors' Plot against Soviet leaders, which implicated several Jews, had just been denounced by *Pravda*). But if I were to accept the claim that trial victims were chosen on the basis of anti-Semitism, what was I to make of the fact that Rákosi, the man who started the series of trials, was a Jew, and that a key figure in his circle, Ernő Gerő, whom I knew from Spain, was also a Jew, as was of the Minister of the Interior in Poland and the Minister of Justice in Czechoslovakia at the time of the trials?

The penny only dropped a few years later when I was in Moscow. Johnny Gibbons, a British Communist living and working in the Soviet Union and who knew a great deal but had a habit of never saying much, arranged for me to meet the only surviving member of the Soviet Jewish Anti-Fascist Committee. We were to meet in the small park area before the Bolshoi Theatre. At the appointed time, I could not see him for the crowds gathered at the funeral of some military senior figure. When they dispersed, there he was, a very, very frightened man. He told me that motor car accidents had been arranged for two committee members in order to fulfil Stalin's wishes. The rest, apart from himself, had been rounded up and shot after a trial held in secret.

Margaret was not the only one uncertain about what I had been reporting. The Communist Party General Secretary Harry Pollitt, with whom I had always had a good personal relationship, asked to see me when I got back to London from Prague. I went to his room at the top of the stairs in the Party's King Street offices. He wanted something first-hand from the courtroom. 'What was it like in the trial?' he asked. 'How did Slánský conduct himself?' I started to reply, but he took me to the landing outside, presumably hoping to avoid whatever bugging he thought MI5 had installed. Harry listened to me for a while before interrupting.

'I knew Rudolph Slánský when I was in Moscow. I would never believe that he was a British or any other kind of spy'.

That Pollitt did not appear to believe the basic charge did not lead to either him, or me, changing the way we acted. It was, therefore, difficult reading when, in 1968, Marian Šling wrote in *Truth Will Prevail* of her interrogation and more than two year's detention, much of it in solitary confinement.[2] Yet she said that, up to Khrushchev's denunciation of Stalin in 1956, 'I had taken the "confessions" [by Otto and the others] to be a truly "Bolshevik" gesture of taking responsibility for damage unwittingly done'. She described 'the web of mystification blinding my vision' and how she 'ultimately came to believe he must be guilty. I convinced myself that it was my duty as a Communist to put personal feelings aside, to face things as a steeled revolutionary'. She concluded: 'I was a prisoner, physically and mentally, of those who had enacted the gruesome tragedy'.

Marian had not been physically tortured, and tough for me as her account was, it was nothing to the painful experience of reading Artur London's *On Trial*.[3] One of the three in the Slánský trial to escape a death sentence, he and his wife Lise had both gone to Spain to fight Franco, both had been in the French Resistance, and both had spent years in Nazi concentration camps. Back in Czechoslovakia, he had become Deputy Foreign Minister, and at the trial, she denounced him in a written statement, something which must have been of unimaginable pain for both of them. His book gives a detailed account of the calculated brutality used to break him down. I had realised by then that those who appeared in the courtroom as the accused, or as witnesses against them, were broken physically and mentally. They had been brought to a state in which they were prepared to accept detailed rehearsal for a fully scripted trial in which they condemned themselves as traitors

136 Believing the Unbelievable

to the cause they had sought to serve, most of them through the whole of their adult lives. I came to know Artur, who had to drag himself around painfully on crutches, but he never renounced his faith in 'Socialism with a human face'.

In his account he made clear the way in which the survivors of the International Brigades were an especial target. They were regarded as suspect simply because they had been in Spain. This was borne out, also in 1968, when I discovered that Czechoslovak Ministry of the Interior files, opened as part of the 'Prague Spring' that year, revealed instructions listing membership of the Brigades as equivalent to membership of a Czech fascist organisation. But back in 1953, though I had seen that victims like Šling and Rajk had been in Spain, I could point to the importance in the Rákosi clique in Hungary of Gerő, a leading figure in the Brigades who had upbraided me in Barcelona for complaining about my broadcasts that were never transmitted.

What linked the different trials, as well as anti-Semitism, was the way in which the masterminds behind them were able to twist into something suspicious the constant movement of Communist activists around Europe in the years between the October Revolution and the end of the 1940s. These people could be in jail and out of it. They put their lives on the line repeatedly, fought in Spain, worked for the Comintern in far-flung places, acquired double identities, smuggled money, people and publications across frontiers, lived lives that were often in illegality, and, above all during the Second World War, worked with those who, in other circumstances, had been their bitterest enemies, all in order to defeat the Nazis. Some, a very small minority, did spy for one side or the other (and in some cases for both). Most were, like me, political activists who thought they were doing their bit to change the world.

The Slánský trial, as it happened, had a beneficial personal consequence at the time: my promotion in the pecking order at the paper. Derek Kartun, the Foreign Editor, left in the wake of the trial. The reason he gave was a remark in the proceedings by Otto Katz naming Claud Cockburn as a British agent. It had been the only untoward moment for me in the courtroom. I included Katz's words in my telephoned report, and the editor got the worst of both worlds when he put the reference in the first edition but cut it out of the second. I did not believe Kartun's reason for leaving and thought he had decided there was no future on the *Worker* and wanted out. The editor called me into his office to tell me Kartun was not leaving in order to better himself, nor was he leaving because 'comrades of Jewish origin' were being removed from leading positions, and he did not want any speculation on the matter.

As usual, a farewell collection was taken, which was my responsibility as NUJ Father of the Chapel. Two bright sparks, Lew Gardiner and Leon Griffiths, asked me to explain why Kartun was leaving. When I said I could only repeat what the editor had told me, they coined the brilliant phrase 'No donation without speculation' and acted accordingly.

On Friday 13 February 1953, I took over as Foreign Editor but it was not my promotion that saved me from further stupidities. Stalin died just three weeks later. The day his death was announced, I had already arranged to meet a woman from the Soviet embassy. We got drunk on North African 'arak', which I have never drunk since. *Sotto voce* she said to me: 'He wasn't all he'd been cracked up to be'. However, Stalin's death was a moment of great emotion at the *Worker*. When the news came through, I had started to write his obituary. Luckily for what might have been left of my reputation in later years, I was taken off the job and the editor put pen to paper. A mere mortal like me was not sufficiently august a figure to take on such a task.

Stalin's corpse was hardly cold before things began unravelling. The Doctor's Plot, over which *Pravda* and I had foamed at the mouth in January, was suddenly nothing of the sort, and our man in Moscow, Ralph Parker, explained that 'the investigation into the charges against the doctors is seen as stemming directly from Beria's appointment as Minister of the Interior'. Three months later Beria, Stalin's head of the secret police, was himself arrested.

Trying to make my way through this maze in later years, I recall the intense paranoia on both sides of the Cold War, which affected my thinking. The same editions of the paper that carried my reports from Prague had stories on American attempts to conduct a witch-hunt among UN officials in New York, on the drive for absolute power by the apartheid government in South Africa, and on the burning of villages by British forces in Malaya and shootings in Kenya. Those ex-Brigaders in Prague were not the only ones to end up in court. In the US, John Gates, who later became editor of the New York *Daily Worker*, and Bob Thompson, a leading Party figure who had been wounded twice in Spain and went on to get a distinguished service cross for his role in the US Army during the war in the Pacific, were put on trial. Such things are no excuse for my gullibility, but they were real.

As were my feelings as an anti-Zionist – and a brief digression on anti-Semitism may help explain why I didn't change my mind on this until my days in Moscow. In the '30s, as an anti-Zionist, my view had been that fighting fascism alongside others was the way forward for the Jewish people in any one country and internationally. That was why I had gone to Spain, from where I wrote a Jewish friend that it would be impossible to establish a Jewish 'home' in Palestine as 'this must of necessity be based on British bayonets and on the subjection of the Arab peoples'. When the World War was over, the landscape had changed completely. The vast majority of European Jews had been murdered by the Nazis and their collaborators. Many of those still alive wanted only to go to Palestine. They could not face trying to resume their lives where they had been persecuted.

In 1948, I supported the *Worker* backing for British withdrawal from Palestine and the creation of a bi-national state bringing together Jews and Arabs, two separate states in an economic union that hopefully might join together in the not too distant future. But the Arab regimes, none of them in any way democracies, had no intention of allowing the Palestinian Arabs to set up their own state alongside the Jewish one, and used force to intervene. Washington recognised Israel on the first day after its declaration in May 1948, Moscow on

138 Believing the Unbelievable

the second. Zionist extremists of the Stern gang and Irgun, organisations that targeted ordinary Palestinian Arabs, assisted by the Arab invasion, helped create tens of thousands of Arab refugees, and the first UN resolution to be rejected by Israel was the one of autumn 1948 calling on the new state to accept the return of all the Arab refugees who wanted to go back to their homes. Instead, a different road was chosen by the new authorities in Tel Aviv. It was one that led to the war against Egypt in 1956, the Seven Days War in 1967 and, ever since then, the occupation of the rest of Palestine.

In the early 1950s, at the time of the trials, I was still an anti-Zionist, and I believed that the arguments of Zionists saying Jews did not belong where they were born but belonged in Israel, which had the right to speak in the name of Jews everywhere, was a profoundly reactionary argument and one that played into the hands of anti-Semites. I saw it more and more as an aggressive approach that, in turn, encouraged aggressive attitudes on the part of the Arab peoples and states surrounding Israel. So, I didn't change my mind.

In later years as Foreign Editor, I remained an anti-Zionist but was never enamoured of the Palestine Liberation Organisation. The first PLO leader Ahmad Shuqeiri wanted to shove all Jews into the sea, and in our silence we either condoned this attitude or pretended it didn't exist. The Israeli CP was very pro-Soviet too, especially over Czechoslovakia. Though Palestinian terrorism was totally unacceptable to me, I believed it was the policy of successive Israeli governments that put the security of the Israeli people at risk. I never got to visit the region but from the desk in London I wrote many articles warning of the consequences of Zionist expansionism, that is its desire to move the frontiers of Israel outward while seeking to draw in as many of the Jews of the world as it could, those from the Arab lands coming first in the '50s and '60s followed, in even greater numbers, by those from the Soviet Union. My view remained the same throughout: occupation and expansion would not guarantee the safety of the people of Israel. Whatever else I might have misjudged, I don't think I got that one wrong – though it gave rise to many a bitter argument with those Jews who were among my friends and even with some of my closest relatives.

But I also wonder: if I had been from central Europe, with my Jewish origins and as a Brigader, maybe I would have been put on trial and probably executed. And, maybe, I would have gone to the scaffold or before the firing squad still believing as I did at the time of the trials. I have sometimes supposed that I would have. It is certainly preferable to thinking I might have played the role of a determined prosecutor like the young woman Ludmila Brožová-Polednová I watched at work in Czechoslovakia. Unfortunately, at the time, I was a lot closer to being her than it is comfortable to remember.[4]

Notes

1 Ewer had been a Communist Party member in the very early days and had been in Petrograd covering the 1917 Revolution for the *Daily Herald*, interviewing Trotsky

on the steps of the Smolny Institute, the Bolsheviks' HQ at the time. Sam learned much later that Ewer had run a network of agents in the 1920s. When MI5 got wind of this, he was not prosecuted, and Sam thought that perhaps explained one reason why Ewer became so devout a 'trusty' of the Foreign Office.

2 Marian Šlingova, *Truth Will Prevail* (London: Merlin Press Ltd., 1968).

3 Artur London, *On Trial*, transl. Alastair Hamilton (London: Macdonald, 1970).

4 Ludmila Brožová-Polednová was tried and found guilty twice (in 2007 and 2008) for her part in the trial. She was pardoned in 2010, aged 89, while serving her prison sentence.

9

THE 'SECRET' SPEECH

By the time of the Berlin Foreign Ministers conference in 1954, it was already decided that I would take up the post of the *Worker* Moscow correspondent. The job was to last almost four years and for much of that time I was the only resident correspondent of a British national newspaper. It was my second university after Spain and despite all that was wrong there I learnt a lot and loved the city.

As soon as I knew of the vacancy I immediately put in for the posting and was accepted. My going, however, was delayed by various things, such as trips abroad for the paper, including one to China, travelling with a Labour Party delegation, on which I met the man I was replacing in Moscow, Ralph Parker, who did not seem at all put out at the impending change.

More importantly, Margaret was worried about what would happen to our then three-year-old daughter Ruth and about the arrangements to let out our London flat in a way that would make it available when we returned to Britain. There was also the issue of her career. She was better trained than me (and was qualified to become Chief Nursing Officer in London), and going to Moscow would interrupt, if not ruin, her career. However, I had taken the decision to go, and go we did.

When I finally arrived in Moscow in December 1955, Parker was covering a session of the Supreme Soviet, which still had some days to go, but the *Worker* editor insisted I take over right away. Parker stayed on in Moscow, where he eventually died, and worked for some other papers. Quite a few people presumed he was still the *Worker* man, and that created some awkward situations. I did not know this at the time but Parker, a KGB man, had written a book published only in the Soviet Union that included a fearsome attack on the British embassy in Moscow. As a result, he had become persona non grata at the embassy, which had probably figured out what his role had been. That made it difficult for him

DOI: 10.4324/9781003243380-10

The 'Secret' Speech   **141**

to do the sort of job both the paper and probably the Soviets wanted him to do. Moscow had agitated with the *Worker* for a staff reporter to replace him. It would not cost the paper because a flat and all facilities would be provided by the Soviets.

Looking back, it is hard to remember exactly what and how I heard things but it was becoming clear straightaway that Stalin's role was being questioned. There were rumours of people being released from the camps but nothing I could get hold of for a story. My Russian was not good enough to pick up what people were saying in the streets but there was a distinct atmosphere of expectation looking forward to the Party's 20th Congress, which was to be held in a couple of months. When I spoke to the editor, Johnny Campbell, on the phone during the first weeks of my time in Moscow, I remember saying in Aesopian language (because I knew we were being tapped) that we should be careful to lay off stories praising Stalin, though I was not clear in my own mind as to how he was to be challenged.[1] Campbell either was not interested or did not want to know what I was saying.

In a kind of dry-run, I had a story surreptitiously put my way not long after I arrived, which was mangled in London. My secretary Lyosha Lipovetsky told me he happened to pop into a bookshop and had, quite by chance, seen a booklet on the abolition of the Special Tribunal, which examined cases without the presence of the accused, and which, under Stalin, had been a key instrument of the terror. Lyosha was pretty obviously put up to tell me about it.

Having read through the booklet, I asked for an interview with the Procurator General Roman Rudenko, who had been the chief Soviet representative at the Nuremberg War Crimes hearings. I was surprised to get it because interviews with people of such rank were a rarity in those days. I was even more surprised to have the President of the Supreme Court Lev Smirnov sit in on the interview. Afterwards, he offered me a lift, and in the car told me he had been the State Prosecutor in Leningrad during the siege. I said they must have been difficult times. 'The most difficult problem we had', he replied, 'was cannibalism'.

I had not then heard of that, though there has been mention in the histories since. Ordinary people, he said, came to be able to recognise the look of people who had been indulging in it. The problem was there was nothing in Soviet law that made cannibalism an offence. 'The problem was also that evidence was hard to come by', he continued.

> When someone had died from starvation, the only really edible part of the body left was the liver, but just because a body had had its liver removed did not prove it was eaten for breakfast. Anyway, the whole issue of law in the siege was irrelevant. People were living in conditions worse than any prisoner could have endured, so what punishment would have been relevant, even if we could have proved what had happened?

At first my piece on the 'norms of Socialist legality' did not appear and then it did but only in much truncated form. I was fighting both the editor in London as well as the Soviet system, though I didn't see it like that at the time.

142 The 'Secret' Speech

During the Congress itself in February 1956, in the open sessions, there were plenty of hints, some very broad indeed, of what was to come but they were missed in London. When Anastas Mikoyan spoke, a key member of Stalin's inner circle for more than two decades, he had barely got into his stride before he was saying: 'For nearly 20 years we did not actually have a collective leadership because the cult of the individual ruled the roost with us'. The words formed the lead of the story I phoned in but I was told this could not lead the story 'because it would come as too great a shock to the readers'. The version in the paper buried Mikoyan's point on an inside page, bizarrely headed 'We too made foreign policy mistakes'.

Mikoyan also ran down Stalin's prize little volume, *The Economic Problems of Socialism*, a bible so far as Communists then were concerned. After I had filed my report, the deputy editor Mick Bennett came on the phone to say that Mikoyan had got it all wrong. I suggested he ring up Mikoyan and tell him. The report appeared without these references.

Pravda was then two days behind in its reporting of the Congress, as the paper did not have enough pages to report immediately the more than lengthy debates. None of the Western correspondents were allowed on the inside of the sessions and so they were reporting things some days late too. When *Pravda* got round to publishing the Mikoyan speech and Reuters put over the *Pravda* version, Bennett suddenly wanted the story, and lengthy extracts from the key points made by Mikoyan appeared on the *Worker*'s front page.

Khrushchev's 'Secret Speech' denouncing Stalin was something I knew about the morning it was made. No other foreign correspondent in Moscow learnt of it that quickly, but I did not know anything like its full import and unfortunately I missed what would have been a world scoop of the greatest importance – except the *Worker* would probably not have printed it. Within days, I realised its significance, and it changed my views and opened up new hope for millions.

Only Congress delegates and selected *apparatchiks* were there to hear Khrushchev and only a handful of his closest allies knew that he was going to let fly. As was usual for all Communist Parties, the last day of the congress was a closed session. Journalists like me, and the international delegates such as Harry Pollitt, had to fill in time elsewhere. Harry had invited me for lunch with the usual joking greeting he had given me ever since Spain: 'I suppose you are *still* hungry?'

To get from my own rooms to the flat he was using in Gorky Street, I had to walk across the huge open space of Red Square. Somewhere in the middle of that vast parade ground, I bumped into a Soviet journalist whom I had got to know quite well. I speculated that in the nearby Kremlin, Congress was merely going through the formality of electing a new Central Committee.

'On the contrary', he volunteered. 'I understand Khrushchev has just made a special speech'. When I asked what it was about, all he would say was that the Soviet leader had 'crossed the t's and dotted the i's on the question of the cult of personality'. 'Cult of the personality' was a phrase which was on everyone's lips in Moscow at that time as a coded reference to Stalin and his rule, so I knew what

The 'Secret' Speech **143**

he meant and that it might be important. 'Let me know if you hear any more', was my parting shot as I walked off. He said he would.

Once the guards let me inside the building, I was ushered into Pollitt's flat by the housekeeper. Harry was at a table with a few bottles and, more importantly, Nikolai Matkovsky, the head of the section in the Central Committee International Department dealing with the British Communist Party and those of the former British empire countries. Small as the British Party might have been in terms of its membership, in the world Communist movement it had a certain status as the Party in the country at the centre of a still powerful empire. Matkovsky I knew, and, unlike many of his colleagues, he was easy to get on with.

Pollitt teased me in a blusteringly cheerful sort of way:

> 'You're the great journalist, what is going on at the Congress? Just the elections I suppose?'
>
> 'As a matter of fact, Harry, I understand that Khrushchev has made another speech.'
>
> Matkovsky's eyebrows shot up. When I added that it was a matter of crossing the t's and dotting the i's on the cult of personality, the eyebrows nearly took off, though whether at the news, or my knowledge of it, I do not know.
>
> 'Ha,' he mocked, 'Sam Russell, the *Daily Worker* eagle!'
>
> 'Not an eagle,' I hit back. 'Only an ordinary sparrow hopping around and picking up a few crumbs that fall off the table.'
>
> Pollitt quickly switched the conversation onto more mundane matters and we proceeded to eat. He left Moscow the following day.[2]

Within a week of the end of the Congress, two British colleagues working in Moscow, Dennis Ogden and Johnny Gibbons, called saying they needed to meet me urgently. They had been invited to take part in a meeting of the Communist Party members at their workplace, the Foreign Languages Publishing House. This was the first time they had ever received such an invitation. The Secretary of the Party Committee there had read out what he said was the text of a speech by Khrushchev. No notes were to be taken and no questions would be allowed.

Dennis and Johnny were able to give me a full report. It was the sort of speech you remembered, whether or not you took notes, and Dennis came with five foolscap pages already typed up from memory. Though I had been fore-warned of the subject, I was astounded by the content. It was a moment of truth for all of us as Communists. Stories about the speech began leaking and the rumour mill in Moscow was alive. Given that there were similar meetings across every workplace in the Soviet Union and in all the localities where there was a Communist Party organisation, this was inevitable. Khrushchev needed to act quickly in order to gather support for his move. Within a fortnight of the end of the Congress, millions of Soviet citizens had heard that their world was being turned upside down. It is hard to think of any parallel in history.

144 The 'Secret' Speech

John Rettie of Reuters told me he had heard rumours about the speech and had tried to get stories through to his agency's main office in London, but could not. All his references to the 'secret speech' had been blue-pencilled, and he knew that if he tried to restore them, his phone call would have been cut off. Full censorship covered reports phoned over by all the foreign correspondents but it was ended for correspondents from Communist Party papers some months before I got to Moscow. Rettie told me he would be taking leave a fortnight or so later and I knew immediately this meant he would send a story as soon as his plane landed outside the Soviet Union.

This was probably the most sensational story I could ever expect to have in my lifetime as a journalist. But it was also a dagger at the heart of what had up till then been the central beliefs of the world Communist movement, and I was a journalist who saw his work as part of his practice as a Communist. If I could not say I had the approval of the Soviet comrades for what I was sending over, how was I going to get my story accepted by the comrades in London?

Raising hell to try to get some movement on it, I asked my secretary to ring Mikhail Suslov, the Politburo member with ultimate responsibility for the International Department of the Soviet Party. Lyosha assured me there had never been any such speech. He would definitely have heard of it. Given that half of Moscow was by that time doing nothing other than talking about the speech, he must suddenly have developed a particularly acute case of cloth ears. And, of course, he would already have attended one of those 'inner party' meetings to receive the report back on that speech. Lyosha did, reluctantly, agree to ring Suslov. Word came back from Suslov's secretary that the message would be passed on. Nothing happened. I told Lyosha to phone again. No answer. I insisted on a third call. Lyosha, white as a sheet, said he was in terrible trouble and that the reply was 'Don't ring us, we'll ring you'.

Not getting anywhere, I went to see the head of the Foreign Ministry Press Department, Leonid Illychov, and told him I knew of the speech. He chose to argue with me in a silly way. 'I don't know what you are talking about', was his stonewalling reply. There were stories going around Moscow about this speech, I reminded him, and sooner or later it was going to get out. Better to put it out sooner, and through friendly sources, than have someone else spill the painful beans. He was not interested. Reuters had the story, I said, but it was being cut by the censors.

'Censors? What censors?' asked Illychov.

'If Rettie does his minimum duty as a Reuters correspondent', I said, 'the moment he arrives in Stockholm he is going to unload this story, or as much of it as he knows'.

Illychov turned to me: 'Well, what do you want me to do? Stop him from leaving?' That was not the point, I argued. 'The speech has been made. Your Party has made it. All your attempts to conceal it are not going to succeed. It is going to come out and we in the foreign Communist parties are going to have to deal with it. And, in that situation, we should try to deal with it first'.

The 'Secret' Speech **145**

He just shrugged his shoulders and said, 'I'm afraid there's nothing I can do to help you'.

Later on, I discovered he had sent a report to 'my friends' – the International Department of the Soviet Central Committee – saying I had come to his office drunk, smelling of vodka and making a *bolshoi skandal*, a great scandal or scene.

The following day, I asked Lyosha to get back to Suslov's office. Much against his will, he eventually did so.

'I was told not to bother them again', he pleaded. 'You will get me into a lot of trouble'.

'Either you call that office or you don't come back to work for me', I said.

When he was on the phone his face went white. Lyosha told me only that the reply had been along the lines of Sam Russell will get all he needs to know from the comrade he usually sees at *Pravda*. This was *Pravda* Foreign Editor, Yuri Zhukov, a deputy editor of the paper. As I had been Foreign Editor before leaving for Moscow I thought I could pull rank but it turned out to be of no help at all. He had been *Pravda*'s correspondent in Paris and spoke very good French, which meant we usually talked in French rather than English. He greeted me with a show of friendship, asking why I had come.

Hadn't the Central Committee people told him, I asked. Well, yes, he said, it was about Khrushchev's speech. Before my hopes were raised, he started to give me a summary of the public report Khrushchev had made to the Congress. He knew full well that I had sat through the whole thing in the Congress hall, but proceeded to repeat the details of pig iron production, house building and crops of wheat. I interrupted, saying I had heard all of that, I had been there. What I wanted to know about was the speech to the private session of the Congress.

'The trouble with you, Comrade Russell', he said, looking me directly in the face, 'is that you pay too much attention to the stories you hear from the bourgeois correspondents and the tales going around the British embassy'.

I persisted, but he insisted he did not know what I was talking about. I had, I explained, a pretty good copy of the speech in my pocket and would give him a few sentences that I had remembered by heart, just to prove my point.

When I had finished, he said coldly and sternly, still in French: '*Comrade, it does not mean that because you are a friend you have the right to look in our* – he hesitated for a moment, lapsing into Russian, and I offered the word – *cupboard*'. It was a straight indication of my role with the added and careful insult of the formal French 'vous' rather than the personal 'tu' which was used for real comrades.

'If that's your attitude', I said, trying to keep my dignity and self-control,

> there's nothing more you and I have to say to each other. You won't be able to keep the speech secret. Unfortunately for you and for us, your cupboard is full of skeletons. When the door bursts open, those you call "bourgeois" correspondents will be there to report the event, but we will have to clean up the dirty mess and deal with the consequences.

146 The 'Secret' Speech

He shrugged and I left with the knowledge that everything hurled against Stalin by our enemies was not so much true but a gross understatement of the truth, and that there was little chance of anyone in Moscow helping me decide what to do. The British Party delegates to the Congress had all already left for London, so I could not discuss with them, and not having a solid source for the story all I could do on the phone to London was drop more hints that were not picked up. I decided to pester Suslov again, and wrote him a letter, pointing out the *Worker* had already published letters from readers raising questions about 'the cult of the individual' and that a Reuter correspondent was leaving Moscow and would communicate what he knew, or thinks he knows, to his office.

Rettie got out that same day, and the following evening, to protect him, Reuters put out a story datelined 'Bonn' which claimed that, according to 'well-informed Communist sources' there, Khrushchev had made a secret speech about Stalin. When the Reuters copy arrived at the *Worker*, they tried to get in touch with me. At the time, I was living in a hotel and the reception said I was not in my room when, in fact, I was there the whole evening.

It was only the next morning that I heard of Rettie's report, on the BBC's morning news, and I decided I had to do something about the speech. That afternoon, a telegram from the *Worker* was delivered to me, asking if I could confirm anything. 'Reply earliest'. Given the wording, it must have been sent as soon as the paper could not get hold of me and had been held back.

The *Worker* had responded to the Reuters story with a short item on page 3, headlined 'Strange story about Stalin'. The editorial offices were closed that day (a Saturday) and it was only on the Sunday that I was able to get on to Campbell, the editor, and tell him I had got what I knew to be a fairly accurate account of the speech. He wanted to know what was in it. I told him I could put it over to the stenographers. 'No', he said. 'What we want to do is to "carry the story forward"' – talking about the speech as if it was a minor matter. Pretty annoyed about this though I was, I had little option but to comply, and produced an emasculated version.

While I was on the phone, the stenographer interrupted. Campbell had said that when I had finished putting my report over, I was also to put over 'what I had spoken to him about earlier on'. It was then that I put over the full story. I learned later Campbell had instructed the stenographer that my second report was to be for his eyes only but the Features Editor Malcolm MacEwen had come into the stenogs room, looked at the copy, ripped it out of the typewriter, and rushed into the newsroom shouting 'Look what Sam has been putting over'. Campbell came out of his office and took it away. A copy was sent to Pollitt. At a British Communist Party Congress, which, by chance, had already been scheduled for a few days later, Harry told delegates he did not know anything about the 'secret speech' until I had put the story over, but the *Worker* still only carried a travesty of what I wrote.[3]

The Soviet side did not interrupt or stop my phone call, even though they must have been listening in. Did someone want this cat out of the bag? After

The 'Secret' Speech **147**

all, if Johnnie Gibbons and Dennis Ogden were invited to that meeting, it was obvious they would get in touch with me. What is more certain in my mind is that had I filed the story straight away, Campbell and the Party leadership in London would not have run it without 'guidance' from Moscow, and, on 'the speech', that guidance never came and never would have, a feeling surely justified by the way they handled my copy when I did dictate the story that Dennis Ogden's notes had given me.

The Soviets pretended for years that the 'secret speech' was an invention of the CIA. The British Party leadership went along with that view and the full version of my story never saw the light of day. It was so stupid. Perhaps what annoyed me most is some sort of amour-propre because Campbell made me look a bigger fool than I really was. But then, as they say in the newspaper world, the editor's decision is final.

Even if the speech itself never appeared in print in the official Soviet media, within a few weeks of the Congress everyone actually knew what Khrushchev had said. This was part of the parallel worlds that formed a basic element of Soviet reality – people knew, people thought, people had opinions, discussions were held, but nothing was said and the official image of what was going on could be something entirely different.

Just after the speech, in early March at a Kremlin ceremony to sign a Soviet trade deal with the Danes, I was the only journalist present for a long conversation that involved key members of the Soviet leadership – Khrushchev, Bulganin, Molotov, Kaganovich, and Mikoyan. At one point, Molotov turned, saw me and said to the others: 'Don't forget that what you are saying is not secret, for the *Daily Worker* correspondent is listening'. Was Molotov referring to the fact that I knew about *that* speech?[4]

It wasn't until mid-June that I found a Soviet publication carrying something saying the speech had been made, and then it was a translation in *Pravda* of an article from the US *Daily Worker* which mentioned the US State Department publishing a version of the 'speech', with a footnote referring to the 'speech' as a 'so-called report'.

In the immediate aftermath of the Congress, there were dramatic policy changes backed by the drip, drip of criticism of 'cult of the personality', which was responsible by the time of Stalin's death, some historians have calculated, for one in six of the adult Soviet population having had some experience either of imprisonment, of life in the prison camps, or of life as a special deportee. Many had relatives, close friends or colleagues at work who were executed or simply disappeared. Within weeks of Stalin's death, Beria, the direct boss of this system, had arranged a massive amnesty covering many tens of thousands. People began to arrive in Moscow and other cities with terrible tales to tell. After the 'secret speech', tens upon tens of thousands more made their way out of the camps but the overwhelming majority were not allowed to come to Moscow. Those few who did, along with their relatives, were very, very leery of speaking to any foreigner. A lot of them, understandably, could not imagine a foreign Communist

148 The 'Secret' Speech

journalist as being anything other than a spy for the authorities. Those who did speak to me, however, served to reinforce the message in Khrushchev's words.

Optimism

Given that the terror was receding, I could share an intense optimism in the Soviet Union at that time. Even before Khrushchev had moved the goal posts with his secret speech, there had been a rising mood among many in Moscow. It compensated for the terrible backwardness that confronted the newcomer like me. It was not just the promise of reform held out by Khrushchev that gave the feel of a society going somewhere. There was promise of new openings internationally. One of my first reports from Moscow was on a Soviet invitation to the Football Association in England to send a squad to Moscow in the summer of 1956 for the first ever match between the two national teams. Technological talk was everywhere: space research was advancing and nuclear-powered icebreakers were announced in February, a vision of the future held out at the moment when Khrushchev was about to denounce the nightmare of the past.

Just about the first interview I had arranged for me had been with one of the grand old men of Soviet technology, 77-year-old Professor Alexander Winter of the Power Research Institute. His ability to talk big in terms of the future and plans was infectious. The vision of a Siberia transformed into a source of hydroelectric power and industry was overpowering. With his younger colleague Arkady Markin, he set out plans that, with hindsight, reflected not so much optimism but rather the way in which Soviet thinking was rooted in a belief that the world could simply be reshaped in whatever way one wanted. They were going to irrigate the Sahara, dam the Mediterranean at Gibraltar and prevent cold currents from the Arctic entering the Pacific while creating a warm current flowing from the Pacific to the Atlantic. These ideas were grandiose delusions of the worst kind. I can't remember now whether I really believed it all, but I wrote in my report that I felt that it was 'one of the most exciting interviews' I had ever had! For once with hindsight I can say that when the paper published my report but without these wilder musings I can be happy that the cuts were made.

The sense of power and progress was present and palpable and not restricted to the Party leadership and its official announcements. Almost as soon as the 20th Congress had ended the giant GUM department store put on a display of the latest silks and dress designs from factories in the Moscow area. Queues had formed up in the store for the cloth and for pre-cut patterns that could be sewn up at home. Having sat through hours of debate, listening from Balcony Number 1 to the lengthening litany of plans for the Soviet consumer, I decided to join the queue and see what was on offer in the very antithesis of the image of the Soviet Union at the time – fashions for women.

A regular fashion parade was put on so that customers could see what they were buying. Putting on the air of a seasoned fashion parade journalist – not that I had ever been to one before – I took up position in the front row to watch as

The 'Secret' Speech **149**

each of the mannequins came in to show off dress after dress to the music of a pianist and fiddle player hidden in a corner. They seemed to think that 'Johnny's the Boy for Me' was the best tune with which to introduce these products of Socialist industry. The shows were held once every hour and there was a long queue waiting for the next show as my one ended. Outside in the street, it was ten below centigrade with the snow swirling around in a biting wind. Inside, the show was of light silk summer dresses, dresses for school graduation ceremonies and full-length evening robes. Watching it, the grandiose claims made at the Congress that a Sixth Five Year Plan would transform life for the Soviet consumer seemed believable.

My mood was reinforced by the fact that optimism was felt by so many ordinary people. Towards the end of June 1956, I was woken by what sounded like all-night revellers returning from a party. People were singing at the top of their voices and someone was playing an accordion. By the third night of this cacophony, I decided to investigate and found myself in the street as dawn was breaking over the city surrounded by young people. I spoke to three of them: Misha – he had been on the accordion – Galya and Natasha told me they had all successfully completed their final school exams and were now off to work as volunteers in Siberia.

They were just a tiny part of the response to the huge call for volunteers that came at the same time as the camps of the Gulag had been opened and the military forces were being reduced at a rate of something like 100,000 a month. The volunteers were off to Omsk and Tomsk, to Biisk and Bratsk. The latter was a huge hydroelectric dam in the wilds of Siberia that needed tens of thousands of workers. The fields and crops that Khrushchev hoped would take the USSR past America in terms of agriculture, needed even more. The dams and irrigation canals, the transport systems and the mines in Siberia or Kazakhstan were the areas to which the Gulag had drawn its labour. People did not speak of that to me. It was an unspoken background to so much that was going on around me, and one which I came to see only bit by bit.

The volunteers from Moscow left via the Yaroslav Station and, invited by those midnight revellers, I went along. Some I met there were completely inappropriate. Three of the young women on the first of the trains were from the Red October Sweet Factory. One was a charge-hand in a workshop, yet I watched as she went off to Krasnoyarsk to labour by hand shifting earth on the vast site of the dam there, not exactly the best use of her skills. Seeing Misha and his friends off a bit later, I found he was playing his accordion leading a group of over 100 young men and women in singing a romantic melody popular among young Russians at the time: 'Nothing can stop us on land or sea; We fear neither tempest nor ice'. Their enthusiasm was utterly infectious.

While these volunteers were leaving the capital, massive new electricity supplies started to come in the other direction from the opening stages of a dam at Kuibyshev. For a short while after it was completed, this was the world's most powerful hydroelectric dam. Many of the Moscow volunteers I helped wave off

150 The 'Secret' Speech

would be working on five others that were in the pipeline. Each one was to be even bigger than Kuibyshev. The electricity meant that the streets were actually properly lit at night – a more than symbolic part of the opening up across the Soviet Union in the wake of Stalin's death.

When I went east in August 1956, following the route of the volunteers, I realised that England, and even the wider reaches of Spain, had given me no idea of the utter vastness of the Soviet Union. Travelling for a month around Soviet Central Asia and Siberia, it seemed as if there was no end to the distances. I flew on the then revolutionary passenger jet, the TU-104, which opened the first regular passenger jet service in the world with my flight from Moscow to Irkutsk. A country that was only just a decade out of the most destructive warfare human history had known, was doing things in style at the very frontiers of technology. To cap that sentiment, in place of the disease ridden, illiterate and backward central Asia of the past, I saw vast industrial plants, power stations, huge agricultural projects and mass participation in education.

One image stuck obstinately in my mind. Driving out from Tashkent across the so-called Hungry Steppe, the car churned up clogging clouds of dust that covered us from head to foot. On one stop to get the dust out of our eyes, noses and mouths, I saw what I thought at first was a mirage – a giant excavator on the horizon in all this nothingness. Yet that was just what it was. Eight others of these goliaths were due to arrive as part of a project to widen an irrigation canal, the Kirov Canal. The task would require shifting more soil than had been moved in making the Panama Canal, and that was to complete just the first stage of the project. Some days later, I watched at night as workers, many of them volunteers, housed in tents with few if any amenities, just got stuck in under search lights to keep the machinery moving. They were from all parts of the Soviet Union.

A couple of days later I was at a new hydroelectric dam, the Kairak-Kum, where over 37 nationalities were said to be represented in the workforce under their Jewish director Jacob Flugelman. Standing on the edge of the growing emerald green sea behind the dam, I thought of all those poetic stories about making the desert bloom like the rose – and about how Soviet power was doing just that. There was an infectious romance in the growing scale of the plans the engineers talked about. 200,000 hectares of barren land, they told me, had already been irrigated by the time of my visit.

The canal and the dam were just part of what Khrushchev hoped would be a Soviet agricultural revolution, solving its food problem by a crash programme to extend the area of cultivation through Virgin Lands on the vast unploughed steppes of Russia and the dry lands of Central Asia. Later the same month, I was in Novosibirsk, 12 hours east of Moscow by plane. It was night as we drove 100 miles deep into the countryside with searchlights sweeping the steppe on either side as hundreds of combine harvesters worked through the dark to bring in the first crop of wheat from this new farmland. Along the road we passed combines that had literally just come off the production line in Novosibirsk and were bring driven, under their own power, to the fields. Others were being brought in by rail and river from southern parts of the Soviet Union where the harvest was already over. It was a colossal effort.

The farm I was going to see, the Proletarsky State Farm by the village of Krasny Yar, employed 500 workers to cover 85,000 acres of what been nothing more than rough pasture just three years before. Locals, it was said, claimed that the land would not grow anything worthwhile, but I could see wheat waving in the wind as far as they eye could see.

The combine drivers were racing to complete their part of the task and some teams were reporting they had reaped double their daily target – they got paid more if they over-fulfilled the targets. That also made it likely that they would reap grain that could not then be moved. Rain came pelting down on several occasions during my visit to the region. This was just the opposite of what was needed to get the crop from the fields to the silos in a good, dry condition. Anything that could be used for transport was mobilised into the fields. As well as the lorries, there were horse-drawn carts lined up to take the grain from the harvesters. Across the region, army units had been sent in with their lorries and field kitchens. Student volunteers had come from all over the USSR. Factory workers from Novosibirsk were sent out with the lorries from their works.

Organising this effort, making a success out of a desperate chaos, was something that needed more than raw enthusiasm or wild orders from Moscow. Progress was slow and, despite the torrent of statistics, it was not clear that this would change. 'The Siberian autumn is approaching fast, bad weather has already begun and this, together with high winds, is causing increasing losses in the grain still standing uncut in the fields, although it has been ripe for some time', was the way I put it in the paper. I was still caught up by the enthusiasm of those midnight revellers but the fundamental errors at the heart of Khrushchev's campaign were all too plainly visible.

The scale of it all was even more difficult to comprehend in the Kostanay region of Kazakhstan. To get to one farm, I was driven for four hours across the steppe and the only trees I saw during the whole journey were two recently planted shelter belts of young saplings. Sometimes racing over good dirt tracks, sometimes crawling at a snail's pace over deep ruts or through clouds of dust, the only sight was of wheat stretching to the horizon in all directions. Three years earlier, the region alone had claimed to have around three million acres under the plough, by this harvest that figure had reached 13 million – which was in fact more than the whole area of arable farmland in Great Britain.

The incredible sacrifices people were making to take part in this enterprise were striking. There were teenage women from almost every part of their Soviet Union, whose blistered hands told of their hard work, tradesmen and labourers from all parts. On one farm, they told me 39 different areas and cities of the Soviet Union were represented with 16 different nationalities. A few of the longer established farms in the region, dating back to the 1930s, had more housing, mostly built by the workers themselves on the back of loans and subsidised materials from the state. These were the exception.

152 The 'Secret' Speech

At the Urneksky State Farm 100 miles further into the steppe, I found a population of over 3,000 with a ten-form school already built and another under construction. Yet the farm had only started in January 1955 when the first group of 76 men and women pitched their tents in the middle of this seemingly endless plain. As on other farms I visited, large numbers of workers and their families had to put up with crowded and poor hostel accommodation at best and sometimes tents at worst, before they could get a chance at building their own home in their spare time. Workers repeatedly told me that was something they wanted to do, but it hardly meant that their life would be easy. For many of them, the working day was already 15 or 16 hours long. The results I saw were also not necessarily of good quality. Even at the Kostanay Sovkhoz, which had been first established in 1930, the director told me it would be three years before the housing problem was 'solved'.

Virgin Land farms were not the only places where a tempest of work was underway. I spent a day watching giant excavators ripping off the topsoil to get at rich iron ore deposits at Sokolovsko-Sarbaisky, some 30 miles from the town of Kostanay. As with the war and the Virgin Lands farm programme, the challenge of building these huge new projects was met by hurling everything available at the problem. The lists of figures of the tractors apparently sent here and there, the combines mobilised from one region to another, filled the local papers. But lorries and railway trucks were standing idle – and, as with the harvest cut but unmoveable, the excavators could dig out the earth but there was little point if there was not enough properly organised transport to take it away.

One could, at least for a while, put the difficulties down to teething troubles, to inexperience or to the urgency of the task. It was particularly easy to do that when talking about it in Moscow. And we did not yet know enough to understand the uneasy parallels between the lives of these new settlers dropped in the middle of an ocean of land and those who two decades earlier had been dumped in similar situations as part of the terror approach Stalin had unleashed in the drive to destroy peasant agriculture and build industry.

Khrushchev held out the promise of reform and created the feel of a society going somewhere through his Virgin Lands policy aimed at meeting the food shortage problem and in giant industrial projects, building hydroelectric dams, for instance, and launching nuclear-powered icebreakers as well, all of which I reported on.

How could writing forward-looking splash after splash for my paper have been anything other than compelling? I knew this was the job I wanted and that I was right to have lobbied for it. To say I was on a roll, would be an understatement. It helped mask my disappointment over the treatment of my secret speech story, and of my own difficulties in confronting the implications of Khrushchev's denunciation of Stalin. That there should be greater democracy at local level, in the factories, in the collective farms, and in culture was out in the open, and there was extensive criticism in the print media of individual failings by individual officials. The prospect of reform and a new international

The 'Secret' Speech **153**

approach – rapprochement with Tito that led to his visiting Moscow in June 1956, the possibility of peaceful coexistence across the barriers of the Cold War – reinforced this optimism, but then events in Hungary put a brake on the positive outcomes of the Khrushchev speech.

Hungary

The Soviets had responded to pressure from within Hungary and removed the hated Party leader Rákosi in July 1956 and replaced him with Ernő Gerő, who continued the same policies; this, and fuel shortages and a poor harvest, kept dissatisfaction alive. Poland experienced similar unrest and, against a background of riots, Soviet intervention was threatened but avoided when the apparently reform-minded Władysław Gomułka was given power. In solidarity with the Poles and to urge their own demands for change, Hungarians held a demonstration in October 1956 that was 100,000 strong. A new and popular leadership was put in place under Imre Nagy but his reforming government was forced out by Soviet tanks just before I arrived at the end of November amid strikes and a continuing uprising. He had announced the withdrawal of Hungary from the Warsaw Pact in reprisal for the Soviets sending in more troops to Hungary than Moscow had agreed with his government, and this had been a step too far for Khrushchev.

The first coverage in the *Worker* was by general reporter Peter Fryer. He had been in Hungary in July and August of 1956 and came back with the first real indications of the scale of the problems, yet his news that Hungarian living standards were lower than in 1949 did not get into the paper. Peter returned in late October and left a fortnight later. He was now totally on the side of the Hungarians who had risen up against the regime and resisted the Soviet troops. He arrived back in Budapest just after Soviet tanks had withdrawn and was knocked back by the dead bodies he saw. He filed reports that the paper did not use, replaced by stories that reflected the Soviet view. When Soviet tanks returned a few days later, Fryer, with other correspondents, took refuge in the UK embassy and was taken under escort to the Austrian border. He resigned from the paper and I was told to go in his place.

I was flown from Moscow by military plane along with Soviet top brass, who would not talk to me or Orfeo Vangelista from the Italian Party paper *l'Unità*, who was also there. We arrived in the dark and were told we were staying the night by the airport. There was no sign of fighting. The menu at the hotel was in Russian and the waitresses were Russian, as were the labels on the drinks. 'Isn't that going a bit far?' I wondered. I went for a stroll and round the other side of the building was a red neon sign saying Lvov. We had not made it out of the Soviet Union.

We reached Budapest the next morning. The airport was surrounded by tanks. We were taken in an armoured personnel carrier to the Party hotel, which was guarded by a small military unit and a tank back and front. On my last night,

154 The 'Secret' Speech

I was nearly shot by the Soviet machine gunner guarding the hotel because I was returning late.

At the Soviet embassy I was given money, a military pass to go wherever I liked, and a revolver. I refused the gun and was told 'it's orders'. I replied that the orders *allowed* me to carry arms but didn't *oblige* me. I had been in similar situations and carrying a weapon is a death warrant. As both Vangelista and I continued to refuse, the Soviets gave way. I went to the loo and in the pan found revolver bullets. It gave me quite a turn. Even the trilby hat I bought had a bullet hole in it.

The first stories I sent from Budapest largely represented the view of the Soviet side and of the new Hungarian leadership they had just installed led by János Kádár, who had been part of Nagy's government. His role alongside Nagy gave him enough of the appearance of a reformer to stand some chance of keeping the population on his side. But he was also prepared to run along with what Moscow demanded. When I interviewed him, his argument, which to me seemed reasonable, was that if counter-revolution had triumphed, world war would have broken out.

A long walk that night, just before the curfew came in at 7 pm, showed me the streets were deserted. But it was not a simple situation. The city was a tragic sight as a result of the terrible damage inflicted by the fighting – damage so bad that some of the streets reminded me of London during the Blitz. But I had also seen butchers' shops open and stocked – some waiting for customers to come, a rare site for someone from Moscow. The overhead lines for trams and trolley buses were being restored and roadblocks were being cleared. With Rákosi and Gerő gone, errors had been admitted, and I thought things were getting better.

On 23 November, a month after the start of the bloodshed, the whole of Hungary came to a halt. Councils had been spontaneously established in workplaces and many towns. They had real support. Kádár could not just get rid of them, so he moved to incorporate them in his regime. New elections were organised in the factories, and I visited several, meeting workers and those elected onto the new committees. A general strike was still in force, with different voices urging different ways forward. Some of those returning to work were physically attacked. Others, like the newly formed leadership of a steel workers' union that I met were for a return to work but only on the basis of a programme that included independence for trade unions, the right to strike, withdrawal of the Soviet troops, and workers control in the factories.

I had been to Hungary for the paper briefly in 1948 when I was shown the country impressively rebuilding. This time at the Goldberger textile plant, which I had visited in 1948, I again heard workers young and old speak of their pride in the new Hungary they felt they were building after two decades of home-grown fascism. I met Geza Kesseg, a chemical engineer and chair of the works committee, who said that, while the Goldberger had been in favour of an end to strikes, this did not mean they were enthusiasts for the new, Soviet-imposed government. 'People fear a return of what happened here before', he told me.

The 'Secret' Speech **155**

'Kádár has said many times that the crimes of the past will never be repeated, but people are waiting for deeds to show that the old regime will not return'.

What did he and his committee want to see happen? I could hardly have got a more direct answer, which I reported in the *Worker*:

> 1, ensuring the independence and sovereignty of Hungary; 2, the defence of the country's Socialist achievements; 3, friendly relations between all Socialist countries on the basis of full equality; 4, freedom of the press and radio, and freedom to travel abroad.

With the journalists from the French and Italian parties and a Hungarian interpreter, I went to the Cspel industrial complex on an island in the Danube, which was on strike and was opposed to the Red Army and the new Hungarian leadership around Kádár. With 18 different factories, it was the key industrial centre in Budapest. We went to a motorcycle plant and couldn't find the Party secretary so I said let's talk to the workers. One bloke said we're not talking to you. 'You're Communist correspondents and they're all liars'. Others did talk, about not being paid while on strike, the stopping of food parcels and, the main industrial issue, the piece-work rates and production bonuses. Workers said they wanted their factories to remain Socialist property but they had harsh things to say about the constant acceleration of the pace of work, with piece-work rates being made harder and harder to achieve. The setting of norms or targets for piece-work was a problem all over the Socialist countries, especially where people were coming to factories from the land where the rhythm of work was different. Norms were set low initially and were quickly surpassed so new norms were introduced, but workers never knew what they were going to receive in their pay packet and this led to resentment and fiddling.

These workers didn't believe what I said about the situation in our factories in Britain. They had been listening to Radio Free Europe and were deeply misinformed about the West, and this reinforced my feelings about the situation. Based in West Germany and funded by US authorities, the station was encouraging Hungarians to believe the US cavalry would come riding over the hill to save them but the US never had any such intentions.

The following few weeks saw a game of cat and mouse, of provocation and counter-provocation. Some Hungarian Party members I knew were uneasy about the situation because of the fascist elements involved. At the start of December, I had to shelter in the first doorway I could find when men opened fire with Tommy guns on a demonstration in support of Kádár. A few days later Kádár imposed martial law and banned the Budapest Central Workers Council, saying it had been 'plotting' a new general strike. Most of the factories across Budapest came to a standstill in a protest at the ban. Among those workers I found at the Cspel complex who were on the island, the atmosphere was one of nervousness and mistrust. The island's workers' council was in session and I was told the chairman had gone to negotiate with the local Soviet commander, who

156 The 'Secret' Speech

had asked for the names of council members. Those I spoke to were fearful this would mean their arrest and deportation.

I did have my own interpreter as well. Arthur was an ex-Comintern agent in Canada who had been wounded in defence of the Party headquarters in Budapest. When the Soviet tanks withdrew on New Year's Eve, we couldn't understand why. Arthur had a line to a Soviet commander, who said, 'It's so you know what it's like when we're not here'.

Leading Hungarian Party members had been flown out by the Soviets and then returned. I knew one of them, the editor of the Party paper, whom I saw in the hotel lobby. As I went up to him, Arthur went past me and hit him across the mouth and then again with the back of his hand. 'These bastards ran while we were fighting', explained Arthur.

I stayed in Hungary throughout December and into January, watching a slow shift to acceptance of working with the Kádár regime and trying to sort out whether the failure of factories to resume work was more down to workers' opposition or to shortages of coal. Many tens of thousands were still refusing to return to work while many tens of thousands had chosen to leave the country. Ten weeks of strikes, turmoil and fighting meant fuel, food and supplies were at a minimum. I wrote my New Year story in my hotel room, dressed in my winter great coat as the collapse in coal production meant that I, like most Budapest families, had no heating despite the winter cold.

Passivity gradually returned under the weight of the blunt reality of the Soviet military presence. The members of all the workers' councils in Cspel resigned en bloc early in January. They said they could not carry out the decrees of the Kádár authorities. This action was about the last of the protests. With the help of the Red Army, Kádár had got his way.

A few weeks after I got back to Moscow, I was sent to Budapest again, for the 15 March commemoration of the 1848 revolution in Hungary. There were insistent rumours that the anniversary would be used to mount strikes and demonstrations but the Kádár regime interned thousands just before hand and nothing happened.

Hungary was difficult. I did not know the country or the language, and the West seemed to be exaggerating the deaths and the situation in general. Unlike Peter Fryer, I had not shared the experience of the peaceful mass involvement in the initial collapse of the Rákosi regime. At a host of major industrial centres – the Tatabanya coal mining trust, the iron and steel works at Dunapetele, factories around Budapest and particularly Cspel – I was given many stories of former members of the Hungarian SS reappearing to exploit popular anger. Unlike in Czechoslovakia, the Hungarians had little progressive history since the failed Béla Kun government of 1919. Of the East Europeans, they had lived longest under fascism, from the 1920s to 1945, and had been allies of Hitler with minimal exposure to Socialist ideas. The argument put by Kádár that the context was wider also greatly influenced me. Four days before the Soviet forces moved in to flatten the Hungarian rebellion, British and French paratroopers had landed

The 'Secret' Speech **157**

in Suez, and I had to cover those events from Hungary. I persuaded myself that great strategic issues were at play. I did think it was a counter-revolution then but I changed my mind. However, I'm not convinced it was the popular uprising it was said to be.

There is a footnote to this Hungarian story. Imre Nagy took refuge from the Red Army in the Yugoslav embassy and emerged later under what he was assured was a safe conduct agreement backed by the Russians and Kádár personally. It was nothing of the sort. He was held prisoner by the Soviets until he was secretly returned to Hungary, secretly tried and secretly executed in 1958. By chance, I happened across someone else in Soviet hands: Rákosi, who had quietly been taken into exile in the Soviet Union when he had been removed from power. I had a ticket to see a film in a Moscow, 'closed' cinema for the elite, and spotted him a few seats in front of me. He was not executed like Nagy, nor like so many other Hungarian Communist figures for whose deaths he had been responsible. Instead, he was allowed to die in his bed.

Notes

1 There was also, Sam said, a special phone link between the editorial office of the *Worker* and the Party offices, a line that was permanently open, by-passing the newspaper's switchboard. This line was part of the phone system provided by the General Post Office, which then ran the whole phone system in Britain. The line, therefore, was not 'secure' and probably made it easier for the government's phone tappers to zero in on the conversations worth recording.

2 In Sam's MI5 files (KV 2/3747), a report of a conversation between Harry Pollitt and George Matthews (the British Party's Assistant General Secretary and a member of its contingent at the Congress) on their return to the UK about Russell and the 'secret speech' confirms Sam's version of events.

3 The telephone line from Moscow was atrocious and mistakes were inevitable. Sam insisted the stenogs set aside a carbon copy every time he dictated a story, and he had them sent to him in weekly bundles. He used them to try to clear his name whenever disastrous mistakes had been made.

4 It was not the only surreal moment, according to Sam:

> Danish Premier Hansen attended a reception at the Danish Embassy for the Soviet leadership. Premier Bulganin and Foreign Minister Molotov turned up. I happened to be standing near the trio when the toasts began. Hansen emptied his glass and, in traditional Danish fashion, threw it straight behind him. I was in his line of fire and it hit me on the wrist. Bulganin's glass followed immediately and before I could duck, it shattered the champagne glass I had in my hand. Molotov's followed and splattered more champagne over my trousers. Only at that point, did they bother to look behind them, with the consequence that having two Premiers and a Foreign Minister simultaneously offering their apologies was a first for me.

10

TROUBLE IN MOSCOW

Back in Moscow after Hungary, I should have watched my p's and q's but could only react in my own way to the stifling idiocy of the system I continued to encounter. What I saw in Moscow was, of course, a life of privilege compared to the vast areas of the Soviet Union beyond, but one had to be perversely blind if one was living long in the Soviet capital and still thought that Stalin had established a Socialist paradise on earth. I suppose I saw myself as pro-Soviet, there to report on the achievements of the first workers' state. My aim was to report in a positive way, but to do it in relation to what I knew to be the type of things of interest to the readers of the paper and the generality of members of the British labour movement. Many incidents occurred that, taken together, sharpened the contradiction between the image I had brought with me of life in the Soviet Union and the reality I was discovering.

After Margaret had arrived with our daughter Ruth six months into the posting, we moved out of the hotel room I had been allocated and into a flat in the Mozhaisk Chaussée, the great road heading west out of central Moscow along which Napoleon had come in 1812. The flat was in a block that backed on to the River Moscow and was used to house Central Committee personnel. I was told that within an hour of us moving in, there were a couple of dozen phone calls from people in our block wanting to report that these foreigners had moved in. An old lady courier delivered news copy from TASS three times a day. When a news printer was installed it made a terrific noise, which irritated Margaret a lot. My battles with bureaucracy – shouting on the phone and the rest – also upset Margaret greatly.

The block had a baker, and in front of his shop there was always a queue of people with sacks who had come from out of town, not for bread to eat but to feed to animals – a sign that the Socialist economy was topsy-turvy. In my family, you ate every bit of bread and used crusts or old bits in soups and puddings.

DOI: 10.4324/9781003243380-11

We paid the ordinary Russian rents which were ridiculously low – something that triggered early doubts; it seemed the housing policy as a consequence had to be completely cockeyed as it meant that decent housing could not be built and maintained. The waiting lists were enormous but never published, though one got to hear plenty of tales through the grapevine. A bit further down the river there were homes that were little more than shacks, which made a stark contrast with our Central Committee block.

At that time enormous numbers of blocks of flats were being built in the south-west of the city near the Moscow State University and the idea was, I heard, that the people would be moved in a military style operation from the shacks to the flats. A fleet of lorries lined up to move them. Each shack had a notice at the door giving the name of the head of household and the names of people in the family. But chaos ensued when the officials in charge of the operation found more than double the number of people they had originally counted up for the move. People had to have permission to live in Moscow, but large numbers had come into the city to live illegally or got temporary permission and rented a 'corner' in a room in one of these shacks.

Moscow Mayor Bobrovnikov, Chairman of the City Soviet, was put on trial for corruption in relation to housing soon after I returned to London and he got a long prison term. While I was in Moscow I heard him in action at one fascinating Moscow City Soviet meeting. With me on the press bench were just two Russian reporters. A deputy got up and asked for guidance from the Chairman as to the space allocation per person, which should be given in the new housing. The calculation was based on 'living area', that is useable rooms not corridors, kitchen or bathroom. Bobrovnikov said the official allocation was nine square metres per person but in the difficult circumstances of the housing shortage in Moscow if you cannot give nine, well then you give eight, or seven, or six, but not less than five.

A voice behind me whispered to somebody else: 'That means the norm is five'. True, anyone who did get five square metres often thought it was paradise, but I decided to go to see the flats to which the local shack dwellers had been moved. The construction was very shoddy, the buildings looked as if they were just slung together. That made me decide to interview the Chairman of the Moscow City housing committee. I put it to him that the allocation of space was essentially on the basis of one family one room. 'Comrade, when we will have achieved that, we will have achieved a great deal', was his reply.

The older blocks built before the war I had been in were places where the Russian term 'a kitchen quarrel' really did mean something. There were three or four families sharing a flat with one room each and jointly using the kitchen, bathroom and toilet. The rooms were often quite large with a high ceiling and some space. The new blocks going up when I was there had smaller rooms on the basis that the flat as a whole was designed for one family, though in fact it was still in practice one room per family. I did a piece and made the point about having seen for myself that the flats were clearly being occupied on the basis of one family per room.

160 Trouble in Moscow

A couple of weeks later there was a conducted tour of the blocks laid on for all correspondents in Moscow. The presentation was on the basis that they were one family flats. Reuters did a piece saying that and I got a call from the paper in London complaining that I had done a story earlier suggesting that it was only one room for a family not one flat!

The background to the housing crisis was the destruction of the war only ten or so years earlier, the inheritance of poor housing and the movement of masses of people from the countryside to the towns. But the way the system worked, whether it was agricultural policy or housing, meant that only the number one man could take decisions. And so it was Khrushchev who decreed the approach to the crash programme on housing. The argument had been put to him that one of the big costs in construction, which could be saved, was the installation of lifts. The decree duly came ordering blocks of flats no more than five stories high but without lifts. So when the shacks were cleared near our flats, up went a series of blocks five stories high but without lifts. Speed was also of the essence, it was argued, and so quality was never at a premium nor, probably, was safety for the construction workers. The Ukraina Hotel built while I was there was covered with ceramic tiles, which started falling off while I was still in Moscow. Coming down 20 stories the tiles would give anyone unfortunate enough to be hit rather more than a nasty headache, so the hotel was surrounded with a network of wire to catch the tiles.

Naturally, living in the shadow of Stalin affected my professional work, which I learned straight away. After some years of reporting home affairs I had an interest in issues like health care. I found an increase in alcoholism among women and an appalling abortion rate, which was the main contraceptive method. Facts were not easy to come by, as I discovered when I enquired about the infant mortality rate, a quick and reasonable indication of the general quality of life. I asked for figures. Nobody knew them. The Press Department of the Ministry of Health said they did not have the statistics. It was a state secret, they told me.

Infant mortality figures were one set of vital statistics every state is expected to issue as part of the overall United Nations data. A lot of countries may have been cooking the books, but at least they gave the impression of trying. The Soviets simply never offered any figures. The Tsarist regime had developed quite a good statistical service but the Soviet regime that followed may have been able to put rockets into space but could not deliver a straightforward population statistic. The same problem arose with maternal mortality, another taboo subject, talk of which was deemed 'immodest'.

Russian women, however, were amazing – in some villages there were very few or no able-bodied men or animals. The women would harness themselves to get in the first harvest and then they would queue to discover what had happened to the men who had been taken away in the night.

Another difficult subject was tuberculosis. The Supreme Soviet held a debate, apparently for the first time, on the Soviet Budget. After the Ministerial speeches outlining the figures, the Minister of Health, who had been a practising doctor earlier in her career, made an intervention on the issue of tuberculosis. She explained the streptomycin drugs that were now available but said there was an anomaly. When tubercular patients were admitted to hospital, the drugs were free but because the hospitals did not have enough space for all the large number of tubercular patients in the Soviet Union many were treated at home and when this was the case they had to pay for the drugs, which were very, very expensive. She asked for an amendment to the budget to allow those treated at home to get the drugs free as well. There followed the sort of exchanges which one gets anywhere in response to such a point. A finance minister explained that yes, of course, we would like to do it, but….

When Vincent Buist of Reuters tried to send his report of this session the section dealing with the Health Minister's intervention on TB was blue pencilled by the censorship authorities. In contrast, all I needed to do was to go home, dial the international exchange, give my account number, which was the *Pravda* account number – the Soviet Party paper was paying all my expenses – and I was connected through to the *Worker* in London. I filed the same story and it was published.

The Minster announced a press conference soon after and I told her press people that I wanted to ask a question on infant mortality, still having got nowhere with the officials. Quite unusually, I was phoned back but the response was more to be expected: the official did not think it would be a very good idea.

There was one press official at the Foreign Ministry called Muravyov who was always doing that sort of thing to me. His usual response was simply, 'Comrade Russell, I have informed my superiors of your request and there is no possibility of fulfilling your request'. It got so ridiculous that I would prance around our tiny flat singing out loud, 'No possibility, no possibility, no possibility, says Comrade Mu - rav - yov'. Once he had called me 'Mr', that is *Gospodin* or Citizen, and not *Tovarisch* or Comrade. Forms of address were important. Not to lose face, I tore him off a strip for that.

At the press conference, the Health Minister kicked off by listing the achievements of Soviet medicine: diseases cut back and the like. Then she announced that infant mortality had been cut by umpteen percent. The *Chicago Tribune* correspondent got in with the obvious question – by what, to what? Her reply was to apologise and say they did not know. But how could that be? If they knew the reduction in percentage terms they must know the figure before and that after? She went red in the face and repeated that she did not know. The Soviet side spread it around that I had put the *Chicago Tribune* up to asking the question, which only showed what a sorry attitude they had as any fool could see it was the obvious point.

Trips outside Moscow were all closely chaperoned. Even when the Press Department of the Foreign Ministry had organised the trip you still had to go to an outfit called OVIR, internal passport and identity card control, and get your official Foreign Ministry press accreditation and authorisation to leave Moscow, which was then stamped by the local militia at your destination. Another stamp was put on it when you left there and the whole lot was presented back to OVIR on return to Moscow.

One of the first trips was to Leningrad and involved both the Communist and the bourgeois correspondents. The Agence France-Presse correspondent was a man called Alexei Chiré (if I remember correctly), whose father had been a prince in Tsarist times. It was the end of winter but still very cold. In the cloakroom of one place we visited, the State University of Leningrad, the porter was so old I assumed immediately he must have been there since before the Revolution. We handed in our coats and were about to start on our tour when I noticed Chiré was standing transfixed with tears rolling down his cheeks. He was overwhelmed by the thought that his father must have stood in exactly the same spot and had his coat taken, perhaps by just the same man.

When the Leningrad visit was over, we Communist correspondents were told that we would be taken on to the Baltic States and off we set, closely shepherded by an official from the Foreign Ministry. At one stop – Kovno in Lithuania – the Dean of the Faculty of Medicine at the local university was put up to talk to us. After his presentation on the great advances they had achieved I asked him whether he could possibly tell us what the local infant mortality rate was. The ministry man immediately intervened declaring, 'The Minister already dealt with that question in Moscow'. The Dean's face went white as a sheet and that was the end of the press discussion. I demanded that the ministry man never interrupt my questions again or I would get on a train back to Moscow. Reluctantly he agreed, though we did not have an opportunity to test him.

FIGURE 10.1 Sam with the Italian Communist and journalist Giuseppe Boffa in Lithuania.

Source: Family archive.

Trouble in Moscow **163**

London had asked me to find out about the deportations of the Baltic people because Ivan Serov, director of the KGB and Khrushchev's chief bodyguard, was about to visit Britain ahead of a visit by Khrushchev and Bulganin. The British Press were digging up dirt on Serov, who had been responsible for transporting Baltic people to camps. As I drew a blank on infant mortality, imagine what would have happened if I had asked about that. I should have left and returned to Moscow as I had threatened but I stayed and tried to make the best of a bad job. The articles I wrote, however, were below my usual standards.

Some while later when in Dushanbe, the capital of Tajikistan, the Dean of the Medical Faculty at the university told us how they had abolished trachoma, an eye disease which had been endemic in the area. When it came to questions I asked what the venereal disease situation was. Very interesting I should ask, he said. 'When teaching medical students we have had a real problem as we have not been able to find a single case of venereal disease to show our students'.

On a Communist correspondents' only trip to Samarkand and Siberia, we went by air via Lake Baikal and saw the pollution of the lake caused by the vast paper mills pumping their waste straight into it. I saw a grandiose Communist Party headquarters being built among slums, a stark contrast of party wealth and public squalor. After touring several towns and factories we agitated to see some farming. In the meantime I had worked out a way of getting some articles written while I was out there, having a pilot of one of the Aeroflot planes take them to Moscow and get them to Margaret via the Central Committee offices for her to dictate to London.

When I was interviewing the Chairman of a Collective farm, I found he had two books of accounts, one with the real figures for his own use so he did know what was actually going on and the other set to give nosey parkers from outside or those from the Ministry who wanted inflated figures to boost the plan reports. I wrote some sunshine stories about progress and advance because I had seen some things, which, on the surface of it, were very impressive. Issues like the pollution at Baikal did not strike me then any more than it would have been picked up by most journalists and I did not feel able to go into the farm chairman's points without getting him into trouble as much as myself.

Soviet officials in my experience did not just follow obtusely obstructive practices, they lied habitually. It was second nature to almost everyone. They would lie, as would their political masters. It got difficult when they knew that I knew that what they were saying was a lie, but they still went on saying it. Whatever anyone else may have thought of the stories I wrote, I myself was trying to write them on the basis of what I understood to be the truth. I never sought to lie – quite the contrary.

Early in 1957, I was asked by *Inostrannaya literature* (*Foreign Literature*), one of the legion of Soviet literary magazines, to prepare an article for a Lenin anniversary. Recalling a book by his widow Krupskaya, *Memories of Lenin*, which had been on my bookshelves in London, I decided to pop along to the Lenin Library, the greatest library of the Soviet Union. Registering as a member was no problem.

164 Trouble in Moscow

Come back in 20 minutes, the assistant said. When I did, all she could tell me was that they did not have the volume. I had asked for the English version, so what about the Russian text? After filling in three forms – one for the Russian, one for the French, and another for the Spanish translations – and another wait of 20 minutes, all the forms were returned with the message that the volumes were not stocked in the Lenin Library. At my insistence, the library superintendent appeared, and assured me the books did not exist on their shelves or, indeed, in their records. I had the same bad luck with Clara Zetkin's *Reminiscences of Lenin* and Maxim Gorky's *Days with Lenin*. These works on the central individual in Soviet history by three of his best-known contemporaries, one the woman who had shared his life for quarter of a century, had vanished into thin air.

On the way back from the library, I ran into a Canadian who had been working in Moscow since the 1930s. I told him of my difficulties. To him it was obvious: under Stalin, Krupskaya's book had been banned as the hatred between her and Stalin was clear. Worse, she had quoted Lenin as referring to Trotsky as the 'young eagle'. However, the Canadian said, he had a copy and offered to have one of his children bring it round. The following day there was a ring on the door and there was a lad on the doorstep offering me a book in a brown box binder. On the spine was written 'Karl Marx *Volume III*'. I protested that it was a mistake. The boy insisted I take it. Inside the box was a book with the hard covers removed: Krupskaya's *Memories*, disguised from the prying eyes of the secret police, should they have come.

While I was doing the piece, I bumped into an older Russian who told me of a veteran Bolshevik, Nikolai Alexeyev, who had been with Lenin in London. 'He had been sent away for a long time, but is now back', was how Alexeyev's history was explained to me. Getting the old man's phone number, I arranged to see him in the communal flat where he and his wife lived. Most of the space was taken up with a grand piano and mountains of books. He loved Beethoven's piano sonatas and his wife played for us as we had tea and talked. They were a wonderfully gentle couple, and I had the feeling of being in touch with the old Russian liberal intelligentsia which had been the backbone of the revolutionary leadership in Tsarist times but which, I was beginning to understand, had been treated in a most brutal, ruthless way after the Revolution. We spoke for over two and a half hours – his English was beautiful. Not once did he offer the slightest reference to what he had been through.

Lenin's main preoccupation in London had been the production of the illegal newspaper *Iskra*, which was printed in London and smuggled into Russia. Alexeyev contacted Harry Quelch, leader of the London Society of Compositors and editor of the Social Democratic Federation journal *Justice*, which was produced from a small building in Clerkenwell Square that, many years later, became home to the Marx Memorial Library. Lenin's team were welcome but Quelch told Alexeyev his union members would not work with people who were paid below the union rate. Alexeyev recalled the exchanges in which he acted as go-between with Lenin, explaining that the exiled Russians could not afford the rates. Quelch took the message to the compositors and they accepted the situation. To me the story was a good one, particularly as it was parallel to the situation we had at the *Worker* where the print workers were paid high wages at the insistence of the unions while we journalists were paid well below the union rate.

Putting together bits from Krupskaya's book and what Alexeyev had told me, I sent the piece off. Chasing a fortnight later, the magazine editor told me the article was a touch too long. I was happy to talk about cuts, I said, but had been particularly pleased with the material from the Old Bolshevik, as I did not think it had been published before. 'Our expert on Lenin tells us that Alexeyev is dead', the editor said. 'It was a good idea, but in view of what our expert says we had better drop it'. I offered Alexeyev's address and phone number and they agreed to go back to their 'expert'. Another fortnight went by and I had heard nothing, so I phoned again. The expert was apparently insistent that the man with whom I had spent such a wonderful evening was dead, no longer existed and could not possibly have been interviewed. The piece could not be used. Enraged at the suggestion that I had cooked the whole thing up and at the way the Old Bolsheviks were being rubbed out, I exploded. In the end, I could not prevent them publishing the text I had handed in, shorn of all references to Alexeyev. I saw him again and explained, but there was nothing we could do. He may have come back from the camps, but he did not exist so far as those in control were concerned.

How ludicrously I – as well as other journalists – were treated was again well demonstrated when Bulganin, Chairman of the Soviet Council of Ministers, sent a letter to the British Prime Minister Harold Macmillan. These things were usually issued with an embargo for midnight Moscow time, which was 9 pm London time. This meant that with our early press deadlines we would miss items that could be picked up by the others with later editions.

I was particularly keen to get the Bulganin item for the following day's editions. I contacted TASS, the official news agency, which had announced that the letter had been sent. I was told they were waiting for the text. I said you announced it, so you must have the text already. They said they were waiting for it from *Pravda*. I 'phoned *Pravda* who said they were waiting for it from TASS. As I had never been able to persuade the Soviet officials to give me any dispensation on deadlines, and this was to be no exception, I contacted a journalist at Moscow Radio whom I had known in London and whom I knew would have a copy ready for broadcast. He invited me round.

There was an armed guard at the entrance in Pushkin Square and it was snowing. The rules meant that I had to wait outside for him to come down to show his pass to the guard before I could be let in. I 'phoned up on their internal line and he said he would be down in a moment. He did not come. I rang again. He would be down soon. After more time freezing in the snow I rang again and he had obviously taken the phone off the hook. So I found a phone booth in the Square and rang through to his direct line from the external phone. He kept pleading that the story might change and he could not give the text in advance.

166 Trouble in Moscow

I protested that the story could not possibly change as the letter had already been delivered to Macmillan. He finally agreed to give me the text and I dashed back to the flat by taxi getting there with ten minutes to go before the final edition.

Some while later my contact dropped dead and at his funeral one of the other mourners told me that he had got into a lot of trouble for enabling me to 'phone a story to London ten minutes before it was released in Moscow. Instead of getting the Order of the Red Banner of Labour for our efforts in helping the cause of getting the story into the one paper in Britain which might support the contents of the letter, we were both marked out as people to be watched and disciplined.

And watched I was, and very nearly disciplined – severely – when later in 1957, in October, the Soviets had an even bigger problem with my reporting. Marshal Zhukov, the Red Army's war time commander, was one of the few accepted heroes of the Soviet Union, both within the Soviet Union and internationally. This was probably why he had been sent to the sticks by Stalin at the end of the war as commander of the Odessa garrison. Khrushchev brought Zhukov back to Moscow and made him Defence Minister – only Trotsky had previously been Defence Minister and commander-in-chief – and there were stories going around: Eisenhower, Supreme Allied Commander on the Western Front, was now President of the US, perhaps Zhukov might try to emulate him.

Zhukov played a very important part in helping Khrushchev defeat what became known as the anti-Party group, the quartet of Molotov, Malenkov, Kaganovich and Shepilov, and the rumour went that Zhukov was going get to a big promotion as a reward. Zhukov, meanwhile, went off on a visit to Tito with whom relations had been mended under Khrushchev. On the Saturday of Zhukov's return, I heard on Moscow Radio that Marshal Malinovsky had been appointed Defence Minister and Zhukov had been appointed to 'other duties'. I thought it odd. Just a few moments later TASS rang saying they had an important announcement, which they would like me to go round and collect. I asked what was it about and the man said he was not allowed to tell me on the phone. 'Was it by any chance this thing about Malinovsky?' I asked. There was a shocked silence until I put the guy out of his misery and explained that I had just heard it on the radio.

Pierre Hentgès from *l'Humanité* came on the phone to ask what sort of story I was going to write. He started telling his angle: the preparation of Zhukov as a new conquering hero, precisely the story which had been doing the rounds. The more he spoke, the more I didn't like the sound of it. In *Pravda* the following morning on the back page in the last column, sandwiched between what's on at the Bolshoi and the result of the football match at Dynamo, there were two paragraphs on Zhukov under the one-word headline, the Russian word 'Chronica' or 'News'. This was certainly not the way you announce a new conquering hero. Giuseppe Boffa of *l'Unità* came on the line to tell me the same story as Hentgès.

When I came through to the *Worker*, Alan Hutt was on the line. 'It's a bit late, there's no need to bother', he said. 'I suppose you have been enjoying yourself.

Reuters have put over a story from *l'Humanité* and *l'Unità* and I have knocked together a piece from them'. I told him I was sure it was not the true story. He went off like a rocket complaining that he had had the whole story set in metal and it would cost 16 pence and a ha'penny to have it reset. To his credit he agreed to carry my alternative, which flannelled around rather than take the Hentgès/Boffa line.

On the Monday, as I was deciding not to ask the officials for any statement, as that could just tie my hands, Misha Kobrin, a Russian journalist with whom I was very friendly, asked to meet for lunch and told me the story. While Zhukov was away in Yugoslavia, Khrushchev had decided to cut him down to size and held a quick meeting of the Praesidium to achieve this.

I deliberately missed the first edition so the other dailies would not be able to pick it up. The chief-sub in charge said he would have to consult John Gollan, the new Party General Secretary, and the story appeared. I was able to hear the BBC report the following morning that the paper had carried the story under my by-line.

A few days on, the doorbell rang and it was Frede Klitgård, the correspondent of the Danish Party paper *Land og Folk – Land and People*, who had picked what he had wanted out of my reports from Hungary when Margaret had had to take them down in long hand. I had shared the Zhukov story with Frede, but on this occasion he had decided it would be a waste of time trying to get his paper to run it in advance of any official say so. Now here was Frede behaving in a very strange way. He insisted on whispering to me. 'You're in deep trouble', he murmured.

Who should reappear just that week at the door of his flat than a Russian he hadn't seen since the war when Frede had been the contact, through this man, between his Resistance network and a group of escaped Soviet PoWs. After the surprise, the hugs and the kisses, the first thing the man said was, 'Do you know Sam Russell?' He wanted to know who my friends were, who I saw, who might be my contacts. 'By the way', the Russian said, 'not a word to Sam Russell about this, please'.

A little later, *Pravda* confirmed everything I had written when it carried a big announcement from the Central Committee. Then the trouble started. Nobody said anything to me, but things began to happen. Margaret had become very friendly with the lift women in our block of flats, who were all police informers of one sort or another but were also friendly to her. But there were now other, strange people around in the courtyard as well. I thought she was just imagining things.

That November in 1957 there were big shenanigans for the 40th anniversary of the Great October Revolution. Communist Party leaders came from all over the world. Pollitt had been kicked upstairs to become Chairman of the British Party and Gollan had taken over in the crisis following the 'secret speech' and the suppression of the Hungarian uprising. They both came to the celebrations and after the festivities Gollan went back to London but Pollitt remained for medical treatment. In characteristic fashion, invited me round for a meal.

168 Trouble in Moscow

His words of greeting were: 'Why is it every time you go abroad you create trouble?' I did not have a clue what he was talking about. He explained that when he and Gollan had arrived at the airport, Besedin, my contact at the Soviet Party Central Committee, got into their car and said straight away, 'I must tell you comrades that the Central Committee requests you withdraw Sam Russell from Moscow'.

When they asked why, he simply said, 'Speculation'.

'In foreign currency?'

'No. Yellow press speculation'.

They quarrelled all the way to the hotel and it became clear the problem was actually the Zhukov story. Gollan apparently argued that the Soviet Central Committee had issued a detailed statement saying more or less what the *Worker* had reported.

'Ah', came the reply, 'but when Sam Russell reported it he could not have known what the Central Committee was going to say, therefore it was yellow press speculation'. Besedin insisted the matter would be taken further and also that I was not to be told the matter had been raised.

Some days later Pollitt and Gollan had a meeting with Pyotr Pospelov, one of the secretaries of the Central Committee and a most unpleasant piece. In the course of the conversation, Pospelov said he understood they had refused the Soviet request to withdraw me. The ding-dong resumed and when he got nowhere, Pospelov insisted, as had Besedin, the matter would be taken further and again that I was not to be told anything.

Before Gollan left he and Pollitt had a meeting with Khrushchev. Ushered into the presence, they chatted about this and that. As they were talking, one of the secretaries came in and put a bit of paper in front of Khrushchev, who looked at it saying, 'Oh, yes, our comrades tell me that you have refused our request to withdraw your correspondent, Sam Russell, who has caused so many problems with his speculation'. Gollan said that in his view I had done nothing wrong.

'Ah', says Khrushchev, 'it does annoy us when a thing like this appears in the *Daily Worker* before *Pravda*'. Gollan said that the Soviet side ought to take correspondents like myself into its confidence. If this had been done and still I had gone ahead and reported it, then I would not just have been withdrawn but sacked and expelled from the Party as well.

Khrushchev wound up the meeting: 'Tell Comrade Russell not to break confidences' to which the only reply was 'Can we tell him?' It was then agreed between the three of them that I would be told – which Pollitt did over that meal, saying I should learn how to be more diplomatic. From then onward it made it very difficult for me with Besedin, who was, after all, just the messenger boy for others.

The Soviets were desperate to find my source for the Zhukov story. This was a serious leak. People had been executed for less. Misha told me later they did manage to track it down to him. Misha, who had already done a 12-year stretch in Siberia, was called up before Pospelov but told him: 'If you really want, you can

Trouble in Moscow **169**

send me back to Siberia'. Given what that meant, it was a sign of real courage – and nothing happened to him.

Curiously, when my younger brother Frank had been reporting from Moscow for the *Worker* just after the war, he *was* withdrawn, unlike me. He was not, however, told the official reason. He was even more of an awkward sod than me and already had a clearer view of things. He covered, for example, the first elections in Poland and saw what sort of elections they were. He told acquaintances in Moscow he did not consider Tito a fascist beast, and attracted complaints because of some of the people he associated with, for example members of the Jewish Anti-Fascist Committee, most of whom were executed. Surplus to requirements back in London after a 're-organisation' at the *Worker,* he defied the Party and went to work for the Yugoslavs, though he made it clear to them that while he did not believe Tito was a fascist agent – the Party line – neither did he think the sun shone out of his behind. Surprise, surprise, they had a 're-organisation' too and – thanks to his wife being a teacher – he was able to return to college and became a pharmacologist.

What puzzled me over the years was why, if the Soviet authorities effectively expelled Frank, did they allow me in a few years later? I may have written under the name of Sam Russell but all my papers and my registration with the Soviets carried the same surname of Lesser. Being Jewish and having fought in Spain, I was in a particularly vulnerable category but nothing happened to me. Later, I was told by Bert Ramelson, the British Party's Industrial Organiser, the Soviets had tried to get me withdrawn before the Zhukov affair, but he did not say why. I have also wondered whether Gollan and Pollitt refused to withdraw me for reasons of self-protection or because they wanted me to act more independently. They could have withdrawn me like my brother Frank, so perhaps some credit is at least due to them for putting up a bit of resistance.

11

FAREWELL TO MOSCOW

In January 1958, the month in which Soviet coal production was said to have effectively equalled that of the US, great plans were announced bringing together the USSR, Eastern Europe, and China in an economic powerhouse for the future. Sputnik 2 was on its 1,000th orbit of the earth when Soviet rocket scientists announced plans for a voyage to the moon. The optimism of the Khrushchev reforms had persisted and he caught the mood of much of the public. 'We shall not sit around drinking tea' was his phrase in response to claims by US President Eisenhower that the Americans would outdistance the Soviet Union in technology.

More concretely, Khrushchev put forward plans for a giant science city on the outskirts of Novosibirsk in Siberia and soon after *Pravda* proudly carried a full page setting out how Soviet space scientists were now confident that they had solved the issue of the safe re-entry into the atmosphere of satellites, a key step on the way to real space exploration and human space flight. Sputnik 3 was up a couple of weeks after that article, weighing over a ton to the 31lbs for the first US satellite. 'You cannot deny us our national pride at the fact', Khrushchev quipped more than once. I met no one in the Moscow streets who disagreed with him.

In August that year, I went to the final opening ceremony of the gigantic new hydroelectric dam on the Volga at Kuibyshev. Its size was difficult to comprehend. What I could see was a vast concrete wall from one side to the other of one of the world's largest rivers. As the sluice gates were opened and the water cascaded down in a flurry of sand-flecked foam, the awesome feel of raw power was all too real. One of the workers who spoke declared: 'The Communist Party told us to build the biggest power station in the world here. Well', he added, turning towards Khrushchev, 'here it is. We built it, we ordinary Soviet people with our own hands'.

DOI: 10.4324/9781003243380-12

That autumn, word began to be put about of an even faster rate of growth in the Soviet economy with Khrushchev speaking of 'a gigantic leap'. This saw the light of day in the form of a new Seven Year Plan from 1959 that would, I wrote, 'open up the practical possibility of the Soviet people being able to achieve the highest standard of living in the world in the years following 1965'. It was not to be, but for the moment neither I, nor the Soviet public, foresaw the stagnation that was to come under Leonid Brezhnev.

My final reports from Moscow covered continued successes for Khrushchev: record harvests which appeared to justify the Virgin Lands policy; the introduction of a 40-hour week; an announcement that Soviet national income had gone up by 8% over the previous year; plans for new, atomic power stations; a preview of the first Soviet designs for space suits. These were probably the most optimistic years in the Soviet Union's history.

Cultural Life

Looking back on my time in Moscow, cultural life was one of the things that I really enjoyed, but it had its problems, too. I went to the ballet as often as I could. Tickets were always sold out and I could only get tickets in the most expensive seats at the front of the stalls, though even they were dirt cheap compared to anything on offer in London. The two great experiences of the Bolshoi ballet were *Swan Lake* and *Romeo and Juliet*, and the first time I saw *Romeo and Juliet* with Galina Ulanova, the company's leading ballerina, it was truly fantastic, but she was someone I was never allowed to interview despite trying over and over again.[1]

I also failed to interview Ilya Ehrenberg, one of the grand figures of Soviet letters, but that was my fault. Margaret and I were sailing back to Leningrad after some leave in London, and I was asked to take some garden plants and bulbs to him. When the Soviet immigration, health, and agriculture officials came on board to check us before landing, the few bulbs I disclosed led to a careful inspection by the chief inspector, who compiled a list of every bulb complete with the English, Latin, and eventually the Russian name. They were then carted away. When I unpacked in our Moscow flat I discovered some more of them in the clothing. I got hold of Ehrenberg's secretary and was invited round to meet the writer. 'Is that all?' he asked when I handed them over. I explained what happened. 'Why on earth were you so foolish as to tell them?' he asked. I left with him muttering what a stupid bastard I was and I did not get the interview.

One British entertainment trade union delegation included the comedian and actor Jimmy Edwards. As was the custom, they were taken to the Bolshoi. Back stage during the interval there was caviar and champagne – the only alcohol you could get there. 'Where's the fucking vodka?' shouts Edwards. Ulanova asked the interpreter, 'What did the comrade say?' Jimmy had more success the following night when dining in the restaurant of the Ukraina Hotel. The band was playing and Jimmy, already well-oiled after a day's visiting and toasting, produced a

172 Farewell to Moscow

trombone mouthpiece from his pocket, borrowed an instrument from one of the band, and he performed impromptu as only he could.

Of the many cultural events, meeting the painter Siqueiros at a Mexican embassy dinner, a Paul Robeson concert, and a conference of Afro-Asian writers stand out. John Osborne visited when *Look Back in Anger* was performed, and the British embassy was furious because they hated it. He behaved badly because there was no hot water for shaving.

Correspondents needed to watch these events from the news point of view as well. When the Party leadership turned out there was always a message contained in exactly who was there and what order they were in, particularly if it was the whole politburo.

The rise to fame of the young poets group, of whom the best known outside the Soviet Union was Yevgeny Yevtushenko, came after my time, but their public readings in Mayakovsky Square were already being pioneered by Yevtushenko while I was there. In contrast, I never got to any of the clandestine art exhibitions. By the time I heard about one, it would have been taken away.

When with other Communist correspondents I met the president of the Soviet Academy of Art, who was himself an artist, I immediately noticed from the gaps and markings on the walls that many pictures had been removed from his office and was told afterwards that these had been his own drawings of the now out-of-favour Stalin. I asked him what he thought of Picasso. 'As a campaigner for world peace and understanding between peoples, he is a fine comrade', intoned the president, 'but unfortunately as an artist he cannot draw'.

Battles with writers were always savage because Stalin and his heirs recognised their importance. There was a great thirst for literature and literary magazines always sold out. When I arrived in Moscow I was told that whatever publication I wanted I could have delivered, so I ordered the lot. After I got authorisation from the Central Committee to receive foreign papers through the post, the office in London also sent me the London papers and I had a huge mountain of waste paper every day. Once they had piled up for a while, I took them down to the bottom of the lift in the block and put them there with all the other rubbish for collection. That brought Boris Dorofeyev from the Central Committee International Department hurrying to me: there was a problem and 'people' were complaining, he said. I had just left the papers lying there and, horror of horrors, *anyone* could just come along and help themselves. In the end the matter was solved by the Dean of the English Faculty at Moscow State University, Zoya Zarubina, arranging to come on a regular basis in a big ZiL car and collect the English language papers direct from our flat – I was expressly instructed never to take them down to the entrance in advance.

I was in Moscow during the heyday of the monthly *Novy Mir*, edited in these years by Konstantin Simonov and Alexander Tvardovsky, although Tvardovsky's most remarkable achievement – the publication of Alexander Solzhenitsyn's *One Day in the Life of Ivan Denisovich* – came in 1962 when I was back in London.[2] My Russian was never good enough to cope with what they called the 'thick'

Farewell to Moscow **173**

magazines like this, so I relied on others to tip me off. Someone suggested I read an interesting piece on Machine Tractor Stations in *Novy Mir*. Quite what such a topic had to do with literature was not clear and it was not easy to get a copy as it was said to have sold out. After some time of trying, I was able to add the relevant issue of *Novy Mir* to the pile of papers delivered to me and discovered that, right at the back of the magazine, there was indeed an article on Machine Tractor Stations, the great instruments for bringing Socialism to the countryside under Stalin's collectivisation programme of the 1930s by keeping political commissars in agriculture. Khrushchev had sent two journalists to tour the countryside and report back and he used the articles as a lever to abolish the stations. The article was, apparently, the first indication that Khrushchev was thinking that the Machine Tractor Stations had served their day and the system had to be changed. But this article appeared in *Novy Mir*, a literary journal not an agricultural paper.

In the summer of 1956 in three successive issues, *Novy Mir* published Vladimir Dudintsev's *Not by Bread Alone*, a novel concerning an inventor and his struggle with Soviet bureaucracy. It is tame now but was dynamite then as one of the first such works of literature to openly question the Soviet system, and it could only appear with Khrushchev's permission. It remained at the centre of discussion for some time and when published in book form it immediately sold out. It became a marker of Khrushchev's 'thaw'.

Yet, just after getting back from Budapest, I was at a reception for Zhou En-lai at the luxury Sovietskaya Hotel, and while toasting the Chinese delegation, Khrushchev was provoked by Bulganin into speaking about Stalin: 'I consider that as a Communist, as a fighter for the class interests of the working class, Stalin was an example to every Communist'. It was a sign that Khrushchev had by then turned against the argument presented by Dudintsev, whom Khrushchev accused of offering a partial account. Dudintsev had been exciting the Soviet public just as the Red Army was about to engage with the uprising in Budapest, and things began to go into reverse, it seemed, as the tanks rolled in Hungary.

Other critical writing appeared that made Dudintsev's look like a cold potato but these hot potatoes became the target for attack by those hoping to keep as much of the old order in place as possible. By the summer of 1957, came the sacking of the whole editorial board of *Questions of History*. The Board members were accused of having put Stalin on the same level as Grigori Zinoviev, the old Bolshevik pushed out of the leadership in the 1920s and then executed after one of the key show trials in the '30s. *Questions of History* had also failed to deal with the events in Hungary 'from a historical-scientific point of view'.

Alexei Surkov, who had kept his position as secretary of the Writer's Union from before the time of Stalin's death until after I left Moscow, vented his spleen against a poem by Semyon Kirsanov, 'Seven Days of the Week', which mocked bureaucracy under Stalin. Surkov declared that 'an ideological struggle is on' and writers like Dudintsev and Kirsanov were making 'grave and great mistakes'. Surkov had been the kind of writer Stalin liked, praising the show trials and turning out patriotic poetry and songs during the war. That he was kept in

174 Farewell to Moscow

his position was an important sign. The Communist Party's theoretical journal *Communist* confirmed the limits to the changes when it published a major think-piece in June 1957 that sided clearly with Surkov and his friends.

While works of literature exploring the horrors of Stalin's rule were published in this period, there was also a renewed attack on the composer Dmitri Shostakovich. There were, indeed, a great many icebergs in Khrushchev's thaw.

The hottest potato was one that never saw the light of day in the Soviet Union but that everyone, including the official press, seemed to keep talking about: *Dr Zhivago* by Boris Pasternak. His poetry was immensely popular, which meant there was a full-scale offensive against him and acres of print about a novel no one could find on the bookshelves.

There had been rumours about the book for some time and when I first met Pasternak at a reception in the British embassy he was understandably very private and circumspect, though he had presumably been given permission to attend. Then *Dr Zhivago* appeared in the West. *Novy Mir* had turned it down, and it was published in Italian, at the end of 1957 after the text had been taken out of the Soviet Union by the *l'Unità* number two in Moscow. There were immediate attacks on the novel in the Soviet media and on its author, ostensibly for having 'smuggled' it to the West, although he had handed over the manuscript in the belief that the novel was going to be published in the Soviet Union. After a report in the *Times* from their Rome correspondent about the way it had been published, the *Worker* wanted me to interview Pasternak, although I had not read the novel – and could not. The idea was I would get him to accept that it was anti-Soviet. Karl Staf, the correspondent for the Swedish Communist Party paper, *Ny Dag – New Day*, came with me to Pasternak's dacha at Peredelkino, the writers' village outside Moscow. Pasternak received us quite amicably. He spoke quite good French and a bit of English, but Karl started interviewing him in a very aggressive fashion.

There was a piano in the room. Pasternak was very nervous. Every so often he would go to the piano and dash off a few bars. This annoyed Karl more and more, and he became even more aggressive. At one stage Pasternak asked, 'Have you read the book?' Karl said, 'No I haven't, but I know all about it'. Pasternak looked at me and asked had I read it. I could only say, 'No'. Pasternak then said to us both: 'Here you come to interview me about the book and you have not even read it'. He then asked us whether we had noticed the pictures in the room. There was a series of small watercolours. He said they were illustrations that his father had done for Tolstoy's book *Resurrection*. Karl said rather belligerently: 'What's that got to do with it?' Pasternak's reply was, 'They had the same fate as my book'. Karl's reply was, 'So what?' In Russian you can say the answer to 'So what' as 'What so', in other words in this case, 'well there you are, things have not changed, my father's illustrations to *Resurrection* went unknown to the public because of Tsarist censorship and my own book has suffered the same fate under Soviet censorship'.

I decided there and then that I was not going to have any part in this attempt to pillory Pasternak. Karl did a really swinish article, but I refused every request from London. I said I would not write anything until I had read the book. The authorities persecuted Pasternak and his friend Olga Ivinskaya, particularly after he was awarded the Nobel Prize in 1958, and these attacks turned out to herald the re-freezing of the waters of creative literature and art before the Khrushchev thaw had been able to penetrate very far below the surface of Stalin's savage permafrost.

My time in Moscow was spent under Khrushchev, who himself suffered censorship and failed to prise open the system. That played a key part in his downfall in 1964. As the prospects of deeper change opened up, Khrushchev's failings came to the fore. Still, he was head and shoulders above the other Soviet leaders. He had the courage to stand up to the Politburo and he tried, not very successfully, to decentralise. He pursued self-financing through self-governing councils at local and regional level – with the old slogan 'All Power to the Soviets' – and he tried to tackle agriculture. He cut back the armed forces and opened the prison gates. He began a thaw in the arts despite his own conservative views and attacked the bureaucracy, laying the seeds of perestroika two decades later under Mikhail Gorbachev. His adventure over the Cuban missiles, believing US President Kennedy to be a pushover, was, however, disastrous. He had been up to his ears in blood himself as one of Stalin's most reliable instruments, especially in the Ukraine, and so it is not surprising, perhaps, that while he may have played the crucial role in securing a break with Stalin's terror, he could not complete the job.

Navigating the Thaw and the Icebergs

Personal contacts were very important to many Communist correspondents who tried to find out what was going on in the First Workers' State and navigate their way through the thaw and round the icebergs, especially if, like me, their Russian wasn't very good. The usual reaction of Russian citizens to foreigners was not to talk to them, but rather to report their presence. It had never entered my head before going to Moscow that that I might get ordinary people into trouble by just meeting them.

Early on I had met up again with Raya, a young woman I had known when she had been an attaché at the Soviet embassy in London. The ambassador, Yakov Malik, had been very interested in an Edgar Wallace play, *The Frog*, and wanted a copy of the text. The ambassador had been invited by Princess Margaret to a charity showing of the play and Raya needed to read the text to make sure it was not some sort of anti-Soviet provocation. I discovered a second-hand book shop with a copy of the original novel by Wallace which helped to put his mind at rest and ensure that Princess Margaret had a good night out.

In Moscow, Raya was working at the Foreign Languages Publishing House. Her parents had both had a bad time during the Stalin years. She was living with her mother on what was then the outskirts of Moscow near Sokolniki Park, one of the oldest in the city. I would visit and talk away in French to her mother. One

176 Farewell to Moscow

day she saw me in the Soviet television report of a press conference. She told her neighbours that her daughter knew me – which only got all of them warning her that they had to be very careful having anything to do with foreigners, even if they were Communist journalists.

That atmosphere was ever present but it still caught you unawares. One night when I was out with my secretary Lyosha, and to my surprise was able to leave the restaurant unaided though we had a few beers and vodkas, I insisted that we visit Raya. I called a cab. It was the middle of winter and Sokolniki in those days was more or less in the country. I stepped off into the snow toward the flat and fell into a ditch. Lyosha yanked me out. I proceeded, telling them I would just be five minutes and he should wait. I had a cup of tea and some jam and chatted away to Raya for a while, certainly for more than five minutes. When I came out again there was poor Lyosha with his back to the cab on this lonely country road with snow drifts piled up high facing a group of four or five men with red arm bands over their coats from the *drushniki*, the volunteer militia who kept an eye on things. The *drushniki* had refused to believe his obviously untrue story of my madcap escapade. I produced my papers and managed to pacify them, but Lyosha was really in a state.

He evidently forgave me as he was still prepared to give me a tip off that was not too obviously from above. After one all-night party I got to my flat completely drunk. The phone rang. It was Lyosha drawing my attention to a story in *Trud*, the trade union daily. It turned out to be a story about Laika, the first dog in space. My head absolutely banging, I got through the story, despite my poor Russian, and sent over a story to the paper. It turned out to be a scoop in the Western press and the following day it was as if every Western correspondent was on the line. Henry Shapiro, the great expert from United Press, led the way. I did not tell them I had just lifted it from the trade union paper.

Having written for *Literaturnaya Gazeta* when I was in London I went along to see their Foreign Editor, Boris Leontiev. Amongst his fellows he was known as Bleontiev, a pun on the Russian word for to vomit. He did not speak English and a woman in his department whispered to me on the side that a battle was going on between a majority of those working in the Foreign Department and Bleontiev over an article the paper had carried. She wanted my opinion, which I gave, without knowing that it was not that of Bleontiev.

Some while later I was invited to a meeting of Communist correspondents in the Union of Journalists building. We had access to the Soviet journalists' professional club, which actually had quite a civilised atmosphere and was a good contact point for all of us. The Foreign Editor of *Pravda* was in the chair at the meeting and explained that the general aim was to have a useful exchange as to how the Soviet side could help us in our work. Giuseppe Boffa from the Italian paper *l'Unita* was first into the fray. It was soon clear he had been set up as the first speaker. He was followed by a Romanian and someone from China. The chairman then invited contributions.

This prompted me to get up and tell the story of the exchanges I had had with the previous Foreign Editor of *Pravda* on how to handle Khrushchev's 'secret speech'. At this point the current Foreign Editor who was in the chair began to be engaged in a most close scrutiny of his watch, announcing that it was very interesting to listen to what I might have to say but that time pressed and he had an urgent appointment. Bleontiev got up and said he was amazed at the remarks of 'Comrade' Russell and at the fact that I had made them in English (my Russian was nowhere near good enough for me to attempt a speech in Russian, which Boffa could and had done). He claimed that *Literaturnaya Gazeta* had had a staffer who had gone to Vietnam and within weeks was speaking the language perfectly, yet Sam Russell not only decided to insult them but to give injury to the insult by doing so in English.

The other Communist newspaper correspondents were more secretive in relations with me than I found with capitalist correspondents, who nevertheless did not understand the problems we had, believing we all enjoyed a hot line to the Kremlin. How wrong they were!

Pierre Courtard, who followed on from Pierre Hentgès as *l'Humanité* correspondent, thought he indeed might have a hot line when he came out to Moscow but was soon disillusioned. In Paris, where he had been the Foreign Editor of *l'Humanité*, he had become very friendly with Yuri Zhukov, the *Pravda* Foreign Editor I had come up against over the 'secret speech'. Courtard thought that this friendship, the thaw in Moscow and his own status back in France would all work to offer him chances to offer positive coverage of developments in the Soviet Union. It was not to be. In Moscow he was just a correspondent and he found that hard to take. With Zhukov he found the same experience as I had. Zhukov sought to close rather than open doors – eventually he was put in charge of one of those particular institutions that the Soviets had developed, a friendship committee to develop good relations with the relevant target country. Being responsible for a friendship committee did nothing to change his attitude. Of course, as an official in the Soviet system he had to be careful not to put a foot wrong. Having known of colleagues who had ended up on the road north from Magadan, he was understandably not keen on viewing the same scenery. Magadan had been a key staging post for prisoners in the Siberian Gulag.

Courtard was particularly disillusioned by the anti-Semitism he ran into. It was a small thing that triggered the real political awakening for him. He happened to be friendly with the Gromykos through some past connection and this continued in Moscow where Andrei Gromyko had become Soviet Foreign Minister and a politburo member. He was invited to dine with Gromyko and his wife. Mrs Gromyko mentioned over the dinner table that the course was a typical Russian soup. Pierre said he had had it before when he had been with some Russian friends who he named. 'You couldn't have had a real Russian soup with them', replied Mrs Gromyko, 'they're Jews'. Pierre told me afterwards that he just could not believe his ears. Here was the cultured wife of the Soviet Foreign Minister, an honoured guest in capitals around the world, not some uncultured peasant from a distant *kolkhoz* (collective farm) in the Russian steppe, engaging in blunt anti-Semitism.

178 Farewell to Moscow

Then came the saga of his car. Having written stories for several Soviet papers over the years he had amassed quite a quantity of roubles which he could not use outside the Soviet Union. He decided to buy a car and like several of the other correspondents in Moscow he used the *Pravda* garage. But when he put it in for some repairs first one week went by and then another without the work being done. Had he put a bottle of vodka in the glove compartment, I ventured to ask. He accused me of taking anti-Sovietism too far but did agree to do so. Next time I saw him he had his car back.

The correspondents of the international Communist press were there as guests, with their living expenses, rent and a small wage paid by the Russians. In Soviet terms we were privileged but we were certainly no better off than we would have been on our 'party wages' at home. The mainstream Western papers paid substantial rents for the flats they had for their correspondents and sometimes asked how we were able to sustain a correspondent in Moscow given the feeble resources of the Worker. I always replied that it was a reciprocal arrangement with *Pravda* based on the assistance we gave to the *Pravda* correspondent in London!

Our money came from different sources. All my phone calls were made on the *Pravda* account. The wage, however, had to be collected from the Soviet Red Cross. This was explained to me by an official on one occasion as being the result of the need by Soviet regulations for everyone to be in a category and the category we were put in was that of 'political refugee'. Occasionally, on one of my monthly trips to the Red Cross offices, I would run into one or other of my colleagues from another Communist Party paper. One of them always had the same puerile joke: 'Had I come to pick up my ration of bandages?'

Like other party journalists I needed to earn a bit of extra money, which I did editing English translations at *Moscow News*. The paper had an office in Pushkin Square from the balcony of which, one of the staff whispered to me once, Trotsky would address the masses.

I was in the office one day when a friend, Philippa Griffiths, who worked for *Moscow News* and was the wife of Pierre Hentgès, just happened to ask where Magadan was.

There was a silence across the room. And then in a very quiet voice one of the Russian colleagues said he would show her where it was. There was a certain tone in his voice and all the other Russians in the office remained silent. He got up from his chair and went over to a map on the wall and pointed out the place.

Slowly conversation came back and when we had finished our work and we were leaving I asked him if he cared for a beer, Pushkin Square having the only *pivnaya* or pub in Moscow then. There was big notice at the entrance saying 'No Vodka On Sale'. Russian customers would come in with bottles of vodka and plead for a glass to drink it – 'we Russians are cultured people', I used to hear them say. 'We do not drink vodka from a bottle'. The quid pro quo was that the customer left the empty bottle, which the waitresses were able to sell.

I asked him to tell me about Magadan while we had our beer.

'With all respect to you foreign Communists', he said, 'You do not know what has happened here. Khrushchev's speech did not even begin to tell what it was like'. To every Russian in the room Magadan had meant a hell, which they had either experienced themselves or known of from people close to them as relatives, friends or neighbours. He had been outside the Soviet Union and had seen a better life in countries like Britain. A small man with a face lined with years of experience, he could not understand why anyone should think that what was being done in the Soviet Union was anything other than a disaster. After some years in the army, he was discharged and ended up being 'sent away'.

Taken to Magadan by sea, people were trucked or marched off to timber felling camps. He talked of the violence, the suffering, the numbers who died. The others had preferred to keep quiet. After all in their minds would have been the thought, perhaps such things might come back again. Silence might not guarantee safety, but it had to be less dangerous than talking.

My British contacts, aside from Dennis Ogden and Johnny Gibbons, also included Johnny Campbell's stepson, Willy, a Clarion cyclist who had come to the Soviet Union in the 1930s to escape unemployment and better serve the proletariat and, once there, building on his perky Glaswegian humour, had become Villi the Clown. He struck up with a Russian ballerina, Elena, who became his wife, giving entertainment to Red Army troops during the war. Although friends and colleagues disappeared, he survived and was awarded medals, until Stalin's post-war anti-foreigner witch-hunt forced him off the stage. Now he was working in Moscow Radio under the name Bill Kaye and had a programme on sport in the English service beamed to India. I met him often and in these days he saw the Soviet leaders as a shower of bastards.[3]

Shortly before Johnny Campbell was due to lead a high-level British CP delegation to Moscow in 1956 I met Willy, who was living in really bad conditions with his wife and sister in law. Knowing the delegation was coming, I told Matkovsky, head of the Central Committee section responsible for the British Party, they needed moving from their hovel, and he saw to it. I imagine Willy would have been very cautious in any letter he sent to Johnny back in Britain, but meeting face to face as they did then, one assumes more was said.

In the very first meeting with Soviet officials, Campbell raised the issue of Len Wincott. The leader of the Invergordon naval mutiny in 1931, he had gone to the Soviet Union where after the war he was charged with being an agent of British naval intelligence. Campbell said he wanted to see Len and there would be no discussions on anything until he was produced. Apparently Matkovsky replied that there were tens of thousands coming out of camps and the authorities did not know where everybody was. Campbell said he could not believe that but the delegation left Moscow without seeing Len, having accepted an undertaking he would be brought to Moscow as soon as could be.

While I was in Budapest, Len, freed from the camps, tracked down where we were living and called on Margaret unannounced. She spent a day feeding him and listening to his story. One day, when he was on a train, he said, two men had

180 Farewell to Moscow

come into the carriage and told him to leave with them. He protested the train was on the move. They pulled the alarm and off he was taken into the Gulag where he worked as a water boy in a coal mine run by the prison system.

On the first day I saw him, I could not get him to stop talking, which was all very well and interesting, but I needed to sleep. With his coat on, I had to keep edging him towards the door. When he eventually saw the inside of the front door he cried out in horror, protesting that we only had one lock and that we had not used the bolts, which were stuck with paint. It turned out that, before the war, a friend of his working at home in Len's flat had heard a scratching sound which would not stop. Looking for a mouse, he realised it was coming from the door. A hacksaw blade was coming through near the lock, going round it. Taking up the chain for his dog, he wrapped it round the wrist of the person who put their arm through the hole and fixed the chain onto a hook in the doorframe.

While phoning the local militia, he heard the most horrible yelling and screeching from the other side of the door, which died away before the thump of boots coming up the stairs. He unhooked the chain and opened the door only to see a headless body falling away at the feet of the militia – the gang had made their getaway, taking the identity of their colleague with them. All this was told by Len at midnight with Margaret standing open mouthed beside me. Whether or not it was a true tale of Moscow crime in the 1930s, Len told it as if he believed it and still lived in fear of it happening again.

Others from Britain living in Moscow also had bitter tales to tell. George Hanna, who had been in the army in India and later left for Moscow to work with the Comintern, was arrested in the 1940s and was only let out when I was *Worker* correspondent. Those of us in Moscow had a small convivial lunch for him at the Astoria, which was part of what had been the famous old Lux Hotel in Gorky Street. George told us that his interrogator said at one point: 'You say you are a member of the British Party. Can you tell us who would stand guarantor for you?' He nominated Harry Pollitt. The interrogator pulled out a book and, after turning over quite a few pages, said, 'Ah. Harry Pollitt, a well-known agent of British intelligence'.

George went down for a long stretch, and Rosie and his two children were thrown on to the streets. As happened in those days, ordinary Russians helped them, giving them what was termed 'a corner', literally a corner of an already crowded room. When he was released he set to redecorate a small flat they had been given. Rosie was ill with a chronic degenerative illness, but was still an amazing person, having kept herself alive through those years. George invited me over to see how well the flat was turning out. It was a flea pit, but to him after years in the camps it was like the Ritz, a most moving marker for me of how bad things had been. He died shortly after.

I saw a lot of Johnny Gibbons, who knew a great deal about what was wrong with the Soviet system. He had been present at the Katyn disinterment in 1943 and was suspicious when the Soviet doctors used the livers of the dead to determine the time of death and therefore the Nazi culpability for the massacre of thousands of Polish officers buried there. Johnny did not live to see Soviet guilt established. His son Tommy, named after one of two uncles killed in Spain, died in a tragedy as a volunteer in the Soviet Virgin Lands in the 1950s. As grain fell off a truck, which was overloaded so that the driver could more than fulfil the target, it created a road surface like ice. The truck in which Tommy was riding over-turned and his skull was smashed. A Central Committee contact phoned me to tell me of the accident. Johnny was in Prague. His wife was in a mental hospital in Moscow. They wanted me to meet Johnny at the airport and tell him the news. There was a funeral in the Great Hall of the Moscow Lomonosov State University. It was massive, a sign of the support this family, who devoted themselves to the cause, had from all who knew them.

One of the most significant friendships in my life also began in Moscow. A lunch with Mark Petrovich Frazer in the Leningrad Hotel was the start of what became a very important part – and, at times, a very disturbed part – of my life in Moscow. Mark Petrovich Frazer was the pseudonym used by Donald Maclean when he was working at the Foreign Languages Publishing House writing articles for the monthly journal *International Affairs*. His presence in Moscow was a scoop I did not get. In February 1956, with Guy Burgess, he was introduced to British journalists for the first time since they had left Britain. The ones who were given the scoop were Sydney Weiland of Reuters and Richard Hughes of the *Sunday Times*. Donald and Guy Burgess had prepared a statement which was wired around the world by TASS. They denied they had ever been agents for the Soviet Union when, for a while, they had been members of the Communist Party at Cambridge University. They implied that they had never acted as agents when they were with the Foreign Office, only referring to 'differences' they had had with official British policy. That was all very well and very carefully constructed by the Soviet controllers, but did not explain in the slightest why they had left Britain for Moscow nor why they continued to stay there.

Donald had famously fled to Russia in 1951 with Guy Burgess. His wife Melinda joined him after two years and they were sent with their three children to Kuibyshev, a closed city to the east of Moscow. Donald had insisted on working and earning his way from the very start. In Kuibyshev he taught English in a teachers' training institute, learning Russian at the same time. When he came back to Moscow, he joined the Institute for World Economics and International Affairs where he was highly regarded. My introduction came through Dennis Ogden, who had met him when he was working at the Foreign Languages Publishing House.

Donald's family and mine became close. I even wondered if the authorities had deliberately put us in a flat nearby. The first we were offered was in the next block and the one we eventually chose was only just up the road.

When Donald learned that James Klugmann was to visit Moscow, he wanted to see him and asked me to be the go-between. Donald worshipped James, who became the leading intellectual working for the British Party but had been hopelessly compromised by his writings attacking Tito. Donald and James had

182 Farewell to Moscow

been at school together, were best friends, and had joined the CP together, and James had helped the Soviets recruit Donald and the other Cambridge University spies.

James, it turned out, was reluctant to see Donald but they did meet eventually. James was still uneasy and, according to Melinda, very stand-offish. She was in tears because she had heard so much about this most wonderful man and here he was acting like a shit.

Donald missed England – he had a hand organ, not a piano, on which he would play the Eton boating song, and at his request his ashes were returned to the church in Penn, Buckinghamshire where his parents were buried. He also had a magnificent cook provided by the government and I recall a wonderful whole perch she served. He chain-smoked and periodically was catastrophically drunk. Melinda was in a very difficult situation. She was claustrophobic and could not get in a lift, always walking up and down the stairs. Margaret got very friendly with Melinda, who would rely on us to help when Donald went off the rails. Once Melinda telephoned after midnight begging me to come. The children were on the stairs outside the flat in tears and Donald, a very strong man physically, was inside in an uncontrollable rage. Margaret was very good at handling him, I wasn't. The Russians successfully treated him for booze because he wanted to do something about it, whereas Burgess didn't.

He saw little of Burgess, who lived with his boyfriend in Kuibyshev. Guy lived his own life and, unlike Donald, didn't feel the need to earn his keep. Donald always thought that it had not been necessary for him to leave Britain and blamed Guy for being panicked by Philby.

In contrast to the awful times when Donald was drunk – and could be very unpleasant – there were more moments when Donald was enthralling, particularly as he went along with the general development of Communist ideas on the basis of Khrushchev's disclosures at the twentieth congress. Our discussions, often walking the streets of Moscow late into the night, would last until one or two in the morning hours. I remember asking him in the middle of one of these conversations in his flat whether the place was bugged. 'I don't care', he said. 'Any way it will do them a lot of good listening in'. He was concerned for me, however, and when, for example, I took him to a concert given by the British conductor Malcolm Sargent, Donald worried that it would affect my relationship with the British embassy top brass, all of whom were there.

Donald was dismayed at the Brezhnev succession after Khrushchev, and when Brezhnev died, Donald thought the more realistic Andropov was, in the circumstances, progressive, although he had been in charge of persecuting Sakharov and the other dissident intellectuals. Andropov only lasted 15 months and Donald died before him. Donald had felt that a new generation of potential leaders and intellectuals was emerging in the Soviet Union who would be capable of overcoming the heritage of Stalin and the succession of idiots who ran the country and Socialism into the ground in the 1960s and 1970s. But that generation proved to be incapable or unwilling. The Soviet Union seemed only to produce leaders of terrifying brutality or banality, and in the 1980s the current crop were rightly swept away when Mikhail Gorbachev unleashed *perestroika*. What makes it all so disappointing is that from the ruins of that mediocrity all that emerged was its mirror image in the shape of Boris Yeltsin and then Vladimir Putin of the KGB.

For years after my stay in Moscow, I would meet Donald regularly, either on periodic visits or when I was passing through the Soviet capital on trips elsewhere. His views became increasingly strong. He stood out against the invasion of Czechoslovakia in 1968. For the regime it was an absolute that there had to be a meeting of everyone in every institution at which all had to vote in support of the military action as justified and necessary. Donald escaped confrontation because his boss arranged for him to take some leave. He knew the Soviet Union had gone wrong but that didn't shake his belief in Socialism as potentially a higher form of society. He supported the programme of the British Party, 'The British Road to Socialism', and the approach of Eurocommunism.

The one major point of disagreement I ever had with Donald was when Jaruzelski declared martial law in Poland in 1981 and to my utter surprise Donald was very strongly in favour, saying the Poles needed to be taught a lesson. That was an exception to his stand on human rights – he campaigned against the treatment of scientist Vladimir Bukovsky in psychiatric prison – and his general and increasingly clear criticism of the lack of democracy in the Soviet Union's sphere and of its foreign policy – he also opposed the invasion of Afghanistan and the introduction of Soviet SS-20 missiles into Europe. His oppositional views meant that by the time he died he was very much out of favour with the Soviets.

He told me at one stage that he would have been in real trouble with the Soviet authorities if it had not been for the intervention of George Blake, the British spy who was smuggled out to the safety of the Soviet Union in the mid-1960s. I had met him once before in Moscow and met him again at Donald's dacha. He was an amusing man and held similar views to Donald but not as ideologically well developed. As far as I knew, unlike Donald, he didn't help dissidents or their relatives. Donald left his library to him.

Donald's big conflict with the authorities came over the treatment of the Medvedev brothers, Roy and Zhores. On my way to Tokyo in June 1970 I visited Donald, who told me the story of how Zhores had got into a mess with a regional Party secretary and was taken off to the psychiatric ward in response – that was the sort of thing regional Party secretaries could easily do. Donald wrote in to protest to Yuri Andropov, then head of the KGB. Large numbers of intellectuals were doing the same. Donald suggested that, as I was on my way to Tokyo, I should write up a detailed story about the protests when I came back through Moscow in a few weeks' time. By the time I returned, Medvedev had been released. Donald was visited by one of the senior KGB generals to remind him of his supposed duties to the Soviet Union.

Wilfred Burchett, the celebrated left-wing Australian journalist, wanted to interview Donald and the message was passed via Pierre Hentgès and then

184 Farewell to Moscow

myself to Donald. Donald invited Burchett for a weekend visit in the country. A few days later I met a livid Donald who demanded to know why I had not warned him about 'that bastard'. Burchett had put up the idea that he, Burchett, could have a number of sessions with Donald and write his biography from that. Officially Burchett was the correspondent of the *National Guardian* weekly in the US, but he had a flat in Moscow in one of the Stalin skyscrapers right near Red Square where it always seemed to me that the other residents were either Red Army generals or ballerinas in the Bolshoi. That meant that someone from on high was financing him. It was alleged that he was a KGB man, and − although he did some important things for the movement, especially in his reporting from Vietnam − I believe he had become one.

Burchett told Donald he had discussed it with the comrades at the head of the Sovinform bureau, the Soviet feature news agency. Burchett apparently put the pressure on, saying it had been agreed at the top level. Donald would not budge even when the Sovinform chiefs themselves sent one of the officials to see him, offering as a parting shot the threatening '...well comrade we shall discuss this further and you will hearing from us...' Donald told me his refusal was mainly to protect the British Party.

Of course, it was a bit late to start thinking like that after the damage was done, but at least he was not prepared to be used in whatever press stunt the KGB might dream up, as they did later with Kim Philby, who was decorated by Franco as well as by the Soviets. Philby loved that self-celebratory glamour side of things. Donald did not and was opposed to the media promotion of Philby by the KGB. He spent his time working in a serious attempt to deal with the issues that all of us as Communists needed to confront. His Soviet minders had other ideas.

Philby supported the Czech invasion and went on working for his spy bosses, unlike Donald. I never met Philby but often wondered if he had been responsible for the notion that I was a Soviet sleeper, which kept me out of the British army; had he fingered me to divert attention from himself? Melinda, who was not a Communist but stood by Donald for many years, later married Philby. One day I saw her and she said she had a message from Philby: I was a bloody bad journalist. After she left Philby, Donald used the English money he had to get her a flat, and she and Donald remained friends.[4]

I was opposed to spying, and I didn't talk about it to Donald, but I saw in a paper he wrote that, given the international and national situation at the time, he believed he had done the right thing. For example, the first file he saw was about Rio Tinto, a major player in Spain. The Spanish Civil War had just begun, and in the file, he saw something useful to pass on to the Soviets on the Non-Intervention Committee. He had friends like John Cornford in the International Brigades, and in his way Donald too felt he was in the IB. However, I had the impression he had doubts about his world by 1939 and he thought the Nazi-Soviet pact criminal. The problem for me is that I recognise the Soviet Union like all countries needed spies but I am against it. Maybe I would have spied if asked but that does not make it right.

Donald visited KGB headquarters at the infamous Lubyanka Prison only once and was shown the room where his messages had been kept. The minder said there were piles of them, so many at one time that they couldn't always shut the door. The problem was that many were unopened. Apparently Stalin, who had a high regard for British intelligence, thought Donald was being duped or was a double agent – so perhaps his sacrifice had been in vain.

As a person, Donald was impressive but what I liked about him was that he was not going to talk to the press. He did not want to harm the Communist Party in Britain, of which he had been a member before being asked to go underground and which he still felt he belonged to. He was not like the figure in the Alan Bennett play *Single Spies*. He was sincere and willing to give his all, including his life, for the cause.

I last saw him in 1981 when he showed me something he had written on Soviet foreign policy, corruption in the Soviet Union and the possible development of internal democracy. Within Party circles it was ahead of its time. He wanted it published in Britain and had thought of sending it to the *New Statesman* but had changed his mind. With his agreement, I said I would offer it to the British Party journal *Marxism Today* under my name. The editor Martin Jacques, who didn't know the background, published the first part in June 1981 but he turned down the second. Later, when I told Jacques who really had written it, he said he would have published it under Donald's name but I doubt he would have got away with it. In 1992 the Institute of World Economics and International Affairs, where Donald had worked, released it in an archive. Donald must have circulated it there as a memo in which he elaborated his reform ideas and predicted perestroika and greater democracy in the Soviet Union but not its eventual collapse.

After Donald's death in 1983, Robert Cecil called me. Cecil had taken over from Donald as head of the Foreign Office's American desk when Donald legged it to the Soviet Union in 1951, and he was now researching a book. I invited him round and soon he got his notebook out. I told him to put it away, but I did talk to him about Donald and Melinda and told him that, contrary to what had appeared in the media, she had known about Donald's activities from the word go. This revelation appeared in Cecil's book. I am certain that I was the only source for this piece of information – and I am thanked in the acknowledgements though not directly for this.

Returning Home

My time in Moscow came to an end in 1959. I was torn about coming back but Margaret had made up her mind.[5] I handed over to Dennis Ogden, whom Besedin, my Central Committee contact, had been rooting for as my replacement for a long time. He was absolutely convinced that Dennis was a 'reliable comrade'

186 Farewell to Moscow

unlike myself. When Dennis came out with his exclusive story about the first cosmonaut in space and refused to divulge his source, Besedin learnt his lesson.

I returned to the *Worker* as a spare part and was sent to cover the general election. I didn't ask for my old job back but the editor, George Matthews, said I should have it, and the incumbent, a Party organiser who had been brought in as a stop gap, took it badly. I guided coverage of Soviet affairs as Foreign Editor, and one of the few pleasures of the sub-editors was listening to me giving the Moscow correspondent a bollocking for not being tough enough on the Soviets. I encouraged them to put over all they knew so that the paper would tell as much as the editor would allow.

I went back to Moscow on many occasions. I covered Party congresses with an increasing sense of the absurd. The last Soviet Party Congress I attended – in 1981, which I wangled as an excuse to see Donald – was the final one of the Brezhnev era and the most corrupt one I knew. Brezhnev, sweating like a pig, could hardly walk and all the applause was piped over the tannoy. They couldn't even trust their hand-picked delegates.

My critical report was published but with some cuts made by the assistant editor Chris Myant. The editor Tony Chater called him at 7 am when he saw the paper and tore him off a strip for what had been published, which he saw as anti-Soviet. Chater repeated it all to me on the phone. Later that day I told Gordon McLennan, General Secretary of the British Party, who was in Moscow for the congress, and he said Chater was right. The criticism was very low key, so I realised then that the Party under McLennan was going nowhere.

He and the International Secretary Gerry Pocock had come to Moscow with a strict brief from the Party leadership in London that any speech McLennan made had to include the British Party's criticisms of the Soviet invasion of Afghanistan in 1979. The tradition in the world Communist movement was that a visiting 'fraternal delegate' would make a speech to the congress with the text being handed over in advance for translation, so a text was duly prepared. On arrival in Moscow, it was handed in by Pocock 'purely for translation purposes', as the Russians would say. But within minutes of getting the text, Dzhavad Sharif, the Central Committee official responsible for relations with Britain and the British Party, came tearing back demanding the section on Afghanistan be cut out. There was a heated argument. McLennan agreed to water down the formulation and the Soviets finally said that they would let it pass.

McLennan was called on to make his speech and I listened to the Russian version given to delegates. After he finished there was a break for delegates to get a bite to eat and Pocock came thundering down the stairs from his seat. He had been listening to the French version and the bit on Afghanistan had been removed. I told him it had been removed from the Russian version as well and that that was the version used for all the other translations. He was furious and seemed surprised. Gerry complained and was told there had been an error and it would be corrected when the speech came to be reprinted in *Pravda*. I was later told that the editions of *Pravda* sent around the country had the Russian text as read out at the Congress with the Afghanistan reference removed. A small number, however, were printed with the reference included and McLennan was presented with a copy from this limited edition. Such was the way of life in the Soviet Union.

Notes

1 Even in the early 1980s, Sam said, his successor as Moscow correspondent could not get permission to interview a chess grandmaster who lived in the same block of flats and to whom he talked daily when they fixed back the windscreen wipers they had carefully removed the night before to avoid them being stolen.
2 Simonov was editor from 1954 to 1957 (as well as 1946–1950) and Tvardovsky 1958–1970 (as well as 1950–1954). Sam tried to interview Tvardovsky on several occasions but he always refused.
3 In the late 1970s, Willy and Elena left the Soviet Union and settled in Britain. Having been starry-eyed with illusions, said Sam, Willy left thoroughly disillusioned and wrote a book, *Villi the Clown* (London: Faber & Faber, 1981), about his time there.
4 Sam mentioned Maclean's concern for others and said that on one visit he had left a winter great coat with him but before he returned to claim it Maclean had given it to a dissident friend just out of a long spell in the camps who had need of some warm wear.
5 Sam's daughter Ruth says her mother had determined that she should start school in London and that she and Margaret left the Soviet Union in September 1958.

12

MEETING CHE

As the Cubans crowded back onto the plane, there was a final security check for any guns. The flight to Havana went via Prague, and we had also stopped at Shannon in Ireland. The Irish police ordered everyone to hand over any weapons. Judging by the arsenal that was collected, the Cubans must have been armed to the teeth, but back in the plane during the silence before the engines warmed up, one of them in the seats in front of mine whispered in Spanish to his colleague 'I've still got two of mine!'

At Gander in Newfoundland for the next stopover, the Canadian Mounties went through everything all over again. There was one big box marked as part of the Cuban diplomatic bag. A Cuban official refused to allow it to be opened but the Mounties ordered it be opened and opened it was. It looked to me just like the sort of box that would have guns in it and, when the lid was finally prised off, the wood shavings underneath made the Mounties feel even more certain they were on to something. Given that this plane was making its journey in the middle of the Cuban missile crisis, their excitement was perhaps understandable. But, while history might have been being made in the Caribbean, on the tarmac at Gander it turned out that this supposed consignment of Soviet arms was nothing more than several enormous sausages.

The Cuban missile crisis had already exploded when I arrived in Havana in early November 1962 – the only British correspondent there as far as I was aware. The Cubans were boiling, expecting the US forces to arrive at any moment. Why was I not wearing a war correspondent's uniform, they asked, and only partly in jest?

Attempts at radical revolution in the Americas were usually suppressed by US backed military coups and on occasion by direct US military intervention. Cuba under Castro was the great exception, and he was getting closer

DOI: 10.4324/9781003243380-13

to the Soviet Union, thanks in part to a US trade blockade. In May 1962, Khrushchev decided to put Soviet nuclear missiles in Cuba but when challenged, the Soviet Foreign Minister Andrei Gromyko speaking at the UN General Assembly denied their existence. The British Communist Party and the *Worker* backed the Soviet position. When the first US spy plane pictures of the launch sites were issued, the Soviets explained them away as football fields and the like. Colleagues at the *Worker* spent many hours examining the pictures carefully and saying, yes, that obviously was the case. In October, the first verifiable pictures of missile launchers in Cuba were taken by US U-2 spy planes, triggering the missile crisis of that month and a fortnight of confrontation between the two major nuclear powers. At the end of October, a letter from the Soviet leadership was delivered to Washington committing the Soviet Union to withdraw the missiles and First Deputy Chairman Anastas Mikoyan, one of Khrushchev's closest allies, was sent to Havana when Cuban frustration and anger at this decision was at its height.

Almost as soon as I arrived, Mikoyan, the typical Soviet leadership figure, was going to address an official rally marking the 45th anniversary of the 1917 Revolution. It turned out to be quite unlike the formal ceremonials in Moscow. There was even a particular Cuban lilt to the 'Internationale'. The Cubans were expert at making every political slogan into some sort of rhyming cha-cha-cha type rhythm. The chant today was *'Fidel, Khrushchev, estamos con los dos!'* – 'Fidel, Khrushchev, we back them both!' – accompanied by rhythmic clapping.

The Cuban speech was made by the General Secretary of the youth organisation, quite a young chap called, appropriately enough, Rebellion. The United States, he said, was going to be wiped out. He finished with a resounding cry of *'Patria o Muerte, Venceremos!'* – 'Homeland or Death, We will Win!'

Then, about 20 decibels lower, came Mikoyan. He was, he explained, pleased to be in Cuba. He talked about the successes of the Soviet Union offering a finely tuned version of the usual Soviet leadership speech with detailed statistics on pig iron production or the extent of Virgin Lands covered now by corn or cotton and the square meterage of new flats.

The following day there was a reception in the Soviet embassy to mark the anniversary. We were in shirt sleeves in the garden, as it was far too hot for an indoor event. Mikoyan finished his formal address by proposing that we all take a toast. 'Don't let us drink to death', he said. 'Let us drink to life and the glorious Socialist future'.

The Cubans were palpably furious. Mikoyan had effectively sneered at the basic slogan of the revolution: 'Patria o Muerte' – 'Homeland or Death'. By rather more than implication he was having a go at their whole approach to politics. Outside in the streets if they could have got hold of Mikoyan – or perhaps even Khrushchev – they would have hanged him on the nearest lamp post. The universal attitude was that he had sold them out to the US.

That same evening, my host suggested there were good things to be heard at the university after midnight.[1] He did not explain what might happen but

190 Meeting Che

when I arrived the students revealed the cause of the excitement: Fidel would be there soon. It was all part of the romance of this unique revolution. After a tiring day's work, Fidel liked to go and be refreshed through discussion with the students.

They fired the questions. In the most obscene language – even for Cubans – they asked why Mikoyan had been invited to Cuba. 'He has nothing between his ears and less between his legs'. Fidel said they should not worry. They pressed him. It was very boring, Fidel agreed. 'You know how it is', he said. 'You have to humour these Russians'. The students insisted. 'Why not send him home?' 'That was a bit difficult given the situation with the planes and so on', Fidel said. 'What was Mikoyan doing? Was he plotting against Cuba?' 'No', said Fidel. 'Of that you can be absolutely sure'. He would have no time for plots because we are sending him around to pig farms, including the one run by my brother. By the time he has gone to all the pig farms we have lined up for him, he will be coming to us on his hands and knees pleading.

In the meantime, Khrushchev had other ideas. Although Mikoyan's wife died while he was in Cuba, he was told by the Soviet leadership to stay and was not allowed to return for the funeral. One of his sons, Sergei, was an expert on Latin America who I got to know very well. From conversations with him, it was clearly a very close and attached family and whatever one may think of Mikoyan, that refusal must have been painful, especially as he was subjected to some really insulting treatment by the Cubans. The message from Moscow was grin and bear it until Fidel and his people cool down. Their calculation was, correctly, that Castro would have to accept a deal between Khrushchev and US President Kennedy because the Soviet leadership were the only friends he had.

One of my key contacts was Carlos Franqui, who had been with Fidel in the Sierra Maestra mountains as one of the leaders of the 26th of July Movement that spearheaded the Revolution. Turning up one time to see him, I found an *Izvestia* correspondent, who spoke magnificent Spanish, had beaten me to the appointment. Franqui was taking the piss out of him in a merciless way. The man from the main Soviet daily paper decided eventually he had had enough and left. As I talked to Franqui, a colleague of his came in and whispered something in his ear, at which Franqui said: 'Come with me and you will see what bastards these Russians are'. He took me into a room that was full of radio equipment.

At that time the Soviets were withdrawing their missiles on the decks of merchant vessels. When they got to the Cuban 12-mile maritime limit they would pass US destroyers on patrol. It turned out that the Cubans were listening in to the communications between the Soviet and the US ships. Franqui gave the headphones to me and I could hear the conversations between the ships carried out in English.

The US Navy ships were given the name of the Soviet merchant ship and would order it to 'uncover'. The missiles on the decks under tarpaulins would be exposed for inspection by the Americans. The US officers could be heard giving the numbers painted on the sides of the rockets on the Soviet ships, each and every one. As the number was read off, the US officer would say over the radio 'OK, cover up and proceed'. Only then were the Soviet ships allowed to continue on their way. Franqui denounced this as 'striptease on the high seas'.

The Soviets said they had had to take an urgent decision and do what they had to do, but to the Cubans, the Soviets had sold out. Part of the deal was that UN observers would be in Cuba. The Cubans were categorical: no UN observers would be allowed in and the US had to be content with surveillance beyond Cuba's 12-mile territorial waters limit. In the streets, the Cubans had put up posters with the slogan 'Cuba no es el Congo' – 'Cuba is not the Congo'. It was not long after the independence leader of the former Belgian colony, Patrice Lumumba, had been murdered with the connivance of the CIA, and his death had been followed by a disastrous UN military intervention.

I wanted to find out more about the background and went to see Carlos Rafael Rodriguez, one of the very few old Cuban Communists whom Fidel trusted and who was Minister of Agriculture. In the course of the discussion about farms that was the excuse for the interview, I asked him about the rockets. What I could not understand was how the government of which he was a member took the decision to have the Soviet missiles in the first place.

'It was like this', said Carlos.

> We had a meeting one day after the Bay of Pigs. The Soviet comrades were at the meeting and said their information was that Kennedy was going to have another go at an invasion and we needed to take precautions in order to deal with that. We asked what they might suggest. They suggested they could put in some rockets, which could help us. We had almost finished the meeting having agreed with the idea, when one of the Cubans present, I cannot remember who it was, asked the Soviet advisers whether they were aware that the US was flying planes over the island all the time taking photographs and that, surely, the US would see all the installations that the rockets would require. The reply of the Soviets was that the US would probably not know what the missiles were, and even if they did, all that Kennedy would do would be to shout. So on that basis we went ahead.

It was a gross miscalculation by both the Soviets and the Cubans if ever there was one.

There was a history of tense relations behind the scenes between the Soviets and the Castro government. Castro had thwarted the Soviet game plan for a leadership in Cuba based on the old Communist Party elite who had denounced Fidel when his movement was launched. A number of members of the Communist leadership, however, had objected to the Party line and joined Fidel in the Sierra Maestra. Rodriguez was among them.

192 Meeting Che

Stories of the faction fighting within the Cuban revolution continued over the years, with the Soviets trying to gain complete control, as they had achieved in most of Eastern Europe. The Fidel leadership had a tail put on the movements of the Communist leader Anibal Escalante, who was charged with treason but allowed to leave for Moscow where, the Cubans believed, he was being kept in the Soviet cupboard as a possible alternative leader to Castro.[2] Such arrangements were not unusual. The Soviet leadership wanted to control the whole Communist movement, whether in power or not. It interfered in the affairs of individual Communist Parties, backing dissident groups which were more supportive of its approach than the existing CP leaders, and keeping 'in store' ageing figures who might one day prove useful, such as Wang Ming as a possible replacement for Mao, and Mátyás Rákosi, the brutal, deposed Hungarian leader, kept alive in the Soviet Union just in case.

The US blockade pushed Castro into the arms of the Soviets, and he sidled up to China during the Sino-Soviet split but fell out with them and then again played the Soviet game instead, especially in Africa and after Czechoslovakia, backing the invasion 200%.

My first report from Cuba was on the arrest of US agents who had come by boat from Florida bringing arms and explosives with the apparent intention of sabotaging the Cuban copper and nickel mines. At the same time, what really got my attention were the US flights over the island at low level. One largish US plane spent a good 15 minutes over Havana Bay. Whether or not the intention in Washington was to provoke the Cubans into opening fire so the US side could claim an excuse for a full-scale attack rather than these pointless attempts by agents who seemed to be easily rounded up was not easy to divine. In any case the Cubans held their fire, despite dozens of these flights.

They let them be until mid-November when Castro sent a formal warning to the US via a letter to U Thant, at the time the Acting UN General Secretary. 'We are defending the rights of small nations to be treated with equal consideration', Castro declared. The day the letter went off, we heard no over-flights by the US Air Force, but the tension was extreme. Everyone knew that if the Cubans attacked a US spy plane then a 'serious situation' could develop. The Cuban argument was simple. The missile sites had been dismantled, so there was no need for Havana to tolerate provocative spy flights.

The Cubans kept making the same point: no need for you to fly, you can come and look at things here on the ground any time you want with just one proviso – we are given the same rights to look at Guantanamo, the giant US base on Cuban soil, and the bases in Florida and Puerto Rico from which you have been sending people to attack us.

On the day Castro's letter went off to New York, the Cuban press reported the presence in Miami of Manuel Sosa, the Guatemalan Chief of Naval Operations. Cuba should be invaded 'now', he was reported to have declared. 'It will be a blood bath with perhaps 10,000 killed in the streets of Havana, but we cannot wait any longer', were his friendly words. His threats were made even more real a couple of days later when a Cuban cargo ship was attacked in international waters. A plane dropped 11 bombs, luckily all of them falling harmlessly into the sea. Planes like that did not come from nowhere.

Castro had already put five points for a peace settlement on the table: there should be an end to the US blockade of Cuba (which he did not achieve); an end to US-backed sabotage and subversion (which also continued over the decades); an end to private attacks on Cuba (another failure); a halt to US over-flights of Cuban airspace (also set to continue); and, supported most enthusiastically by all the Cubans I talked to, the evacuation of Guantanamo, which had been leased indefinitely by a government in Havana in 1903, a government put in place after a Washington invasion of the island. What Castro and the Soviets did secure was an acceptance by the US that its attempts to unseat the revolutionary regime in Cuba would not amount to more than perpetual skirmishing, dangerous, destructive and distracting but never terminal.

That the popular sentiment in Cuba was overwhelmingly behind the new authorities was obvious wherever I went. Walking past anti-aircraft guns along Havana's famed Malecón, the broad boulevard that skirts the sea shore round the city's beautiful bay, I came across a group dismantling a giant eagle of the kind that adorns the front of every US embassy entrance. They explained that it was going to be replaced by a replica of Picasso's *Dove of Peace*. Beside the boulevard, gardens had been laid out on what had been wasteland under Batista – the deposed dictator had been keeping the land aside for developers to build their hotels and casinos. Now they were playgrounds for children – but with army watchtowers beside many of them. The docks were busy with Greek, West German, Soviet and various East European registered ships; one I noticed was named *Lidice* after the Czech village destroyed by the Nazis in reprisal for the assassination of the SS boss Reinhard Heydrich in 1942.

Sailors on two Cuban war ships in the harbour's naval base – all very young, most of them just 17 or 18 and trained in the Soviet Union – left me in no doubt as to their determination to fight, if that proved necessary, nor as to the skill with which they could use their weapons. There were militia guards everywhere. At night I could look down from my room on the 17th floor of the Hotel Havana Libre, which had been the Havana Hilton three years before, and see how well the waiters, lift boys, cooks and kitchen hands from the hotel were progressing in their drill practice in the empty car park, lit up for all to see by searchlights. It took me back to my first days in Madrid in November 1936, less than 30 years earlier, with the same sense of danger and threat coupled with gaiety and determination, both of them unquenchable.

Cuba's revolution was approaching its fourth anniversary. In just 48 months, one could not change everything but there were already powerful symbolic signs of change. I went to the new Ministry of Education. It had been the former HQ of the Batista general staff. Previously Columbia, it was now Ciudad Libertad, Freedom City. Each of the seven main military headquarters of the old regime had been converted into these 'school cities' boasting schools, nurseries,

194 Meeting Che

FIGURE 12.1 In Cuba, 1962, Sam talks to sailors ready to defend their country.
Source: Family archive.

FIGURE 12.2 Sam at a meeting in Cuba, 1962.
Source: Family archive.

Meeting Che **195**

workshops, and study rooms, changing over from bullets to blackboards. In the newspapers and on billboards around Havana, slogans called on the Cubans to educate themselves. 'To be educated is to be free' was a popular one. Batista had left a population where the majority could not read or write. The revolutionaries set out to change that with a determination that was astonishing.

Mercedes Alper, a young literacy activist who took me around Ciudad Libertad, had been working with a small group of adult illiterates in a village near Playa Giron, the Bay of Pigs, when the invasion took place in April 1961. Ciudad Libertad had been a CIA target at the time. Aircraft flying from Florida had machine gunned the ministry buildings leaving bullet scars that were all too obvious as I walked around. In the workshops in this new Freedom City Chinese engineers were putting together lathes, Czechoslovak technicians were helping Cuban teachers prepare a scientific project while Soviet specialists were setting up equipment for a physics laboratory. In what had been the cavalry stables, a young woman, her hair in curlers, was bending over a motorcar engine – one of many women there learning to become engineers.

Under Batista, the economy depended on imports from the US of food and virtually every sort of manufactured item imaginable. The revolution and the subsequent US blockade created painful shortages. The early measures taken by the Castro government meant a huge increase in the purchasing power of ordinary people. Agriculture was being reorganised and food production would increase but not overnight, not least because 1961 and 1962 brought a 14-month drought, the worst on the island for 40 years. The boycott and blockade imposed by Washington meant no spare parts for all the US manufactured machinery that in 1959 dominated Cuban life, whether it was a bus deep in the countryside, a lift in a Havana hotel or a water purification plant in a provincial city – hence the drive for engineers. The Cubans had been given a lot of metal working machinery by the Soviet Union but a lack of skills had meant that much of this was quickly rendered useless. The skills were what I could now see coming through.

Out in the countryside, many of the huts that characterised the rural housing in the old Cuba were still there, but in Havana building of a different sort was already underway. The terrible shanty town of Las Yaguas which in 1959 had been home to some 15,000 families was being emptied. A few were still there when I looked out across the hillside on the outskirts of the Cuban capital. It was the worst housing I had ever seen. That was the kind of change that made the farm worker Benino Pilato tell me in no uncertain terms that life on his Granjas del Pueblo, the state-owned farms that had taken over from the largest landowners around a third of all of Cuba's agricultural land, meant that Kennedy simply would not understand why Cubans backed the revolution. He was some 50 years old, had a new house and a small vegetable plot for which he was then paying a nominal rent. 'It is like the difference between night and day. Only God and I know what I suffered before the Revolution', he told me.

He had heard over the radio the previous day the comment by Kennedy that 'Cuba will one day be really free' and he was in full angry flow over this as

196 Meeting Che

we talked in Spanish. He had been 'really free' for four years, he announced. His hovel had been replaced by a house with *separate* rooms. He had work. 'I've got dignity as a human being', he said. 'We don't want Kennedy's kind of freedom'. For him, that would have meant a return to the kind of life before the Revolution and he had no intention of letting that happen. To emphasise the point, he explained that he had just spent 32 days in the trenches on guard against another attempt like that at the Bay of Pigs, an attempt that he feared the CIA would try to make, whatever the public pronouncements from the White House.

I went back to Cuba a decade and half later and something was missing. In 1962, I could look out of the window each morning and see just off shore the ominous presence of the US destroyer *Oxford*, but the city was vibrant with sound. The vital thrust of an Afro-Cuban beat seemed to express all the sense of heroism against impossible odds that characterised the Cuba of Fidel and Che in those early years. In the summer of 1978, that music was gone. For some reason it had vanished from the night clubs and the bars, a sign of changing times, I thought.

This second visit was something of a mess. There was no one there to meet me when I arrived so I had to stage a hunger strike to get some attention! Old Havana, despite nearly 20 years of Castro's government, was still the crowded warren of narrow streets with tenements and former merchant houses packed with families. 'Make no mistake about it', I told the readers, a fair percentage of whom did not want to hear this sort of thing,

> Cuba is not flowing with milk and honey. While restaurants are full on Saturday nights, rationing of food and clothing is still strict, shoes are of poor quality and shortages occur from time to time, such as a shortage of soap and toothpaste while I was there.

Of course there was the impact of the US blockade, but there were also significant policy errors by the Cubans themselves. Castro and his colleagues always found it difficult to give room for private initiative. They tried to run relations between public enterprises on the basis of a 'no money economy'. Indeed for a whole decade up to 1976, they had ignored the need to have a national budget. 'So', I was told by Manuel Garcia, vice chair of the Central Planning Commission, 'no one knew what was happening'. There was no 'economic consciousness', as he put it, since people engaged in production did not need to bother with thinking about the costs they were racking up. They had added to their problems by hoping that the vastly inflated sugar prices of 1974 and 1975 might continue. Then, a pound of Cuba sugar could get 65 US cents on world markets. By the time I was on the island in 1978, that figure was down to 7 US cents, a catastrophe in any one's language. Throughout the decade, the Soviet Union had come to the rescue selling oil to Cuba at below world market prices and buying Cuban sugar at rates well above those prices.

Cuban sugar came mainly from large state farms which had, before 1959, been the vast estates of US companies like United Fruit and a small number of Cuban landowners who dominated the world sugar markets. These estates amounted to about 40% of the farmland on the island. A further 30% of the farmland was nationalised in 1963 when all farms over 150 acres were put in state ownership. At Pepito Tey sugar farm near Cienfuegos, roughly in the middle of the island, I joined a machete team cutting the cane in a temperature of 40° in the shade and soon discovered how back-breaking the job was. One of the workers, Felix Hernandes, showed me how it was done. Watching him, it all seemed very easy, but ten minutes with a machete and I was done for. That was bad enough, but the cane was then processed in a mill that looked as if little had changed since the farm was established by a US firm in 1847. I came away with a deep appreciation both of the scale of the task Cuba faced in taking this industry forward, but also of the achievement they had notched up in raising production in the way they had.

Despite the urgency of economic reform, the optimism of the early days still counted. Cuba was playing an important role in world affairs. There was a wide-ranging programme of technical and medical assistance to those states in Africa and Latin America that were prepared to work with Cuba. For some states, this Cuban presence was effectively their health service. While countries like Britain were sucking out the medical talent in a huge brain drain, Cuba was providing a unique flow in the other direction.

Cuban Foreign Minister Isidoro Malmierca was at pains to point out to me that the first assistance Cuba had provided to newly liberated Africa was a group of 54 medical specialists who went to Algeria in 1963 to help set up a health service and that the humanitarian presence was what Cuba was most proud of. He did not shy away from the strategic importance of the Cuban troops then fighting in Angola. The white racist regime of Ian Smith was still in charge in Zimbabwe, Namibia was a colony of Pretoria and South African troops were directly fighting in Angola against the newly independent and radical government that had taken over from the Portuguese in 1975. With the support of US-funded mercenaries, the apartheid regime's troops had a good chance of deposing the new government. They were stopped by Cuban and Angolan government forces, at some considerable cost in lives to the Cubans.

Malmierca explained it like this to me: 'Our help was a way of ensuring that South Africa's racist regime troops did not advance northwards and extend their frontiers far from Namibia and thus exercise a negative influence over the whole of South-West Africa'.

The first Cuban revolutionary to go to fight in Africa was Che Guevara, Castro's charismatic comrade. Che was then one of only 15 survivors from the first group of 80 revolutionaries who landed with Castro from the *Granma* on the Cuban coast and started the guerrilla campaign that toppled Batista. He later went to try to help those seeking to keep alive the legacy of Congo's murdered independence leader Lumumba. Che, the icon of romantic revolutionaries

FIGURE 12.3 Sam interviewing Che Guevara in Cuba, 1962.
Source: Family archive.

everywhere, eventually died a miserable, lonely death in captivity in the hands of the Bolivian army in 1966 after failing in his attempt to repeat the experience of the Cuban revolution.

Of all my memories from Cuba, the most powerful is of my meeting Che in 1962 at the height of the missile crisis. It was the first interview he had given to an English language journalist since the start of the confrontation, and I was able to talk to him in Spanish, which helped us both relax and forget formalities.

I say interview, but in a way it was nothing of the sort: it was a chaotic, infuriating, moving and utterly unforgettable encounter. Che started talking at 10.30 pm and was only brought to a halt at 3.30 in the early hours. At first, we had to deal with the ministerial business. After all, that was the excuse for the interview. He was then in charge of Cuba's economy. Immediately after the victory of the revolution in 1959, he had set out the basic principle by which he thought the island's economy should be transformed: ending what he termed the monoculture of sugar cane production that dominated the economy. 'We are the slaves of sugar cane, the umbilical cord that ties us to the great northern market', he later wrote in the last pages of his *Episodes of the Revolutionary War*.[3] The theme was his obsession when we met, and, even though the cord had been slashed by the US blockade, the island was still imprisoned by its reliance on sugar being bought in huge quantities by the Soviets.

We soon left the economy behind and got on to politics. He was nothing if not completely frank and sincere, and his line throughout was that had the US so much as lifted a little finger against Cuba 'and if the rockets had been under our control, we would have fired them off'. I remember thinking, as he said it, 'Thank Christ they were not!' Luckily it was not the sort of ball game the Soviets ever played.

His analysis was that Washington wanted to liquidate the Cuban Revolution and was trying to assess what the cost of doing that might be: would it be greater than the cost of leaving the new Cuban regime in place? The Cubans had to be able to show they were ready to inflict the maximum damage on the Americans in the event of a new invasion, and that could mean a fight to the death. Yes, he said, this could sound highly emotional, but during the tensest days of the crisis the Cuban people understood that that they were faced with the possibility of nuclear annihilation, that they were in the front line, and that their determination to resist meant they could die. 'We are under no illusion. We know we cannot exist on our own. We depend on the solidarity of the Socialist camp and of the whole world'.

But hadn't there been differences between the Cubans and the Russians, I asked, given that Castro had suggested there had been 'misunderstandings' or 'discrepancies' between the two leaderships? Using the formal language of the kind Moscow engaged in, Che replied that the discussions had been 'frank and full' – that is, there had been fierce arguments. However, 'the discrepancies are past and will not be of importance in the future'. Part of the 'discrepancies' had no doubt been the move by Fidel, Che, and their colleagues to control the old leadership of the Cuban Communist Party. The former CP General Secretary Escalante had been pushed out of his post not long before the missile crisis.

Che did not only have those like Escalante in his sights. 'Yes, I know about you Western Communists', he said, challenging me. 'I know that you in Western Europe are patting your chests (he was thumping himself on the chest at this) and saying we are alive'.

'Excuse me', I said, 'but I do feel very much relieved to be alive'.

'Ah', he said, 'you think you are. But because of your betrayal ...' I protested that I had betrayed no one.

'No', he said.

> Your friends and their betrayal, you are making another world war absolutely inevitable. It will come, it may be in one year or two years' time, and, as a result of the betrayal of you and your friends, the international working-class movement is going to be in a much worse situation.

He went on to denounce the concept of a peaceful transition to Socialism by the parliamentary road, the idea that had become dominant in the Western European Communist Parties.

200 Meeting Che

> Let's take, for example, in some country of Western Europe where you carry out this policy. You Communists, you work away at propaganda, you have elections, and, say you get 20 Communist delegates elected. Very good. So you keep on working away as it proves the possibility. Say four or five years later you get 50 or 60 deputies, then you say, well it is all very good, so you carry on working away but just before the next elections the bourgeoisie passes a law making the whole thing totally invalid and you are back to square one because through your policy you have led the working class into a trap and in that trap the working class have become the prisoners of the bourgeoisie inside the factories where you once had your main organisations.

The only thing, he said, was to organise revolution, something he tried to do.

There were, I said, Communist Parties in Latin America, which were surely working to get members elected to parliaments.

'Los Partidos Communistas de America Latina son la mierda' was his reply. 'The Communist Parties of Latin America are shit'. His whole approach was to suggest that by even hinting there was a possibility of peaceful transition, a Communist Party was betraying the working class. At the time there was going to be a conference of the Communist parties of Central America in Havana, so I asked Che about it. 'Son cuatro gatos' – they are 'four cats' was all he would say, using a term of general contempt. But he did say there were two countries in Latin America where there was a possibility of peaceful transition – Chile and Uruguay.

However little he might have known about the economy – he just wanted to nationalise everything – and however little we might have agreed on political strategy, Che was a very impressive person. Here we were sitting in the comfort of the ministerial office – coffee and cigars brought in whenever we needed them – and every now and then, gasping for breath, he would produce an old-style asthma spray and use it until he could breathe freely again. How on earth he survived, either in the Sierra Maestra, or in Bolivia where he eventually died, let alone in the jungles of the Congo, I cannot imagine.

I sent the text of the interview by cable to London before leaving Havana, and also gave a copy to Joe North, the correspondent of the New York *Daily Worker* in the Cuban capital. An old mate of mine from Spanish Civil War days, we had shared many stories. I was no hero of independent thought in the Communist movement, but Joe was at the very opposite end of the spectrum and more so than most. He did not use the story.

Any other newspaper would have grabbed the interview with both hands but when I got back to the office in London, I discovered it had not been used on our side of the Atlantic either. The editor, George Matthews, said in the usual casual way that editors have, that I should do it up again. I did so and handed him the new copy. Because it did not fit in with the British Party leadership's view of the world, he made substantial changes and the version finally published in the *Daily Worker* was a travesty, bearing little resemblance to what I had heard from Che. Again, in the way that editors often have, George did not consult me about the changes.

Some while later a letter arrived from the New York *Daily Worker* which George showed to me complaining about my interview. The New York paper said the US news agency United Press (UP) had put out a story claiming the version published in London was censored. It also claimed that in the course of the interview Che had said that if the Americans had moved their little finger we would have fired every one of the rockets on Washington and New York, a remark which did not appear in the London version.

I was puzzled. How did UP know about it? UP eventually issued a statement from their Diplomatic Correspondent in London saying that I, Sam Russell, had been in one of the House of Commons bars, drunk, and had let the whole story out. The UP Diplomatic Correspondent was a good acquaintance and we used to meet up at Foreign Office functions. When we next met my question was direct: 'What the hell had he been up to?' He said that the story had nothing to do with him, and it was then the penny dropped. The CIA or some other US agency must have had a transcript from the cable and leaked it to UP.

When I had had my run-in with Leonid Illychov in Moscow over the Khrushchev secret speech, he had put in a complaint that I had come to him drunk, smelling of vodka. Here was the American CIA confronted with a similar situation and jumping to the same excuse: Sam Russell was on the bottle again and could be held up to international obloquy as one of those alcohol-hazed hacks everybody knows so well.

Years later, I was able to see that my interview had indeed been picked up by the CIA and had been an issue in the discussions between Kennedy and the Soviet leaders long before anything appeared in the *Worker* itself.[4] CIA Director John A McCone personally dropped into the Oval Office a note he had prepared for Kennedy in which he reported three 'indicators from Cuba that worry me'. One was Che Guevara's statement to the London *Daily Worker* that 'Cuba will pursue the armed struggle already taking place in a number of Latin American countries'.

The interview also came up when the US UN Ambassador Adlai Stevenson met Vasili Kuznetsov, the Soviet First Deputy Foreign Minister, a few days later, as reported in the official files, giving my telegram as the source reference. A minute of a meeting in January 1963, when Kennedy met Kuznetsov, records that the President referred to small bands of guerrillas acting as a catalyst in a large number of Latin American countries and read out a quotation from the interview himself.

The bitter irony was that the very points which excited the top Americans were among the bits that George Matthews had cut from the published version.

Vietnam

The other great liberation struggle of the time, the symbol of the 'first' world versus the 'third', of capitalism versus Communism, was Vietnam. My first visit was in 1970. By that time there had been no American bombs dropped on North

202 Meeting Che

Vietnam for a while but evidence of the earlier years of heavy bombing was everywhere as were efforts at reconstruction. Around Hanoi, the craters that had pot-marked the paddy fields were filled in and the transplanting of seedlings for the second rice crop of the year was well underway. Down Highway Number One, the road from Hanoi to the South, masses of people, mostly women, were working by hand, spade and basket to repair the roadway, fill in the craters in the fields and get the buildings back to a useable state.

On a hillside overlooking the Ham Rong or Dragon's Jaw bridge across the Ma River about 100 miles south of Hanoi, I could still see the words 'Determined to fight, determined to win' set in limestone letters ten feet tall.

When I reached the province of Quang Binh, then the dividing line between the North and the South, the province's capital, Dong Hoi, had vanished because of the bombing. What remained were some low, grass-covered mounds, that and the shell of the Catholic Church with a crucifix still somehow standing on high, a silent witness to the devastation all around. A small town of 7,000 people, its schools and its hospital, its homes and its shops had been wiped away by the US Air Force's high explosives, napalm and fragmentation bombs.

Someone took me to some piles of rubble that they said had been the hospital, though how anyone could locate a particular spot amid this chaotic desolation I could not be sure. The staff and the patients had been evacuated to villages around but four doctors were then killed in one raid on a straw hut operating theatre.

Some craters I saw at the Dai Phong co-op farm were being used for duck ponds – nearly every crater I saw in Vietnam was filled with water. One farmer laughingly told me the bombs had helped them diversify their production; they now had ready-made reservoirs, fish ponds and just the right sort of place to grow the kind of water-spinach that seemed to come with just about every meal. The co-op's one and a half square miles had been the target for some 27,000 bombs but their anti-aircraft batteries had shot down three planes. One patch had been nicknamed 'The Houses of the Five Fires' as the homes there had been bombed, rebuilt and bombed again five times. Yet there, smiling, like all the others I met, was the new assistant doctor, a 20-year-old young woman who proudly reported to me that she had just helped at her first delivery of a baby.

Just back from the coast, the youngsters of a famous Girls Militia Unit, all 39 of them, were resting with their long-range guns in a reserve position. With their secondary education interrupted by the war, they had had to learn the principles of artillery ballistics before they were able to leave five US warships at the bottom of the sea. To be with these cheerful girls, ready for whatever might be thrown at them and confident that they could deal with it, was to be with people for whom it seemed no danger was too frightening.

This optimism was dauntingly overwhelming. Perhaps I could not cope with it easily because I remembered only too clearly my own optimism even in the final days of the retreat over the French frontier from Barcelona in 1939, an optimism that was horribly wrong.

If the terrible cost of the war, in the South and in the North, got me down, it did not seem to dishearten the people I met. I was pointedly but politely reminded that, as Ho Chi Minh in Hanoi declared Vietnam independent on 2 September 1945, a British general was landing in Saigon in the South with a force that set about re-arming Japanese troops to hold the country for the return of the French. It was nine years of massacre and war before the French left. And in 1970 the Vietnamese could count only a handful of years of attempted reconstruction after the devastation left by the French before another decade of war overwhelmed them.

I interviewed North Vietnamese Premier Pham Van Dong and met a leader whose energy and enthusiasm belied rumours being spread by the Nixon administration in Washington that he was seriously ill. In March of that year, the Cambodian King Norodom Sihanouk had been deposed in a US-engineered coup, and US and Saigon ground forces had been sent into the country. 'Whatever happens', Dong told me, 'we shall continue our chosen path and we shall not depart from it. We shall continue our fight. It will be stronger and it will be victorious'.

The heroism of the Vietnamese people was overshadowed for me by the bluff and double bluff of the leadership in a war enmeshed in the tensions of the Sino-Soviet split. The Soviets wanted dialogue with the US yet the US bombed Hanoi when Soviet Premier Kosygin was there and the Soviets did nothing. Mao wanted war not talk. As he had done over Korea, he calculated in terms of birth rate v losses and thought victory was certain. It was the same line on nuclear war: if we lose three million, we still have three million left. Yet the 'no talk' stance was not even Marxist-Leninist. Following the Revolution, after all, Lenin had negotiated with the Kaiser straightaway.

The Vietnamese backed Mao opportunistically, believing they would always get Soviet aid because the Soviets couldn't refuse, but they might not always get Chinese aid, so Dong spoke to me about their eternal friendship even though there was an ancient antagonism with the Chinese, celebrated in the National History Museum I visited in Hanoi. This 'big power' mentality in the region had other consequences. The Vietnamese used both Laos and Cambodia, expecting them to get bombed too, and the people of Cambodia and Laos are still paying for this Vietnamese arrogance. It was related to the Vietnamese 'we did it ourselves' line, which was a con. The Vietnamese expended considerable energy on removing the country of origin stamp from cranes and other goods they received in order to perpetuate the myth.

Four years after my first visit, I was back, going even further South and crossing the dividing line between the two halves of Vietnam. I was, I believe, the first British journalist to cross the 17th parallel to liberated areas of the South where I saw the atrocious conditions people had to survive in.

I visited a hospital in Dong Ha, capital of the most northerly province in the South, and blitzed repeatedly by Nixon after the Saigon and US forces were forced to leave it. Like most of Vietnam, the area was littered with tiny anti-personnel bombs scattered from the air, and in the hospital I met victims still being brought in nearly two years after the last plane had come raiding. A saline

204 Meeting Che

drip was keeping a woman alive, but only just. Her eyes were covered and the lower part of her body was swathed in bandages. She had been planting out rice seedlings when she had triggered one of these tiny bombs hidden at her feet in the paddy field. Her chances of recovery? The doctor just shook his head. It felt indecent to ask for her name. In the bed beside hers was an 11-year-old boy, Nguyen Hung. On his way home from school a few days before, he had spotted something in the undergrowth. When he reached to pick it up, the explosion took his right hand off and tore out his right eye.

To cross into this province was to enter an abomination of destruction. The muck and debris of modern warfare stretched out to all points of the compass without exception. What had once been an American base at Ai Tu was a grotesque graveyard of rusting metal and wrecked hangars reaching as far as my exhausted eyes could see. For a length of three miles, I walked through destruction so pointless it took the breath away. After the base had been taken by the Vietnamese, the American planes came in wave after wave to reduce to nothing what they had been forced to leave behind. The landscape all around was a wasteland. This was where the US Air Force had spread defoliation chemicals to strip the place of its trees and vegetation, to eradicate the jungle and poison any crops attempted by those foolish enough to think of growing them; where lines of huge bulldozers had shaved away all that remained of civilization and life. This had been a rich, green province of teak and mahogany, of tea and coffee and of pepper plantations. It was all gone, all bombed into a bleak and blasted barrenness. I had fought on battlefields, but here was something else. I had experienced the Blitz in London, but what I could see was beyond my understanding.

From the summit of just one scene of combat that had been marked as Hill 241 by the Vietnamese – Camp Carroll apparently to the Americans – I could survey a panorama of death, desolation and decay. With every step, cartridge cases rattled under foot. Crazy lines of barbed wire hung out in all directions. There was not a hut or habitation on the horizon, just jumbled mud interrupted by the silhouettes of rusting howitzers, of tanks, of concrete bunkers. How human beings had survived to fight in this hell of nothingness, I could not imagine. Yet fight they had. Before this vista of man's inhumanity to man, I wanted to cry out to the silent skies above me at such senseless savagery.

The statistics of the war were mind-boggling: the weight of bombs dropped was greater than throughout the Second World War. I thought of this when Dr Henry Kissinger, the policy architect of so much of this, published the successive volumes of his memoirs, where the heartless hypocrisy of his practice in power was rehearsed in two verbose volumes. I ploughed through page after page in preparation for a press conference he was to give in London to mark the publication. 'America', he wrote, 'contributed to the disaster in Cambodia, not because it did too much, but because it did too little'. From that I could only conclude that he wanted even more towns and villages razed to the ground, more silent cemeteries under the moon as monuments to his mastery of the correct conduct of diplomacy. I could draw not even the slightest glimmer of remorse from him. His fish-like stare and guttural monotone did not falter when he delivered a two-word reply to my challenge that he recognise at least some error in the ruination he had imposed on Vietnam, Cambodia, and Laos. 'Gross exaggerations', was his answer.

When the Americans finally left Vietnam in 1975, the old Vietnamese rivalry with China and the 'big power' mentality in the region broke out into the open. The Vietnamese, who knew, like everyone else in the region, about Pol Pot's massacres in Cambodia, eventually moved to topple him in 1979 and were rewarded by an attempted Chinese invasion of their own territory – the Chinese teaming up with the US to try to get Pol Pot back into power.

The *Morning Star* (as the *Daily Worker* was renamed in 1966) spiked stories about the atrocities of Pol Pot because the editor didn't want to carry them. Then Vietnam invaded. I suggested an interview with its ambassador, who, in true party style, insisted on written questions. I was flabbergasted by his cynicism. The Vietnamese, Soviets, Chinese, and Cambodians all knew about Pol Pot but kept quiet – and thousands died because of this. 'There are tactical considerations and there are strategic considerations', said the ambassador in justification. The US were bastards in Asia but they were not alone.

China

I made only two visits to China. The first was in 1954 – the year of my trip to Geneva, my first major assignment abroad as Foreign Editor and the year I first was given a regular by-line. It was extraordinary that it took place at all, as I was travelling with a Labour Party delegation and only five years after the revolution. I went because Alan Winnington was persona non grata with the British embassy – Winnington had gone to China in 1948 to report on the advance of the People's Liberation Army and in 1950 had been the first correspondent to report on the US terror bombing and use of germ warfare. Under US pressure, the Tory government had refused to renew his passport.

The Labour Party delegation was very high powered and included the former Prime Minister Clement Attlee, the General Secretary Morgan Phillips, and the former minister Edith Summerskill. They wouldn't talk to the press because they had signed up with papers to write their own articles when they returned. On this trip, I saw the racism of the Russians towards the Chinese and wasn't surprised by the split at the end of the decade.

My second visit came in 1979, a few years after the end of the Cultural Revolution. It was for the 88th birthday of a remarkable woman, Rose Smith, ex cotton mill worker and Hunger Marcher who had been a journalist on the *Daily Worker* from its very first days in 1930 up to her retirement in 1955. She had built a new life in China, and, as with other foreigners, she got into trouble during the Cultural Revolution in the 1960s, though she was not gaoled and the Chinese made amends later.

Rose, whom I had known at the *Worker* after the war, invited me to celebrate her birthday. I raised it with the British Party's Foreign Department, because we had no relations with the Chinese Party, having sided with the Soviets in the split, but nothing happened. She persisted and sent a message saying come via a friend involved in Sino-Anglo trade. It was Byzantine. He made the arrangements, and the Chinese embassy said if Rose wants you to come, come you shall, which meant the visit had tacit Chinese Party backing. The visit might have signalled a rapprochement between the two parties.

I couldn't go via Moscow because of the split, so I went via Hong Kong. I was the first Western European Communist correspondent to visit for several years. I was met by Rose at Beijing airport with a man from Xinhua, the official news agency, who arranged an interview with the first deputy foreign minister. He spoke excellent English but didn't use it except to correct the interpreter (a favourite device of some top Party cadres.) Needless to say the interview was anti-Soviet, but I typed it up and sent it back.

Getting a full picture of what had happened in the decade of the Cultural Revolution from the mid-60s to the mid-70s was impossible. That there had been profound disruption and a great deal of violence was evident. My visit was before the massacre in Tiananmen Square and before it became clear that China's economy was moving toward becoming the workshop of the world, but things were obviously changing fast. Some of the industrial developments I saw in places like Daqing and Changzhou were deeply impressive, with an emphasis on quality of product that contrasted strongly with my experiences earlier in the Soviet Union, and the driven focus on education was awesome.

FIGURE 12.4 Sam on the Great Wall of China, 1979.
Source: Family archive.

FIGURE 12.5 Sam visiting a Chinese factory, 1979.
Source: Family archive.

The skills of the old China and the promise of the new came together in Changzhou, halfway upstream on the Yangtse River between Shanghai and Nanking. It was the home of an ancient artisan industry making combs out of the particularly high-quality boxwood that grows in the area. By all accounts, these combs had been produced in Changzhou for over 2,000 years. I sported a fine moustache in those days and I came away with one of these hand-made and painted combs specially designed for the purpose. Alongside vast amounts of heavy manual labour – scores of men portering great sacks on their shoulders on the wharf side of the Grand Canal moved deftly along flimsy planks that bucked and swayed as they moved from wooden barges up to hand-drawn barrows – were the beginnings of something very bold at the cutting edge of technology. From that quayside I was taken to the town's computer factory which had a completely new workshop. Workers were already being trained for it, some of them sent off to university, others at intensive classes and study groups. At the entrance, our shoes were replaced by special slippers and we put on overalls that sealed completely, before passing through a wind tunnel with a force 6 gale designed to remove every speck of dust an employee might bring with them. The technicians explained their target for useable circuit production was the level achieved in Japan and the US, which, at the time, was some three times higher. This was just the start of China's not so long march into the front line of modern production techniques.

But the whole visit was heavily coloured for me by something quite different, an intense obsession with military preparation in case of attack. In a crowded street in the commercial centre of Beijing we pushed our way through a vast mass

208 Meeting Che

of people into an equally crowded clothing store, until we came to a particular counter. Someone pushed a button in the wall and a large trap door opened before our feet, revealing a flight of concrete steps down deep under the shop. There were what could only have been miles of tunnels stretching out as far as they eye could see. We walked along one of these to a room where I was given a special presentation. It would take me three hours walking to get to the end of the network at the edge of the city. They were now working on an additional network twice as deep which would have dormitories capable of hosting tens of thousands of people. The first network already had full lighting, ventilation, water supply, lavatories, and clinics.

At the great northern industrial city of Harbin, I was taken to a similar tunnel network under a crane factory that stretched out to the residential areas of the town. Here, I was told, they aimed not only to protect the workers from nuclear radiation but also to ensure that factory production could continue. Who, I wanted to know, was going to do the attacking? 'As Russia wants to dominate the world, we have to maintain our vigilance and be prepared', was the reply.

The most chilling part of the trip was talking to survivors of the Cultural Revolution. The politics of absolute control were still in command of even the most basic things. One consequence was that even in private conversations there was not a great deal of openness. Conversations took place in the presence of interpreters and minders who would report back on how both I and my interviewees behaved and on what was said. Although what I did not get was the scale of the cruelty and killing, one hint of it did come when I was talking to the film scriptwriter Shi Fangyu, who was sent to a farm to shovel pig sties clean and was paraded with a dunce's cap. Some had to wear an iron dunce's cap and if it didn't fit it was made to. The phrase 'persecuted unto death' kept cropping up – people were either shot or committed suicide, as many of Shi's colleagues had.

On my return to London, the *Morning Star* editor Tony Chater refused to announce I was doing a series of articles on China until he had read and agreed all of them. He edited the foreign policy interview heavily and wrote bits in, including quotations, to make sure we had nothing to do with this anti-Soviet stuff. The articles were reproduced in whole or in part in several European Communist papers.

I received a letter from Rose dissociating herself from what had appeared under my name. Clearly she was incapable of criticising the Chinese Party. Eventually her note was published but the attempt to renew relations between the two parties had failed because we handled it badly.

Notes

1 Sam's host was Orlando Perez, a former student activist from the days of the dictatorship whom he had met in Moscow when Perez had helped set up the Cuban embassy there in 1959.

2 Escalante later returned to Cuba, was tried and given a prison sentence.

Meeting Che **209**

3 Che Guevara, *Episodes of the Revolutionary War* (New York: International Publishers, 1968).

4 McCone note CIA, DCI/McCone Files Job 80-BO1285A; (http://history.state.gov/historicaldocuments/frus1961-63v11/pg_574); Stevenson-Kuznetsov meeting: Telegram 1531 from London, December 7; Department of State, Central Files, 737.00/12-762; Department of State, Central Files, 737.56361/12-1262 (http://history.state.gov/historicaldocuments/frus1961-63v11/d245); Kennedy-Kuznetsov meeting: Department of State, Presidential Memoranda of Conversation: Lot 66 D 149 in Department of State, Central Files, 033.1161/1-963 (http://history.state.gov/historicaldocuments/frus1961-63v11/d266). Dates may appear inconsistent because they relate to when the interview took place, the time the telex was sent, and the time the monitoring systems forwarded the details to Washington.

13

DEMOCRACY MURDERED

Czechoslovakia

I first returned to Czechoslovakia, a country that was to play an important part in my political thinking, in 1965. It had not experienced even the limited opening up that other East European states had enjoyed to one extent or another immediately after the 1956 revelations about Stalin. The thaw eventually came during the 1960s, especially in the cultural field, as I discovered when I interviewed the playwright Václav Havel, who was to become the figurehead of the dissident movement and then President of his country.

Everyone I spoke to, whether they were factory managers, economists in the university or technicians and workers on the shop floor, all said the same thing: the system had to learn how to make room for individual initiative from below, the system had to become more democratic. It was what I had heard in the debates in the Soviet factories during my time in Moscow, and what I had heard on my trip to Yugoslavia earlier that year, looking at the self-management system under Tito, and it was what I was to hear every time I came to Eastern Europe over the following years.

In January 1968, Antonin Novotny, General Secretary of the Communist Party since the 1953 Slánský trial I had covered, was removed from power and Alexander Dubček was elected as CP General Secretary. He ushered in what became known as the Prague Spring, promoting 'Socialism with a human face', which offered an apparent rebirth of a democratising Socialism in Eastern Europe. This upset the Soviets, and what they had gained before through internal means – an obedient Czechoslovak Communist leadership which murdered democracy at the Kremlin's behest – now had to be imposed by tanks through the front door. The Soviets invaded with massive military force in August 1968, and I went to Prague that September.

DOI: 10.4324/9781003243380-14

Alan Winnington, the *Worker* correspondent in East Berlin, had gone to Prague before the invasion and had filed anti- Dubček stuff. Alan was temperamentally and politically opposed to the Prague Spring and barely talked to me again after my coverage. I had no guidelines from the editor so I set off to find out what was going on and to report what I found. Chatting with people wherever I went, from Prague in the north-west or Bratislava in the south to Ostrava in the north-east, visiting factories and other workplaces, or just walking in the street, I did not come across any voices in support of the invasion. I detailed the large number of factory meetings where workers protested about the Soviet invasion, at places such as the CKD Sokolovo Locomotive Factory 20 minutes from the capital, the Klement Gottwald Ist Brno Engineering Plant, the Matador rubber factory at Bratislava and the Kladno Iron and Steelworks.[1]

I cannot remember exactly when I became aware that all my reports were being broadcast by Radio Free Europe in every relevant language including Czech, Slovak, and Russian. That must have resulted in pressure from the Soviet embassy in London on the British Party leadership and hence a request from the editor, who had received letters from readers complaining about my anti-Soviet pieces, to do a story on views from the 'other side' to that of the Prague Spring in order to provide 'balance'. That was a problem. The 'other side' was just not available to be interviewed. The invasion had no observable support, and there was no sign of the leadership the Soviets were hoping to get in place. At no stage did the supposed 'majority' that had allegedly 'invited' the Russians to arrive with their military might dare to show its face, even with the presence of huge numbers of Warsaw Pact troops and tanks in the streets.

Soviet Deputy Foreign Minister Kuznetsov was sent to Prague and unofficially acted as a kind of viceroy. I'd known him as head of the Soviet trade unions and thought I would try to interview him. The request was 'being considered' when I saw him at a reception held on the anniversary of the founding of Czechoslovakia. To the great consternation of those around him, I went up to Kuznetsov and said I had been trying to interview him. He remembered me, he replied, and the request was still being considered. I turned to see the ex-Czech ambassador to the UK, now Culture Minister, who was grinning.

'You've got a nerve', he said. 'Why do you want to see Kuznetsov?'

'I thought I'd go to the man in charge', I responded. The Minister laughed but I did not get my interview.

Eventually, I was served up with a nobody called Josef Jodas, part of the Novotny old guard and known in Czechoslovakia as Judas because he organised meetings against Dubček. My interpreter, who was pro-Dubček, refused to interpret so someone else had to be found. Jodas delivered a giant interview of stunning stupidity, which I reported back to the paper in its full length. The editor had his balance, but even he cut the interview down.

The British Party and the *Morning Star* opposed the invasion and paid the price in terms of its relationships with pro-invasion CPs and lost orders for the paper. Like the events of 1956, the invasion disrupted long-standing friendships and

212 Democracy Murdered

associations, both in respect of those who stayed at the paper and in the Party and also those who left. Old friends became new enemies.[2] At a staff meeting in 1956, I had been denounced as a Soviet stooge by some because of my reporting from Hungary and in 1968 I was denounced as anti-Soviet. But Czechoslovakia was a defining moment for me politically. The invasion put an end to any idea that a positive, fundamental change in Eastern Europe and the Soviet Union might take place. It made me realise that the only future for the Party was a complete break with the Soviet Union.

Chile

I was witness to the snuffing out of another Socialist experiment a few years later, this time in a different continent and by a different hand.

I had not been to Chile but wanted to go because I was deeply frustrated reporting on the Popular Unity government under Salvador Allende, which had been elected in 1970, just using agency copy from sources like Reuters and the Soviet news agency, TASS. Clearly it was a volatile situation.

Since Chile had won its independence in 1818 there had been ten successful coups – the last in 1932- and four civil wars in addition to many other revolts. Despite such a record, Chile was envied by other Latin American countries as one of the few with a history of elected government and long periods of stability, then running into 40 years. In the twentieth century, US business took over from the British both as the principle economic power and as the schemer behind the scenes, manipulating and funding those trying to get their hands on political power.

The 1964 Presidential election in Chile saw the CIA spend $2.6 million in support of the winning candidate, Christian Democrat Eduardo Frei, although the details of this involvement were not known at the time. Frei won 56% of the votes. The left candidate, Salvador Allende, won 39%. He had been a minister in a Popular Front government elected in 1938 and had already stood twice for President, in 1952 and in 1958. Backed by a Popular Unity front of left parties in 1970, Allende's vote of 36.6% was down on his 1964 total but the vote for the Christian Democrat candidate had collapsed to 28% with the right-wing National Party candidate gaining 35%. Under the Chilean constitution, where a directly elected President had executive powers and a Congress held the legislative powers, if no Presidential candidate secured an absolute majority, the leading candidate had to be confirmed by the Congress before they could take office. The Christian Democrats voted for Allende but not before the Army Commander-in-Chief had been murdered in an unsuccessful pre-emptive coup attempt by a group of leading officers.

Inaugurated on 3 November 1970, Allende's government proceeded with nationalisations, reform of land ownership, social programmes and other radical reforms. The initial response was enthusiastic. In municipal elections in April 1971, Popular Unity gained a fraction over 50% of the votes.

Helped by extensive funds and advice from the CIA and US corporations, right-wing opponents of Popular Unity had as their key political target reversing the left slant in Christian Democracy and bringing the Party into an alliance with the right. They orchestrated a wide-ranging campaign, blocking key actions of the government in the Congress, denying the government finance internationally, stoking up inflation internally, and bit by bit creating an atmosphere of violence and tension with bombings and other terrorist attacks. Stoppages by road haulage owners, funded by the CIA, twice brought the country to a near halt. Unable to pursue radical budgets because they were voted down in the Congress and unwilling to follow orthodox deflationary policies, the government lost control of budget deficits and inflation. Far-left groups added to the atmosphere of tension by their own unrealistic actions.

When Popular Unity candidates won 43.4% of the votes in Congressional elections in March 1973, the situation became extremely volatile. On some walls in Santiago, the slogan 'Ya viene Djakarta' – 'Jakarta is coming' appeared, a reference to the US-backed massacres of left-wingers and Communists in Indonesia in 1966. As 1973 proceeded, the situation was getting more hairy. There was even talk Allende might resign and hold another election. On 4 September 1973, the third anniversary of Allende's election victory, Popular Unity held a massive rally in which the whole of the centre of the city was flooded with people.

Unfortunately, when I asked the paper if I could go, the answer was no. As Foreign Editor I followed events as best I could but it was difficult because the paper could not afford to send me beyond Western Europe without the trip being paid for, which usually meant by the Soviets, and as requests were referred back to Moscow, I had to ask in advance, and you never know about important events in advance. Sometimes it was possible to run a trip on the back of holiday travel promotions, but holiday companies did not usually promote package tours to the world's trouble spots.

By chance, I noticed one day that the Soviet airline Aeroflot had extended its regular scheduled flights from Moscow to Havana down to Chile. It meant a total journey time of 32 hours but the result could be interesting stories, even if it meant a cap-in-hand visit to the Soviet embassy in Kensington Palace Gardens.

Stopping over for a few days in Moscow, the Chilean ambassador there told me everything had been arranged, including the comrades who would meet me at Santiago airport. When I arrived, there were lots of Soviet officials with flowers to greet a group of Bolshoi ballerinas but there did not appear to be anyone for me.

I waited until the ballerinas had gone, which was something like 3am. Having exchanged some money and found a taxi, the only thing I could think of doing was to ask the driver to take me to the Chilean Communist Party paper, *El Siglo* (the Century). 'Never heard of such a paper', he said. 'Are you sure you're not confusing it with an insurance company?'

214 Democracy Murdered

As we drove through dingy unlit or barely lit streets in the depths of the early morning, he asked me had I been in Chile before. When I said I hadn't, he explained that Chile had once been a lovely place until the Communists took over. He gave me a diatribe but did eventually find the printing works for *El Siglo*.

The only person I could find there had never heard of any visitor being expected. He phoned his colleagues and told me not to worry. They had said to put me into a hotel and they would sort things out in the morning. The comrade took me to the Carrera Hilton and left, giving me a copy of the paper that was just being printed. There was no room booked but there were vacancies. The receptionist gave me a map with my room key. Whacked as I was, I thought I ought to see where I was before turning in. Looking out of the window I realised that I was in the square bang opposite the Presidential Palace, the Moneda.

'Nice place', I thought. 'I'll have a look at that later after I've had a sleep'.

Just as I got into bed there was an enormous explosion. Whatever lights there had been in the square had gone out and I could see nothing. The reception rang and told me that the manager's office was telling everyone to go down to the cellar in view of an emergency. I could not be bothered, as I was so tired. I decided for some reason, however, to open the door of my room and then turned to go back in to try to see what was going on.

At that moment a man appeared and asked if I could see the square from my room. Did I mind if he came in? He was a former Argentine army officer working, or so he said, for the fire security department of Shell Petroleum. As we both looked out I could see tanks coming across the square and shooting started up in earnest. They were shelling the palace at point blank range.

The hotel management tannoyed for everyone to go down to the basement, but we decided to stay put. The Argentinian then cocked his head to one side and said, 'Look. Your planes are coming now'. True enough, I could see Hawker Hunter jets, which Allende had ordered, dropping bombs on the palace in what looked like a well-rehearsed rocket attack.

I rang up *El Siglo* and asked them if they knew what was happening. They put me through to the person I had spoken to some hours earlier. I told him of the gunfire but he said he could not hear anything. They had no clue, and indeed it appeared that so many involved in the Popular Unity movement were caught completely off guard, both by the coup itself and its terrible violence.

I finally joined the other guests in the kitchens in the hotel basement. A group of them, obviously quite wealthy Chileans, were listening in to a radio and heard the first communiqué of the junta led by Augusto Pinochet, who had been made Chief of Staff of the Army by Allende because of his supposed loyalty to the constitution. There were reports on the radio that Allende had been killed and the wealthy group let out an enormous whoop of joy. One demanded: 'Champagne!'

Waiters stood there, frozen. A couple of the waitresses were openly crying. Some of the young women working in the kitchen were also weeping.

'Come on hurry up', the manager shouted to the waiters. 'Didn't you hear the gentleman?'

The way the waiters and waitresses looked at him conveyed a deep but now – of necessity – sullen hatred. He rushed off and the guests were soon toasting the news.

Fed up with the guests in the kitchen, I prowled around and later, while I was wandering around the deserted upper floors of the hotel trying to work out what to do, I came across a group of the hotel staff gathered round a television set, watching a junta news announcement. 'Son fascistas', said one of them, 'They are fascists'.

I discovered there were other British correspondents in the hotel, including the BBC's John Humphrys and Hugh O'Shaughnessy, who was for many years the Latin America expert on the *Financial Times*. I didn't make myself known to them. We were not allowed to go out, but after a few days when the curfew was lifted a notice appeared on a hotel board announcing a press conference.

I was in a particular and awkward quandary. I was in Chile with a return ticket to Moscow. I had managed to get through to the British embassy over the phone to ask them to contact Margaret in London and to tell the paper to book me back to London on the first available plane. I decided to go to the press conference but not to declare myself as a reporter for the *Morning Star* – that seemed like tempting fate unnecessarily, especially as I could not get any stories back to London. While comrades were being shot and killed in the streets outside, I might survive in the hotel, as my passport was under my own name, Manassah Lesser, not my professional name.

A colonel who spoke impeccable Oxford English presided at the press conference. Humphrys laid into him in an impressively aggressive way. O'Shaunnessy also asked some questions but I decided not to, out of self-protection.

Once the curfew was lifted after three days, I managed to get to the Bank O'Higgins and take out some money the paper had sent. Ludicrously I was able to get it even though it was sent not under the name on my passport but under the name I used in the paper, Sam Russell. Worse, the paper's accountant had wired the money via the London branch of the Moscow Narodny Bank. When I protested to him on my return to London, he opened his eyes wide in surprise and explained that the Moscow Narodny had been £4 cheaper than Barclays – 'the choice was obvious'.

There were dead bodies in the streets, deliberately left by the military. The soldiers looked like thugs in their dress and general manner. I could only think of the Nazi Storm troops. I heard an officer say that over 5,000 'Marxists' had already been killed. In some streets, soldiers had lined up teams of young men who, with rifles pointed at their backs, were being dragooned to clear the walls of political posters and paint over the graffiti of political slogans. Back in the hotel, I watched an announcement on the television saying this was a 'spontaneous gesture by the population to clean up the city'.

Before the coup, there had been food shortages because of stoppages by lorry owners. Now the army was making sure those same lorry owners had the roads

216 Democracy Murdered

clear. Some stall holders had already set up their stalls of fruit and veg. One chap selling apples was shouting in a very mocking way the slogan *'Allende, Allende, el pueblo te defiende, Ha! Ha! Ha!'* in derision of the same Popular Unity chant. Outside one shop, a queue for food went round two blocks as people waited patiently for their turn to go in. The troops got impatient at the crowd in the street and started using their rifle butts. They must have then decided the pavement had to be cleared as, without any warning, they started firing into the air, leaving me a wreck, the queue disintegrating and women and children trampled underfoot as people fled.

At night, you did not have to strain your ears too much to hear the gunfire. Some of it may have come from the national stadium, which was being used as an open-air prison camp, interrogation centre, and murder ground. I did not get to see the morgues stuffed with those shot, nor to tour the embassies crowded with desperate refugees. It was not possible for a journalist to get into the hospitals, one heard of these things from frightened contacts, and I was able to meet a few, despite the terrifying atmosphere.

One was the mother of a Party member in the Chilean embassy in London, and she gathered three or four others together. They told me about arrests and shootings. Once the Moneda Palace had been reduced to a smoking ruin with Allende dead, the junta troops were switched to the working-class suburbs. Well-known centres of militancy, like the Sumar and Yarur factories, were savagely attacked. Prisoners came out with their hands behind their necks but, I was told, they were still shot in cold blood. I walked to the factory area, and all that was left was congealed blood on the pavements. On the way, just 200 yards from my hotel, I saw the body of a worker shot during the night, his corpse left like the others as a warning. Soldiers smoked and joked around his bullet-ridden remains as I passed by.

The brother of one man I knew in London told me what had happened at the State Technical University. A hurried meeting of students and staff decided armed resistance was not possible but when junta troops arrived the military opened fire anyway and rounded up everyone they could find. Those arrested were made to lie down in the courtyard and told that anyone who moved would be shot. After some hours, the women were told to leave and as some of the men raised their heads to say goodbye, perhaps to their wives, the soldiers machine-gunned them.

There was to be a 'Te Deum' in the Santiago Cathedral and I went along, finding a place at the back. The members of the junta now in power filed in with Pinochet along with the commanders of the each of the armed services. Archbishop Silva Henrique delivered a sermon that, in coded language, distanced himself from the coup. Stuck at the back, I could not see what Pinochet's reaction to it was, but he cannot have liked it when the Archbishop declared: 'Let there be no reprisals. Let there be taken into account the sincere idealism which inspired many of those who have been defeated'. My contacts were quite dismissive of such signs of opposition. As in Spain in the 1930s, many on the left seemed to prefer to alienate the church rather than find ways of working with it. Subsequently the

Archbishop was made a Cardinal and the Vicariate under him became a centre of opposition to the junta.[3]

Ignoring the Archbishop, the junta began a mass purge of all government employees the day before I left. There were huge queues outside the offices of the different ministries, the publicly owned banks, and the nationalised industries. Troops with machine guns covered the columns of people as they slowly moved forward, checked at each of the entrances I saw by armed police. At one office, police dogs were snapping at the heels of those standing in line to be processed and told of their fate. Soon I was watching as streams of people began coming out, women weeping, men grim-faced. Those who did not move away fast enough had rifle butts thrust into their backs

As for me, I could do nothing other than pick up such stories, and try to do so without endangering anyone who talked to me. The only telex was in the hotel guarded by two gorillas with sub-machine guns. No heroics, I thought. As soon as there was a flight out, I left without too much difficulty. Worried that I might be stopped at the airport, I resisted the temptation to take my copy of *El Siglo* – the last edition, as it turned out to be – and instead hid it with other CP material I had gathered under a prayer cushion in a church near the hotel. Just as well, because at the airport every bit of luggage was thoroughly turned over. I was asked my profession, which was in my passport so I couldn't risk lying, and then which paper. I said *Morning Star* and thought my time was up but they let me through. I doubt they had ever heard of it, whereas if it had still been the *Daily Worker*, I would have had to invent something.

Back in London, I went straight to the paper from the airport to get a story in that day's edition, but when I arrived I was mentally and physically washed out and just could not think what to say. This after, all was, where I came into journalism: a vicious and fascist general using military might to sweep away democracy rather than allow a democratic government to gain in popular support and, perhaps, consolidate a long-term majority.

It was one of those rare moments when I was grateful to the editor: 'It's obvious', he said. 'You just start off: I saw democracy murdered…' And that is what I wrote.[4]

Some good while before the coup, I had interviewed in the Chilean ambassador's residence in London one of the key Chilean Communist leaders. Pacing up and down the magnificent salon, Volodia Teitelboim had assured me that everything was under control. When I looked back on the interview, with his claims that the army was with the Allende government, it read like what it was – utter idiocy. It made one of my next assignments very hard. Luis Corvalán, the Chilean Communist Party General Secretary who was taken prisoner some weeks after the coup and was subsequently exchanged at Zurich Airport for the Soviet dissident Vladimir Bukovsky, came to London in the mid-1970s and I had to interview him. It was impossible. I kept trying to deal with the core issue: what should a reforming government do when it gets into power with only 36% of the popular vote?

218 Democracy Murdered

In Italy at the time, Enrico Berlinguer, the Italian Communist leader behind the idea of the 'historic compromise' (an unfortunate phrase – 'historic understanding' might have been better), was saying that a left government could not successfully govern with only 50% plus 1 of the votes. The majority needed to be a significant one, bringing together people across the nation in full support of the process of change. How on earth one might achieve such a majority remained the unanswered question. What was certain, though, was that in Chile, the Popular Unity government tried to transform society with too little support. And though its vote was up a bit in the elections of 1973, the population was deeply divided, with a substantial group, approaching half the population, slipping progressively into opposition.

Allende, his Socialist Party and the Communists had made a mess of it in Chile, but Corvalán could not discuss it in any helpful or sensible way. Whatever their grand and good intentions, the bitter reality was dead bodies in the streets. It is no service to the downtrodden if a government sets about liberating them in such a way that the military jackboot is able to slam down on them ever more harshly. Corvalán seemed quite unable to face the fact that such self-criticism did not in any way weaken one's anger at the horrors imposed by the Pinochet coup and the dictatorship that followed. Nor did it weaken one's criticism of the activities of the CIA and its role in fostering, if not actually guiding, the coup, a role confirmed by a 1975 US Senate inquiry.

Later, some senior Chilean military people on the side of Popular Unity told me they felt the Soviets had known all along what was going on. There is no means of knowing, but it is hard to believe that Soviet intelligence did not have some idea and were repaying a debt to the CIA for the Americans letting the Czech invasion of 1968 happen. I asked a former general in the Chilean Air Force years later at a reception if the Russians had known, and he said of course they did and of course they didn't tell us.

Soviet inactivity over Chile, like US inactivity over Czechoslovakia, was the price paid for a world order based on spheres of influence.

Poland

The Soviet invasion of Czechoslovakia put an end to any idea that a positive, fundamental change in Eastern Europe and the Soviet Union might take place. The different party leaderships and governments still had to deal with the same problems they had been discussing in the middle 1960s, and all toyed in one way or another with exactly the changes in economic management that had been embarked on in Czechoslovakia. The crucial, damning, difference was that they were not prepared to give anything away on the political front. Eastern Europe became a time bomb, slowly ticking away. What was needed was quick, profound and democratic solutions, but those could not come until Moscow agreed. When Moscow finally did under Mikhail Gorbachev, it was too late.

By then I was no longer on the foreign correspondents' beat. All I had been able to do in the meantime was listen to the trigger ticking away. I did not go back to Czechoslovakia. It would have been possible, but I refused. I did go, though, to some of the other countries of Eastern Europe and a couple of times to Moscow. They were depressing occasions.

In Poland in July 1981, I watched queues that seemed to get longer by the day, the shelves in the shops emptier each time I looked. In December, martial law was declared.

Poland was the country of birth of my parents and where my grandparents were undoubtedly murdered by Nazism, but, while that reality was never far from my mind, whenever I was in Poland, I never wrote about it in that sense. No one could escape the evidence of the suffering that the people of this country, and particularly its Jewish population, had endured.

In 1954, I had walked around the old St Anne's Church in the heart of Gdansk, still surrounded by the ruins from the fighting in the war, only to see it 11 years later rebuilt in its full medieval splendour. On this second visit in 1965, I wrote that

> Life may not be very easy yet for the people of Poland's western territories [this was the land transferred from Germany to Poland in 1945] and there are still many difficulties and shortages. But when the older people look back on the road covered since they arrived in the ruined towns in 1945 with a bundle on their back in battle-stained uniforms or striped concentration camp clothes, they can see that it is an achievement of which they can be proud.

Poland was in many ways quite different to other East European countries. The patchwork pattern of tiny farms and fields was a striking contrast to the extensive fields of the collectivised farms in the other Socialist countries. Given the huge numbers of people involved in Polish agriculture, it was not economic to push or persuade Polish farmers into cooperatives, which would leave large numbers unemployed.

I got this message loud and clear during a visit to farms in different parts of the country towards the end of 1972. A long-standing system of compulsory deliveries to the state had finally been abolished at the start of the year. Ministry of Agriculture officials, who told me they had long opposed the system, were confidently predicting a 7% increase in farm output as a result. Instead of the state requiring farmers to produce what that state thought it needed, farmers had been freed to produce what they knew they could do best.

Talking to one farmer, Tadeusz Stangreciak, who had 50 acres on good land in the village of Słotwin not far from Warsaw, I found that for him the prices for his potatoes had gone up by 50%, for his grain by somewhat more but for his pig meat by four times. That was bad news for consumers but good news for him, even if it still did not give him enough money to invest in modernising his

220 Democracy Murdered

farm. Worse, the average size of Polish farms was then around 12 acres and their technical level was very low and productivity rock bottom – one of the reasons behind successive social outbursts triggered by rising food prices.

Reporting at the same time on the astonishing growth of the shipbuilding industry, the Gdansk I had seen in 1954 was long gone. In its place was an internationally important industrial centre with vast shipyards. The yards, however, had been successful partly because managements had competed on price by pushing down piece rates, pushing up work targets and investing little in even the most basic facilities for the workforce. That was the background to the strike by the 16,000 workers in the city's Lenin shipyard to two years before that ended in terrible massacres. Some changes were now underway, but the workers I spoke to were wary about the future. Their working conditions were bad, as I could see for myself. Their equipment was out of date. Outside the yards, the housing estates were terrible – no shops, no kindergartens and no schools. The city's sewage system was a disaster. Work to replace it was not scheduled to start until after 1975. Despite what I saw, I little suspected that years later I would be witnessing the role the shipyard workers were to play in ending the power of the regime.

Going to Katowice in Polish Silesia, one entered a Hades world of almost unbelievable pollution. True, it was somewhat better than when I had been there over a decade earlier, but this area was turning out a fifth of Poland's coal output and, while there was talk of improving things, the focus was on driving up that output, not on reducing pollution. Coal might have been king in the Polish economy, but the Mysłowice miners were not treated like princes. Coalface workers I spoke to were insistent that their unions had been useless up to the strikes and food price riots of 1970. We were talking as delegates were elected to the first trade union congress after those December events. Leading trade union officials in Warsaw told me that, up to then, the union representatives in plants had been essentially management yes men and that the lack of communication between union leaders and the rank and file had been 'disastrous'. This was good stuff and suggested that perhaps there might be real changes.

That was not to be. I was told by one leading Party member that trade unions were a nineteenth-century concept and that, while there might be 'some role' for them at a local level, there was nothing for them to do at a national level which was not already being done by the party. This was the idea that 'the leading role of the Party' was the best guarantee for everything.

When I returned a decade later, the problems were the same. This was my visit in July 1981, a year after the Solidarity trade union movement sit-ins had brought Poland to a halt. Shoppers were queuing for up to six or seven hours for meat. Milk, butter, cheese, soap, washing powder, toothpaste, matches, and even bread, were also running short and the authorities were unable to honour ration coupons. There was anger over this breakdown of the rationing system and at the fact that, to get some necessities, people had to pay rocketing prices on a growing black market. Understandably, there was talk of strike action, of hunger marches and protests.

I was in Warsaw to cover a Party congress. I listened as the Deputy Premier Mieczysław Rakowski responded to demands from delegates for an honest picture of the economic situation. He could hardly have been blunter. It was a frightening picture of increasing social tensions and repeated breakdowns in production. The figures he cited were devastating. Poland's coal output had dropped by 21.8% in the first half of the year. It was hardly believable. Indeed, I found many people did not believe even these, at long last honest, official statistics. Cynicism and distrust of the authorities was such that, even while people faced acute shortages, many thought the figures were a lie issued to frighten the public into doing what the authorities wanted. Others were telling me that, in reality, the situation was far worse and the official statistics were just a cover up.

Rakowski was not calling for another Prague Spring but the stick of dynamite he threw into the debate was to say that those in the Party leadership and structure who had been, and were, opposing change were the cause of Poland's problems. Democracy was the crunch question. The huge applause that greeted the speech showed it was the most important moment in the congress. And if I needed another indication of its significance, then I got it from Moscow where the press reported plenty of speeches but somehow not that one. There was a real degree of open debate and a major renewal of personnel at the top, the removal of the 'compromised and incompetent', as one delegate put it. However, I finished my main report by saying that the delegates left the congress with high hopes that the new leadership 'would initiate the far-reaching changes that the country requires. But time is running out'.

General Wojciech Jaruzelski, a professional soldier who had been Defence Minister for years and had masterminded Poland's participation in the invasion of Czechoslovakia, had been promoted to the Premiership in the February before the congress and became Party General Secretary that autumn. In December, he declared martial law and abolished all trade unions. Rakowski, still Deputy Prime Minister, reported to the Polish Parliament on what he saw as the result of a debate on the kind of trade unions Poland could have in the future. They should be 'autonomous' and 'democratic', he said, and bemoaned the fact that few members of the banned Solidarity movement had taken part in the debate, forgetting to add that the key Solidarity figures had been dumped in detention camps after the imposition of martial law. Any new unions, he added, had to 'accept the leading role of the Party' and 'the country's existing alliances and foreign policy'. This hypocritical and impossible house of cards was kept upright only by Moscow's veto on fundamental change, and when Gorbachev removed that veto, the house collapsed.

To add a personal note to this sorry history, I recalled that Jaruzelski became Defence Minister in 1968 on the resignation of Marian Spychalski, the prisoner who had appeared in the 1951 Polish trial that I attended and who had later been rehabilitated. The note is personal not because I had seen Jaruzelski's predecessor in a Warsaw courtroom but because his resignation as Defence Minister was part of a campaign from which Jaruzelski benefited organised by a group of leading

222 Democracy Murdered

Polish Communists in which hundreds of officers were dismissed along with other public functionaries on the grounds that they were Jews. I was told that Spychalski resigned when he was 'accused' of being a Jew (which he was not). Once again, anti-Semitism had played its ugly role in stalling democracy and progress.

Notes

1 Sam told his daughter Ruth that some people were arrested or disappeared after he had spoken to them.
2 Sam particularly remembered a blazing row with leading South African Communist Joe Slovo at the airport in Prague in 1968 as he was on his way back to London; Slovo was vehemently supported the invasion.
3 The Archbishop helped found an ecumenical human rights committee that was closed in 1975 on the orders of the junta. The following day, the Archbishop established the Vicariate of Solidarity with the same purpose and staff. Lying within the jurisdiction of the Catholic Church, it was protected from the junta.
4 The editor at the time was George Matthews.

14

BACK IN SPAIN

The day I arrived in Spain in 1972, the first time I had been back since the Civil War, the building sites of Madrid started a series of strikes in the run up to May Day. Those taking part showed real courage. The sites were covered by armed police. I watched the notorious Civil Guard surrounding one site, their winged, patent leather hats making it look as if they had just stepped out of a comic opera. This look was belied by their ever-present sub-machine guns. The previous September, a striking building worker, Communist Pedro Patino, had been shot dead by the Guards. This time they had tried to head off the action by arresting what they hoped was the 15-strong organising committee. The men had been using the flat of leading actress Julia Pena to hold their meeting, so they arrested her too, dragging her off the stage of the Goya Theatre where she was performing in *Lysistrata*, the anti-war play by Aristophanes first performed in Athens in 411BC and, nearly 2,500 years later, playing a role in poking fun at Franco. The strikes went ahead anyway.

On May Day itself, a giant protest rally had been called for Atocha Square, a very busy crossroads with lots of traffic which was thick with police. A helicopter hovered overhead and armoured water cannons were at the ready. Police in riot gear waited in the streets off the square. Suddenly there were shouts, smoke bombs landed among the police, and a group of students and young workers appeared with their banners. The truncheons were out and plenty of arrests were made, but I could hear slogans still being shouted nearby.

With a friend, I drove around on the lookout for more protests, trying to appear as unremarkable as possible. Eerie groups of armed police waited at the corner of every one of the six streets that lead into the square formed by Madrid's Cuatro Caminos crossroads. The plain-clothes members of Franco's Special Branch stood out like a sore thumb. Tension was everywhere. When a car

DOI: 10.4324/9781003243380-15

224 Back in Spain

backfired, we all jumped, thinking the worst. Then, a group of some 20 young people appeared, the couple at the front carrying a red banner. We could hear their shouts clearly: '*Libertad! Libertad!*' – '*Amnesty for the prisoners!*' Then came the whining scream of police car sirens and across the flow of traffic I could see one vehicle with uniformed and plainclothes police hanging on outside making for the group. With short, reinforced rubber truncheons, the Special Branch men began lashing out at all and sundry, demonstrators and passers-by alike. Most of the young protesters got away but three were left on the ground being systematically beaten and kicked by the police. It was all over in little more than a couple of minutes. It felt like a disaster. Every time more than a handful of people gathered, they were savagely dispersed by the police.

The outlawed Spanish Communist Party had called for a national strike and the Party's paper *Mundo Obrero* – which, contrary to the propaganda we all indulged in was prepared and printed in Paris and smuggled into Spain – had talked of mass demonstrations. This was my reason for deciding to return, which was now deemed safe. Comrades in Paris had given me contacts in Spain and when I arrived I found other foreign Communist correspondents there too. One from *l'Unità* made a phone call from her hotel and was picked up the next day. I asked Simon Sanchez Montero, leader of the Communist Party underground in Spain, about the failure of the demonstration. But it was difficult to challenge him in such circumstances. He was a brave comrade who had been tortured and was risking his life every day. How could I challenge him on the stupidity of the Party? 'One doesn't talk of rope in the house of the hangman', as the French say.

Franco was a dictator whose regime began amid blood and continued in the same way. Many leading figures in the West refused to accept the extent of that bloody beginning, and carried on doing so even when, some three decades after the collapse of the regime, the mass graves of slaughtered Republicans began to be excavated.

As a full-time correspondent on the *Daily Worker* and its successor the *Morning Star*, I had done a great deal to keep the issue of Spain alive through their pages and at the same time help maintain a grossly over-optimistic idea of the overthrow of Franco. I did believe this was possible at the start but later it was no more than lip service, with me simply reporting what the Spanish Party was saying.

I had not returned before because I had to recognise that if I did not meet any activists there, I would not see what was going on, and if I did meet any activists there, I could put them in danger. To prevent further deaths, sometimes even I, trusted as I might have been, was not privy to the real identities of the people I interviewed when they came on their way through Britain. At the end of 1969, three young activists met me just before they went back into Spain. As I wrote at the time, these were people 'whose names I cannot give, whose photographs we dare not print'. They had come partly to tell me about the fate of Horacio Inguanzo, a leading trade unionist and Communist in the Asturias region. Captured in 1938 during the Civil War, he had been condemned to death by a Franco tribunal. The sentence had been commuted to imprisonment and he got out of jail in 1943. From then on, he was in the underground resistance to Franco, collecting a couple of lengthy prison sentences 'in absentia' before finally being caught again in 1968. What they wanted from me was publicity to try to ensure he did not join the list of other democrats sentenced, once again, to death by the regime.[1]

During the decades of clandestine activity, the strategy for people like Inguanzo of how to topple the dictator changed. The greatest blow was the defeat of fascism at the end of the Second World War and with it the vain belief in Spain that the Allies would turn on Franco.

It took a long while for Spanish Communists and others on the left in Spain, as well as us on the outside, to realise that military action was not going to bring about the downfall of the regime. Guerrilla war continued for years. Comrades I had known in Spain, or who I met later in France before the Second World War, returned to Spain by the dangerous mountain paths across the Pyrenees. Many of them died, either executed after torture or shot during gun battles. There was a moment of optimism as France was liberated in 1944. Copying the French National Resistance Council that brought together the Gaullists, the Communists, and others, all the Spanish anti-Franco parties were joined in a Supreme Junta. There were reports of risings, of guerrillas who had liberated whole areas of the country.

Nazi German troops had fled across the border into Franco's Spain and the Free French units were eager to pursue them. Just for a moment it felt as if, with fascism crumbling in the rest of Europe, the job might also be done in Spain. The restrictions on journalists going into wartime France meant that there was no chance for me to see things on the ground at that time, but my friend and mentor from Spanish days, Willy Forrest, was reporting from Paris for the *News Chronicle*. He reminded us all of the role Spanish Republican exiles played in the French Resistance: on the first day of the Paris rising that threw out the German occupiers it was a Spanish Republican who died in storming the Hotel de Ville, the town hall. When the first tanks of de Gaulle's army reached that same spot a few days later they were crewed by Spanish Republicans and were painted with the names Guadalajara and Belchite, battles in the Spanish war. 'Your liberation heralds our own', the Supreme Junta declared. It was the first of a long line of futile hopes. Though Spanish guerrillas serving in the French Resistance forces had liberated towns and villages in the French far south, they were soon made to fall back from the frontier with Franco. His overthrow was not what Churchill and Roosevelt, or de Gaulle for that matter, actually wanted.

There was bitterness for me in some of the stories I ferreted out in those early years. After having tried to alert British public opinion to the treatment of the Republican refugees, soldiers, and civilians at the hands of the French government after Franco's victory in March 1939, it was deeply saddening in post-war Britain under Labour to come across Spanish Republicans who had fought in Spain, been interned by the French, used as forced labour by the Germans finding themselves interned once again after D-Day by the British. In

226 Back in Spain

August 1946, I publicised the case of one group still being held in a detention camp in Britain and who, incredibly, were being held alongside German Nazi prisoners of war.

A contribution I felt I could make was to hammer away at the business links between Britain and Franco Spain. Norton Motorcycles provided all the technical specifications for its bikes to a Spanish company so they could be manufactured there, with Franco's military as a key customer. In several factories – like Metro Vickers in Manchester (home of the famous engineers' rhyme: 'The wages of sin are death and a curse. The wages at Metro Vic are a bloody sight worse') – workers refused to proceed with orders destined for Spain. The mood just after the war was such that the executives of both the electrical trades and the engineering unions backed their members at Metro Vic.

When Franco held a referendum in July 1947, he prepared the ground against the opposition inside Spain with an order to his regional governors to stamp out the guerrillas. It ended with the statement: 'No prisoners will be taken'. Franco was not immediately successful in destroying the armed resistance. At the start of 1948, I got news of the use of tanks, armoured cars and some 20,000 infantry against Republican guerrillas in the mountains north of Valencia, the so-called Eastern Guerrilla Formation. 'Not only have we resisted all attempts to annihilate us, but we are stepping up our activities and have inflicted serious defeats on the fascist forces' was the message from these brave fighters. It was heroic, but to no avail.

The Spanish Communist Party continued the armed struggle in a disastrous campaign that petered out amid immense sacrifices and it adopted a policy of national reconciliation in 1956. The view was that enough had been lost in Spain, even though the policy played into Franco's hands. But even then there were problems. The old guerrillas would not give up. They had suffered terribly. There was awful torture and executions. After the war was over, Franco's execution squads consumed at least another 200,000 lives.

After the 1956 change of line many exiles wanted to return to Spain. There were secret meetings between the Spanish in Moscow and the Soviet Red Cross about this and the Spanish were furious because their return – not to carry on Party work but just to live an ordinary life – was being hindered by the Soviets. Some had relatives who had already gone back and had not been harmed. The Soviets wanted to help but were not sure about how to facilitate it. One or two ships had sailed from Odessa. Another plan was to go by rail via France but a visiting French Socialist MP Guy Mollet vetoed it. What would happen if they were stopped? Would the French have to insist they went on to Spain? Little by little they did return. The children had learned Spanish in the Soviet Union and maintained their Spanish identity. Some even returned to their Catholic roots while living in the Soviet Union, although there was no religious education there.

Dolores Ibárurri, who went to live in Moscow after the war and became General Secretary of the Spanish Party from 1944 to 1960, lost her son at Stalingrad fighting in the Red Army. I interviewed her for the *Worker* in Moscow in 1962 and one of her grandchildren entered and she told the child, 'We'll be going back to Spain' and the child replied, 'We'll never go back'. Dolores told the child to keep quiet – the Party line must not be contradicted. In the interview that I wrote up, the editor, without any consultation, cut out all references to the use of violence, which the Party still sanctioned in self-defence.

Dolores stuck to her political guns through all the years in exile, particularly after opposing the invasion of Czechoslovakia. Many Spanish comrades had gone to Czechoslovakia, and they formed the largest group of political émigrés there, which is why in 1968 the Spanish Party was the best informed Western Communist Party on the developments in the Prague Spring. It put them at the forefront of what became dubbed Eurocommunism and they suffered gross interference as a result from the Soviets as did all Communist parties that criticised the invasion.

I met Spanish comrades around the world not only in Moscow and Prague. Some went to Latin America, some to France, some to Britain, some to Yugoslavia, some to Israel and so on. In one family I knew, three ended up in different countries, and the one in the Soviet Union had the best life. However, those who ended up living under the rule of the Communist parties suffered terribly as Stalin kept up his repressive measures after the Second World War. The secret police network targeted Brigaders, many of whom were Jewish, as agents of imperialism and a great many lost their lives as a result.

With the change in line in 1956 away from guerrilla war came the inevitable question: what to put in its place? Just sit on the side lines and wait while others did the job? That seemed to be the strategy of the Spanish Socialist Party. But if you set about protesting, claiming the liberties that in Britain were considered basic, the costs for you as an individual, your family, friends, and acquaintances could be catastrophic. Bit by bit ways were developed of mobilising people against the regime, despite those costs, exemplified by the powerful Workers' Commissions.

Independent trade unions were banned, and Communists active in workplace struggles had decided in the 1960s on a combined strategy of working within the official syndicates while at the same time forming local, rank- and-file structures, Workers' Commissions, wherever possible.

Whether it was a building site or one of the modern giant factories that had been opening up like the SEAT car factory in Barcelona, the shipyards at El Ferrol, Michelin tyres at Vittoria or the vast array of engineering factories at Madrid, they were, by then, likely to have had a Workers' Commission formed inside the plant. Though some things had to be discrete, the whole point about these Commissions, the CC-OO in Spanish, was that they were open and public: how could they be anything other than that and yet be elected by workers on the shop floor? A strategy of openness meant one thing straight away. The minute they declared themselves, these worker delegates were vulnerable. As soon as a strike was called, the police moved in to arrest as many members of the local CC-OO as they could get their hands on. The police could impose an immediate

228 Back in Spain

summary fine on them – the going rate at the time was equivalent to £1,500 in 1972, far more than any ordinary Spanish mortal could hope to pay. So in reality, it meant two months in prison which could also mean dismissal by their employer. In Madrid alone, 2,000 workers elected to Workers' Commissions had been sacked by their employers over the previous three years.

British shop stewards knew all about the kind of vulnerability that taking action against a powerful boss could entail. In British factories, the strength of the shop stewards lay in their ability to show that they were needed by those who had voted for them. That meant, as I knew from my own experience in Napier, that they always had to carry the workers with them. Democracy was also the heart of the Workers' Commissions' strength. As a result, they operated in a very different way, and had a very different relationship to the Communist Party, than was the case in many trade union structures in other countries, particularly when it came to those in Eastern Europe and the Soviet Union, but also in many West European countries where trade unions were divided on political lines.

Though it had been Spanish Communist Party members who first developed this form of action, from the start they realised that the movement would lose its strength if the workplace structures became the creatures of a political party. In the Communist movement up till then, trade unions had been seen as organisations that were, in words of Stalin himself, 'transmission belts' for the Communist Party's influence in the working class. Many members of individual Workers' Commissions were Communist Party members. But they did not meet beforehand in private and decide how a CC-OO session should be run and what it should decide – which was the way Communists sought to conduct trade union business in many countries, including in Britain, whenever they had the strength in numbers to do so. My Spanish comrades considered that would be suicide for the movement, ruining the democracy that meant ordinary workers were prepared to put themselves forward for the Commissions.

The prime role for Communists in Spain at that moment was not all to speak the same way, or all to vote the same way. It was to encourage the involvement, the commitment, and the activity of their colleagues on the shop floor. This was an extraordinary if hard school in democracy, not as quick or as exciting perhaps as that described in Petrograd by John Reed in *Ten Days that Shook the World*, but this form of direct, working-class democracy was developing the power that was the context without which everything else happening in Spain could not be understood.

It was a process of slow erosion through democracy from below, and that was what I wanted to see when I returned in 1972, to share again with people in Spain the fight against fascism and its cruelties.

In the flat of my contact I met Manuel Lopez, a Communist lawyer, who became a good friend. Party lawyers like Manuel were very important, especially in helping at labour tribunals, which gave rise to the Workers' Commissions. He told me of an English woman then in prison for her role in the anti-Franco underground, a founder member of the education section of the

Workers' Commissions. She turned out to be Pamela O'Malley, not English, but very much Irish and cousin to the then Justice Minister in the Irish Republic, Desmond O'Malley.[2] She was also a teacher at the Madrid British Institute School. A key Communist trade union activist among Madrid teachers, she had been arrested on 13 March for attending an illegal meeting of teachers involved in a strike and was still being held in the notorious Carabanchel Prison when I got to Madrid.

On 18 April, Norman Tett, who was the Cultural Attaché at the British Embassy, and who also headed the British Council which ran the school, had sent a letter to her home address dismissing her on the grounds of 'unjustified absence from work'. When I talked about her to parents of children at the school one thing became very clear: she had been an outstanding teacher. Managing to get the paper to splash on the case, my interest was not that her sufferings were worse than those of others, but that it had been British officials who were playing the Franco game, sacking trade union activists to try to crush the movement. I quoted 'Friends of Mr Tett' as 'trying to justify his action'.

That phrase, 'friends of Mr Tett', was journalistic double speak for someone at the British embassy who I did not want to name. It was not just that such a phrase was part of the etiquette imposed on reporters by officials who would deny they had ever spoken to you if you sought to identify them, it was also that I really did not want to reveal who my source for this point was.

The British Ambassador in Madrid, Sir John Russell, had been head of the News Department at the Foreign Office when I was regularly attending the Whitehall briefings. In those days, he used to jocularly call me 'Cousin Sam'. I also knew his secretary and phoned her at the embassy: 'Tell him it's Cousin Sam'. He came himself to the phone and called me round. Before I could get to the thing I really wanted to discuss, he began by saying that, if there were free elections, the Spanish Communists would get about 25% of the vote and come in ahead of the Socialist Party – a gross over-estimate as it later turned out. At first, 'Cousin John' said he knew nothing about Pamela, but he then invited me to his home where he became rather more honest. I told him I was going to write the story and in it blame him for Pamela's sacking. He admitted he knew of it, but claimed this was only after the event. He had had to defend his man, he said.

One thing I did get from talking to this 'friend' of Mr Tett was that the said official had only acted after he had discovered Pamela was in prison. He even, Sir John generously explained, visited her in the Carabanchel to tell her she was losing her job. I explained in the report: 'Mr Tett's friends claim nevertheless that it cannot be said that she was dismissed because she had been arrested, but because she was absent from work'. Over the many, many years I had been attending Foreign Office briefings in Whitehall, I had been fed more than enough crap to cover every field in Spain with rich manure several times over. Some of that mountain had come from Sir John himself. What made me so angry this time round was the personal closeness of the relationship involved, the obviousness of the collusion between a British government official and the practices of the

230 Back in Spain

Franco regime and the irritation that I felt at the idea that Mr Tett and his 'friends' thought I would accept this rubbish.

My story with a picture of Pamela given me by her friends was the Saturday splash. The Irish papers got onto the story quickly and there were lots of repercussions. Happily, as unions geared up to campaign for her release, she was freed the following Thursday and I was able to report that the British Council in London had instructed Mr Tett to reinstate her in the Institute School job. I suspected that those deciding this instruction had to be sent did not, at that moment, particularly want to be described as 'friends of Mr Tett'.[3] He himself was, I believe, sent back to London rather earlier than he would otherwise have expected. Being the campaigner that she was, Pamela was back in the Carabanchel the November of the following year, arrested again for attending an allegedly illegal meeting, and that was probably rather later than she would otherwise have expected.

On my trip, I also met students at Madrid University, where for three years all faculties had been patrolled by armed police – part of the regime's response to growing militancy by the students. The movement was particularly strong among medical students. There had been sit-ins, mass suspensions by the university authorities, demonstrations, and running battles with the police since January after a strike had started two months earlier. Meeting the students, meant treading the same ground in Madrid's University City where I had sought shelter in 1936. Between the buildings of the Faculty of Philosophy and Letters and the Clinic Hospital had been the trench from which I could see the helmets and the red fezes of Franco's crack Moroccan troops in their own trenches a few dozen yards away. This time, as I stood there, the trees that had grown up since in the area around the buildings, were being cut down by armed police so that their troop carriers and bulldozers might have greater room for manoeuvre. Jeeps were on patrol with other police, their sub-machine guns at the ready, lolling over the sides.

Yet it was a dictatorship in decay. It no longer had Hitler or Mussolini prepared to send it troops and planes. The opposition to it was far broader than the support for the Republic in the 1930s. Just before I got to Madrid, the Episcopal Council of the Catholic Church in Spain formally asked forgiveness from the Spanish people for the attitude it had taken in 1936. Then it had blessed the bullets that Franco's forces fired at democracy. On my last day in the country on that first time back, the Carlists, supporters of the old monarchy of Spain, whose red-bereted Navarre divisions had provided some of Franco's most fanatical infantry units, held a vast gathering in Navarre where Franco and the regime was condemned hook, line, and sinker. Franco, the Carlists declared in a complete reversal of their approach in the '30s, was now the 'subversive'. Big business also wanted an end to the regime, partly because it wanted to see Spain joining the Common Market, as the European Union was then known. With a fascist dictator still in power, that would not be possible. The US Embassy was hosting diners and lunches hand over fist for all and sundry who they wanted to be part of the future Spain, everyone, that was, other than the underground Communist Party.

Apertura or 'opening' was the name of the game and an extraordinary range of people within the regime were recognising the need for change. There were still plenty of diehards; if they had not been around the regime would long since have gone. However, the real interest was not those who continued to use the language of Franco of the 1930s, but those who talked of democracy.

One illustration of this profound shift was the role of prominent lawyer Don Jaime Miralles. Three of his brothers, officers in Franco' forces during the war like Don Jaime himself, were killed in the fighting. Franco named a street in Madrid after them once he was victorious. For years, Don Jaime had been a pillar of the regime. But just a few days before I got to Madrid he had been released from prison after being held for six days on a charge of 'insulting the armed forces'. He had been asked to act on her behalf by the widow of Pedro Patino, the striking Communist building worker shot by police the year before. Don Jaime investigated the circumstances of Patino's death and, frustrated at the obstruction of the authorities, ended up publishing a dossier detailing what he found and how the authorities refused to let him dig deeper. Taken before a military tribunal, he walked out of the courtroom in protest at the way the case was being conducted. 'Nobody has ever, nor ever can give lessons in patriotism or love for Spain, to those of my blood', he declared from his prison cell in a statement that was being circulated among the lawyers I was with in Madrid. Theirs was a profession, like so many others, in ferment.

At the forefront of my mind was the basic question: how could this ferment be transformed into a movement that Franco could not hold back? Communists spent endless hours and reams of paper debating this. Spanish Communist leaders were caught in a Winter Palace scenario. They thought of the end of Franco's system in the way they saw the Bolshevik revolution in Russia in 1917 and they thought of that revolution as the storming of the Winter Palace. It would be a single moment, a *ruptura*, or quick, total break, not a process of slow erosion. To that end they looked for every way possible to stir up protest. And the more the regime tried to suppress the ferment, the hotter it got, and this formed a real school for democracy from below. Spain was not Russia. Each vote for a new Workers' Commission was one more nail in the dictatorship's coffin.

Freeing up the trade union movement was not the only lesson we all had to learn. Franco – by then being described as 'the unburied corpse' – was trying to ensure some stability for his regime after his own, inexorably approaching death. These moves focused on promoting Juan Carlos as a future King of Spain. Like the opposition inside the country generally, I was contemptuous of this idea. Juan Carlos' grandfather, Alfonso XIII, had been deposed as King in 1931 and the monarchy ended. Franco had brought the grandson forward as a Crown Prince successor, getting him to swear a solemn oath to be loyal to the principles of the regime. When Franco was in his final days in November 1975, I wrote that 'in Spain, nobody really believes that a new monarchy, Franco's death bed gift to a tortured people, can really be on the cards'.

232 Back in Spain

It was not unreasonable to think like this: Juan Carlos had taken the salute alongside Franco on 1 October that year at a military parade, he had been declared head of state at the end of October, and yet the arrests and beatings continued. But how wrong I was. Once the fascist regime was dismantled, he turned out to be a key defender of the change, resisting attempts from within the right wing among officers to reverse the process, however negative his role might have seemed while Franco was still alive.

In the end, it was Franco's heart that gave out not his regime's preparedness to use violence. His death on 20 November 1975 was followed by weeks of frantic manoeuvrings as different senior figures in the regime tried to construct a future for it. I got to Madrid in March 1976 to find a capital city smelling of tear gas and resounding to the chants of demonstrators and the declarations of opposition coalitions.

It was the beginning of open politics as people began to hold rallies, give press conferences and do the sort of things that are normal in a democracy. On one giant protest rally, we walked through streets with every corner for miles having its own police patrol. Tear gas, smoke grenades, water cannon, and batons were all used to intimidate people. Ominously uniformed special police stood around in their German Nazi-style helmets, attacking the marchers every so often. Leading figures in the two opposition blocks, one, the Democratic Junta, based around the Communist Party, and the Democratic Platform, based around the Socialist Party and the centre right, were at the head of a group that handed in a letter to the Ministry of the Interior.

This Minister was Manuel Fraga who had been the Franco Ambassador to London until November. He banned street demonstrations and meetings in public places, only to see striking workers hold their assemblies in some of the country's large churches, in some cases through a whole day or night. The more of them I attended, the more impressed I was. Everyone was encouraged to take part, no decision was taken without full participation and the strikers leaders did nothing before they had got as many strikers as could be crammed into a church or church hall for yet another assembly. Sometimes the meetings were held twice so that all who were on strike could join in. There had not been anything like it in Spain since the mass participation in the mobilisation against Franco's coup attempt in July 1936.

I watched as workers on different building sites in Madrid took strike action and elected delegates on the spot, delegates that managements, who up till then had felt able to ignore their employees' claims, were now forced to negotiate with. You could almost feel the strength of popular involvement as something in the air. A measure of that was the insistence on 'no victimisation' clauses in the agreements being forced on their employers. This was going to be vital, as it was obvious that ministers like Fraga had no intention of handing democracy on a plate to the Spanish people.

I met the Workers' Commissions' leader Marcelino Camacho, a metal worker who had been jailed in the Carabanchel Prison just outside Madrid in 1967 for his

Back in Spain **233**

trade union activities. Released in March 1972 he was re-arrested three months later along with nine other Workers' Commission leaders, who became known as the Carabanchel Ten. He and two others had been let out by King Juan Carlos just as Franco died. I had reported on the Carabanchel Ten, a story underplayed by *Mundo Obrero* until my pieces appeared.

Strikes and rallies continued on and off for seven months before Franco's last Prime Minister, Carlos Arias Navarro, resigned in July 1976. His departure did not save the regime and I was back in October to cover the widening political campaign for real change. Some 40 demonstrators had been killed by the police at different protests since my previous visit; the Communist and Socialist parties and papers of the left were still banned; fascist groups appeared to have a free rein to attack progressive bookshops; some 200 political prisoners still languished in jail; and, just a week after I arrived, employers were given the right to sack workers as they wished.

In a brutal killing towards the end of January 1977, a far-right terror group murdered five labour lawyers in the office of Manuel Lopez. The murders triggered a wave of strikes. The murders came just after a delegation representing all the democratic political parties, including the still-banned Communists, had met the then prime minister Adolfo Suarez and issued an unprecedented joint statement with him saying that violence would 'put obstacles in the way of Spain's democratic normalisation'. All five lawyers had been members of the Communist Party and their funeral cortege of over 200,000 became the largest rally against the regime in 40 years. The police stayed away and the discipline of the Spanish Communist Party that was evident on that day made it impossible not to legalise it.

Over the five months that followed, the Franco regime was dismantled bit by bit, the Communist and Socialist parties were legalised, and I was able to cover an election campaign in June 1977 for the country's first democratic parliament since the 1930s.

There were candidates for the left who had emerged after a generation of clandestine activity; some were exiles like Dolores Ibárurri, just back in Spain after half a life time away; others were young militants who had no knowledge of anything other than the fears and misfortunes of illegal struggle. Messages of change and hope were everywhere.

Not that the right was silent. Manuel Fraga had been re-incarnated as a possible future leader of Spain. Crammed in between supporters of his Popular Alliance in Madrid's Vista Alegre bullring that held some 25,000 spectators, I had to endure repeated chants of 'Fraga, Fraga, Fraga' mixed up with those of 'Franco, Franco, Franco'. Next to me was a distinguished-looking lady who was chanting for Franco when the others around us were shouting for Fraga. She stopped halfway through a triplet when she seemed to realise that she was out of step. She apologised to her friend in a half whisper before adding 'Oh, well, it's the same after all'.

In contrast, it was an astonishing experience to attend a Communist election rally of 40,000 in a football stadium in the industrial suburb of Villaverde, and,

234 Back in Spain

just a fortnight later on the outskirts of Madrid, amid torrential downpours, the final Communist Party election rally, which was a quarter of a million strong. There were enormous meetings to hear CP leaders but heroism is not enough to win elections. People flocked to those first monster meetings – Dolores Ibárurri and Santiago Carrillo, the Party General Secretary, needed a police helicopter to get to one – because the Party had been the main force opposing Franco but this understandable interest was misread as a key to political support for the Party. Carrillo overestimated the electoral strength of the Party and dismissed the Socialist candidate for Prime Minister, the lawyer Felipe Gonzalez, as a mere boy. It may have been true but it was not clever politics and the Communist Party suffered. Its votes did not match its aspirations – or the predictions of Sir John Russell. It came away with only just over 9% of the votes.[4] The percentage was higher in some industrial areas, up to as much as a third of the total votes in some of them, but the lesson was clear. A private calculation that I made at the time was that many more people attended the Party's election rallies than actually voted for it.

There were all sorts of reasons for this, including the continuing friction between the Socialists and Communists, which dated back to the Civil War. One point Carrillo made at some rallies was that, after 40 years of illegality and 40 years of anti-Communist propaganda, the Party had had only 40 days of legality to try to set the record straight. Another reason was put to me by a leading member of the Socialist Party, which got three times the number of votes as the Communists.

> There is no doubt that the Socialist Party benefited from the work of the Communists in keeping the flag of freedom and Socialism flying during the dark years of the dictatorship. But many people were still afraid to vote too left for fear of what the army and the Franco fascists, still entrenched in the state and the municipal apparatus, might do.

Weren't there other reasons as well? In my report for the *Morning Star*, I quoted an editorial from the formerly ultra-right newspaper *Arriba*, now part of the intelligent anti-Communist right, to use the terminology then being bandied about in Madrid. Ending the ban on the Communists – which had ensured that the election could go ahead as the other main parties would have boycotted the polls if the ban had been kept in place – meant 'the full normalisation of our political life' and was 'a triumph of realism over fears and nostalgia'. It meant 'not just a change in the rules of the game, but letting the game be played by everybody'.

Playing that game proved to be a lot more complicated than myself, or my comrades, imagined. Trying to find ways of doing so was the reason behind what many called Eurocommunism, which was a focus of many hopes, especially in Italy and Spain.

In October 1977, I was back in Madrid's Casa de Campo, the scene of the battles I took part in 41 years earlier. This time it was to join some two million

Spaniards in an explosion of joy at a special festival that sprawled across Madrid's giant park. It was a fiesta of freedom, amnesty, and national reconciliation. People rushed into each other's arms, people who had not seen each other for years, in some cases not since the end of the war in 1939. They were kissing, hugging, crying, laughing, singing, and dancing all around me. But they were also talking and discussing. There was food from every region of Spain, toasts in every drink Spain could produce, with stall holders working like people possessed to keep up with the requests from all who came. This was above all a political moment. Authors whose works were banned over many years were hard at it signing thousands of copies. Singers whose voices had once been silenced were turning this parkland, in my memory a place of gunfire and the cries of agony of the wounded and dying, into something that could speak of the beauty that human beings can create, not the cruelty.

Then there were the set piece speeches, the climax of the day. Carrillo reported on talks underway with Premier Suarez to explore an agreed way forward to consolidating democracy. 'Are we doing the right thing?' Carrillo asked. A mighty '*Si*' came from tens of thousands of voices.

Listening to the intense debates at the Spanish Communist Party's congress the following April was hard. It was the first legal conference of the Party in the country for 46 years. Carrillo told the delegates that he wanted to see a party which was 'neither social democrat nor Stalinist' and that others on both sides of that divide, those in the Spanish Socialist Party and those who hankered after the old Soviet-dominated ways, could not deliver the solutions the Spanish people needed. But while he talked democracy for Spain, within the Party itself he refused it. The united 'Yes' he drew in Casa del Campo was replaced by expulsions from the Party's ranks, furious arguments over the way forward, and resignations.

Carrillo, who served as General Secretary from 1960 to 1982, used Stalinist organisational methods to 'de-Stalinise' the Party. There was a huge cultural and generation gap between those who joined in the 1960s, including many young independently minded, middle-class people who had nowhere else to go under Franco, and those like Carrillo who had lived in exile. He battled with the renovators, who he believed wanted to turn the Party into a debating society. At the congress, as I had seen in France and Italy and the Soviet Union, the Party system of democratic centralism was manipulated to achieve a monolithic unity as Carrillo pushed through his unpopular policies on backing the old Spanish flag and removing Leninism from the Party's statutes. Perhaps there, above all, lay the secret of the Spanish Communists' failure to make the shift from the great party of the struggle against Franco to one that the Spanish electorate might trust to shape the future of a democratic Spain.

Spanish comrades became disillusioned with Carrillo. His attitude was often found offensive, particularly by the lawyers, who, unlike him, had first-hand knowledge of Franco's repression and of the workers who suffered it. A lot of good Party work, for example on education and the role of the church, was

236 Back in Spain

thrown away after legalisation. At the second congress, the renovators came into the open and were defeated. Problems regarding the role of the Party in the regions and the tension between a central state and local autonomy came up – a question peculiar to Spain but with parallels elsewhere – and were used by Carrillo and his supporters to purge the Party of the renovators. Carrillo was defeated at the next municipal elections and resigned. The only 'ruptura' was within the Party.

At the first legal meeting of the Party after Franco's death, Dolores Ibárurri had been amazing. No other party had such a leader. She also presided over the first session of the new Spanish parliament. It was very sad for her to see the Party in total disintegration.[5]

My last tryst with the embers of Spanish fascism came by chance. I was on holiday in Madrid in November 1978 and a referendum on Spain's first democratic constitution since the death of Franco was about to take place. Thousands of his supporters had called a rally to mark what their leaders had hoped would be a successful fascist coup, codenamed 'Operation Galaxia' after the Madrid café in which the conspirators met. After an evening of eating, drinking, and talking with an old friend in the Communist Party leadership, I went back to Pamela O'Malley's flat where I was staying. I was woken by a phone call from my dinner host giving me the broad details of the plot and how it had been stalled. The Defence Minister General Gutierrez Mellado had faced down those senior military figures who were thinking of taking action. That was a bit of a turnaround for him. When I was journeying to Madrid in 1936, Gutierrez was a lieutenant, acting as a Franco intelligence source inside the Spanish capital. It was difficult to sleep after that phone call. The coup ploy flopped but, while the vote in favour of the constitution was an impressive 88%, around a third of the electorate did not take part, an abstention rate that gave continued hope to the far right.

Portugal

In neighbouring Portugal, the Communist Party took a different approach. Franco's fascist ally, António Salazar, had created a regime that lasted even longer. He died in 1970 and a final blow to the weakened regime came in the spring of 1974 as officers in the Portuguese military, radicalised by the impact of their failing attempts to control Portugal's vast African colonies and organised as the Armed Forces Movement, got rid of his successor, Caetano. As with Spain, I had only been able to cover events in Portugal before the 1970s through information provided by exiled members of the illegal opposition parties. The Portuguese Communist representative in Britain, known to me only as 'Big Albert', would give me his latest news in strangely separated snatches. Sometimes, the process took hours. I learned afterwards that he would phone the paper from a call box near an underground station in London dictating just the opening paragraphs before moving on through the tube network to another phone to give me a bit more. Old habits die hard and Big Albert continued this way of communication

Back in Spain **237**

for some weeks after the fascists had lost power in Lisbon, and only afterwards did I finally discover the method behind these maddening conversations.

I got to Portugal in mid-April 1975, just before elections to a constituent assembly that was charged with drawing up a constitution for the country. Radical military officers and the newly freed political parties were grappling with the creation of a new democratic system supported by basic welfare state rights, which the fascist regime had blocked. They were also bringing an end to the colonial wars in Africa.

As I arrived, the Armed Forces Movement and the coalition government, which included all the major parties, were planning a major nationalisation pro-gramme. It was supported by a number of powerful factory occupations and huge demonstrations in the major towns. In this heady atmosphere, the Communist Party General Secretary Álvaro Cuñhal told me that this new process of public ownership offered 'a real perspective for a profound democratic transformation of our society'.

The night before we were talking, over 100,000 had marched through the capital in support of the nationalisations, while that day in steel works, power stations, and other workplaces employees were holding mass meetings to set out their views on just how the nationalised enterprises should be run.

At one company taken over by its workers, a building firm in Lisbon, a young employee, Maria Laura, told me that she had learned more in the year since the fall of fascism than in the previous 20. The staff themselves had taken over the company in December during a row with the owner and she was now a key fig-ure in the Workers' Commission running the company. As we walked around the premises with other employees asking her advice on this or that, she told me that a year earlier she had just been an ordinary woman with two children, a home to run and job to keep. 'I kept my mouth shut at work. I never dreamed that I would have any say in anything other than what to shop for the next day's meal'.

Lisbon, of course, was a relatively modern capital city, but the background to Maria's remarks was not only the previous repressive regime, but the backward conditions in parts of the countryside where whole areas were still in many respects in the Middle Ages with illiteracy running at up to 40%. Not only were factories being taken over by their workers, but a real sense of excitement and change was created by the way some big estates in the poverty-stricken country-side were already being expropriated ahead of the new law due to go into force providing for all Portugal's larger estates to be taken over.

The mood across the country was electric. The weekend I arrived saw over 400 meetings organised by the Communists throughout Portugal, let alone what the other parties were doing. One I attended was a family festival in a park beside the presidential Belem Palace in Lisbon that drew upwards of 300,000. People around me were in tears when one of Portugal's most popular actors, José Viana, a Communist candidate in the elections, spoke of how throughout the years of dictatorship he had longed for a moment such as this, a moment when he could say what he wanted, not what had been scripted by the regime.

238 Back in Spain

The days of campaigning for what were the first free elections in half a century were filled with passionate debate and mass meetings. On the last night of campaigning, I was at a Communist Party rally with over 150,000 crammed into the city's May Day Stadium and overflowing into the United States Avenue outside. Groups had come with banners and placards from factories, offices, housing estates, many of them marching through the streets. Unlike the leaders of the Italian and Spanish Communist parties, Cuñhal and his colleagues had not been associated with Eurocommunism. They had, for instance, approved of the Soviet suppression of the Prague Spring in 1968. Clearly, the Portuguese Communists had huge support: as in Spain, theirs had been the only effective underground network opposing the fascist regime.

Amid the optimism, there was also considerable tension – a key general had tried a counter coup in March – and on election day, 25 April, exactly one year after the so-called Carnation Revolution, the atmosphere was one of great restraint and dignity. Long orderly queues moved slowly through the polling stations from the moment they opened, and in many areas over three quarters of those on the electoral role had voted by midday. The turnout was a stunning 91% of the six million electorate and voters gave an overwhelming majority to the left with a total of 56.7% of the votes. However, within that left majority, Cuñhal did not get even a fraction of what he wanted. The Communist Party came away with only 12.5% of the total votes as against the Socialist Party's 38%. This result effectively spelt the end to Cuñhal's dreams. Whether through fear of what the far right might do or through a clear-sighted assessment of the meaning of democracy, the electors on the left wanted a step-by-step road to greater democracy and social rights, not Cuñhal's leap into the kind of Socialism that could be confused with Soviet tanks.

Although the situation was different to Spain, there were similar illusions in Portugal when the Communists proved unable to capitalise properly on their popularity as the chief and heroic anti-fascist resistance movement. In the Iberian Peninsula as a whole, the two Communist parties could not forge an alliance because of the animosity between Cuñhal, a very impressive man of great intellect but a terrible hard-line Stalinist, and the Eurocommunist Santiago Carrillo.

Italy and Eurocommunism

I was in Rome in 1970 when the Catholic trade union confederation – like most continental countries, the Italian trade union movement was divided into separate national confederations according to religious or political affiliation – had voted to break its formal links with the Christian Democrats. Their policy was now to seek 'radical changes in the structures of capitalist society and this radical alternative can only come through a process leading to Socialism'. Sitting down with leaders of this organisation, formed in 1945 on the instructions of the Vatican to split the trade union movement in Italy, and to hear these words was strong stuff. That we were in a former convent, just a little walk from the Vatican itself, only reinforced the sense of being a witness to some profound changes.

Back in Spain **239**

After that visit, I had opened my report with the words 'Can Chile happen in Italy?' By that I had meant: could a united left government take power in Rome as it had done in Chile? By my return in 1976 for the Italian elections, the same question meant something very different and much more ominous, and in Chile I had seen why.

Following the coup in Chile, Enrico Berlinguer, leader of the Italian Communists, proposed the idea of the 'historic compromise' involving an alliance of the Communists and the ruling Christian Democrats, and said that a left government could not successfully govern with only 50% plus 1 of the votes.

I had great admiration for the Italian Communist Party, from its resistance to Mussolini, which gave the Party and its leader Palmiro Togliatti (whom I'd known in Spain) tremendous popular support, through to its post-war role and its relative independence from the Soviet Union. The Italian Party, as well as the French, had once been the number one party in its country but they couldn't build on that. After the war, the US helped kick the French Party out of government and worked with the mafia to thwart the Italian Party, which, with deep roots in the Italian countryside, in industry and in the intellectual world, was the most influential within its own country of any non-ruling Communist Party around the world. (The only possible rival was the Indonesian Communist Party, whose members were subjected to a terrible and terminal massacre in the 1960s when they set about playing with military power under the influence of the Chinese.)

The 1976 election in Italy was dominated by debate around the core challenge in Italian politics: the role the Communists might have in any future governing structure. The whole campaign by the Italian Communists at that moment had a very serious and careful air: everyone sensed the importance of the moment and the dangers it held. The Italian Communists secured their highest ever vote (34.4% for the Chamber of Deputies, 33.8% for the Senate), coming second to the ruling Christian Democrats. Berlinguer argued after the results were declared: 'We will have to deal with the Christian Democrats and they will finally realise that they have to deal with us'.

The Christian Democrat government accepted Berlinguer's 'historic compromise' and ruled with Communist support. But two years later the political situation changed when Christian Democrat President and former Prime Minister Aldo Moro, who had headed the first left-of-centre government in Italy in 1963 when the Christian Democrats linked up with the Socialist Party, was kidnapped by the Red Brigades. After nearly two months held prisoner, he was killed by his captors.

All sorts of questions remain over what happened and who was behind the kidnapping. It was a murky world, drawing together big business corruption, secret service intrigue from different sides of the Cold War, and far-left idiocy. The month following Moro's death, the Italian President, Christian Democrat Giovanni Leone, resigned over his possible involvement in a massive bribery scandal involving the US aircraft company Lockheed, and a week later I discussed these issues with one of the leading Italian Communists, Giorgio Napolitano, who himself became President of Italy in 2006.

Napolitano was careful in his replies. His focus was on ensuring that public institutions in Italy be reformed in open ways that reinforced democracy, not on scoring political points against a corrupt political opponent. In successive interviews, he told me how Communist MPs took up positions as chairs of parliamentary scrutiny committees, how parliamentary oversight improved, how the left in the Rome Parliament supported a minority Christian Democrat government as long as that government put in place a number of key changes, but how a strong right within the ruling party was opposed to any such changes. It was a difficult balancing act between trying not to push things too far before the left became politically strong enough to be able to prevent a coup of the type in Chile, while, on the other hand, mobilising for the fundamental changes that would prevent frustration, disillusionment, and violence from the downtrodden. The stakes were high. We all knew, through leaks from the entourage of Henry Kissinger and others, that there were more than whisperings in Washington about doing what was necessary to stop the Communist Party getting into government. Napolitano pointed to the deep-seated economic and political problems in Italy as a fertile breeding ground for both right and left extremism. There had been a series of riots, particularly in areas where the local government was led by the Communists, and he was clear attempts were being made to destabilise Italy.

Berlinguer was no more successful in changing Italy in the way he wanted than other Western European Communist leaders were in their own countries and he abandoned the 'historic compromise' in 1980.

The ideas at the heart of what was often given the label Eurocommunism came out of the debates in the Italian Communist Party in the 1960s and 1970s. Chile as well as Czechoslovakia had a big effect on the development of Eurocommunism, the changes in approach made by most Communist Parties across Western Europe as we tried to understand how to combine our desire for fundamental social change and our commitment to democratic means to achieve that with the fact that power in the media and the state was not on our side.

Its heyday was a meeting in 1977 in Madrid of Berlinguer, Santiago Carrillo, the Spanish Party General Secretary, and Georges Marchais, the French Party General Secretary. The French Party, like the British, didn't like the word Eurocommunism – or the concept – and, by attending the Madrid meeting, Marchais was being opportunist. I had admired the French Party in the 1930s but then I saw how centralised and rigid it was, and, in fact, Marchais was a brake. There was never a meeting of all the Western European parties on Eurocommunism. Much more discussion was needed, particularly to isolate those like the West German, Portuguese, and Luxembourg parties, which were pro-Soviet. A public break with the Soviet Party was crucial but this never happened.

Notes

1 Horacio Inguanzo was released by Adolfo Suarez, Spain's first post-Franco, democratically-elected Prime Minister, and remained active in politics. He died in 1996.
2 Pamela O'Malley and her husband Gainor Crist went to live in Spain in the early 1950s. Crist, the model for Sebastian Dangerfield in the novel *The Ginger Man* by J P Donleavy, died in 1964. She took on the role of host, mentor and guide on things Spanish for many visitors, especially those from Ireland, including the poet Seamus Heaney, who wrote several poems about staying at her flat overlooking one of Madrid's busiest fish markets. Sam stayed at the flat on his subsequent visits to Spain.
3 *The Times* (10 May 1972, p. 5) reported the reinstatement: 'Informed sources said the publicity given to the case [i.e. Sam's story] had influenced the Institute in changing its mind. The British authorities had appeared to be cooperating with General Franco in persecuting a woman for her political beliefs'.
4 The election was won by the Union of the Democratic centre led by Adolfo Suarez with 34.4% of the vote. The Socialist Party came second with 29.3% of the vote, followed by the Communist Party with 9.3%.
5 Carrillo himself was expelled from the Spanish Communist Party in 1985. The following year, the Party joined as a founding member the United Left coalition.

15

EPILOGUE

Now that we're together
I'll say what you and I know
and often forget:
we've seen fear
be the law for everybody.
We've seen blood
-which begets only blood-
be the law of the world.
No,
I say no,
let's say no.
We don't belong to that world.
We've seen hunger
be the bread
of the workers.
We've seen
locked in prison
men full of wisdom.
No,
I say no,
let's say no.
We don't belong to that world.
No,
let's say no.
We don't belong to that world.

DOI: 10.4324/9781003243380-16

In 1976, 40 years almost to the day after I had crouched in a Madrid trench with a small group of British volunteers and one machine gun, I was in the Spanish capital again and heard this song, 'Let's Say No', sung in Catalan by its author, Raimon. The concert hall echoed to the rafters with defiance against a fascist regime that still held the country in its grip. The words of Raimon's song meant much to me. They were deeply etched, biting in the immediacy of their meaning for his Spanish audience, but no less powerful for me as an elegy on the history I had – and have – lived through. I had gone to Spain in 1936 as a volunteer against fascism, carrying my family name, Manassah Lesser, a Jewish name from Poland. As Franco imposed his grip in the spring of 1939, I left Spain as Sam Russell, a journalist.

When Stalin dismissed the Spanish struggle as 'no longer of importance', he was wrong. Successive generations have looked back with an increasing interest and emotion to the time when a few thousand men and women from around the world put their lives at risk for what they believed in. Democracy is the stronger today because of what we did. Knowing that warms the heart. But it does not make it easy to remember all those names on that terrible, long casualty list typed up in Albacete, which I carried with me to London in the spring of 1937. Nor to sort out why, at the same time, other, longer, lists were being typed out in Moscow as Stalin's Great Terror got under way.

For those of us involved in spreading the good news about what we thought was a new vanguard for human society, confronting the reality of terror and oppression which lurked behind that veil of progress is an especially painful process. Under the resounding slogan of 'ending the exploitation of man by man', Soviet-style Socialism shackled the spirit and sullied the vision that inspired the struggle of countless millions the world over.

Looking back with honesty is not easy. Like so many others, I took part in perpetrating a lie about Stalin's Russia. I did not do so cynically and knowingly, as some people did, but rather, like most of those committed to the Communist movement in Britain, with an anger over what I thought was wrong with the world, an anger that helped to obscure, or make me ignore, other, terrible crimes carried out in the name of the very cause I was trying to serve.

I believe the overwhelming majority of Communist Party members in the Socialist countries would not have been Communists if they had been in my situation in the West. The Party card was the job card and they made Communist into a dirty word and debased the whole idea of Communism, which has come to mean institutional corruption and terror. In the Soviet Union, the nomenklatura or ruling elite were promoted over the dead bodies of the Red Army, and they knew it, and their children, who joined the elite like our ruling class, knew it too.

An iron curtain was indeed rung down across Europe and around those parts of the rest of the world that followed, or were forced to follow Stalin's model.

244 Epilogue

It turned the fine ideals that drew millions into action for a better world into a cruel con-trick. Those who followed the ideology but lived outside the physical reach of Stalin's secret police regimes carried their own iron curtains within their minds. Communists were quick to stand in line when it came to denouncing Trotsky, condemning Tito or whatever other turn of policy and programme was demanded. We excelled in excoriating yesterday's comrades who had become today's enemies as 'fascist beasts', 'running dogs of imperialism', or 'hirelings of the capitalist class' – the list of the insults is long. And we kept our minds closed to the terrible truth. If we did not know about the millions in the concentration camps across the Soviet Union from Vilnius to Vladivostock, it was because we did not *want* to know.

Communists ruled a third of the globe for nigh on 70 years. During that period, they developed some of the most evil regimes the world has seen. From Stalin to Mao Zedong, from Brezhnev to Deng Xiaoping, from Enver Hoxha in Albania to Kim Il Sung in North Korea, along with Cambodia's Pol Pot, Romania's Ceauşescu, East Germany's Honecker, Bulgaria's Zhivkov, the leaders praised as heroes beyond parallel were in reality mediocre people who ranged from the incompetent to the bloodthirsty, and sometimes both. Above all they were people who, while proclaiming the values of democracy, proved unable ever to loosen their personal grip on power. Any who showed a spark of originality, a degree of openness or anything else that might seem to threaten the security of their colleagues in power became themselves victims to the machinery of oppression.

My own views changed during my time as a journalist the more I saw of what was being done in the name of the cause to which I was committed.

In Britain, the Party failed to recognise capitalism's ability to regenerate. It wasn't the old pattern of the rich getting richer and the poor poorer but of a general rise in living standards, even if the 'poverty gap' grew. When there was support for Communists as shop stewards, usually by open and fair vote in recognition of their fight for better pay and conditions, the Party mistook it as a vote for Socialism. The purely trade union struggle was dismissed as 'economism', yet that was what we were good at, and better than the social democrats who we criticised for focusing too narrowly on that struggle.

The Party was too romantic about the working class – for example, during the great miners' strike of the 1980s, it didn't openly criticise the adventurist tactics of the miners' leader Arthur Scargill. Families fought for their sons to avoid the mines, so why go on about wanting to send more lads down the pits? The decline in mining was already a fact. Instead, we could have fought for alternative jobs, better retraining, and support for the communities.

The Party also turned a blind eye to many scandalous rackets that have gone on in our trade unions, like ballot rigging. To my mind the most scandalous was always the racism. This was the case in Smithfield, the central London meat market just down the road from the *Daily Worker/Morning Star* offices, a depressing sign of the level of political education in the local membership of the Transport and General Workers' Union in those days.

The British Party was always cautious, and on international affairs waited to see what the French or the Italians said, even on Czechoslovakia. We should have broken with the Soviet Union then. People in the leadership knew what went on through their personal connections: General Secretary Harry Pollitt had a Russian friend Rose Cohen who vanished, and when he tried to inquire was told not to; *Worker* editor Bill Rust's second wife was a Russian, and probably had NKVD/KGB links, and his daughter Rosa by his first wife was found working at the bottom of a copper mine in Kazakhstan; leading Party member Bob Stewart's daughter was married to a Russian who vanished; the Party's Industrial Organiser Bert Ramelson was Ukrainian and had two sisters vanish in Russia; John Gollan, General Secretary after Pollitt, knew both Marian Šling, who was imprisoned in Czechoslovakia, and her husband Otto, who was executed, and so on.

The revelation in 1991 that, like other Western parties, the British Party – contrary to what it had always maintained, and unknown to all but a very few of the top leadership – had, as many of us suspected, received money from the Soviet Party from 1958 until 1979, some of it going to the *Daily Worker* and the *Morning Star* and therefore paying my wages, just rubbed salt in the wound.

I was never active in the Party as such; all my political activity was carried out through working for the paper, and I increasingly became aware of the troubled relationship between being a Communist journalist and being a Communist Party member. The Party saw the journalists as having the same status as Party workers. Except that, as we were constantly reminded by the Party leadership, we were in the privileged position of receiving our Party wage on a regular weekly basis, whereas many of the direct Party employees had to raise their own meagre salaries from members' donations and the like, and had consequently to cope with significant backlogs of unpaid wages. (Party workers, however, could take wives – or husbands – on Party-paid holidays, a reward Party journalists were denied.) Remarkably, the Labour Party did not have its own daily paper, so with all its internal and external problems, the continued existence of the *Daily Worker* and then the *Morning Star* was all the more surprising. It was rightly dubbed 'the miracle of Fleet Street'.

The clearly held view of the Communist Party leadership was that we journalists needed to be kept firmly under control. There was always a struggle between the paper and the Party, which seems true of all CPs. After all, if you are asked to analyse and criticise as your profession, you might turn those skills on the party's activities. The Party leadership quite simply never fundamentally trusted any of the journalists on our paper, however brilliant at their craft they may have been.

On a number of occasions when I needed to consult the editor, as I came to his office off the large, open newsroom where we all worked I would have the door literally slammed in my face because he was talking on the direct line to King Street, the Party HQ. It was all so stupid. The phone line was obviously tapped. MI5 was privileged to know, but I, like the rest of the Communist Party

FIGURE 15.1 Celebrating Sam's 40 years' service to the *Daily Worker/Morning Star* with other staff members at the paper's offices, 75 Farringdon Road, London.

Source: Family archive.

membership, was not! Such incidents were evidence of collective make-believe which infected the Party leadership.

For much of that time I was the Foreign Editor of the paper, a post I saw as little more than a glorified office boy because every editor of a Communist paper wants – and has – to be his or her own foreign editor. Thwarted in the news and feature columns, I used obituaries and book reviews, especially in the 1970s, to say what I really thought, and I carried on when I left the *Star* in December 1984, outlining my views in articles for Communist papers like the weekly *7 Days*.

After Czechoslovakia, I saw no more role for the CP but I had never been inspired by the Labour Party.[1] I was rather schematic in my views: I thought you should only stay in the CP if you attacked the Soviet Union, and being critical of the Soviet Party became a bit of an obsession – maybe because I felt guilty at being conned before.

The world I have seen is a world of hatred, of war, of slaughter, of empires and of poverty: a world I set out to change. This memoir relates how I went about trying to do that, the things I saw and witnessed others trying to do, the lessons I learned, the mistakes I made – errors, I would like to hope, others do not need to repeat. But it is also a world of beauty and friendship, where I have joined those who imagined and dreamed, watched those who worked to try to make things better for themselves and others, reported on their efforts, sometimes getting it terribly wrong, always intending to get it right, always hoping. For without hope, a human being is nothing.

As a child at the start of my century, in the years before Hitler and Stalin, I used go to with my mother to a Yiddish theatre at the Peoples Palace in Mile End Road near our home in London's East End. On the bus back, we would join in a chorus of the signature tune at the performances. It stayed in my mind, a chorus from one of the musicals that were such a part of that Jewish world brought to London by those fleeing pogroms in the East:

> Yidele, Yidele,
>   Little Jew, little Jew, never give up hope ….

FIGURE 15.2 Sam at 94, a year before he died.
Source: Marshall Mateer.

Now it will be for others to learn and to practice what I was not able to.

Note

1 The Communist Party of Great Britain disbanded in 1991. Sam later joined the Labour Party when it was led by Tony Blair, whom he admired at the time.

APPENDIX: LETTERS FROM ABROAD

Sam Russell wrote many letters to his wife Margaret while he was abroad but only a handful survive. Here are two examples:

Room 1016

International Hotel

Shanghai

Thursday August 26th 1954

My Darling Mag,

Arrived from Peking by air a few hours ago after a five hour journey and now we're here, I can't quite see what the point is, but I suppose we'll find out. The place is a complete contrast to Peking. While Peking is an old Chinese city with its Imperial palaces and gardens, Shanghai is the complete Western type port and financial centre - although most of the glory has departed or what the British commercial community consider glory. It was very funny to pass just now a huge skyscraper and see the name Sassoon House and a small board stating that it is British property. Just what the delegation is going to do here no one seems to know and although it's 8pm they apparently have no schedule yet. In the meantime some of the press gang have already got cracking interviewing some of the few British businessmen who remain and I suppose tomorrow you'll be reading heartrending stories about their trials and tribulations.

It's interesting the way the press gang has somehow naturally divided itself into two groups. One group is composed of the racketeers MacColl (*Express*) and Ridley (*Telegraph*) and Gale (*Guardian*) [...] They are all equally viciously opposed

250 Appendix: Letters from Abroad

to everything that is happening in China today, jeer and sneer most of the time. Because of his experience MacColl is of course a much smoother operator and it's really a sight to watch him at the innumerable banquets and receptions we're attending performing the well-mannered gentleman act, gesticulating smoothly and with the greatest urbanity and suaveness of manner. Then later he tells you what he really thought.

The other group is composed of Harris (*Times*), Winterton (*Herald*) and myself with Fraser Weighton (Reuters). This latter is as worried an old woman as I've ever met. Of course being an agency man, he's got to keep filing stories and has to think of evening as well as morning newspapers. He's had quite a few tiffs with the racketeers group but he's getting everybody down a bit. Harris and Winterton of course don't agree with me on China, in fact we've hardly discussed the politics of the business, while I've had a number of ding dong arguments with the racketeers going on until the very early hours, neither side convincing the other. Harris of course has the great advantage of knowing Chinese and he certainly knows China in all its aspects and knows many people.

I've now definitely made up my mind not to go to Japan. But I shall not be coming back via Hong Kong, but go back to Peking where I have a number of things to do and then return via Moscow. Whether I shall stop off at Warsaw I still don't know, but once I've finished what I have to do in Peking I'd like to get back home as quickly as possible.

I had hoped to have had a letter from you before leaving Peking but I suppose you didn't get my letter in time. Here's hoping there's one waiting when I get back there. I hope you've been getting the rare letters I've sent and that Ruth [Sam's daughter] has been getting her postcards which are the only ones I can get.

[…]

I thought it was hot in Peking but when we stepped out of the plane here, the heat just hit us in the face from the tarmac, and it's apparently much worse in Canton. I thought with all the sweating I've been doing I must have lost some weight but before getting on the plane this morning I stepped on the scales and tipped them over 80 kilos - I really must get down to some slimming when I get back.

Had myself measured for a pair of shantung silk trousers, which'll be ready in 24 hours. Also went with Harris to his shirt maker of old, found he was still there and ordered two silk shirts [made to] measure. Harris had Japanese silk but I stuck firmly to Chinese. I'm hoping to get a length of silk for a dress for you but I'm blowed if I know what colour to get. I was thinking perhaps something in peacock blue or green, we'll see.

I've a very nice room here at this hotel which used to be called the Park Hotel before and was the main American hotel in town. I forgot to tell you that the hotel in Mukden was a shocker. The usual reception on arrival in a new place is on tonight so I must dress and first try and mop up some of the sweat. Goodbye darling, wish you were here. I miss you terribly. A big hug and kiss for you both.

Love Sam

Room 314

Hotel Savoy

Moscow, USSR

February 25th 1956

Darling Mag,

Now that the Congress is over I can at last start writing again and reply to your letters of the 15th, which arrived on the 22nd, and letter card of the 6th and letter of the 9th which arrived together on the 15th. Please forgive the delay and the typing, but I'm so on edge I can't write and it's easier to type.

It must be miserable for you with all this ghastly weather and it seems that it's still the same. I hope by the time you get this it will have improved. I'm hoping that Harry Pollitt [British Communist Party General Secretary] will take it so that you can get it quicker. Here it's much warmer and today is only 10 degrees below [zero] compared with 15–20 below in the past few days. It's a beautiful sunny day and I'd like to go for a walk in the country but I've got to stick around in case something happens. During the Congress I've been walking to the Kremlin every morning from my hotel which takes about 15 minutes to the Borovitsky gate through which I go and so I've been able to get some exercise apart from my daily toe-touching. On my way to the Kremlin I pass by Red Square and then through a little garden which skirts the Kremlin wall and which must have been a moat at one time and […] must be very pleasant in spring and summer. Yesterday (Saturday) there were lots of children playing in the snow in the brilliant sunshine and there's a slide that young children can use for tobogganing and generally it's very jolly.

The Congress was pretty hectic starting at 10 a.m. every day and going on till 7 or 7.30 p.m. with a two-hour break from 2.30 to 4.30 and a half hour about 12 when I usually had a couple of oranges and watched visitors from the public gallery buying enormous quantities of sweets and chocolates. For the first week I was nearly bursting a blood vessel three times a day because, although I had been given a card to attend the session, I could not get a card for my interpreter and was I sitting […] like an idiot not understanding a thing. The fraternal delegates sitting down below and on the rostrum had simultaneous translation over headphones but this was not laid on to press gallery until, after a week of Pollitt and others raising blue murder, they finally ran a wire to the press gallery - but by then the best part of the Congress was over. Fortunately George Matthews [British Communist Party Assistant General Secretary] was taking a very full note and so each day I rushed along to the flat where he and Pollitt were staying which was about halfway between the Kremlin and the Savoy, got his notes then rushed to the hotel to telephone, and although this was a good arrangement it was obviously not as good as reporting it first hand.

252 Appendix: Letters from Abroad

But you can imagine what I felt like when I kept on speaking to umpteen people to try and get some translation facility and only met with a blank wall each time and had to sit there reading novels and not knowing what was going on. I'm afraid I've not made much progress with my Russian but now the Congress is over I hope to get down to it and do two hours every day.

The worst business of the lot was over the Mikoyan speech where the uncomplimentary references to Stalin's Economic Problems came right at the end of the speech and where Matthews notes were not very full. Nevertheless I had my story on the strong condemnation of the cult of personality which […] two other leading blokes had made before him and especially singling out the Mikoyan statement that there had not been any collective leadership in the Party for 20 years. But when I got on Arthur Clegg [Foreign Editor] told me that the story would not be led that way because "it would come as too great a shock to readers" and so it was buried out of sight. Of course when the following Sunday [Edward] Crankshaw [in the *Observer*] made such a fuss about it, Mick Bennett [Assistant Editor] – who I believe was the one responsible for the decision to re-lead the original story and bury the par about collective leadership […] – was on the phone raving about why I didn't give Mikoyan's speech and claiming that in any case Mikoyan had misquoted Stalin. You can imagine what I felt when I saw the paper and I told them just what I thought.

I do hope that you've now got out of your flat spin and that now you've [sorted] out the question about the flat you won't worry about it. I haven't heard anything more about the flat here, but I should think that now the Congress is over things will begin moving. Anyhow I'm glad I haven't had to move into a flat before you come and am still hoping […] that you'll be able to come before April. Perhaps you'll feel better about going to Gdynia and Warsaw when the weather gets better.

I am rushing around quite a bit and find it quite impossible to relax at all. Could you please get in touch with Sheila Lynd [Features Editor] and ask her to ring the BBC and get a transcript of this Stephen Wynburne talk [a radio item on Russian women] you mentioned and ask her to send it on to me. It would be most useful to see what it's like because I'm trying to think of particular women's angle stories. […] And how about getting that picture of yourself and Ruth done by Henry Grant [photographer, married to Rose Grant, who worked at the paper] that you promised to let me have. I know it hasn't been possible before because of Ruth being ill and the weather, but please try and do something about it now, darling.

You must have been in a spikey mood when you wrote your last letter. I don't remember what motivated your question about what people do when it's so cold and they can't afford a taxi. But anyhow, they go by Metro which is very warm or by bus or trolleybus which are heated of course but most times crowded. […] I've given George Matthews a couple of toys for Ruth and I hope she likes them.

All my love, Sam

POSTSCRIPT: MI5 AND MY FAMILY

*Ruth Muller**

> *Every individual, whatever their office or political persuasion, may dispose of their personal papers as they see fit ... Here, however, a whole class of individuals ... have had clandestine state functionaries provide the service for them. In redacting the files, they may protect the identities of their fellow operatives, but show no such compunction regarding the most intimate affairs of their subjects. In every case the collection of this information is without their consent and often it is without their knowledge.*[1]
>
> Prof. Kevin Morgan

At the end of October 2012, almost exactly two years after my father Sam's death, the UK National Archives made a now-routine announcement:

> This is the 29th Security Service records release containing a total of 77 files and bringing the number of Security Service records at The National Archives to 5,003.

Under the heading 'Communists and suspected communists, including Russians and communist sympathisers' was just one entry:

LESSER, Manassah, aliases Mortimer LESSER, Sam LESSER, Michael de LESSEPS, Sam RUSSELL, Stuart RUSSELL

- Catalogue ref: KV 2/3741
- Date: 22/08/1935–09/05/1961

A member of the Communist Party from 1934, he first came to notice in 1935 while a student at University College London, as a member of the executive committee of a student group at LSE which published 'Student

---

* **Ruth Muller** is Sam Russell's daughter.

Front'. In 1937 he was wounded serving in Spain in the International Brigade, and as Sam Russell began to write from there for the Daily Worker in 1938. Later, he was the Daily Worker's correspondent in Paris and Brussels and worked for the paper in the UK as its diplomatic and later foreign correspondent from 1943, concurrently providing broadcast material for Polish Radio. From 1955 to 1959 as the Daily Worker's Moscow correspondent he was friendly with Donald Maclean, before he then returned to London as foreign editor. The file contains much of Sam Russell's intercepted correspondence and transcripts of conversations at Party HQ referring to him. The files span KV 2/3741 to KV 2/3750.

Sam had, of course, always suspected, as had all Communist Party of Great Britain members, that someone, somewhere was keeping tabs on him and had done so for many years. He'd even tried to find out, with the assistance of former *Morning Star* colleague Chris Myant, and one of his own nieces, if such files existed but to no avail. The Service waited until 51 years after the date of the closure of the last file (1961) to provide a vast amount of concrete evidence that such was indeed the case.

The first I knew about the release was in early November 2012 when a cousin sent me a short piece from the *Jewish Chronicle* headlined 'High on the MI5 Radar' alongside a photo of Sam taken in the 1930s. The article began: 'The tones of a balalaika could be heard in the evening air as Guy Burgess and Donald Maclean … entertained friends at a Moscow flat' and going on to mention the documents concerning Sam now in the possession to the National Archives and fully open to the public.

It took some months for me to be able to obtain copies of the more than 1,000 pages of 'information' that had been collated on Sam, with my mother Margaret and myself, as well as the rest of the family and a wide circle of close friends, friends, acquaintances, contacts, fellow journalists, comrades, and casual 'passers-by' featuring as what might be called 'collateral damage'. When the parcel eventually arrived at my home in South Africa in 2013, I received it with a complex mixture of feelings: astonishment, anger, distress, perturbation, curiosity, and overarching everything else – great relief that yes, indeed, we *were* always being watched, listened to, and reported on. My parents had not imagined it all.

The thing is that, for my mother at least, it went beyond imaginings and caused her severe psychological distress and anxiety – adding to the nightmares that remained from her time in Spain (1937–1939), London during the Blitz, and her work with Yugoslav refugees and in the Displaced Persons camps of southern Germany. Her suspicions also made her wonder who of her fellow Party members, neighbours, friends, and even relatives might have been prevailed upon to report on our activities to the authorities. In the course of the prolonged, largely unsuccessful, psychiatric treatment she received in later life, much of this was erroneously put down to paranoia and bi-polar disorder. Margaret's MI5 files have not been released to the National Archives, though their existence is not

Postscript: MI5 and My Family   255

in doubt as her Personal File number, PF 711,420, is much in evidence in the detailed reports on Sam from 1951 onwards.

I think Sam saw it more as a hazard of his job as a Communist journalist and, being able to travel a great deal, it didn't weigh as heavily on him. Nevertheless, even as a young child, both my parents made it clear to me that I had to be very careful what I said on the phone, certain things and people were never to be mentioned. Given that the CPGB 'family' was also, in a way, our family, I knew from an early age that Communists were not viewed with equanimity by government, and that made us 'different'. Despite the fact that being a Communist was never illegal in the UK, the 'Cold War' atmosphere was such that announcing one's political inclinations to friends, as I once did, age about eight, resulted in the notable reduction of my social circle. The erstwhile 'friend', Leslie, announced that I couldn't be a 'person' if I was an un-christened Communist and I retorted that if that was how she felt, she couldn't come and have the tea that my Mum had prepared specially for us: mashed-banana-on-brown-bread sandwiches!

So aside from the effect on the lives of thousands of families at the time all the 'snooping' took place (and of course, it still continues both electronically and in more 'conventional' forms), there is the issue of the publicising, many years later, of uncorroborated statements, allegations, and observations, when the 'subject' is no longer around to refute or comment on them.

Kevin Morgan, Professor of Politics and History, Manchester University, puts it very clearly:

> An Operational Selection Policy (OSP) was produced in 2001, providing generic guidance for the preservation of selected historical files and none at all for their release into the public domain. The main priority groups identified are senior officials of 'subversive' parties, targets of 'intrusive' surveillance, agents of hostile intelligence, any individual or their relative not given security clearance, and those achieving positions of 'public eminence'. No information is provided as to the number of individuals falling within each class, and [MI5's] voluminous official history does not even contain such basic information as a listing over time of the bodies that were deemed subversive. [Its official historian] alone has been granted access to such information, but under conditions of confidentiality ... No other historian is able to request a file, or even to establish that it exists, or has existed, as Eric Hobsbawm was able to confirm on being denied access to his own. Hobsbawm's files have, as it happens, been made accessible since his death, subject to what appears to be an implicit fifty-year rule. By policy or good fortune it appears that we are not (except by oversight) to have the benefit of any subject of a file being able to comment upon its contents ... MI5 remains exempt from the provisions of the 2000 Freedom of Information Act ... [and] ... retains complete control over its own records and has never engaged in any public consultation with specialists having either an interest or an expertise in radical political movements.

> Its role in recent British history remains controversial and it makes no secret ... of its manifest continuing interest in the validation of its historical role as a form of public advocacy in a post-Cold War world.[2]

In mid-2020, I discovered by chance whilst accessing material on the National Archives website, that a further, small 'tranche' of papers concerning our family had been 'released' – this time by the Foreign Office in 2019. What I have been able to access shows that we weren't just being spied on – but that the government, in the guise of the notorious International Research Department (IRD) of the FO which was set up immediately post-WWII to specifically target Communists (and not just British ones), was engaged in 'dirty tricks' too. In this case, a family holiday to the Soviet Union in the summer of 1962, and a meeting with friends, Donald and Melinda Maclean, was to be leaked to trusted media sources (Reuters was suggested as the most 'responsible' and 'with the best facilities for widespread replay afterwards') in an attempt to embarrass the CPGB. Cables and letters were flying back and forth from the FO to the British Embassy in Moscow even as we were boarding the Soviet passenger ship *Baltika* to sail to Leningrad. Photos were to be taken and our movements closely watched [UKNA Ref. FCO 168/654/1].

I recall part of this in an incident on a boat going down the Moscow River. Mimsy Maclean and I were instructed to hide under the benches we had been sitting on after Sam and Donald spotted the FO-instructed news-hounds lurking on the back of the top deck of the boat, camera at the ready. Interestingly, the Foreign Office is still not prepared to release to me the part of these documents that they have retained, citing Sections 23 (1) and 24 (1) of the Freedom of Information Act, which relate to exemptions, security bodies, and the public interest. The FO says,

> it is not appropriate in the circumstances of this case to confirm which of the two exemptions is actually engaged as to do so is likely to undermine national security or reveal the extent of any involvement, or not, of the bodies dealing with security matters. Therefore this response does not confirm which of the two exemptions is engaged.

The letter to me (August 2020) goes on to say that, 'having reviewed the material, there is a stronger public interest in protecting national security' than in allowing access. No explanation was forthcoming as to what aspect of 'national security' still needs protecting after 58 years! At the time of writing my appeal is in process.

Notes

1 Kevin Morgan, 'Communist history, police history and the archives of British state surveillance', in *Twentieth Century Communism*, Vol. 17, 2019, pp. 67–89 (https://www.research.manchester.ac.uk/portal/files/173655804/K_Morgan_Communist_history_police_history.pdf).
2 Morgan, op cit.

INDEX

Note: Page numbers in *italic* refer to figures; page numbers followed by 'n' refer to notes.

Abetz, Otto 87
Abramsky, Chimen 134
Acton Gazette 103
Afghanistan 183, 186, 187
Agence France-Monde 83, 84, 86, 91, 94
Agence France-Presse 162
Aitken, George 41
Alexeyev, Nikolai 164, 165
Allende, Salvador 2, 212–14, 216, 217, 218
Alpàri, Gyula (Julius) 83, 91
Alper, Mercedes 195
Alvarez, Santiago 68
Amalgamated Engineering Union 100, 101, 104, 107, 109
anarchists 32, 72–74
Andropov, Yuri 182, 183
Anglo-Italian Pact 52
anti-fascism 36n3, 48, 69, 85, 90, 92, 93, 135, 238
anti-Semitism 1, 11, 13, 60, 87, 88, 114, 116, 134, 136–37, 177, 222
Aragon, Louis 95
Armed Forces Movement 236–37
Arriba (newspaper) 234
Arter, Fred 101
Arthur (interpreter) 156
Arthur, Max 36n6
Association of Volunteers for Liberty *38*
Attlee, Clement 31, 205
Auschwitz 5, 84, 109n2
Azikiwe, Nnamdi 124

Barman, Tom 128
Batista, Fulgencio 193, 195, 197
Bay of Pigs 191, 195, 196
BBC 107, 108, 114, 116, 117, 128, 146, 167, 215, 252; Bush House 107–08; World Service 107
Becker, Artur 44, 84
Belgium 57, 92, 93, 95, 96; Brussels 1, 91–99, 107, 254
Bennett, Mick 142, 252
Beria, Lavrenti 137, 147
Berlinguer, Enrico 218, 239, 240
Besedin, Grigori 168, 185, 186
Bevan, Aneurin 117, 119
Bing, Geoffrey 77
Birnbach (Lewin), Dora 39, 60n1
Blackshirts 11, 13; *see also* Mosley, Sir Oswald
Blake, George 183
Blieck, René 92, 95
Bobrovnikov, Nikolai 159
Boffa, Giuseppe *162*, 166, 167, 176, 177
Bolshoi Ballet 166, 171, 184, 213
Bonnet, Georges 88, 90
Bramley, Ted 96
Brezhnev, Leonid 171, 182, 186, 244
British Council 229, 230
British Library 23
British Medical Aid 77
British Medical Association 116–18
British Museum 23

258 Index

Brits Who Fought for Spain, The (TV documentary) 26, 36n6
Brocq, Norman Le 114, 115
Browne, Felicia 15
Brožová-Polednová, Ludmila 131, 138, 139n4
Brugère, Fredo 20, 21, 22
Buckley, Henry 45, 59, 67
Buist, Vincent 161
Bukovsky, Vladimir 183, 217
Bulganin, Nikolai 147, 157n4, 163, 165, 173
Burchett, Wilfred 183–84
Burgess, Guy 181, 182, 254
Burke (Cooper), Edward 23
Bush, Alan 9
Butler, RA 50

Caetano, Marcello 236
Camacho, Marcelino 232–33
Cambodia 4, 203–05, 244
Campbell, Elena 179, 187n3
Campbell, Johnny 3, 110, 141, 146, 147, 179
Campbell, Willy (Villi the Clown/ Bill Kaye) 179, 187n3
Cambridge University 17, 19, 20, 27, 66, 181, 182
Campesino (Valentin González), General 55
Carrillo, Santiago 234–40, 241n5
Carroll, Nicholas 128, 129
Carey, Victor 114
Casablanca (film) 133
Casanova, Danielle 84
Casanova, Laurent 84
Castro, Fidel 188, 190–99
Catalonia 41, 47, 48, 55–57, 66, 67, 71, 82
Catalonia Communists *see* Unified Socialist Party of Catalonia
Cave, Cissie 115
Cayton, Alf 96, 121
Ce Soir (newspaper) 89
Ceaușescu, Nicolae 244
Cecil, Robert 185
Chamberlain, Neville 49, 52, 54, 57, 68, 82, 85, 92, 93
Channel Islands 1, 3, 114–116, *116*; Jersey 114, 115; Guernsey 114, 115
Chapayev (film) 26
Chater, Tony 2, 186, 208
Chicago Tribune 161
Chile 2, 200, 212–18, 239, 240
Chilton, Sir Henry 30, 31
China 2, 20, 36n7, 140, 170, 192, 205–08, 250; Beijing 206–08, 249–50; Changzhou 206, 207; Harbin 208;

Shanghai 207, 249; *see also* Cultural Revolution
Chiré, Alexei 162
Choury, Maurice 84, 108
Churchill, Winston 22, 102, 109, 117, 129, 225
CIA 147, 191, 195, 196, 201, 209n4, 212, 213, 218
Clark, Jock 19, 22
Clegg, Arthur 252
CNT (trade union body) 73
Cockburn, Claud 3, 29, 51, 110, 125n1, 136
Cohen, Jack 16
Cohen, Judd 111
Cohen, Rose 244
Cold War 120, 122, 127, 137, 153, 239, 255, 256
Cominform 129, 130
Comintern 1, 16, 17, 22, 36n7, 36n9, 41–46, 69, 73, 74, 81n2, 82, 83, 91–93, 96, 129, 133–36, 156, 180
Communism xvi, 1, 4, 11, 36n7, 93, 144, 182–85, 199–200, 201, 243
Communist Party of Belgium 92
Communist Party of Chile 213–18
Communist Party of China 20, 206, 208
Communist Party of Czechoslovakia 130, 133, 210
Communist Party of Denmark 167; *Land og Folk* (Land and People) 167
Communist Party of Germany 44, 69–70, 84; West Germany 197
Communist Party of Great Britain Great Britain 2, 3, 4, 11–17, 33, 35, 38, 41, 44, 45, 47, 69–71, 83, 85, 92–97, 101, 106–07, 122, 129, 133, 134, 143, 146, 147, 157n2, 167, 169, 179–86, 189, 200, 205–06, 211, 245, 246, 253–56; History Group 96; King Street 16, 122, 135, 245, 247n1
Communist Party of Indonesia 239; Jakarta 213
Communist Party of Luxembourg 197
Communist Party of the Soviet Union 69, 121, 140–45, 148, 161, 163, 168, 172, 192, 240, 245, 246; 20th Congress 141–49, 157n2, 182, 251; 26th Congress 186–87
Communist Party of Sweden 174; *Ny Dag* (New Day) 174
Communist Party of the USA 70
Confessions of a Nazi Spy (film) 88
Copeman, Fred 71
Cordon, Colonel Antonio 57

Cornford, John 16–17, 19, 21, 26, 33, 34, 184
Corvalán, Luis 217, 218
Courtard, Pierre 177
Coutanche, Alexander 114, 115
Coward, Noël 133
Cox, Geoffrey 29, 45
Cox, Idris 96
Crankshaw, Edward 252
Crossman, Richard 108
Cuba 2, 188–201, 208n2; Communists 191, 192, 199; Guantanamo 192, 193; Havana 188, 189, 192, 193, 195, 196, 200; US blockade 189, 192–96, 199; *see also* Bay of Pigs
Cuban missile crisis 2, 175, 188–92, 198, 199
Cultural Revolution 205, 206, 208
Cuñhal, Álvaro 237, 238
Cunningham, Jock 19, 28, 32, 41
Czechoslovakia 2, 4, 49, 68, 83, 90, 91, 129–36, 138, 156, 183, 184, 192, 195, 210–12, 218, 219, 221, 227, 240, 245, 246; Cspel complex 155, 156; invasion of 183, 184, 192, 211, 212, 218, 221, 222n2, 227; Prague 120, 131, 133–35, 136, 137, 181, 188, 210, 211, 222n2, 227; Slánský trial 133–136, 210; trial of Social Democrats 131; *see also* Prague Spring

Daily Express 28, 31, 45, 63, 108
Daily Herald 45, 127, 138n1, 250
Daily Telegraph 45, 95, 134
Daily Worker (London) 1–4, 29, 30, 41, 44–46, 54, 57, 65, 66, *78*, 82–85, 87, 92, 94–96, 99–102, 105, 107, 109, 110–29, 133, 134, 136, 137, 140, 141, 142, 143, 146, 147, 153, 155, 157n1, 161, 165, 166, 168, 169, 174, 180, 186, 189, 200, 201, 205, 211, 217, 224, 226, 244, 245, *246*, 254; Alfie cartoon 96–97; Cayton Street 82, 110; Farringdon Road 121–24, 128, *246*; People's Press Printing Society 121; Swinton Street 110; *Workers' Notebook* 110
Daily Worker (New York) 46, 54, 83, 95, 137, 147, 200, 201
Dain, Guy 118
Days with Lenin (book) 164
de Gaulle, General 100, 125
Death of Uncle Joe, The (book) 3
Delage, Luis 58, 68
Delasalle, Gaston 72
Delmer, Sefton 28, 29, 45, 46, 108
Democracy and Fascism (pamphlet) 11

Deng Xiaoping 244
Der Zeit ('The Times') 7
Dimitrov, Georgi 70, 81n2
Don Quixote de la Mancha (novel) 33
Dong, Pham Van 203
Dorofeyev, Boris 172
Dove of Peace (Picasso) 193
Downing, Miss (teacher) 11
Dr Zhivago (novel) 174
Driberg, Tom (William Hickey) 63
Dubček, Alexander 210, 211
Dudintsev, Vladimir 173
Duke of Kent 102
Dumont, Jules 21, 22
Duret Aubin, CW 114, 115
Dutt, Rajani Palme 11, 92, 93, 97

East–West trade 120
Eastern Europe 3, 120, 130, 170, 192, 210, 212, 218, 219, 228; Warsaw Pact 153, 211
Economic Problems of Socialism, The (book) 142
Ede, Chuter 115
Edilli, Ladislau 55–56
Edwards, Jimmy 171–72
Ehrenberg, Ilya 171
Eisenhower, Dwight D 166, 170
El Shatt refugee camp 79
El Siglo (the Century) 213, 214, 217
Elliott, Lon 66
Enemy Within: The Rise and Fall of the British Communist Party (book) 2
Episodes of the Revolutionary War (book) 198, 209n3
Escalante, Anibal 192, 199, 208n2
Eurocommunism 2, 183, 227, 234, 238, 240
Evening Post (Jersey) 114
Evening Press (Guernsey) 114
Ewer, WN (Trilby) 127, 128

fascism 11–13, 17, 20, 21, 22, 49, 65, 68, 70, 73, 74, 81n4, 85, 89, 125n1, 130, 136, 137, 154, 155, 156, 225, 228, 232, 236, 237, 243
Fermina (radio secretary) 68, 90–92
Financial Times 215
First World War 5, 22, 26, 36n7, 36n8, 71, 76, 83, 90, 93
Flugelman, Jacob 150
Foreign Languages Publishing House 143, 175, 181
Foreign Office 18n5, 30, 50, 96, 97, 107, 126–29, 138–39n1, 181, 185, 201, 229, 256

260 Index

Forrest, Willy 45, 59, 67, 127, 128, 225
Fox, Ralph 33, 34
Fraga, Manuel 232, 233
France 16, 22, 31, 37, 47, 50, 51, 57, 59, 63–69, 71, 72, 74, 82–84, 87, 88, 89, 92–96, 99, 102, 108, 127, 177, 225, 227, 235; Agde 39; Argelès 67, 85; Cerbère 64, 67, 82; Paris 1, 3, 16–8, 23, 37–39, 51, 68, 83–95, 107, 108, 126, 129, 133, 134, 145, 177, 224, 225, 254; Perpignan 17, 18, 39, 64, 82; Perthus, Le 65; Pyrenees 18, 37, 39, 47, 50, 56, 64, 76, 225
Franco, Francisco 15, 16, 23–28, 30, 32, 39, 40, 45–49, 51, 52, 55–60, 63, 67–76, 84, 89, 90, 92, 120, 135, 184, 223–26, 229–36, 241n2, 243
Franqui, Carlos 190, 191
Free French forces 35–36n2, 100, 225
Frei, Eduardo 212
French Communist Party 3, 16, 17, 21, 26, 35–36n2, 39, 72, 84–86, 89, 90, 92–95, 99, 130, 155, 239, 240
Fried, Eugen (Clement) 92–96
Frog, The (play) 175
Frost, Terry xvi
Fryer, Peter 4, 153, 156

Gale, George 249
Gallacher, Willie 85, 93
Galton, Sir Francis 11; Galton Society 11–12
Garcia, Manuel 196
Gardiner, Lew 136
Gates, John 70, 137
George V 14
general strike 11
Geneva 127, 128, 205
German forces 1, 15, 31, 47–49, 52, 55, 58, 59, 61n4, 62, 68, 84, 104, 105, 112, 114, 115, 225, 226
Germany 13, 16, 36n7, 68, 69, 79, 89, 90, 104, 109, 111, 113, 219, 254; Berlin 52, 87, 88, 127, 140; Duisburg 113; Düsseldorf 113, 114; East Berlin 211; East Germany 219, 244; Elberfeld 113, 114; Essen 109, 113–14; Gelsenkirchen 113; Hamburg 113; Ruhr 113; West Germany 155
Gerő, Ernő (Pedro) 41, 43, 46, 134, 136, 153, 154
Geyl, Bill 17
Geyl, Pieter 17
Gibbons, Johnny 135, 143, 147, 179, 180
Gibbons, Tommy 181

Goldfinger, Ernő 122
Gollan, Elsie 133
Gollan, John 97–98, 133, 167–169, 245
Gomułka, Władysław 131, 132, 153
Gonzalez, Felipe 234
Gorbachev, Mikhail 96, 98, 175, 183, 218, 221
Gottwald, Klement 130, 211
Graham, Frank 47
Grant, Henry 252
Greenhill, Denis 96–99, 107, 109n3
Griffiths, Leon 136
Griffiths, Philippa 178
Gromyko, Andrei 177, 189
Gromyko, Lydia 177
Guernsey *see* Channel islands
Guevara, Che 2, 196, 197–201, 209n3
Gulag 36n7, 149, 177, 180

Habonim (Builders) 7
Haldane, JBS 121
Hanna, George 180
Hanna, Rosie 180
Hannington, Wal 109
Harris, Richard 250
Harwell atomic research centre 119
Hastings, Lady Moorea 123
Havel, Václav 210
Henrique, Archbishop Silva 216–17, 222n3
Hentgès, Pierre 166, 167, 177, 178, 183
Hill, Charles 117
Hinks, Joe 20
Hitler, Adolf 3, 15, 16, 33, 40, 45, 48, 49, 51, 52, 56, 59, 66, 68–9, 88, 89, 92–94, 101, 102, 109, 111, 112, 114, 156, 230, 247
Ho Chi Minh 203
Holland 112
Holmes, Walter 110
Honecker, Erich 244
Hong Kong 74, 206, 250
Hope, Peter 128, 129
Horáková, Milada 131
Horder, Lord 'Tommy' 37, 118
Horner, Arthur 44, 46
housing 118–19
How to Win the War (pamphlet) 92
Hoxha, Enver 244
Hoyland, John xvi
Hughes, Richard 181
Humphrys, John 215
Hungary 2, 4, 79, 83, 130, 136, 153–58, 173, 212; Budapest 83, 153–56, 173, 179; Communist party 154–57; Goldberger textile plant 154

Hurry, Colin 118
Hutt, Allen 2, 110, 121, 166
Hyde, Douglas 3

Ibárurri, Dolores ('La Pasionaria') 24–25, 36n5, 49, 226–27, 233, 234, 236
ICI 110–11
IG Farben 110–11
Illychov, Leonid 144, 201
Imperial War Museum xv
Industrial and General Information (news sheet) 107
Inguanzo, Horacio 224–25, 241n1
Inostrannaya literature (Foreign Literature) 163
International Brigades 19–31, *34*, 35, 36n3, 37, *38*, 40, 41, 45–49, 51, 52, 63, 66, 69, 71–77, 81n1, 81n4, 103, 136–38, 184, 227, 254; Abraham Lincoln Battalion 31, 50; American volunteers 50, 51; archives 66, 81n1; Australian volunteers 50; Austrian volunteers 66, 89–90; British Battalion 31, 34, 50, 51, 60, 71, 81n4, 101; British volunteers 68; Bulgarian volunteers 66; Canadian volunteers 50, 51, 56; Czech volunteers 66, 90; Dimitrov Battalion 31; Dombrowsky Battalion 31; French brigade 21; Garibaldi Battalion 31, 36n3, 48; German volunteers 22, 29, 35, 39, 44, 45, 66, 69, 89–90; Italian volunteers 39, 90; medical volunteers 27, 38–39, 49, 64, 77, 79, 81n5; Number 1 Major Attlee Company 31; New Zealand volunteers 20, 27, 50; Palestine volunteers 39, 50; Polish volunteers 39, 66, 90; Saklatvala Battalion 31; Thälmann Battalion 31, 45; Tom Mann Centuria 45
International Brigade Memorial Trust xvi, 75, 81n4
International Military Commission 63, 67, 72
Israel 60n1, 137, 138, 227; Irgun 138; Stern gang 138
Israeli Communist Party 137, 138
Italian Communist Party 30, 46, 61n4, 61n6, 66, 81n1, 130, 153, 155, 176, 218, 239, 240
Italian forces 15, 22, 23, 31, 39, 43, 47, 48, 50, 52, 53, 55–60, 62, 75
Ivinskaya, Olga 175

Jacques, Martin 185
Jaruzelski, General Wojciech 183, 221

Jersey *see* Channel Islands
Jersey Democratic Movement 114
Jewish Chronicle 105, 254
Jewish identity xvi, 3, 5, 7, 8, 9, 10–12, 15, 18n4, 79, 134, 137–138; *see also* Ladino, Yiddish
Jewish National Fund 13
Jodas, Josef 211
Johnson, Hewlett 121, 123
Jones, Freddy 20, 21, 22, 27, 105
Jones, Jack 76, 81n4
Jones, Nell (first wife) 80, 105, 109n4
Juan Carlos I 231, 232, 233

Kádár, János 154, 155, 156, 157
Kaganovich, Lazar 147, 166
Kartun, Derek 3, 136
Katyn 180–81
Katz, Otto (André Simone) 43, 133, 136
Kavan, Pavel 129, 133
Kazakhstan 149, 151, 245
Kennedy, JF 175, 190, 191, 195, 196, 201, 209n4
Kerrigan, Peter 34, 35, 36n9, 44, 45, 53, 71, 101–02, 107; Rose (daughter) 53; Rose (wife) 102
Kesseg, Geza 154
KGB 140, 163, 183, 184, 185, 245
Khrushchev, Nikita 2, 3, 132, 135, 142–53, 160, 163, 166–68, 170, 171, 173–76, 179, 182, 189, 190, 201; secret speech 2, 140–148, 152, 157n2, 167, 177, 201; 'thaw' 172–75
Kim Il Sung 244
Kirsanov, Semyon 173
Kisch, Richard 86–87, 95
Kissinger, Henry 204, 240
Kléber, General Emilio 23, 29–30, 35, 36n7
Klein, Herbert 55
Klitgård, Frede 167
Klugmann, James 181, 182
Knox, Bernard 19, 21, 36n3
Kobrin, Misha 167, 168, 169
Korean war 126, 203
Kosygin, Alexei 203
Krupskaya, Nadezhda 163–65
Kuznetsov, Vasili 201, 209n4, 211

Labour Party xvi, 13, 14, 31, 77, 104, 108, 111, 115, 117, 126, 140, 205, 225, 245, 246, 247n1
Ladino 79, 92
Laika 176
Laos 203, 205

262 Index

Laura, Maria 237
Lawrence, Jack 104
Le Figaro 87, 88
League of Nations 63
Lehmann, Beatrix 121
Lenin, Vladimir 14, 22, 85, 91, 122, 128,
    163, 164, 165, 203; Lenin Library 164;
    Lenin shipyard 220; Lenin School 41;
    Leninism 130, 203, 235
Leningrad 141, 162, 171, 256; siege 141
Leone, Giovanni 239
Leontiev, Boris 176, 177
Les Communistes (novel) 95
Leser (Lesser), Naftali (Nathan, Sam's father)
    xvi, 5, 7–8, 9, 10, 11, 12, 13, 15, 18n1,
    105, 109n2
Lesser, Efraim (Frank, brother) 6, 10, 18n3,
    18n6, 75, 76, 76, 77, 77, 104, 105, 110,
    169
Lesser, Isaac (Ivor, brother) 18n3, 105
Lesser, Manassah (Sam) *see* Russell, Sam
Lesser (Powell), Margaret xv, xvi, 77, 78,
    79–80, 81n6, 106, 134, 135, 140, 158,
    163, 167, 171, 179, 180, 182, 185, 187n5,
    215, 249, 251, 254; Llangenny 77; Order
    of Loyalty to the Spanish Republic 81n5
Lesser, Mira (sister-in-law) 104, 105
Lesser, Miriam (sister) 18n3, 105
Lesser, Polly (mother) 5, 6, 7, 8, 15, 18n2,
    99, 102, 105, 106, 247
Lesser, Queenie (sister) 18n3, 105
Lesser, Ruth (sister) 18n3, 105
Lesser (Muller), Ruth (daughter) 80, 106,
    140, 158, 187n5, 222n1, 250, 252,
    254–56
Lesser, Salom (Sid, brother) 6, 18n3,
    60–61n3, 105
Lesser, Shirley (sister) 18n3, 105
'Let Us Say No' (song) 243
Levin, Bernard 124
l'Humanité 84, 85, 87, 89, 94, 95, 166, 167,
    177
Lipovestsky, Lyosha 74, 75, 141, 144, 145, 176
Lister, General Enrique 55, 66, 68
Literaturnaya Gazeta 176, 177
Lithuania 162, 162
lobby system 126–29
London 1, 5, 7, 11, 35, 37, 73–74, 79, 82, 96,
    99, 100–09, 110, 115, 118–20, 134, 135,
    138, 140; Blitz 104, 105, 110, 112, 118,
    119, 154, 204, 254; County Council 8,
    10; East End 1, 5, 7, 8, 9, 10, 11, 12, 12,
    105, 204, 208, 215, 217, 243, 247, 254;
    V2s 111–12

London, Artur 135, 136, 139n3
London, Lise 135
Longo, Luigi (Gallo) 46, 61n4, 66, 81n1
Look Back in Anger (play) 1, 172
Lopez, Manuel 228, 233
l'Unità 153, 166, 167, 174, 176, 224
Lynd, Sheila 252
Lysistrata (play) 223

MacColl, René 249–50
MacEwen, Malcolm 146
Mackenzie, David 19
Maclean, Donald (Mark Petrovich Frazer) 2,
    181–85, 187n4, 254, 256
Maclean, Melinda 181, 182, 184, 185, 256
Maclean, Mimsy 256
Macleod, Alison 3, 4
Macmillan, Harold 165, 166
Mahon, Johnny 106–07
Malik, Yakov 175
Malinovsky, Rodion 166
Malmierca, Isidoro 197
Manchester Guardian 133, 249
Mao Zedong 192, 203, 244
March, Juan 25
Marchais, Georges 240
Margaret, Princess 175
Markin, Arkady 148
Martin, Kingsley 124
Marty, André 3, 21, 34, 35n2, 46, 51, 66, 67,
    69, 70, 72
Marx, Karl 72, 91, 125, 164; Marx House
    122; Marx Memorial Library 164;
    Marxism 14, 16, 17, 23, 37, 93, 215;
    Marxism-Leninism 130, 203
Marxism Today 185
Matkovsky, Nikolai 143, 179
Matthews, George 4, 98n5, 157n2, 186, 200,
    201, 222n4, 251, 252
Matthews, Herbert 45
McCone, John A 201, 209n4
McLaurin, 'Mac' 27
McLennan, Gordon 186, 187
Medvedev, Roy 183
Medvedev, Zhores 183
Mellado, Gutierrez 236
Memories of Lenin (book) 163, 164, 165
MI5 xvi, 3, 18n4, 36n4, 61n3, 81n6, 97,
    98n3, 98n4, 109n1, 109n2, 109n3, 119,
    125n2, 135, 138–39n1, 157n2, 245,
    253–56
Miaja, General José 32
Mikoyan, Anastas 142, 147, 189, 190, 252
Mikoyan, Sergei 190

Miralles, Don Jaime 231
Misseldine, Len 101
Modesto, General Juan 55, 58, 66, 68
Mola, General Emilio 28
Molesworth, Colonel 67
Mollet, Guy 226
Molotov, Vyacheslav 147, 157n4, 166
Montagnana, Rita 59, 61n6
Montero, Simon Sanchez 224
Mora, Constancia de la 46
Moran, Lord 117–18
Morgan, Kenneth 253, 255, 256n1
Moro, Aldo 239
Moro-Giaffera, Vincent de 88
Morning Star xv, xvi, 2, 4, 96, 125n2, 205, 208, 211, 215, 217, 224, 234, 244, 245, *246*, 246, 254
Morocco 15, 18n5, 25; Moroccan forces 28, 230
Morrison, Herbert 13, 114
Moscow News 178
Moscow Radio 165, 166, 179
Mosley, Sir Oswald 11–12
Münzenberg, Willi 43
Munich agreement 49, 68, 69, 88, 89, 94, 10
Muravyov (press official) 161
Mussolini, Benito 15, 16, 25, 33, 45, 47–48, 51, 52, 56–59, 68, 230, 239
Myant, Chris xvi, 186, 254

Nagy, Imre 153, 154, 157
Napolitano, Giorgio 240
Nathan, George 32
National Health Service 2, 37, 116–18
National Union of Journalists 2, 122, 136
National Zeitung (Basel) 55
Navarro, Carlos Arias 233
Nazi-Soviet Pact 69, 85, 89, 101, 126, 184
Nazis 13, 22, 23, 40, 57, 69, 75, 79, 85, 87–92, 96, 98n2, 101, 102, 104, 108, 111, 112, 114, 115, 126, 130, 131, 133–37, 180, 184, 193, 215, 225, 226
Nazism 40, 88, 102, 104, 129, 133, 219
Negrín, Juan 49, 54, 64, 67
Nehru, Jawaharlal 46
New Masses, The (magazine) 46
New Propeller (magazine) 103
New York Times 45
News Chronicle 7, 29, 45, 127, 225
Nguyen Hung 204
Nigeria 124–25
Nin, Andreas 74, 81n3
Niven, Barbara 115
Nixon, Richard 203

North, Joe 54, 200
Not by Bread Alone (novel) 173
Novotny, Antonin 210, 211
Novy Mir (New World, magazine) 172–74

O'Casey, Sean 121
Officers' Training Corps 14–17, 19, *20*, 21, 22, 27–29, 70, 74, 85, 102
Ogden, Dennis 143, 147, 179, 181, 185
O'Malley, Pamela 229–30, 236, 241n2
On Trial (book) 135, 139n3
One Day in the Life of Ivan Denisovich (novel) 172
Orwell, George 37
Osborne, John 1, 172
O'Shaughnessy, Hugh 215

Pagès, Pierre 84
Palestine 11, 13, 36n9, 39, 50, 137, 138; Palestine Liberation Organisation 138
Parker, Ralph 137, 140
Pasternak, Boris 174, 175
Patino, Pedro 223, 231
Pearce, Brian 14, 85
Pena, Julia 223
Perea, Sebastián Pozas 55
Perez, Orlando 208n1
Péri, Gabriel 85, 88, 98n2
Pétain, General 100
Philby, Kim 182, 184
Phillips, Morgan 205
Picasso, Pablo 172, 193
Pickles, William 108
Pilato, Benino 195
Pinochet, Augusto 214, 216, 218
Pocock, Gerry 186
Pol Pot 204, 244
Poland 1, 2, 5, 7, 10, 11, 13, 36n8, 60n1, 122, 131–34, 153, 169, 183, 218–21, 243; Cracow 5, 132, 133; Galicia 5, 109n2; Gdansk 219, 220; Katowice 220; martial law 183, 219, 221; Ropczyce 5; show trials 131–36; Wawel Castle 133
Polish Workers' Party (Communists) 69, 220, 221–22
Pollitt, Harry 3–4, 16, 63, 66, 83, 84, 92, 93, 100, 101, 135, 142, 143, 146, 157n2, 167, 168, 169, 180, 245, 251
Portugal 197, 236–38
Portuguese Communist Party 236–38, 240
Portuguese Socialist Party 238
Pospelov, Pyotr 168
POUM (United Workers' Marxist Party) 17, 37, 43, 73, 74

264 Index

Powell, Margaret *see* Lesser, Margaret
Prague Spring 136, 210, 211, 221, 227, 238;
 see also Czechoslovakia
Pravda 121, 134, 137, 142, 145, 147, 161,
 165–68, 170, 176, 177, 178, 186
Pritt, DN 124
Putin, Vladimir 183

Quelch, Harry 164, 165
Questions of History (journal) 173

Radio Barcelona 40
Radio Free Europe 4, 155, 211
Radio Salamanca 52
Raimon 243
Rajk, László 130, 136
Rákosi, Mátyás 130, 134, 136, 153, 154,
 156, 157, 192
Ramelson, Bert 169, 245
Raya (attaché) 175, 176
Real Band of Brothers, The (book) 36n6
Red Army 26, 36n7, 36n8, 74, 75, 102, 114,
 130, 131, 155–57, 166, 173, 179, 184,
 226, 243
Red Cross 53, 54, 56, 178, 226
Reed, John 228
Reminiscences of Lenin (book) 164
Resurrection (novel) 174
Rettie, John 4, 144, 146
Reuters 4, 55, 131, 142, 144, 146, 160, 161,
 167, 181, 212, 250, 256
Ribbentrop, Joachim von 88
Ridley, John 249
Robeson, Paul 46, 108, *124*, 172
Robinson, Edward G (Emanuel
 Goldenberg) 88
Robson, RW ('Robbie') 17, 18n6, 38
Rodriguez, Carlos Rafael 191
Romeo and Juliet (ballet) 171
Romilly, Giles 22
Roosevelt, Franklin D 225
Rosier de Madame Husson, Le (novella) 84
Rowland, Jimmy 112
Rudenko, Roman 141
Runge, Fritz 83, 84, 91, 134
Russell, John 129, 229, 234
Russell, Sam xv, xvi, 1, 3; becomes *Daily
 Worker* correspondent in Spain 44;
 becomes Moscow correspondent
 140, 141; birth 1, 7, 18n3; Brussels 1,
 91–96, 98n3, 254; Bush House 107–08;
 censorship 2, 3, 28, 35, 40, 41, 45, 46,
 48, 54, 108, 111, 112, 141, 142, 144,
 161, 163, 166, 174, 175, 208; change of

name 41, 243; Channel Islands 114–16;
 Chile 2, 212–18; China 2, 140, 205–08,
 249–50; Cornwall 99; CP line on
 WW2 92–93, 96–98; Cuba 2, 188–200;
 Czechoslovakia 2, 129–36, 138, 210–12,
 219, 245–46; death xvi, 253; Diplomatic
 Correspondent 126, 129; education
 7, 8, 9, 10; Farringdon Road 121–24;
 first marriage 105; flying with bombers
 112–13; Foreign Editor xv, 2, 3, 127, 136,
 138, 145, 205, 213, 246, 254; France (*see*
 France); general reporter 109, 110–19;
 honorary Spanish citizenship 2, 76;
 Hungary 2, 4, 153–57, 167, 173, 212;
 Italy 2, 238–40; journalism xvi, 1–4, 40,
 44–46, 51, 54, 64, 66, 68, 81, 83, 88, 94,
 96, 107, 109n3, 117, 121, 122, 125n1,
 126–28, 144, 147–48, 163, 176, 178,
 217, 243–45, 255; Lesser, Manassah 1,
 6, 8, 18n3, 30, 41, 60n2, 92, 98n4, 105,
 108, 169, 215, 243, 253; Moscow (*see*
 Soviet Union); Napier *100*, 100–109,
 228; Nightingale House xvi; parents
 and siblings (*see* Leser/Lesser); Paris (*see*
 France); Parliamentary Correspondent
 126; Poland 2, 132–33, 218–21, 243;
 radio broadcasts 40–43, 44, 46, 47, 71, 74,
 104, 107–09, 122, 136, 211, 254; Royal
 Scots 14, 36n9, 74, 99; second marriage
 80; shop steward 2, 102, 103, 106, 122;
 Soviet sleeper suspicion 97, 99, 119,
 184; Soviet Union (*see* Soviet Union);
 Spain (*see* International Brigades, Spain,
 Spanish Civil War); Vietnam 2, 4, 201–05;
 wounded in Spain 32, *34*
Rust, Bill 41, 44, 54, 70, 83, 97, 107, 109,
 121, 125n2, 245
Rust, Rosa 245

Sakharov, Andrei 182
Saklatvala, Shapurji 31
Salazar, António 236
Sampaix, Lucien 87–88, 98n2
Sargent, Malcolm 182
Scargill, Arthur 244
Schechter (Grant), Rose 94, 252
Second World War 1, 40, 68, 74, 80, 98n5,
 102, 136, 137, 204, 225, 227; Eastern
 front 69; Second Front 102, 103; Western
 front 69, 166
Serov, Ivan 163
7 Days (weekly paper) 246
'Seven Days of the Week' (poem) 173
Shapiro, Henry 176

Sharif, Dzhavad 186
Shepilov, Dmitri 166
Shi Fangyu 208
Shostakovich, Dmitri 174
show trials 2, 3, 74, 129–136, 173
Shuqeiri, Ahmad 138
Sicher, Gustav 134
Simonov, Konstantin 172, 187n2
Single Spies (play) 185
Siqueros, David Alfaro 172
Slánský, Rudolf 133, 135
Šling (Šlingova), Marian 133, 135, 139n2, 245
Šling, Otto 133, 135, 245
Smirnov, Lev 141
Smith, Rose 205, 206, 208
Smith, Sam 117
socialists (non-Communist) 7, 11, 72, 73, 118, 218, 226, 227, 229, 232, 233, 234, 235, 238, 239, 241n4
Socialist Medical Association 117
Socialist Party of Great Britain 11
solidarity (trade union movement) 220
Solzhenitsyn, Alexander 172
Sosa, Manuel 192
South Africa 137, 197, 254; apartheid 137, 197
South Wales Miners' Federation 44
Soviet Jewish Anti-Fascist Committee 135, 169
Soviet Union 2, 4, 13, 23, 35n2, 36n5, 45, 68, 69, 74, 80, 81n1, 89, 92, 93, 96, 101, 102, 107, 120, 125, 127, 129–31, 135, 138, 140–187, 189, 192, 193, 195, 196, 206, 212, 218, 226, 227, 228, 235, 239, 243–46, 256; Dushanbe 163; Kuibyshev 149, 150, 170, 181, 182; London embassy 4, 18, 92, 128, 137, 175, 211, 213; Magadan 177, 178, 179; Moscow xv, 2, 4, 16, 36n7, 36n8, 36n9, 41, 44, 74, 79–81n1, 89, 91–93, 96, 98, 120, 130, 135, 137, 140–54, 156–69, 170–86, 187n1, 189, 190, 192, 201, 206, 208n1, 210, 213, 215, 219, 221, 226, 227, 243, 250, 251, 254, 256; Novosibirsk 150, 151, 170; Odessa 66, 166, 226; Siberia 36n7, 148, 149, 150, 151, 163, 168, 169, 170, 177; Sokolovsko-Sarbaisky 152; Tajikistan 163; Tashkent 150; Virgin Lands policy 150, 152, 171, 181, 189
Spain 2, 3, 15, 17, 18, 46, 57, 62, 68, 89–90, 92, 102, 104, 105, 107, 120, 125n1, 130, 133–3, 140, 169, 181, 184, 216, 223–36, 238, 239, 241n1, 241n2, 243, 254;

Albacete 19, *20*, 21, 30–34, 45, 51, 70, 71, 243; Andújar 32; Barcelona 23, 40–84, 104, 107, 111, 136, 202, 227; Barcelona opera *78*, 79; Belchite 225; Boadilla 21, 30; Borjas Blancas 57; Córdoba 32, 33, 72; Cortes 36n5, 64; Ebro, River 47, 48, 50, 52, 75, 77, 81n4' Embassy (UK) 76; Esplugas 57; Estremadura 56, 57; Figueras 19, 55, 60, 64, 65, 66, 67; Guadalajara 48, 225; Guernica 37, 52; Irun 15; Jarama 23, 31, 35, 50, 51; La Jonquera 64, 65, 66; La Roda 21, 31; Linares de Jaen 33; literacy campaign 40; Lérida 57, Lopera 32, 33, 34; Madrid 15, 24–33, 44, 45, 47, 49, 51, 52, 59, 68, 71, 72, 82, 85, 108, 112, 193, 223, 227–35, 236, 240, 241n2, 243; Madrid University City 25, 26, 28, 70, 230; Madrigueras 31; Maqueda 15; Oviedo 29; Popular Front 15, 16, 32, 41–43, 47, 51, 72–74; Port Bou 64, 68; Puigcerdà 51; Pyrenees 18, 37, 39, 47, 50, 56, 64, 76, 225; Republic 3, 15, 16, 18, 24, 30, 32, 33, 36n5, 36n8, 37, 39–41, 44, 47–49, 51, 52, 55, 56–59, 63, 66–73, 77, 81n5, 83, 89, 90, 114, 224, 225, 226, 230; Ripoll 49, 50, 56; Sant Ferran Castle 19, 61n5, 64, 67; Santa Coloma 57; San Sebastian 15; Segre, River 48; Sierra de Pàndols 75; Tarragona 57, 58, 59, 68; Teruel 70, 104; Valencia 25, 41, 51, 52, 68, 226; Valls 58
Spanish Civil War xv, 1, 3, 15, 16, 17, 21, 36n5, 40, 70, 72, 74–76, 184, 200, 223, 224, 234; bombing of civilians 43, 52–54, 56, 57, 64–65; desertion 29, 33, 69, 71; fascist forces 17, 23–25, 28, 29, 30, 32, 33, 43, 47, 48, 51, 55–60, 62–64, 67, 68, 71, 73, 217, 226, 232, 233, 234, 236; fifth column 55, 60, 74, 87; Gurs camp 89; military discipline 19, 22, 30, 48, 58, 67, 70–73; military training 16, 19–22, 27, 28, 31, 32, 70, 75; 'non-intervention' 16, 18, 31, 39, 58, 63, 184; People's Army 47, 48, 49, 51, 55, 56, 58, 66, 67; refugees 55, 56, 60, 62–67, 79, 84–86, 89, 225–26; retreat to France 59–60, 63–68; Service of Military Information (Servicio de Información Militar) 55; *see also* International Brigades
Spanish Communist Party 25, 32, 36n5, 37, 42, 43, 46, 60n2, 59, 60, 66, 69, 72, 199, 223–36, 240; *Mundo Obrero* (Workers' World) 224, 233
Spanish Socialist Party 227, 229, 232–35

266 Index

Springhall, Dave 60, 93
Spychalski, General Marian 132, 221, 222
squatters 118–19
Staf, Karl 174
Stalin, Joseph 2, 3, 36n7, 68, 69, 72, 74, 90,
 91, 93, 104, 120, 129–32, 135, 136, 137,
 141, 142, 146, 147, 150, 152, 158, 160,
 164, 166, 172–75, 179, 182, 184, 185,
 210, 227, 228, 243, 244, 247, 252
Stalinism 2, 3, 235, 238
Stangreciak, Tadeusz 219
Stevenson, Adlai 201, 209n4
Stewart, Bob 245
Suarez, Adolfo 233, 235, 241n1, 241n4
Summerskill, Edith 205
Sunday Times 128, 181
Sunday Worker 110
Surkov, Alexei 173, 174
Suslov, Mikhail 144, 145, 146
Suvorov, Marshal 75
Swan Lake (ballet) 171
Swanson, Gloria 100
Swanson, Walter 100, 103
Swingler, Randall 126
Swingler, Stephen 126
Swire, Joseph 55
Symes, Robert 27

Taittinger, Pierre 94–95
TASS (news agency) 109, 158, 165, 166,
 181, 212
Teitelboim, Volodia 217
Ten Days that Shook the World (book) 228
Tett, Norman 229–30
Thompson, Bob 137
Thorez, Maurice 3, 85, 88, 93, 94–95, 97
Tillon, Charles 84, 85, 88
Timbaud, Jean-Pierre 109
Times (London) 19, 85, 124, 174,
 241n3, 250
Tito 60n1, 153, 166, 169, 181, 210, 244
Togliatti, Palmiro (Alfredo/Ercoli) 46, 59,
 61n4, 239
Tolstoy, Leo 174
trade unions 3, 36n9, 58, 72, 73, 90, 101,
 103, 110, 121, 122, 154, 171, 176, 211,
 220, 221, 224, 227–29, 231, 233, 238,
 244; shop stewards' movement 103, 228;
 union elections 104, 244
Tréand, Maurice 94
Trotsky, Leon 138–39n1, 164, 166, 178, 244
Trotskyism 14, 60, 103
Trud (trade union paper) 176

Truth Will Prevail (book) 135, 139n2
'Turkish March' (piano piece) 77
Tvardovsky, Alexander 172, 187n2

UGT (trade union body) 73
Ulanova, Galina 171
Unified Socialist Party of Catalonia 41, 42,
 42, 43, 60n2, 72
United Nations 96, 137, 138, 160, 189,
 191, 192, 201; Relief and Rehabilitation
 Administration 79
United Press 95, 176, 201
United States 4, 36n3, 36n7, 41, 46, 87,
 102, 120, 127, 129, 130, 137, 147, 155,
 166, 170, 184, 188, 189–93, 195–97,
 199, 203–05, 207, 212, 213, 218, 239;
 Marshall Aid 119–20
University College London 9–10, 11,
 13–14, 17, 85, 253
Uribe, Vincente 57

Vangelista, Orfeo 153, 154
Viana, José 237
Vichy France 3, 100, 108
Vietnam 1, 2, 4, 87, 177, 184, 201–05; Ai
 Tu 204; Dong Ha 203; Dong Hoi 202;
 Hanoi 202, 203
Vittorio, Giuseppe Di (Nicoletti) 30

Waley Cohen, Robert 10
Walker, Bob 101, 103
Walker, Hooky 50
Wallace, Edgar 175
Walter, General (Karol Świerczewski) 33,
 36n8
Wang Ming 192
Warsaw Radio 122, 132
Watch on the Rhine (play/film) 133
Watson, Keith Scott 45, 60, 62
Weighton, Fraser 250
Weiland, Sydney 181
Weitzen, Perla *see* Lesser, Polly
Werth, Alexander 133
Weston, Reg 122
Weygand, General 3, 88
Wild, Sam 50, 51
Williams, Bert 71
Wilson, Harold 120
Wincott, Len 179–80
Winnington, Alan 205, 211
Winter, Alexander 146
Winterton, Deryck 250
Wooley, Ernie 45

Workers' Commissions 227–29, 231, 232, 233, 237
World News and Views 94
Wyatt, Woodrow 123
Wynburne, Stephen 252

Yates, Steve 20, 27
Yeltsin, Boris 183
Yevtushenko, Yevgeni 172
Yiddish 5, 7, 18n2, 79, 88, 102; theatre 5, 247
Young Communists: Great Britain 85; Germany 44

Yugoslavia 60n1, 79, 130, 157, 167, 169, 210, 227, 254

Zarubina, Zoya 172
Zetkin, Clara 164
Zhdanov, Andrei 130
Zhivkov, Todor 244
Zhou Enlai 173
Zhukhov, Georgi Marshal 166, 167, 168, 169
Zhukov, Yuri 145, 177
Zionism 7, 12–13, 39, 137, 138; *see also* Jewish identity